"My friends Josh and Sean McDowell have a clear understanding of what this generation needs, and they communicate that truth in a logical and compelling way. This ought to be required reading for every high school and college student in America, and quite honestly, it wouldn't be a bad idea if parents read it too!"

—**DENNIS RAINEY,** president, FamilyLife

"There is a growing need for young believers to know what they believe and why they believe as they do…The McDowells have addressed that need with clarity, completeness, and conviction. This magnificent work…addresses crucial doctrinal and apologetic issues within a single volume. That alone is worth the price of the book."

—**DR. J.P. MORELAND,** distinguished professor of philosophy, Talbot School of Theology, and author of *The God Question*

"*The Unshakable Truth* will fascinate and challenge you. It gives you the outline to understand God as the creator, God in the incarnation, and God as our re-creator. You will walk away with a biblical foundation on which to build your worldview…Well done!"

—**KAY ARTHUR,** co-CEO, Precept Ministries International, and author

"Provides a biblical blueprint for believing and living as God designed—a plan for bringing redemption and restoration to our nation through the family and the church. This is a crucially needed resource, one I can heartily recommend."

—**DR. PAT ROBERTSON,** host, *The 700 Club*

"This…catechism, overall…is a very successful one…This material should bring blessing far and wide."

—**DR. J.I. PACKER,** author, professor of theology, Regent College

"Destined to be a classic for every follower of Christ who desires to fortify their faith, develop their discipleship, and expand their effectiveness as a witness of the truth of God's Word. Take the time to devour this book and discover how relevant your faith will become."

—**DR. JACK GRAHAM** pastor, Prestonwood Baptist Church

"Creation, redemption, and being restored to God are all about relationships. Josh and Sean have given us God's ultimate plan—a relational theology to believe and live out in relationship to him and one another."

—**DR. GARY SMALLEY** founder of the Smalley Relationship Center

"Josh McDowell is both a scholarly apologist and a popular communicator. His careful research and artful presentation provide Christians with the ability to be equipped to engage people in relevant and effective evangelism."

—**STEVE DOUGLASS,** president, Campus Crusade for Christ International

"Josh and Sean have nailed the priority of the church and provided pastors and church leaders with a biblical blueprint for ministry effectiveness and relevance."

—Dr. David Ferguson
executive director of the Great Commandment Network

"A big thanks to Josh and Sean for articulating with clarity and conviction the bedrock realities that make our walk with Jesus Christ solid and certain...This book welcomes us to the joy of the no-regrets freedom that His truth cultivates in our hearts and lives."

—Dr. Joseph M. Stowell
president, Cornerstone University, Grand Rapids, Michigan

"Will give you rock-solid answers to the real questions people are asking. Josh and Sean McDowell have made the most important truths of theology relevant, practical, and accessible for seekers and skeptics alike."

—June Hunt, founder, CEO, CSO (Chief Servant Officer)
Hope for the Heart

"*The Unshakable Truth* gives us a model of how to demonstrate the essentials of the faith to our young people."

—Paul Fleischmann
president, National Network of Youth Ministries

"The authors' aim is to state, not only what we believe as Christians, but why we believe it, how it is relevant to our lives, and how we should live it out before the world. In view of their wide lay audience, this goal is well achieved."

—Norman L. Geisler, PhD, provost and distinguished professor of apologetics
at Veritas Evangelical Seminary, Murrieta, California

"This is a most incredible comprehensive handbook to learn and absorb the truth of the Christian faith. Josh and Sean have woven their own life stories into this theological, yet practical, work. There is no doubt in my mind that *The Unshakable Truth* will be one of the classics for this generation."

—Jim Burns, PhD, president, HomeWord
author of *Creating an Intimate Marriage* and *Confident Parenting*

"Addresses the ever-present need to develop and pass on a Christian worldview and shows how to do it transgenerationally. The book...will awaken in the reader an enthusiasm to think clearly and respond boldly to our postmodern culture, which is bent on pushing God and absolutes far away."

—Skip Heitzig, pastor and author

"*The Unshakable Truth* is not just another offering in practical theology or apologetics. It is, in fact, a Bible-college education in one very engaging and readable volume...Read it and reap!"

—Dr. O.S. Hawkins, former pastor, First Baptist Church in Dallas, Texas,
president/CEO, GuideStone Financial Resources of the SBC

"Josh and Sean have created a comprehensive foundation for our faith using basic biblical truth and clever contemporary insight."

—Bobb Biehl, executive mentor, BobbBiehl.com

"*The Unshakable Truth* by Josh and Sean expands Josh's classic work *Evidence that Demands a Verdict* and brings it into the relational world in which we live...It will be of great help to old and new believers alike as we seek to pass on our faith to the next generation."

—DR. DANN SPADER, president, Global Youth Initiative

"Nourishing food for the heart...Truly a practical handbook for living in the truth of God's story, for which each of us were created, and passing it on to others, especially the next generation."

—DR. ROBERT SAUCY, distinguished professor of systematic theology,
Talbot School of Theology

"In many respects our young people have lacked a solid biblical catechism—teachings about God and his Word. And now Josh and Sean McDowell have delivered us such a catechism that can be taught and lived out in front of our kids. This is a much needed book."

—RON LUCE, president, Teen Mania

"A necessity for a lost and broken generation...Josh and Sean very clearly and biblically lay down what it means to have a Christian worldview in 12 easy-to-understand and compelling truths...If you read this book and apply it to your life, you will become emboldened and equipped to carry the truth of Christ to even its most hostile opponents."

—NATE HEITZIG, youth pastor, Calvary Church of Albuquerque

"The authors recognize the greatest apologetic in winning people to Christ—loving one another as Christ loved us!"

—DR. GENE A. GETZ, founder, Fellowship Bible Church Movement
host, Renewal Radio

"An excellent combination of what Christ-followers should believe and why we should believe it. I applaud Josh and Sean's efforts to help present these 12 unshakable truths in such a clear, readable fashion."

—DR. BILL JONES, president, Columbia International University,
Columbia, South Carolina

"I already find myself going back to the 12 truths in this book to help me meet specific challenges I face as my faith is attacked by today's postmodern culture... This resource is a must for every believer, regardless of age, who wants to find the abundant life in Christ."

—GLEN SCHULTZ
Christian educator and author of *Kingdom Education*

"Josh McDowell has long stood for the truth of Christ in a shifting culture. Now, along with his son, Sean, he presents a lifetime of teaching in a volume that represents the Christian faith persuasively and passionately for a new generation. This crowning achievement offers a rock-solid reference for those preparing 'to give an answer' for the hope within us.'"

—DR. JOHN ANKERBERG
president and host of *The John Ankerberg Show* (johnankerberg.org)

The Unshakable TRUTH

JOSH McDOWELL
SEAN McDOWELL

HARVEST HOUSE PUBLISHERS

EUGENE, OREGON

Cover by Koechel Peterson & Associates, Inc., Minneapolis, Minnesota

THE UNSHAKABLE TRUTH
Copyright © 2010 by Josh McDowell Ministry and Sean McDowell
Published by Harvest House Publishers
Eugene, Oregon 97402
www.harvesthousepublishers.com

Library of Congress Cataloging-in-Publication Data

McDowell, Josh.
The unshakable truth / Josh McDowell and Sean McDowell.
   p. cm.
Includes bibliographical references.
ISBN 978-0-7369-2870-0 (Hardcover)
ISBN 978-0-7369-2878-6 (International Edition)
1. Theology, Doctrinal—Popular works. 2. Apologetics. I. McDowell, Sean II. Title.
BT77.M364 2010
230—dc22
                                                                    2010001136

Printed in the United States of America

10 11 12 13 14 15 16 17 18 / LB-NI / 10 9 8 7 6 5 4 3 2 1

ACKNOWLEDGMENTS

A work of this magnitude is not completed without long hours and extensive collaboration with many people. We wish to recognize the following individuals for their valuable contribution to this book.

Dave Bellis, my (Josh's) friend and colleague for 33 years, for hammering out the theme and focus of the book, collaborating with us in the research for the book, writing the rough drafts, rewriting, and overall, guiding and molding the book into its final form. In many respects, Dave could be considered a "third author," and we are deeply grateful for his contribution.

Tom Williams for editing the manuscript, to which he applied his valuable insights, wordsmithing skills, and passionate heart to make words come alive on a printed page.

Becky Bellis for laboring long and hard at the computer to ready the manuscript.

Jason Carlson and Pastor Mark Fitter for their insightful analysis regarding the theological perspective presented in the book.

Rich and Pam Bucha, Regina SirLouis, Blake and Deanna Matthies, Ron Pavlovich, Ken and Debbie Kear, Tammy Bellis, Bryan and Annette Walters, Dave Bellis II, Chris and Charlotte Woofter, Laura Fahringer, Shane and Dawn Meyers, Becky Bellis, Caleb and Jen Nichols, and Angela Farkas for participating in the focus group and providing insights that helped us clarify the message of the book and make it easier to understand and more practical to apply.

Terry Glaspey of Harvest House Publishers for his analytical skills, theological insights, and structural understanding of what makes for a compelling yet practical book. His collaboration with us has been invaluable.

Paul Gossard for the expert editing and insight he brought to the manuscript completion.

Bob Hawkins Jr. and LaRae Weikert of Harvest House for their vision for this work and for all the patience and encouragement they gave us.

And finally, to those on the Harvest House Publishers team who have been involved in copy editing, internal design and layout, cover design, and the many details required to bring a book to press—we thank you.

Josh McDowell
Sean McDowell

CONTENTS

PART III

THE UNSHAKABLE TRUTH OF GOD'S INCARNATION

IIIIIIIIIIIIIIIIIII **TRUTH FOUR: GOD BECAME HUMAN** IIIIIIIIIIIIIIIIIII

IIIIIIIIIIIII **TRUTH FIVE: CHRIST'S ATONEMENT FOR SIN** IIIIIIIIIIIII

IIIIIIIIIIIII **TRUTH SIX: JUSTIFICATION THROUGH FAITH** IIIIIIIIIIIII

IIIIIIIIIIII **TRUTH SEVEN: LIVING THE TRANSFORMED LIFE** IIIIIIIIIIII

PART IV

THE UNSHAKABLE TRUTH OF GOD'S RE-CREATION

FAMILY OR SMALL-GROUP ACTIVITIES

PART I

THE TWELVE UNSHAKABLE TRUTHS OF CHRISTIANITY

What is the Christian faith, really?

▪

What do we believe?

▪

Why do we believe it?

▪

How is it relevant to our lives?

▪

How can we live it out?

CHAPTER ONE

WHAT WE ALL WANT
OUT OF LIFE

I t was a beautiful fall day. The car windows were all rolled down. I (Josh) was in my first year of college, and I was driving some of my friends from campus to downtown. We were laughing and just having a lot of fun. A woman pulled up beside us at the traffic light, rolled down her window, and with a scowl on her face said, "What right do you kids have to be so happy!"

Our Desire for Deep Happiness

Deep down all of us want to be happy. We want to live a satisfying life, a life of joy and contentment. Actually, God wants us to enjoy that as well. Jesus said, "I have told you this so that my joy may be in you and that your joy may be complete" (John 15:11 NIV). Yet the quest for deep happiness often eludes us. Webster's dictionary defines happiness as "a pleasurable or satisfying experience." Happiness is often equated with pleasurable feelings. And of course there's nothing inherently wrong with pleasurable satisfaction, except in how we pursue it.

Focusing on Self

I (Sean, Josh's son and co-author) work as an educator. When I ask my students what they want most in their lives, their typical response is "happiness." I ask them to define happiness, and most of them tell me that happiness is people feeling good and having fun. Many of us would define it that way. If happiness is about a pleasurable feeling or experience of fun, then it should follow that the greater number of fun experiences we have, the happier we become.

But somehow, it doesn't seem to work out that way. For example, the earning power of the baby boomers increased dramatically over that of any previous generation in history. They have had more money, more leisure time, more access to sports, travel, and entertainment than any society has ever experienced. And yet according to happiness expert Dr. Martin Seligman, baby boomers experienced a tenfold increase in depression over any previous generation. The reason for the depression, Dr. Seligman concludes, was that people began a shift toward a focus on self.[1]

When one's mission in life is to pursue pleasure, the result is to become "me" focused. And "me"-focused happiness is generally short-lived. Sooner or later, and for most people it is later, when we focus primarily on our own pleasure, our lives tend to become empty, depressed, and void of any real meaning. We come to experience the reality that a self-centered focus doesn't produce lasting satisfaction, joy, or real happiness. Christian philosopher and apologist J.P. Moreland suggests a conclusion to a self-absorbed life:

> If happiness is having an internal feeling of fun or pleasurable satisfaction, and if it is our main goal, where will we place our focus all day long? The focus will be on us, and the result will be a culture of self-absorbed individuals who can't live for something larger than we are.[2]

Yet this is the current life philosophy that most people have bought into: The individual always comes first, with the number-one virtue being to feel good about yourself. The culture tells you to "be yourself, believe in yourself, express yourself." That's why we have *You*Tube and *My*Space. Self, self, self. The prevailing view is that you *do what it takes to feel good about yourself because that's the most important thing in the world. That is the way to find happiness.*

To some degree or another most of us have bought into that viewpoint. And it's easy to understand why. If the goal is happiness, then why shouldn't we pursue the things that will give us pleasure and thus make us happy?

Focusing on Jesus and His Worldview

Jesus, however, has another view on achieving genuine happiness and joy—one that encompasses a whole different set of priorities. Instead of seeking our happiness first, Jesus tells us to put *him and his kingdom* first (Matthew 6:33). He says we must die to ourselves; that to find our life we must lose it; essentially, that we must look beyond ourselves and pursue him first. In reading such things, many people wonder how we can expect to be happy if we set aside our quest for what gives us pleasure and follow someone who asks us for our total commitment. As a result, they think Christianity might spoil all their fun.

This is emphatically not the case. Jesus said he was "the way, the truth, and the life" (John 14:6) and our source of genuine happiness. According to Jesus, happiness is not based upon a certain feeling. Instead, it is a sense of contentment, peace, and joy that transcends our circumstances and feelings. When Jesus said that his joy would be in us and our joy would be complete, he was defining the true way to happiness—a happiness that does not fade, but grows and expands into true and lasting joy.

> *A worldview is what we assume to be true about the basic makeup of our world.*

He was saying to focus on him and his way—his view of the world. And by doing this we would understand who we are, and thus we would experience our identity as a person of value and worth. We would realize why we are here, and thus we would experience our purpose and meaning in life. We would know where we are going, and thus we would experience our destiny and mission in a life larger than ourselves.

And in this process we will find we have attained something much bigger and better than the way our culture understands happiness, which is based on the pleasure of the moment. We will find true, deep, satisfying, and lasting joy. It will be a joy that remains intact through all of life, with or without pleasures, through ups and downs, through pains, sorrows, and losses. That is something we all want.

The way to achieve this lasting joy is to buy into Jesus' idea of life—that is, his worldview. A worldview is what we assume to be true about the basic makeup of our world. A worldview is like a mental map of reality. We believe certain things about ourselves and God and life, and then we interpret our experiences through them. Everyone has a worldview, even though not everyone *realizes* they have one.

Jesus' worldview—his view of life—is called a biblical worldview. Embracing a biblical worldview means understanding and living life from God's perspective. It means understanding what we were meant to know and be and how we were meant to live. This biblical worldview works because it explains the truth about God and about us. That is what Jesus and the whole of Scripture does—it gives us the truth about life and happiness, and the power to live according to the kingdom of God. As J.P. Moreland says,

> This is why truth is so powerful. It allows us to cooperate with reality, whether spiritual or physical, and tap into its power. As we learn to think correctly about God, specific scriptural teachings, the soul, or other important aspects of a Christian worldview, we are placed in touch with God and those realities.[3]

Nothing works right unless it conforms to reality. A plane flies because engineers design its shape to conform to the realities of airflow and gravity. A boat floats because its designers shaped it to conform to the realities of water displacement. Try to fly a boat or float a plane and the results will be disastrous. It's the same with your life. If you want a significant life, you must run your life in accordance with what it was designed to do. Your life was created to work properly when it conforms to the reality of its purpose. And God has gone to great lengths to show us the reality of our purpose, which is diametrically opposed to how our culture understands happiness. He tells us that when we abandon self-absorption we will find significance. When we seek first His kingdom, all these things will be added unto us (Matthew 6:33). When we find the meaning he intends for our lives, we will gain a deep contentment even in the middle of the pain, loss, and abandonment that characterizes our fallen world. This is why it is vitally important to adopt God's perspective on life. This, and only this, is the path to genuine happiness and deep, lasting joy.

My (Josh's) Path

As a teenager, I (Josh) began my quest for happiness down the wrong path. Yet I sincerely wanted the answers to *Who am I? Why am I here? Where am I going?* So I started searching for answers. I certainly didn't find answers at home. My father was the town drunk. I grew up watching in fear and horror as my father beat my mother and wreaked havoc at home. I experienced sexual abuse from a man named Wayne, whom my parents hired as a part-time cook and housekeeper. As I got older I eventually told my mother about what Wayne was doing, but she didn't believe me. I can't describe to you the pain of abandonment I felt when my mother refused to believe me. Also, growing up I never remember my father saying that he loved me. The only love I ever felt was from a struggling, abused mother who died suddenly when I was a teenager. So my home was not a place to find answers or happiness.

In the small Michigan community in which I grew up, everyone seemed to be into religion, so my search started there. I really got into the church scene. But I must have picked the wrong church, because I felt worse inside the church than I did outside. So I gave up on the church to provide me any answers.

Then I thought that education might have the answers, so I enrolled in a university. I soon became unpopular with my professors because I hounded them with so many questions. But I learned that my professors had just as many problems, frustrations, and unanswered questions as I did.

I remember seeing a student wearing a T-shirt that read, *Don't follow me, I'm lost.* That's how everyone at the university seemed to me. I concluded education wasn't the answer.

Next, I tried prestige. I thought I could find a noble cause, commit to it, and in the process become well known. So I ran for various student offices. It was great at first. People got to know me and I enjoyed spending the university's money getting the speakers I wanted. I also liked the idea of spending the students' money for throwing parties.

But the prestige thing soon wore off. I would wake up on Monday morning, usually with a headache from the night before, dreading the next five days. I endured Monday through Friday just to experience the party nights on the weekend. But every Monday brought the meaningless cycle all over again.

About that time I noticed a small group of people who seemed different from the others. They appeared to know who they were and where they were going. They had a clear set of convictions about what they believed. And what really stood out was that they appeared to be genuinely happy. Their happiness and joy wasn't like mine, which was dependent on my circumstances. I was happy only when things were going great—when I was having "fun." But they seemed to possess an inner source of joy that I longed for, and I wondered where it came from.

I befriended these people and tried to figure out what they knew that I didn't. One day I asked one of these students (a good-looking woman in the group) what made her so different, so happy. She had told me before she hadn't always been that way but she had changed. So I asked her, "What changed your life?"

Her answer shocked me. She used two words as a solution, two words I never thought I'd hear at the university. She simply said, "Jesus Christ." I immediately told her I was fed up with religion and the church and was certain it wasn't a solution. Again, this woman had convictions and she knew what she believed. She shot back and said, "I didn't say *religion*, I said *Jesus Christ*."

She and her friends went on to explain that a relationship with God through Jesus Christ offered what I would come to know as a biblical worldview. They told me it was Christ and his worldview—seeing everything from a biblical perspective—that would answer all the questions I had. They didn't offer to walk me through a shallow prayer or get me to go to "church meetings." What they did was challenge me to intellectually examine the claims of Jesus and to determine, in essence, whether God's worldview written in Scripture was credible. I accepted their challenge out of pride. I wanted to prove Christianity was a farce.

What I discovered was that I was the farce. My quest for happiness and meaning was found in Christ.

Most people who know my testimony know I set out to disprove Christianity, and they assume I came to Christ through the intellectual route. They think my examination of the evidence of Christ's deity, his resurrection, and the reliability of Scripture convinced me that God had spoken and that it offered me a worldview that would establish my identity, purpose, and meaning in life—and therefore I trusted in Christ.

Truth is, all the evidence I have documented in my books did not bring me into a relationship with Christ. The convincing evidence certainly got my attention, but it was God's love that drew me to him. I saw love between a group of Jesus-followers who devoted themselves to God and one another. And God demonstrated his love to me through them. Through the power of the Holy Spirit my life was transformed through a relationship with God. I discovered a whole new way of thinking and living that brought pure joy. This new way of thinking and living was possible as God empowered me to live out truth from his perspective—a biblical worldview.

Most Christians believe Jesus' worldview is what we need to follow, yet we encounter many who seem to have trouble making it work in their lives. Our experience tells us that the following quote represents untold numbers of people:

> "I'm a Christian and I want to find real joy. I do believe I can find it in following Christ, but somehow it doesn't seem to be happening. I do my best to live out my faith. But to be honest, I really don't know a lot about why I believe what I believe. And when it comes to a biblical worldview, there are so many conflicting claims floating around about what that means, I'm not sure I'm forming the right one. How can I be sure?"

Answering these questions that we find on the lips of so many Christians is our first purpose in writing this handbook. We want to demonstrate a way to experience the happiness and joy that every person desires and that God wants us to have. We also have a second purpose in writing this handbook.

Our Desire to Pass the Faith to the Next Generation

We run across hundreds of Christians who tell us something like this:

> "I'm a Christian and want to pass my faith on to my kids. Yet I don't feel very equipped to do that. But I definitely don't want to lose my kids to a godless culture. What can I do?"

The fear of the culture capturing our kids is real. This handbook is designed to better ground you in the essentials of the faith in a way that provides a greater understanding of what you believe, why you believe it, and how it brings you a deeper joy in life. That understanding in and of itself will serve as a platform to successfully instill a robust and active Christianity in the lives of the next generation. We know that passing on the faith is a real and vital need. And it doesn't happen automatically.

Captured by the Culture

Many times we have heard stories similar to the following scenario:

Marsha hugged her son as he prepared to leave. "It's been nice having you home again, honey," she said.

"Yeah, Greg," his father, Mike, echoed. "It really has been good." He stepped in for a hug. "I miss the weekends as a family, going to church and all. But I assume you've found a church home there in the college area by now, haven't you, son?"

Greg swung his backpack onto his shoulder. "Well, Dad, not really," he said hesitantly. "Being a freshman is tough, so I've been really busy."

Sarah, Greg's 16-year-old sister, handed him his duffel bag. "Is college really that hard?"

"Well, I wouldn't say hard, really. You just keep busy, you know?"

Mike gently gripped Greg's shoulder. "If you're too busy to be in church, son, I think you might be too busy."

"Well," Greg responded, "your kind of church just isn't my thing anymore, Dad. I've got some friends and we do a group study once a week and that's enough for me."

"I'd rather do things with my friends too," Sarah added. "Church is a bore."

"Sarah!" Marsha said. "That's a terrible thing to say!"

"Well, it's true!" Sarah said.

"She's right, Mom," Greg said. "Church just doesn't cut it for me anymore."

"Honey, don't say that." Marsha touched her son on the arm. "That college isn't turning you against God, is it?"

"No, Mom," Greg chuckled, "I'm just rethinking a lot of things. God is still important to me, I just believe some different things from you guys, that's all." He adjusted the weight of the backpack. "Hey, I've got to get going."

Greg moved on out the door as Sarah helped him with his things. Marsha and Mike stepped onto the porch and watched their son walk toward the car.

"We'll be praying for you, son," Mike called.

"Thanks, Dad," Greg responded with a chuckle.

Marsha and Mike watched in silence as he backed down the drive and waved to them as he drove away. "I hope we're not losing our son," Marsha said.

Mike nodded. "I hope we're not losing our son *and* our daughter."[4]

If we hear one dominating and recurring theme among the many church leaders and families we come in contact with, it's the fear that Mike expresses above. There is a deep, abiding fear among Christian parents that their kids, having been raised in a Christian family and having spent their childhood and teenage years in the church, will nonetheless walk away from God.

A Generation Gap

The problem is, this fear is becoming a reality. Presently, within ten years of entering adulthood, most teens professing to be Christians will walk away from the church and put whatever commitment they made to Christ on the shelf.[5] This doesn't mean all our young people are rejecting God outright and becoming atheists. That's not the case. It's that they are adopting beliefs and a worldview that are definitely not "the faith which was once for all handed down to the saints" (Jude 3 NASB). A large portion of young people today would echo Greg's remark to his dad: "God is still important to me, I just believe some different things than you." These differences, often referred to as the generation gap, are wider and deeper today than ever before. According to a recent Pew Research Center study, almost 80 percent of adults see a difference between the beliefs and points of view of young people and themselves. Asked to identify where older and younger people differ the most, 47 percent pinpointed the areas of social values and morality.[6]

Consider just some of what today's Christian young people believe:

- 23 percent are not assured of the existence of miracles;

- 33 percent either "definitely" or "maybe" believe in reincarnation;

- 42 percent are not assured of the existence of evil as an entity;

- 48 percent believe that many religions are true.[7]

It is difficult to lead a young person to adopt a Christian worldview when nearly one out of two can't say that Jesus is definitively "the way, the truth, and the life."

And even when our young people do begin to embrace a Christian worldview they are under intense assault from their high school years and up. According to a 2006 study by professors from Harvard and George Mason Universities, the percentage of agnostics and atheists teaching at American colleges is three times greater than in the general population. More than half of college professors today believe the Bible is "an ancient book of fables, legends, history, and moral precepts."[8]

Students are continually told by today's culture that the Bible is unreliable, that Jesus was no different than any other religious figure, and that anyone who asserts there is an objective truth that shapes a worldview is intolerant and a bigot. It is very hard for young people to stand up against such pressures unless they are fully equipped, as the apostle Peter said, "always being ready to make a defense to everyone who asks you to give an account for the hope that is in you" (1 Peter 3:15 NASB). The truth is, few are equipped and ready to face a world that is increasingly hostile to Christianity.

Young people must be led...to adopt the biblical worldview as their guiding principle.

If you have children or work with young people, you know how difficult it can be to get through to them. And it seems at times that all the advantages communication technology has brought us haven't helped a bit. In fact, the pervasiveness of modern electronic communication may be one of the obstacles we must overcome. In his book *Handoff* Dr. Jeff Myers says:

> The young people our organization has studied spend between 27 and 33 hours per week using communication technology—gaming, watching television and movies, text messaging, instant messaging, and surfing the internet. In short, they're overwhelmed with information.
>
> Information overload breaks down a person's capacity for discernment. For example, C. John Sommerville argued that the 24-hour news cycle actually makes us dumber, not smarter. It presents so much information that we find it impossible to figure out what is truly important.[9]

Then Jeff goes on to say:

> With shopping and surfing available 24 hours a day young adults believe they can have whatever they want, whenever they want, however they want, and with whomever they want to have it. Nothing is more than a few clicks away.
>
> Here's the paradox: when there is nothing more to see or do, there is nothing more to look forward to. It's easy to see why surveys of young adults pick up high levels of hopelessness, distrust, cynicism, and boredom.
>
> The unceasing access to pleasure and the consequent unhappiness led evangelist Ravi Zacharias to reference G.K. Chesterton in saying that "meaninglessness ultimately comes not from being weary of pain but from being weary of pleasure."[10]

The task may not be easy, but if ever there was a time to make a concerted effort to instill a biblical worldview into the next generation—a way to think from a biblical perspective—it's now. Their misconceptions and distorted views of what is important in life and what brings happiness and joy must be addressed. The consequences of failing to tackle this problem head-on are disheartening.

Young people must be led to align their beliefs and behavior with ultimate reality, which means, in essence, to adopt the biblical view of the world as their guiding principle. In *The Scandal of the Evangelical Conscience,* author Ron Sider concludes that people who have a biblical worldview live differently—in ways that are highly significant to the temptations today's youth face. They are nine times more likely to avoid "adult only" material on the Internet, three times as likely not to use tobacco products, and twice as likely to volunteer to help the poor.[11] What people believe about God, truth, and the world around them (for example, a biblical worldview), makes a tangible difference in the way they live.

Equipping the Mind

Some might think their young people won't respond positively to addressing their beliefs and challenging them to examine why they believe what they believe. Some think that all today's kids want is to deal with relationships and what they can experience emotionally. This simply is not the case. In the recent "National Study of Youth and Religion," thousands of nonreligious teenagers said they were raised to be "religious" but had become "nonreligious." These teenagers were asked, "Why did you fall away from the faith in which you were raised?" They were given no set of answers to pick from; it was simply an open-ended question. The most common answer—given by 32 percent of the respondents—was *intellectual skepticism.*[12] That is a very high percentage given the fact that this was an open-ended question. Their answers included such statements as "It didn't make sense to me"; "Some stuff is too far-fetched for me to believe in"; "I think scientifically there is no real proof"; and "There were too many questions that can't be answered." Our kids want answers they can grapple with in their *minds* as well as in their hearts.

When it comes to spiritual and character formation, Scripture attaches great importance to training the mind. "Do not conform any longer to the pattern of this world," Paul states. "But be transformed by the renewing of your mind" (Romans 12:2 NIV).

All of us want our kids to be equipped in mind, spirit, and character, able to resist the pressures of this increasingly godless culture so that no matter what temptations and opposition they face, they will live lives we can be proud of—lives that are pleasing to God and others. We want our kids to live out a biblical worldview. Yet actually living out a biblical worldview is impossible apart from a transformed relationship through Jesus Christ. Neither our young people nor any of us have the natural inclination or power in our human strength to live out "the way" of Jesus—his worldview. That means each of us and our young people must place our trust in Christ and surrender our lives to him so we all can stand strong with deep convictions for the unshakable truths of God.

This handbook will provide guidance to lead your young people to such a faith in Christ. Because through a transformed relationship with God they "will no longer be like children, forever changing [their] minds about what [they] believe because someone has told [them] something different or because someone has cleverly lied to [them] and made the lie sound like the truth" (Ephesians 4:13-14). You want to teach and mentor and empower them to think and live as "children of God without fault in a crooked and depraved generation, in which [they] shine like stars in the universe" (Philippians 2:15 NIV).

There is probably nothing more rewarding to us (Josh and Sean) than being able to pass the baton of the Christian faith to our children. Jeff Myers said it well in *Hand-off*:

> The universe is designed in such a way that passing the baton is the only way I can truly experience blessing, fullness, meaning, satisfaction, and joy in life. I may want to believe that serving myself leads to happiness, but my heart knows better. No matter how much stuff I buy, or what kind of house I live in, or where I travel, life only takes on meaning when I live for something bigger than myself.[13]

Use This Handbook as Your Guide

Some books are designed for you to curl up on a couch with them and enjoy a "good read." Others are reference texts from which you glean specific information. This book is a handbook. The best way to use it is first to absorb it, and then to engage in a long-term process of applying its content incrementally in your own life and in the lives of your children, grandchildren, youth group, or others to whom you wish to impart the faith.

This book will present the essentials of the biblical worldview by exploring what we have identified as the 12 basic truths of the faith, which are noted in the 12 sections of this work. The next two chapters will give you an overview of these 12 truths, and then the following 48 chapters will delve into each truth thoroughly.

Each foundational truth will be given four chapters. Some chapters will be short and succinct. The *first chapter* in each section will identify a particular truth and what we as Christians believe about it. The *second chapter* will examine why you can believe it with confidence. The *third chapter* in each section will explore how that truth is relevant to your life. The *fourth chapter* will offer practical ways to live that truth out in the presence of those around you. As you live these truths out more and more in front of your family and friends you will be better equipped to impart them to others.

It is not necessary to read each truth and its chapters in order. There is no problem jumping ahead to a particular truth of interest or to one that applies to an immediate situation in your life. For example, if you are nearing the Easter season you might want to skip to Truth Eight: "Jesus' Bodily Resurrection." Or if Christmas is around the corner you might want to go to Truth Four: "God Became Human." The point is, while each truth of the Christian faith builds off the other, each stands on its own merits. So if a particular time of year makes it more appropriate to address certain truths, or if those around you are raising a certain question that makes focusing on a particular truth more timely, go for it. Eventually, however, we urge you to cover all the truths in this handbook—and to review them more than once.

There is a reason God instructed his people to "repeat [God's truth] again and again to your children. Talk about them when you are at home...away on a journey...lying down...getting up" (Deuteronomy 6:7). No matter how young or how old we are, we will never exhaustively understand the depths and riches of God and his truth. The truths of the faith can become fresh and alive to you again each time you go over them. Absorbing them repeatedly can give them deeper relevance because in the process of filling ourselves with knowledge of his truth we are actually deepening our relationship with a relational, infinite God. We would not mislead you—the McDowells, this father-and-son team, do not claim to understand all the deep truths we present here. Nor have we mastered the Christian life. Far from it. It is important that you realize that we too are on a journey of constantly uncovering the richness of God and applying these truths to our daily lives.

Experience an Enriching Celebration with Your Family

The 12 unshakable truths you will discover throughout this handbook are rooted in the Old Testament, even though most of the passages we refer to are in the New Testament. And to help you instill these truths in your family we have adapted three Old Testament Jewish festivals and made them into mealtime celebrations.

For centuries Jewish families have gathered around the dinner table to celebrate those festivals God had ordained for them. Many Christians today are realizing the benefits and richness of these festivals in aiding us to better understand the meaning of God's plan for each of us. So to help you impart the truths of the faith to your family and friends, you will find in the appendixes to this handbook a Judeo-Christian Feast of Unleavened Bread (Passover), Feast of Harvest (Pentecost), and Feast of Tabernacles. These three mealtime events focus on celebrating the God of relationship, redemption, and restoration, which are all found in the sweeping story from creation to God taking on humanity to Christ's return. We have provided you detailed instructions on how to plan and execute these mealtime celebrations. Take advantage of them.

The development of these festivals has been greatly aided by the help of Harvey Diamond and his "Pathways to Glory" interactive devotional. Harvey has done a phenomenal job of explaining all the feasts of the Old Testament and their relevance to today and to the Christian life. Visit www.ariseinglory.org and click on "Pathways to Glory Relational Devotional." You will benefit greatly from Harvey's teachings and insights.

Our Prayer for You

As you begin your journey, we pray that you will come to know God more deeply, understand your place within him and the world more clearly. And above all, we pray that God will empower you more fully to live out your biblical worldview so you can more effectively impart the living truth of Jesus Christ to your family and those around you. We live in a scary world dominated by pain and suffering, sin and heartache, war and death. But we are not to fear the evils of this world. The only one we are to fear is God himself (see Matthew 10:28). We serve a conquering God who is working in you and me to transform the present kingdom of this world into the future kingdom of God. It is an honor to engage in this mission with you. Let the journey of unlocking the unshakable truth of God begin.

CHAPTER TWO

Twelve Truths That
Define the Christian Faith

I magine an auditorium full of church attendees. You ask them this question: "What defines the Christian faith?" You would probably expect to get a myriad of answers. But what you might not expect is that the answers would be far from what defines true biblical Christianity.

A recent study among Christians revealed that 81 percent said the essence of the Christian faith was "trying harder to follow the rules described in the Bible." Even pastors struggle with this issue. Amazingly, 75 percent of Christian leaders were not able to define clearly the core of Christianity and the process of spiritual maturity.[1] Polls and our own experience tell us that there is a lot of confusion among Christians about what the essence of Christianity actually is. Is Christianity a set of biblical teachings we are to follow? Is it a relationship with God? Is it a philosophical viewpoint? Is it a set of beliefs we should adopt? Just what is the Christian faith, which makes up a biblical worldview?

Embracing the Biblical Worldview

The Christian faith is more than a set of teachings or laws to govern our actions. In his book entitled *The Faith,* author and speaker Chuck Colson said that the Christian faith is "a complete view of the world and humankind's place in it. Christianity is a worldview that speaks to every area of life, and its foundational doctrines define its content."[2] Yet this faith that forms our biblical worldview is not to be understood simply as an idea, a philosophical viewpoint, or a construct. It is about a relationship—a relationship lost in early human history and a relationship re-established by God's intervention. And in experiencing this reconnected God-human relationship, one sees the whole of life illuminated through a new lens that clarifies and defines everything we know and experience.

This is not to say that adopting a biblical worldview defines the essence of Christianity. A better way to put it is to say that being in proper relationship with God defines our worldview. When we are in proper relationship with him, we understand how we relate to one another. We understand his overall mission in the world. We understand his truth about ethics and morality. In other words, adherence to a set of teachings or rules does not in itself form our concept of Christianity and our biblical worldview. Our worldview must be formed out of our relationship with God as defined through Christ by his Word and empowered by his Holy Spirit.

> *The Christian faith that forms our worldview… is a way of knowing and being and living in right relationship with God, ourselves, others, and the world around us.*

The prophet Hosea told the children of Israel, "I don't want your sacrifices. I want you to know God; that's more important than burnt offerings" (Hosea 6:6). Moses told God's people, "You must worship no other gods, but only the LORD, for he is a God who is passionate about his relationship with you" (Exodus 34:14). Yes, God wants us to know his truth, his will, and his commands, but as Moses told us, all these things enclose one central idea: God is passionate about his relationship with us. He loves us dearly. With all his heart he wants to be in a close, loving relationship with us.

Although these verses come from the Old Testament, God's relational purpose did not change with the coming of Christ. In fact, the very reason he came was to restore and solidify our relationship with God. That is the core of Christianity. It is about who we are and how we relate to God, what we believe about him, how we gain a relationship with him, and how living in relationship with him defines all our other relationships. This is the way God designed us from the beginning—for relationship with him. Therefore, it is crucial that we know how God intends for us to relate to him.

When we enter this relationship with God, we begin to embrace our biblical worldview. We begin to truly understand ourselves (who we are, why we're here, and where we're going), how we are to relate to others, and how we are to interact with the natural world God gave us. To put a succinct definition to the Christian faith that forms our worldview, we could say it is *a way of knowing and being and living in right relationship with God, ourselves, others, and the world around us.* It is Christ's "way" that we must regain and recapture; and when we live in that "way," our joy is complete.

Recapturing the Living Story

To understand the true faith and form a biblical worldview we must begin with Scripture. The Bible provides us a clear picture, through many stories, of how God has related to us throughout human history—to the first human family, to the children of Israel in the Old Testament, and to the people who came to know Jesus and his "way" in the New Testament. These stories are God's means of conveying to us who he is. They give us vivid pictures of godly people believing and living out the great truths of God. These stories and the unshakable truths they present define who we are, how God wants to relate to us and wants us to relate to him, and how we are to relate to one another. All this was committed to sacred writings that are now our reliable Scripture. God himself has preserved these truths for us so we can know him and pass the baton of the faith to others.

It is these living stories that provide the basis of our biblical worldview. What we have today in the 66 books of the Bible is "inspired by God and is useful to teach us what is true and to make us realize what is wrong in our lives. It straightens us out and teaches us to do what is right. It is God's way of preparing us in every way, fully equipped for every good thing God wants us to do" (2 Timothy 3:16-17).

Far too many Christians see Scripture as merely a set of rules and teachings. They fail to see the Bible as an expression of who we are as God's creation, and our purpose for existence. Unlock the Scripture, and it provides a depiction of a specific way of life, a way of knowing what is true, a picture of being what God meant us to be, and a pattern of living based on the revelation of who God is in relationship to us. Or, to put it another way, Scripture reveals everything we need to know to see the truth about what the world was meant to be, what it is now, and how it can be restored to his original intention. Scripture shows us that we were originally designed to be in relationship with God, what caused us to lose that relationship, and how it can be reclaimed. It is in fact the sweeping story of *creation, incarnation,* and *re-creation.* Understanding what Scripture reveals about those three foundational truths will give us our panoramic, all-encompassing, biblical worldview.

Discovering Truth That Makes a Difference

The three foundational truths of the faith—God's original creation, his incarnation in our world, and his plan for a re-creation—were first clearly delineated in the teachings of second-century theologians such as Tertullian and Irenaeus. The early church used these three truths as the foundation for building a set of core beliefs that captured the heart of the biblical worldview. And it worked. Incredibly well! These early Christians were so intensely discipled in their beliefs that not only did they experience genuine happiness in their lives, they also successfully passed the baton of the Christian faith from one generation to the next in a movement that expanded like wildfire. Alan Hirsch, founder of Forge Mission Training Network, says that by AD 100, about 65 years after Jesus was on earth, there were as few as 25,000 Christians. Within 200 years their numbers exploded to 20 million.[3] That is an increase of 800 times! Let's explore what God did through these Christians that caused such astonishing change and growth to happen.

By the third century there was a focused consensus within the Christian community as to what the truths of the Christian faith were all about, and there existed a defined worldview that governed how they would live. In order to retain this consensus and prevent a drifting of truth, 300 Church Fathers met in the city of Nicaea in Asia Minor in AD 325 to affirm in writing the essential truths of the Christian faith. The result is what we know as the Nicene Creed. These men produced what is now the most widely used statement of faith ever written. It has been endorsed and accepted by practically every major Christian community in history. In this succinct statement the Nicaean council captured the truth of who God is and who we are (the creation), what God did and our purpose in life (the incarnation), and what God's mission is and where we are going (re-creation).

The Nicene Creed (see the end of this chapter) identified at least 12 basic truths that Christians believed—truths based on the three declarations of creation, incarnation, and re-creation—which combine to form the basis of the biblical worldview. What we have done in this handbook is identify, isolate, and define those truths in such a way that we can easily comprehend them and take them into our lives. Following is a summary of these 12 truths. They illuminate and define the three basic declarations (creation, incarnation, and re-creation) that we have presented in this chapter. Below, we give each declaration—written in the first person as if God were speaking—and beneath each declaration we list whichever of the 12 basic truths illuminate it.

God's Truth Declarations

The first declaration: Creation. *I am God. I have spoken the world into existence and have delivered my words to you accurately so you can know me and my truth. I have created you in my likeness for the purpose of having a love relationship with you. Out of that relationship you will find joy in knowing who you are, why you are here, and where you are going. However, you have not trusted what I have told you. You have sinned by disobeying my truth, and sin has brought you death—a separation from me. This separation has resulted in the deforming of my image and likeness in you, and as a result you have suffered immensely. Because I am a God of relationships this has broken my heart.*

Based on this declaration, we assert and believe these three unshakable truths:

1. **The truth that God exists.** God is the personal creator. He created humans because he wanted us to have a love relationship with him. It is

through this relationship that we find completeness that results in experiencing true joy and happiness.

2. **The truth about God's Word.** God wants a relationship in which we know each other intimately. He has given us his Word to reveal himself to us so that we can know him—experience him in all his fullness.

3. **The truth about original sin.** Sadly, this God-human love relationship came to an end because human disobedience to God brought death/separation between us. The deforming nature of sin has caused both physical and spiritual death, resulting in great pain and misery that ultimately result in the physical death of all humans. God was not willing that death be our final end, and he initiated a plan of redemption.

The second declaration: Incarnation. *Because I am also a God of redemption and want to regain my relationship with you, I have provided the only solution to your problem of sin and death. I have entered the world in human form on a mission to redeem you and transform you back into my image. This requires that I atone for your sin by laying down my own human life. If you accept my provision for your salvation, which I offer in love and grace, you and I can again enter into a relationship with each other.*

Based on this declaration, we assert and believe these four unshakable truths:

4. **The truth about God becoming human.** Before the world was formed, God planned to redeem fallen humans. He would do this by entering our world by taking on a human form—his name was Jesus.

5. **The truth about Christ's atonement for sin.** Disobedience and sin against a holy and just God had to be atoned for. Jesus, the sinless Lamb of God, paid for our debt of sin so we could be reconciled to God.

6. **The truth about justification through faith in Christ.** Because of Jesus' death we can be declared righteous before the just and holy God. Through his mercy and grace we can be justified before him when we place our faith in Jesus. We are saved by grace through faith in the Son of God.

7. **The truth about living the transformed life.** Because of Jesus we are raised from death to new life in relationship with God. He imparts his nature to us and we begin the process of becoming conformed to the image of Christ, his Son. In Christlikeness our joy is made complete.

The third declaration: Re-creation. *I cannot accomplish my mission to redeem you eternally unless I conquer death through Christ's resurrection and establish my eternal kingdom in a new heaven and a new earth. You are to join us—the Father, the Son, and the*

Holy Spirit who empowers you—in our mission to first establish our kingdom in the hearts and minds of men and women. We will accomplish this mission through Christ's body, the church; and upon his return all things will be eternally restored to my original design. I will do this because I am also a God of restoration.

Based on this declaration, we assert and believe these five unshakable truths:

8. **The truth about Jesus' bodily resurrection.** Jesus' death was necessary. But he also had to rise from the dead in order to raise us from our condition of spiritual death. And he did. It is Christ's resurrection that brings meaning and the power of salvation to our faith in him.

9. **The truth about the Trinity.** God is a relationship. God is Father, Son, and Holy Spirit. Father God loved us enough to send his Son. His Son loved us enough to sacrifice himself. The Holy Spirit loved us enough to enter our lives and make our relationship with God real.

10. **The truth about God's kingdom.** Jesus came to establish his kingdom in order to take back the human race from Satan, the one who rules the kingdom of darkness. Establishing his kingdom is not only part of Christ's mission, it is also our worldview. This kingdom is first to be in the hearts and minds of men and women and then later to become our eternal destiny.

11. **The truth about the church.** Establishing God's kingdom was not completed by Jesus. His mission has been passed on to each of us individually and collectively as his church. Functioning as his body with his mission we fulfill his salvation plan for the world.

12. **The truth about the return of Christ.** Christ will one day return literally to set up his kingdom on the earth—a kingdom without end. Even though we must experience physical death, his plan is to raise us up with new bodies that live forever. This is our eternal inheritance. It is a kingdom in which we will live together with God and our loved ones in Christ, free of sin and death for all eternity.

These truth declarations and the 12 statements that support them encapsulate the Christian life and message. They are the core of what the gospel is all about. These unshakable truths of the Christian faith provide for us a worldview that defines what we believe, who we are in relationship with God, and how we should behave. They give us the answers to who we are, why we are here, and where we are going—our identity, our purpose, and our destiny. These are not dry theological concepts for discussion and debate. Rather, this is the true and gripping story proclaimed from Genesis to Revelation, the story that gets to the very heart of what life, relationships, human happiness, and joy are all about.

Living the Dream

Each of us and those we love *can* become the "children of God without fault in a crooked and depraved generation" whom Paul described in Philippians 2:15 (NIV). We can embrace and grow in God's revealed way of knowing, being, and living in the world to the point that it becomes unmistakably clear to those around us as to what Christianity really means. This will bring pleasure to God and true joy and happiness to our lives.

THE NICENE CREED

We believe in one God, the Father Almighty, Maker of heaven and earth, and of all things visible and invisible;

And in one Lord Jesus Christ, the only begotten Son of God, begotten of his Father before all worlds, God of God, Light of Light, very God of very God, begotten, not made, being of one substance with the Father; by whom all things were made; who for us men and for our salvation came down from heaven, and was incarnate by the Holy Spirit of the Virgin Mary, and was made man; and was crucified also for us under Pontius Pilate; he suffered and was buried; and the third day he rose again according to the Scriptures, and ascended into heaven, and is seated at the right hand of the Father; and he shall come again, with glory, to judge both the living and the dead; whose kingdom shall have no end.

And we believe in the Holy Ghost, the Lord and giver of life, who proceeds from the Father and the Son; who with the Father and the Son together is worshipped and glorified; who spoke by the prophets. And we believe in the holy catholic and apostolic church; we acknowledge one baptism for the remission of sins; and look for the resurrection of the dead, and the life of the world to come.

CHAPTER THREE

THE REAL MEANING
OF TRUTH

Nearly 20 centuries ago, a high government official, trained in politics and the law, asked a question that has echoed all the way into the twenty-first century.

Imagine Pontius Pilate, then the Roman governor of Judea, standing in his elaborate palace, magisterially bedecked. He posed a set of serious questions to the man who stood shackled between two soldiers.

"Are you the King of the Jews?" Pilate asked. The prisoner was accused of sedition.

This prisoner, unlike most, stood straight in the presence of the governor and looked him in the eyes as he spoke. "I am not an earthly king...My kingdom is not of this world."

"You *are* a king then?" the governor said.

"*You* say that I am a king," the prisoner answered, aware that his interrogator was in a prickly political position, "and you are right." He looked at the politician with eyes that seemed to read not only his face but his soul as well. "I was born for that purpose," he continued, "and I came to bring truth to the world. All who love the truth recognize that what I say is true."

Pilate responded, "What *is* truth?"

Imagine for a moment that you are in that hall with Pilate and his prisoner. Imagine the words of the governor's question echoing off the marbled walls. Imagine the expression on Pilate's face as he posed the question, scornful at first, then turning serious when the answer did not come quickly.

Seconds ticked by. Still the prisoner and the governor studied each other.

Imagine the governor's thoughts: *Who is this man? Why does he gaze at me so?*

And the prisoner's thoughts: *Have I not just told you? I came to bring truth to the world. Pilate, you are looking at the answer to your own question: I am the truth.*[1]

Truth in Relationship

On that day in his Jerusalem palace when he met Jesus, Pilate was not merely discussing the truth; he was literally looking at it. Truth was standing before him, clothed in human flesh! Just days earlier Jesus had told his disciple Philip, "I am the way, the truth, and the life" (John 14:6). He was saying truth is a person to relate to, that "the way" is a person to interact with and follow, and that he is the only true source of life. Truth, a way of living, and life itself is embodied in the person of God. And the means to obtain the truth, the way, and the life is through a relationship with Jesus.

> To explain a biblical worldview…outside of relationship is to distort and invite error into Christianity.

To explain or present a biblical worldview and the truths of the faith outside of relationship is to distort and invite error into Christianity. Jesus wasn't simply trying to correct the theology of the Jewish leaders with his teachings. Neither was he launching a new philosophy of the Jewish religion. He was offering a way to restore God's original design for a world gone mad. He was offering the means to restore the God-human relationship that had been broken by sin. Relationship was key. And it still is.

A number of years ago Dartmouth Medical School commissioned a scientific study of young people. The project, which was called "Hardwired to Connect," analyzed the results of more than 260 studies of youth. The report stated that 100 percent of all the studies they analyzed showed that from the moment a baby is born his or her brain is physically, biologically, and chemically hardwired to connect with others in relationships.[2] That shouldn't surprise us, since we were created in the image of a relational God for the purpose of relationships. In fact, the healthier we are relationally, the more receptive we will be to God's relational truth.

Mark Matlock, author and president of WisdomWorks Ministries, made this observation about the students with whom he was ministering:

> Some of my students were incredibly intelligent and even showed an interest in Christ, but they never seemed to make a breakthrough. I was trying to convince them of the evidence of Christ, and they just couldn't get it.

Looking back, I realize many of these students were emotionally wounded (or even abandoned) individuals who simply could not connect to what I was saying.[3]

It stands to reason that if truth is intrinsically relational in nature and we experience struggles or dysfunctions in our relational life, it will be more difficult to receive the truth. But the other side of this coin is that receiving the truth in all its relational meaning can overcome the problems in our relationships. Truth not only points out our wrong and corrects us; it brings relational healing as well, because truth is a person who lovingly cares for us.

Not long ago, I (Josh) was speaking at a large church in the Midwest. The church had just completed a building project and moved into their large facility. As I approached the entrance, I noticed a huge banner hanging across the building. It read, "We preach the truth—and the truth only!"

Now, I know there is nothing wrong with declaring the truth, if by truth we mean the whole of the truth in all its dimensions. However, I've heard enough similar statements to be suspicious when pastors make declarations about preaching "truth only." So my first thought on seeing that sign was, *If that sign means what I suspect it means, this church is doomed to failure.* Over the course of the weekend I engaged the pastor about his banner. I asked why he was placing such an emphasis on truth only. He explained that he was concerned about a gospel that was emotionally driven to make us feel good about ourselves but never really addressed people's minds. He wanted to get back to the early church emphasis of proclaiming the truth and only the truth because that, he said, "is what turned the world upside down."

I smiled and shook my head. "No, it wasn't," I said. I went on to explain that he was overreacting to an out-of-balance emphasis on one aspect of the truth. As relational beings we think *and* we feel. We have both a mind and a heart. I told my pastor friend that truth was meant to be proclaimed in the context of relationships so it would reach both our intellect and our emotions. This is the kind of proclamation Paul referred to when he depicted the process that brought the Thessalonians to a vibrant faith: "We loved you so much that we were delighted to share with you *not only* the gospel of God but our lives as well, because you had become so dear to us" (1 Thessalonians 2:8 NIV).

Paul was passing on the faith relationally just as Christ had modeled it. The truth he proclaims to us appeals to our minds by pointing out our dilemma (sin and death). But it goes on to demonstrate a love that ultimately provides a solution—a way to regain a relationship with God. We live in a broken and relationally disconnected culture. Each of us has relational and emotional struggles. "Truth only"—if by that term we mean a set of facts that appeal solely to the intellect—will not solve our emotional and relational issues. Rather, it is truth within the context of relationship that we can believe with our minds and experience with our emotions. It is God's penetrating truth that reveals our true condition, loves and accepts us for who we are, and makes provision to freely forgive us. Relational truth is what each of us needs and craves.

We Have a Model in Forming Our Biblical Worldview

The early church provides the ideal model for how the relational truth of God was imparted so effectively to others. Christianity was birthed from Judaism. Jesus' immediate followers were Jewish men and women who had been raised in a Hebraic model of education. There is a vast contrast between the way we typically learn and teach in our Western culture and the way God instructed the Hebrews to learn and teach. Today practically all modern education in North America, including that of most churches and Christian schools, employs a form of teaching based on a Hellenistic model. Greeks shaped much of how we think today about education and disseminating information. Essentially, this Hellenistic approach is to present a student with rational and logical constructs of information that he or she is required to absorb intellectually. To determine if the subject matter has in fact been absorbed, students are asked to regurgitate the information back to the teacher. This is called testing. If the student can accurately repeat the information, he or she passes the course, and the pupil is said to have been "taught."

The Christian faith…
is an integrated and
organic cycle of intimately
knowing the truth, being
the truth in relationship
with God and others, and
living the truth before
the world around us.

The Hebraic model of education is quite different. The goal of this model is not mere memorization of repeatable facts; the goal is for the truth to become one with the pupil to the point that it is lived out. Under this approach truth is to be learned by practicing it in relationship with others. This means we have not necessarily "learned" a truth simply because we can repeat it to a mentor. We have merely lodged it in our mind. It is learned only when it is reflected in our lives in relationship to God, to others, or to our environment. In this educational model, the testing is in living out what we learn relationally. The question isn't whether we have the information correctly stuffed into our heads, but rather how the truth has transformed our attitude and behavior.

If we see Christianity simply as a worldview to be discussed, debated, and proven on a rational basis rather than demonstrated on a relational and transformational basis, we will undoubtedly not see Christianity as God intended. Nor will we be passing on the faith effectively to the next generation.

Early in the second century the church firmly established a relational model enabling individuals to embrace the faith and pass it on to others. By AD 130 Justin Martyr declared that the Christian faith revolved around a continuing cycle of believing, belonging, and behaving. These three components were not compartmentalized into three disciplines; they were seen as a whole—integrated and continuous.

Believing or knowing the truth is a process of understanding who God is and how we relate to him and others. This truth we believe leads naturally to a transformation of our lives in relationship with God. This is where belonging comes in. Entering into a relationship with God bonds us with others who share that relationship, enabling us to experience a sense of belonging. The apostle talked about the "unity in our faith" by which "the whole body is fitted together perfectly. As each part does its own special work, it helps the other parts grow, so that the whole body is healthy and growing and full of love" (Ephesians 4:13,16). We know the truth, and then we become that truth in relationship with God and others in the body of Christ.

The truth process does not stop with believing and belonging. It continues on and affects our behavior. When we become intimate with the truth, it transforms our very being and how we relate to others in community with them, and that results in godly living. Truth is to be lived out.

The early church saw this as an organic cycle of bringing new converts to spiritual maturity and equipping them to pass on the faith to others. They modeled before their children and a needy world what it meant to be in relationship with God, both as individuals and as a community of believers. A sense of belonging was established. They would then take their children and new converts by the hand and walk them through an intentional, life-changing process by instructing them to know and believe the truth handed down by the apostles. They taught them to live out that truth like devoted followers of Jesus and initiated them into an active engagement of the world around them.

This process naturally embedded within each follower of Christ a biblical worldview. The Christian faith was then and still is *an integrated and organic cycle of intimately knowing the truth, being the truth in relationship with God and others, and living the truth before the world around us, starting in our own families.* This is God's plan to know, to be, and to live his truth and naturally impart that living and transformational truth to others.

This process of forming a biblical worldview and passing on our faith, established in the second century, can still work in the twenty-first century. But we do face some challenges, both in dealing with influences in our own lives and influences in the society we're part of. In order to address those challenges, let's look individually at each of the three elements that make up this cycle we've just outlined and consider how to make them work in the present day.

Know the Truth

Picture a small-group Bible study. The group leader, who has just finished reading a Scripture passage, turns to a group member and asks, "Pam, what does this verse mean?"

Pam, a professed Christian, pauses to reflect on the passage. "Well," she begins after a few moments of careful consideration, "what this verse means to me is…"

Chances are, most of us wouldn't even detect the subtle shift in meaning reflected in Pam's use of the words *to me*. But the importance of those two tiny words must not be underestimated. They are indicative of a condition that exists among most Christians today. Most Christians are not looking to the biblical text in order to know *the* truth; they are actually looking for "their truth." The vast majority in our culture, including many professed Christians, say there is no objective moral truth. In a world with no objective moral truth, one cannot claim that there is any specific truth to be found in a given Bible verse. Therefore, the best we can do with the Bible is use it as a foil to determine a personal "truth" that meshes with our own way of thinking and thus has meaning only "to me."

Many pastors and church small-group leaders have become group facilitators rather than teachers of scriptural truth. It's not so much because these leaders are not intending to share the meaning of scriptural truth—many are. The problem is that many people simply hear the truth through their own "filter," which, strongly influenced by a postmodern culture, tells them that all truth is subjectively and personally determined.

Not long ago I (Sean) was speaking at a youth rally on the topic of sexuality. In the middle of my talk a girl interrupted and echoed the five words I so often hear from young people today: "Who are you to judge?" She was saying I had no right to make moral judgments, because truth is subjective—that is, it was "my truth," which makes all views equal. This girl, like most of us, has grown up in a culture of moral relativism that prides itself on accepting many truths. We have been told we need to be tolerant of all beliefs, without judgment, without being critical, and to think that no one way is better than another. In fact, the moment anyone claims to have *the truth,* he or she is labeled as arrogant, bigoted, and judgmental.

While we reject the idea that truth is personal and subjective, it isn't totally incorrect. Some truth is a personal choice or preference. For example, which statement is true: "Chocolate is the best flavor of ice cream" or "Vanilla is the best flavor of ice cream"? Your answer would depend on your taste preferences, and thus it would be neither right nor wrong, true nor untrue. Chocolate can be the best to you, and vanilla can be the best to me. There is no contradiction here because we are talking about our subjective preferences. This kind of truth is relative to the individual and can change. But when it comes to moral truths, that's another issue.

Gregory Koukl, president of Stand to Reason, has pointed out that a person could believe that ice cream controls diabetes. But the reality is, insulin controls diabetes. A person can believe that ice cream controls diabetes with great conviction, but it doesn't change the objective fact that insulin is the controlling factor. The same is true for morality. Even if someone believed rape was right, it would still be wrong. Moral truth is not based on subjective preferences; it is based upon objective reality.

Moral truth isn't something you or I create or decide for ourselves. In fact, it isn't even something God decides. It is something he *is*. It is God's nature and character that define moral truth. The basis of everything we call moral and right springs from the truth that resides in the character of the eternal God who is outside us, above us, and beyond us.

One of the appealing aspects of subjectively deciding your own truth is that you can embrace it as something that is personally and experientially yours. But discovering a truth outside yourself is even more personal and experiential when you understand that Jesus is the truth—he is the exact representation of his Father God. And when the person of truth—Jesus—enters our lives, he is there to transform us into a representation of himself.

I realize, of course, that we Christians can talk all day about how we know the truth because we have experienced Jesus personally. Yet we cannot expect that claim to convince others that what we proclaim as truth is actually true. They can simply claim it might be true for us, but that doesn't make it true for everyone. We know that God's truth is true for everyone, but unless that truth can be proven or demonstrated to be true, we cannot expect others to get on board with belief. And that is where knowing why we believe that something is true comes into play.

Knowing the truth calls for a balanced mind and heart approach. Jesus wanted his followers to believe in him for who he claimed to be, but he didn't want them to believe in him blindly. He wanted them to be confident that what he was asking them to believe was true. So he appealed to the evidence that established that he was, in fact, the Son of God. "Don't you believe that I am in the Father and the Father is in me?" he asked. Then he urged them to "at least believe because of what you have seen me do" (John 14:10-11). The evidences for believing what God says is true are there to convince our minds that what he says *is* real and true. Yes, as we said above, truth is more than just a set of facts; it is relational and emotional. It brings joy. But it is impossible for our hearts to rejoice in what our minds reject. That is why we need to know not only *what we believe* but also *why we believe it*. Knowing what we believe forms our belief system. When we know why we believe it we develop deepened convictions.

The Bible itself repeatedly invites us to examine why a truth is true so we can form our convictions. The apostle John, who had firsthand knowledge of the truth, wrote, "Jesus' disciples saw him do many other miraculous signs besides the ones recorded in this book. But these are written so that you may believe that Jesus is the Messiah, the Son of God, and that by believing in him you will have life" (John 20:30-31). In other words, John recorded evidences that confirmed Jesus to be the one true God so we could know the truth with confidence and deep conviction.

So as you explore each truth of the faith in this handbook, you will equally examine both the truth you are to believe as well as the evidence for why you can believe it with confidence. Of course, no matter how convincing the evidence is, you still must exercise faith. For example, I (Sean) didn't have exhaustive knowledge about Stephanie before I married her. I couldn't know 100 percent that she was the person of integrity I firmly believed her to be. But I did have sufficient evidence to make a wise, informed decision on the moral character of the person I was dating. And now that we have been happily married for over a decade, I thank God that we each took that step of faith.

You will seldom, if ever, have exhaustive evidence, but you can find sufficient evidence to establish that what you believe is credible and objectively true. That is what knowledgeable faith does—it rests its case on sufficient evidence. Noted author and apologist J.P. Moreland aptly defines faith as "a trust in what we have reason to believe is true."[4] A faith rooted in the truth that we have reason to believe is objectively true will ground us in the knowledge of the truth both intellectually and experientially.

When we know the truth and why we believe it ourselves, we can then offer to others a faith that appeals both to the heart and the mind.

Be the Truth

Simply knowing what we believe and why we believe it is not, of itself, sufficient. The truth that we believe must also become the very core of who we are. Buying into the Christian faith involves *being a living representation of the truth.*

We have a friend named Frank; his son is called Frankie. Frank is a man of few words; so is his son. Frank appears most comfortable when his hands are thrust into his pants pockets; Frankie is no different. Frank is a skilled mechanic; Frankie is fascinated by mechanical things. Not once has Frankie's father ever sat down with him to teach him these behaviors or interests. The son was a representation of his father due to sheer genetics and by simply being in relationship with his dad.

Being a representation of the truth is about allowing the truth of God to penetrate us so intimately that it transforms our very lives. "As the Spirit of the Lord works within us," Paul states, "we become more and more like him and reflect his glory even more" (2 Corinthians 3:18). The purpose of Christ's Spirit—the truth—coming into our lives is to become like the truth-giver. Frankie had the DNA of his father, so it was natural for him to become like his father. When we receive the Holy Spirit of truth, the apostle Peter says we "share in his divine nature" (2 Peter 1:4). Metaphorically speaking, God's very DNA is implanted in us and a process of transformation begins as we "become conformed to the image of His Son" (Romans 8:29 NASB).

There was a college student years ago, we'll call him Chad, who registered for all his classes and moved into a dorm room. Chad was working himself through school and was on a tight budget. So for breakfast, lunch, and supper all he could afford to eat was cheese and crackers in his dorm room. Day in and day out, all his meals consisted of nothing but mice food. After a couple of weeks he grew extremely tired of cheese and crackers, so he decided to splurge for one meal and eat at the college cafeteria. He loaded up his tray with meat and potatoes, salad, vegetables, and a couple desserts. When he came to the cashier he asked, "How much for all this?" The cashier responded, "Do you have your student ID?" "Yes," Chad answered. "Well, it won't cost you anything. All your meals were included in your registration."

From the first day of school Chad had had full access to all the food he could eat. Yet he had failed to understand how the college meal program was applicable to him. There are many believers who have a knowledge of God's truth and may even know why they believe it, but for some reason they fail to understand how that truth is relevant to their lives. Consequently, the power of that truth isn't appropriated to their life. So in the chapters that follow, as we discover step-by-step what we believe and why we believe it, we will also uncover the relevant and transforming nature of each truth when it is applied to specific needs of our lives. That application leads to our "brand-new nature...continually being renewed as [we] learn more and more about Christ, who created this new nature within [us]" (Colossians 3:10). When we know the truth and become a representation of the truth, we are not only beginning to embrace a biblical worldview, but we are also in a position to effectively pass it on to others. Someone has said, "We teach what we know, we impart who we are." And if we become a living representation of God's truth, we will demonstrate it in our lives—we will live it.

Live the Truth

Knowing the truth and being a representation of the truth leads naturally to living out that truth. John the disciple of Jesus said, "Let us stop just saying we love each other; let us really show it by our actions. It is by our actions that we know we are living in the truth" (1 John 3:18-19). Truth is to be lived, and when it is lived it also becomes an example to others.

Lest you give up hope before you even begin, let us be quick to say that being a representation of the truth doesn't mean we must live perfect lives. I (Sean) remember a time when I was still living with my parents, and my dad was in a heated argument with Mom. To be honest, Dad was being pretty awful. At one point in the argument he threw a folder down on the table and said, "I'm out of here." He stormed out the door and drove off. I remember thinking, *Man, is he ever ticked.*

I, along with my sisters, went back to doing whatever we had been doing prior to the "Josh explosion." But it wasn't long before Dad was back and called us all in for a meeting. In front of us all he told my mom how wrong he had been and how sorry he was that he had hurt her, and he sought her forgiveness. He turned to each of us kids and told us how disrespectful he had been to our mother, and he sought our forgiveness too. Now, my dad's earlier actions were far from a perfect model of Christlikeness, but he was, nonetheless, a great model of one who was truly following Christ. How? When he realized his offense and sought forgiveness, he was being sensitive to the convicting Spirit of God. My dad was a model of a person who sincerely desires to be conformed to the image of Christ.

Believe it or not, those around us need to see us fail and humbly seek forgiveness. The Spirit of truth through his Word is there "to make us realize what is wrong in our lives. It straightens us out and teaches us to do what is right" (2 Timothy 3:16). Being a living reflection of the truth in a fallen world means we sometimes mess up, but when we do we must realize it and make amends. The great and spiritual apostle Paul said, "I don't mean to say that I have already achieved these things or that I have already reached perfection! But I keep working toward that day when I will finally be all that Christ Jesus saved me for and wants me to be" (Philippians 3:12).

So as we cover the twelve truths of the faith in the pages that follow, we will not only discover: 1) what it is we believe, but; 2) why we believe it; then 3) how these truths are relevant to life and how they transform us internally; and finally, 4) how we can live truth out before the world around us so that it can be imparted to those we love. As these truths take root in our innermost being, we will be reflecting Christ's way, his truth, his life—living a biblical worldview.

PART II

THE UNSHAKABLE TRUTH OF GOD'S CREATION

God is a personal God who
desires a love relationship.

■

God wants us to know him;
he reveals himself through
his written Word.

■

Sin entered the world and
brought death to the human race.

TRUTH ONE

GOD EXISTS

CHAPTER FOUR

WHO IS GOD?

A s a young teenager I (Josh) didn't like who I was—the son of the town drunk. I hated my father and everything he stood for, and that impacted what I thought about myself in a significant way. As I grew older and left home I took with me the puzzling question of "Who am I really?"

As a skeptic, I questioned the existence of a personal God. So I didn't have a definitive answer of who I was meant to be as God's creation. Yet as I would stare up at the stars at night I wondered how everything got here. Planet Earth orbited the sun in just one galaxy among billions that filled deep space. And I felt so small and alone in such a vast universe. And to be honest I secretly hoped there was some Intelligent Being out there called God who could help me understand who I was and what my life was all about.

Does God Exist?

We do live on a planet in a vast universe. And it's natural to ask where we all came from and for what purpose we exist. Our home on earth seems so insignificant and small, suspended as it is in the vastness of space. Is God out there somewhere in the vastness? Think about space for a moment. It seems to stretch on and on without any possibility of ending. When we try to imagine the size even of the known universe, it's impossible to truly comprehend. But let's try.

Why Does Anything Exist?

The expanses of the universe are so immense that we measure them using the light-year, which is the distance light travels in 365 days. Light travels at the speed of 186,282 miles per second. In a year, that distance, multiplied out and rounded off, increases to 5,865,696,000,000, almost 6 trillion, miles. To put that in a perspective we can almost grasp, it takes a sunbeam just over 8 minutes to travel the 93 million miles from the sun to earth. So what is the size of the observable universe in terms of light-years? Scientists say matter is spread over a space at least 93 billion light-years across. Our Milky Way galaxy is roughly 100,000 light years in diameter. Its nearest sister galaxy, the Andromeda galaxy, is located roughly 2.5 million light years away. And there are probably more than 100 billion galaxies in the observable universe.[1] As finite beings we simply cannot imagine such distances, such magnitude. And the very concept of infinite space is far more than our minds can handle. How was this vast space formed, and why?

Thinking about time presents a similar dilemma. It's impossible to conceive of a beginning or an ending of time because the only thing we can imagine before or after time is just more time. Since everything we experience has a starting and an ending, the concept of eternity is incomprehensible to us.

Time, the vastness of space, and the number of galaxies are for the most part mysteries to us. Could it all be here just by chance? Where did it all come from? If we look right here on our home planet we also find the mysteries and fascination of nature. Take the grass cutter ant, for example. These amazing creatures have developed a complex social structure called a colony, one of which can number in the hundreds of thousands of ants. It requires sophisticated communication and coordination to gather large quantities of food to feed the colony, and each ant is a specialized member of a team that accomplishes that feat.

Scout ants are sent out to find food. When an ant finds a succulent leaf, it scurries back to the colony to deliver the news, frequently touching the ground with its body to lay down a scent trail between the ant mound and the food source. Foraging ants follow that aromatic trail to the food source.

Certain cutter ants use a "song" to communicate the discovery of high-quality leaves that need to be harvested. The ant "sings" by producing a high-frequency vibration with its abdomen against the leaf. Other ants from up to three feet away perceive the vibration through their legs. They follow the vibration to the leaf, and together they cut it away from its stalk and carry it back to the ant mound. Ants can support 100 times their own weight, and these cutter ants will carry plants up to a thousand feet—a distance equivalent to more than three football fields—to get food to the colony.[2]

Cutter ants are indeed a great and wonderful mystery, but an even greater one is your ability to read these words and marvel at the sophisticated communication skills, coordination abilities, and strength of those little creatures. Because inside your skull is a three-pound wonderment. Your eyes blink and follow the words on this page. The words are symbols with specific meaning that string together thoughts, which you can understand as you read. Your heart pumps, you inhale and exhale, your body is digesting and processing food.

All these involuntary muscle movements are controlled by the miracle organ called the brain. Your ability to walk, run, sit, sleep, touch, see, hear, smell, taste, and feel every type of emotion is being processed right now through over 100 billion nerve cells called neurons. Your neurons have the amazing ability to gather and transmit electrochemical signals that tell your muscles to move the parts of your body so it will accomplish what you want it to do. These neurons are like the gates and wires in a computer—only immeasurably more complex. While medical science has made significant advances in understanding how the brain works, most of it still remains a mystery. For example, in a digital computer, information is processed by a small

What or who brought everything into being? And for what purpose?

set of "registers" that operate at speeds of billions of cycles per second. The brain uses its neurons to process vastly more information but at speeds of only around 100 cycles per second.[3] How does the brain function so much more effectively than the most sophisticated and complex computer made today? No one really knows.

Your brain is the most complex biological structure known today. Yet how did it come to be? Where did you and your brain, the tiny ant, the Milky Way Galaxy, and all that is in the universe come from? Why is there *something* in existence instead of nothing? What or who brought everything into being? And for what purpose?

An Impersonal Power?

Some would say that all that exists was created by the universe itself and will one day be reabsorbed by the universe. In this view an entity or being called God does not actually exist. God, they say, is a cosmic life force that includes all the substance of the universe. Nature and the idea of God are the same. This is called *pantheism*.[4] Eight percent of teenagers who identify themselves as conservative Protestants embrace this New Age, Oprah Winfrey philosophy. Further, from this cosmic life force we are all empowered to be god and to be one with the universe.[5] The classic phrase used to describe this belief is "God is all and all is God." This is the view of God that was propagated so effectively in the movie *Avatar*.

Some who disagree with pantheistic doctrine say that a supreme being who is not a part of the universe created everything that exists, but essentially this being is uninvolved in any further way with creation. This is the view of Deists, who typically reject most supernatural events (prophecy, miracles) and assert that God, "the Supreme Architect," has a plan for the universe that is not altered either by his intervention in the affairs of human life or by suspension of the natural laws of the universe.[6]

Ten percent of teenagers who identify themselves as conservative Protestants hold to this Deist philosophy.[7] They believe there is a God, but he is like a master clock-maker who designed the world, wound it up, and since then has let it run on its own. A young person with this view would not bother to pray to God for help in time of need or for strength to resist temptation. In this view God is an impersonal being who has left us to make it on our own.

What We Believe About God

Christians, however, believe that a personal being existed before time and space as we know it. This being spoke the words "Let there be..." and by the power of his will all that exists came into being (Genesis 1:3). We believe those words came from the voice of a personal, infinite God that "created everything there is. Nothing exists that he didn't make" (John 1:3). We believe this God is the Intelligent Designer of all that exists within the universe.

The questions naturally arise, what is the nature of this God, is he knowable, and why did he create us? While a God with the power to create vast universes is bound to be beyond our comprehension in many ways, he is knowable to us finite creatures. But how? Although we cannot know him exhaustively, we can know him truly, suffi-ciently, and with confidence because of *what he has revealed* about himself to us. For example, God is known to us by at least six characteristics.

God is eternal. Eternal means life without beginning or end. There was never a moment when God didn't exist, nor will he ever end. That is impossible for our minds to grasp. Moses could not understand it. He was out on the backside of the desert herding sheep when God showed up in a bush burning with flames that didn't con-sume it. When God sent him to tell the people of Israel he was going to deliver them out of Egypt, Moses said, "'They won't believe me. They will ask, "Which god are you talking about? What is his name?" Then what should I tell them?' God replied, 'I AM THE ONE WHO ALWAYS IS. Just tell them "I AM has sent me to you"'" (Exodus 3:13-14). The great I AM has no birthday and will have no funeral.

The prophet Isaiah said, "Don't you know that the LORD is the everlasting God, the Creator of all the earth? He never grows faint or weary. No one can measure the depths of his understanding" (Isaiah 40:28).

God is omnipotent. God is almighty and powerful. If he wants to do something he can do it. Job said to God, "I know that you can do anything, and no one can stop you" (Job 42:2). King David said, "How great is our Lord! His power is absolute" (Psalm 147:5). The prophet Jeremiah said, "O Sovereign LORD! You have made the heavens and earth by your great power. Nothing is too hard for you" (Jeremiah 32:17). The prophet Isaiah proclaimed, "The LORD, your Redeemer and Creator, says: 'I am the

LORD, who made all things. I alone stretched out the heavens. By myself I made the earth and everything in it'" (Isaiah 44:24). The eternal, never-ending God is also the ever-powerful God who can accomplish anything he desires.

God is omnipresent. God is ever-present. His presence encompasses all the galaxies while at the same time he is with you right now right where you are. King David said, "I can never escape from your spirit! I can never get away from your presence! If I go up to heaven, you are there; if I go down to the place of the dead, you are there" (Psalm 139:7-8). Because we are finite beings it is hard to imagine a being who is everywhere-present, but this is a characteristic of God. "'Am I a God who is only in one place?' asks the LORD. 'Do they think I cannot see what they are doing? Can anyone hide from me? Am I not everywhere in all the heavens and earth?' asks the LORD" (Jeremiah 23:23-24). The ever-present God spans the reach of the universe and yet is there to hear you whisper a prayer.

God is immutable. God by his very nature can always be counted on because he will not change. The psalmist said that the earth will perish, "but you [God] remain forever…you are always the same; your years never end" (Psalm 102:26-27). The writer of the book of Hebrews said, "Jesus Christ is the same yesterday, today, and forever" (Hebrews 13:8).

We can rest secure in a God who does not waver or lie. He will always do what he says he will do. "God is not a man, that he should lie. He is not a human, that he should change his mind. Has he ever spoken and failed to act? Has he ever promised and not carried it through?" (Numbers 23:19). The immutable God is worthy of our complete trust.

God is omniscient. God knows all. Everything past, present, and future, he knows. He has infinite knowledge. He spoke through the prophet Isaiah and declared, "I am God, and there is no one else like me. Only I can tell you what is going to happen even before it happens. Everything I plan will come to pass, for I do whatever I wish" (Isaiah 46:9-10). King David said, "O LORD, you have examined my heart and know everything about me" (Psalm 139:1). Such awesome knowledge is beyond us. Imagine the hard drives of a trillion computers filled with all the information known to humans… and it wouldn't even scratch the surface of God's knowledge.

God is personal. Even though God is the eternal, almighty, ever-present, unchanging, and all-knowing God, he is also a God who desires personal interaction. On one hand his power and awesome might is fearful, yet he is the "God who is passionate about his relationship with you" (Exodus 34:14).

This is actually what I (Josh) was searching for but didn't know it. To know the God of the universe in a personal way would answer so many questions as to who I was, why I was here, and where I was going. God is not an absentee God who created the universe and then left it to its own devices. He is active and involved with his creation. He entered our world in the form of a human; at the moment of salvation he enters our lives in the form of his Holy Spirit; he answers our prayers and gives us strength through the Holy Spirit, he empowers us to resist temptation and wants to fulfill his purpose in our lives. He is a personal, interactive God who desires a relationship with his creation.

Therefore:

> We believe the truth that there is an infinite, personal God of the universe.

The angel that spoke to Mary stated it well: "Nothing is impossible with God" (Luke 1:37). And while he is infinite in his existence, power, presence, and knowledge he wants a relationship with each of us personally. That is what is so amazing. A God who is in need of nothing and can do anything and everything still wants and desires to have an intimate, personal relationship with you and me! That is the God who is and always will be, the God you and I can believe in with confidence.

CHAPTER FIVE

EVIDENCE FOR GOD'S EXISTENCE

We may *believe* a personal God exists, but can we *know* that he exists? It's not possible to offer absolute proof of God by having him materialize before a large crowd and demonstrate his omnipotence, omnipresence, omniscience, and glory for all to see.

Even if that happened many people would not accept it as proof. They would wonder if they were hallucinating. In fact, God *did* show up in human form and demonstrated his deity with miracles and prophecies. And people still doubted that he was God.

God has made himself known for those who want to seek him.

Yet, we are not left without sufficient evidence of God's existence. More than enough convincing data is available for anyone who wants to examine it. God has made himself known for those who want to seek him. Jesus said, "Seek and you will find" (Luke 11:9 NIV). There is evidence of him all around us. His fingerprints can be seen anywhere you look—from the vastness of the universe to the tiniest microscopic cell. Let's look at just four evidences or arguments for the existence of God.

1. The Cosmological Argument

This is also called the *first-cause argument*. The point is made that everything that begins to exist must have a cause. So if you go back in time far enough you will find the first cause—and that cause will be Creator God.

Thomas Aquinas, a renowned philosopher of the thirteenth century, made a similar argument. He said that anything in motion, like the universe, could not have brought itself into motion. He stated that a thing in motion must be caused to move. He concluded there had to be an Unmoved Mover and that Mover is God.

Frank Turek, Christian apologist and author, makes a case that science supports the existence of God as the first cause in an article published in the *Apologetics Study Bible for Students*, of which I (Sean) am the general editor. Not all of Dr. Turek's views are accepted by every Christian. However, we quote from his writing to allow you to evaluate this position for yourself. He states:

> In philosophy, the cosmological argument for God's existence says:
>
> 1. All things that begin to exist have a cause of their beginning to exist
> 2. The universe began to exist
> 3. Therefore, the universe was caused to exist (and by inference, God is the cause)
>
> Does science support this? Absolutely. Overwhelming scientific evidence tells us that the universe exploded into being out of nothing at some point in the distant past...
>
> There are five main lines of scientific evidence—denoted by the acronym SURGE—that point to the definite beginning of the universe. They are *the Second law of thermodynamics, the expanding Universe, Radiation afterglow, Great galaxy seeds in the radiation afterglow,* and *Einstein's theory of general relativity.*
>
> The conclusion that the universe had a beginning is virtually certain (see chapter 3 of *I Don't Have Enough Faith to Be an Atheist*)...According to the evidence, the universe began from nothing—literally *no* thing physical, temporal, or spatial. Once there was no time, no space, and no matter and then it all banged into existence out of nothing.
>
> What caused this creation event? To answer this, it's important to realize that [it] was not an explosion *in* space but the explosion *of* space. It was not an explosion *in* time but the beginning *of* time. It was not an explosion of pre-existing matter, but the creation of matter itself. Therefore, the cause of the universe must be something beyond space, beyond time, and beyond matter—a Being who is spaceless, timeless, and immaterial. Those are attributes of God!
>
> An atheist might ask, "Why couldn't some natural force or process have caused the universe?" The problem is, nature and natural forces did not exist before...so they could not have caused it. That means the cause of the universe must be something beyond nature—something *super*natural.[1]

So, Who Made God?

This brings us back to the question, "Who made God?" It is important to clarify that Christians do not believe that *everything that exists needs a cause*. Rather, everything that *begins* to exist must have a cause. There are many things that exist that are uncaused, such as mathematical truths and the laws of logic. Even if the world had never been created, it would still be true that 1+1=2. The universe had a beginning so it must have a cause. But God by definition does not need a cause—he is uncaused.

Philosopher William Lane Craig comments penetratingly:

> And this is not special pleading in the case of God. After all, atheists have long maintained that the universe doesn't need a cause, because it's eternal. How can they possibly maintain that the universe can be eternal and uncaused, yet God cannot be timeless and uncaused?[2]

As a young boy I (Sean) often wondered how God could be eternal. I concluded that if the universe had a beginning then something must have existed prior to it to bring it into existence. This thought boggled my mind then, and it still does today! While the human mind is not be able to grasp *how* God has always existed, we all sense that something outside the universe had to cause the universe to come into existence. And a God who is uncaused is the most reasonable explanation.

2. The Teleological Argument

This is the argument for design. The point is made that life, the laws of nature, and the whole universe demonstrate immense specified complexity, the mark of design; therefore the universe must have come from a Personal Designer. King David made this point when he said,

> The heavens tell of the glory of God. The skies display his marvelous craftsmanship. Day after day they continue to speak; night after night they make him known. They speak without a sound or a word; their voice is silent in the skies; yet their message has gone out to all the earth, and their words to all the world (Psalm 19:1-4).

Recently I (Sean) collaborated with Dr. William Dembski in writing a book entitled *Understanding Intelligent Design*.* In it we covered the many facets of the arguments for intelligent design. The remaining portion of this section is drawn from that book.

---

* Harvest House Publishers, 2008.

If you have ever visited Disneyland or Disney World you have probably noticed the bed of flowers laid out on a sloping bank. The colors, formation, and particular flowers form a clear resemblance to Mickey Mouse. No one would attribute that gardening marvel to mere chance. Why? First, flowers of that variety and color don't just grow by chance to form the shape and color of the famous Mickey Mouse. The numerous types of flowers and their multiplicity of placements clearly indicate *complexity.* Complexity in this sense is the same as saying it is highly improbable that these flowers randomly grew there or were positioned so intricately.

Second, besides being complex, the floral arrangement is laid out in a very specific manner. Certain flowers make up the eyes, others the nose, and yet others the mouth and the renowned ears. The image exhibits an independently given pattern— it's therefore *specified.*

This combination of complexity (or improbability) and specificity (or independently imposed patterning) is called *specified complexity.* Specified complexity is a marker of intelligence. Like a fingerprint or a signature, specified complexity identifies the activity of an intelligent agent. The huge flower bed at Disney exhibits specified complexity and leads us to believe an intelligent gardener was its cause.

What a Single Living Cell Declares

The more specified complexity a thing displays—that is, the more complex it is and the more its form obviously follows specific patterns—the more it points to an intelligent designer. Take, for example, the building block of human life—a single living cell. Does it have specified complexity?

> Let's briefly look at a cell magnified a billion times. On its surface we find millions of openings, like portholes in a ship. But these are not mere portholes. They regulate the flow of materials in and out of the cell. Cells exhibit nano-engineering on a scale and sophistication that scientists have hardly begun to scratch. Francis Crick, one of the co-discoverers of DNA's structure, described the cell as "a minute factory, bustling with rapid, organized chemical activity." That was in the early 1980s. Scientists now think of the cell as an automated city.
>
> Inside the cell we find a host of raw materials maneuvered back and forth by robot-like machines all working in unison. In fact, many different objects move in perfect unison through seemingly endless conduits. The level of control in these choreographed movements is truly mind-blowing. And this is just *one* cell. In larger organisms, cells must work together for the proper function of organs such as hearts, eyes, livers, and ears, and these in turn must work together for the life of the organism.
>
> If we peer further inside the cell, we find coils of DNA that store the

information necessary to construct proteins. Proteins themselves are remarkably complex molecular systems. A typical protein is composed of a few hundred amino acids arranged in a precisely ordered sequence that then folds into a highly organized three-dimensional structure. That structure enables the protein to perform its function inside the cell.

Biologists today cannot even describe the activities inside the cell without comparing it to machines and other feats of modern engineering. The reason is that nearly every feature of our own advanced technology can be found in the cell.[3]

As we carefully observe the inner workings of the cell, one thing becomes apparent: There is complexity and sophistication that dwarfs human technological innovation today. This is why more and more scientists are concluding that the best explanation for the cell is intelligent design.

Life Requires Vast Amounts of Information

The key feature to life is information. Life, even the simplest of bacterial cells, requires vast amounts of information to function. Cellular information is stored in DNA. The DNA in one cell in the human body holds the equivalent of roughly 8000 books of information. A typical human body has about 100 trillion cells, each of which has a DNA strand that could be uncoiled to about three meters in length. Thus, if the DNA in an adult human were strung together, it would stretch from Earth to the sun and back around 70 times![4]

Supposing there were no Intelligent Designer—how would the needed information for life be assembled? The typical answer Darwinists come up with is, given enough time, matter, and chance anything can happen.

But how much time, matter, and chance are actually available? As early as 1913, the French mathematician Émile Borel argued that a million monkeys typing ten hours a day would be exceedingly unlikely to reproduce the books in the world's libraries. The universe is very old and enormous, according to Borel, but not old and big enough for something that unlikely.

Let's narrow Borel's scope. Instead of focusing on many books, let's consider the works of Shakespeare. Here is the question: How many monkeys and how much time would be required to reproduce one of the works of Shakespeare, or even just a few lines?

Work has been done on this question by MIT computational quantum physicist Seth Lloyd. According to Lloyd, in the known physical universe, chance is capable of producing only 400 bits of prespecified information (this is equivalent to a string of 400 zeroes and ones). This amounts to a sequence of 82 ordinary letters and spaces. Therefore, the longest initial segment of Hamlet's soliloquy that the entire universe—given its size and purported multibillion-year history—could by chance produce is the following two lines:

TO BE, OR NOT TO BE, THAT IS THE QUESTION.
WHETHER 'TIS NOBLER IN THE MIND TO SUFFER...

Clearly, the phenomenon of chance is limited in its ability to explain certain features of the universe. All the chance in the known universe can't randomly type more than two lines of Shakespeare, much less an entire book.[5]

If chance over time cannot create enough information for two lines of Shakespeare, how could it ever create the complexity of even a single primitive cell? A single cell requires hundreds of thousands of bits of information precisely sequenced in its DNA. So those who deny an Intelligent Designer have the impossible task of explaining how the information (specified complexity) in even a simple living organism could arise out of the process of chance and time. Life simply requires too much information to occur randomly. For example:

The information-storage capacity of DNA far surpasses even the most powerful electronic memory systems known today. Molecular biologist Michael Denton notes that, for all the different types of organisms *that have ever lived*, the necessary information in their DNA for the construction of their proteins "could be held in a teaspoon and there would still be room left for all the information in every book ever written." But DNA does not just store information. In combination with other cellular systems, it also processes information. Hence Bill Gates likens DNA to a computer program, though far more advanced than any software humans have invented.

This is why intelligent design best explains the information content of DNA. Imagine you are walking on the beach and notice the message "Sean loves Stephanie" inscribed in the sand. What would you conclude? You might think Sean, Stephanie, or some gossipy stranger wrote it, but it would never cross your mind to attribute it to chance, necessity, or some combination of the two. Wind, water, and sand simply do not generate meaningful information. The most reasonable inference is that it is a product of intelligent design. If we justifiably infer a mind behind a simple message of 15 characters, then inferring an intelligence for the origin of the cell—which requires hundreds of thousands bits of information— is fully justified.[6]

3. The Moral Law Argument

Every human culture known to man has had a moral law. While there is some variety regarding moral practices across cultures, there is a striking universal agreement about the validity of moral principles such as justice, courage, and fairness. Without appeal to a higher source, namely God, what could account for the moral sense that is common to the entire human race through all of history? Where else could morals have come from?

An objective, universal, and constant standard of truth and morality points to an existence of a personal and moral God.

> In *The Brothers Karamazov*, Russian novelist Fyodor Dostoyevsky aptly observed, "If there is no immortality of the soul, there can be no virtue and therefore everything is permissible." In other words, if God does not exist as the foundation of morality, then *anything goes*. This doesn't mean atheists or other nonbelievers will necessarily act more immorally than believers, but it does mean we lose an objective basis by which to make moral judgments. If God does not exist then we lose the right to judge the Nazis and anyone else with whom we disagree morally. They believed they were right. We think they were wrong. Without a higher law above humanity, who gets to decide moral truth? If there is no greater source above human beings, then the existence of morality is an inexplicable illusion.[7]

Yet if God exists, then we have reason to believe in morality. We *ought* to be truthful, because God is true and faithful. We *ought* to do loving acts, because God is love. Morality stems from the character and nature of God and is binding on his creation. The existence of morality points to the absolute of God's existence and character. Only God's existence and character can properly account for morality.

But there are those who would argue that morality can exist independently of God. They contend that we don't need a God in order to be good—or evil. Yet this assertion presents a problem: How do you define good or evil without some transcendent moral standard? Evil, for example, has traditionally been understood as the perversion of good. Just as crookedness implies a standard of straight, evil implies a standard of good. C.S. Lewis famously said that to complain that a stick is bent makes sense only in light of the concept of straight. Similarly, there can be evil only if there is first good. But if there is no God, then what defines the standard of good? Without God, we are all left to figure out the meaning of good for ourselves, and the concept of objective good disappears. Good becomes a meaningless term, for it is simply whatever each of us wants it to be at a given moment, or whatever evolution has blindly wired us to believe.

The universally recognized existence of objective moral values is a strong reason for believing in God. Consider this simple argument:

1. If objective moral values exist, God must exist.
2. Objective moral values exist.
3. Therefore, God must exist.

We know that objective moral values do exist. We don't need to be persuaded that, for example, torturing babies for fun is wrong. All reasonable people know this. Therefore, since moral values do exist, then God must exist as well.

4. A Personal-Experience-with-God Argument

Not long after I (Josh) became a Christian I was in a debate with the head of the history department at a Midwestern university. I was telling him how my new relationship with God gave me meaning and purpose. He interrupted me with, "McDowell, are you trying to tell me that you believe in God and he has really changed that much about your life? Give me some specifics." After listening to me explain for 45 minutes, he finally said, "Okay, okay—that's enough!"

People have asked me, "How do you know you became a Christian?" "How do you know God is real?" For one, he changed my life. This transformation is one way that I'm assured of the validity of my conversion and the existence of a real and personal God.

I'm sure you have heard people speak of the "bolt of lightning" that hit them when they had their first religious experience. Well, it wasn't that dramatic for me. After I prayed, nothing happened. I mean *nothing*. And I still haven't sprouted wings or a halo. In fact, after I made my commitment to God, I felt worse. I actually felt I was about to vomit. *Oh no, what have I gotten sucked into now?* I wondered. I really felt I had gone off the deep end (and I'm sure some people think I did!).[8]

The change in my life was not immediate, but it was real. In six to eighteen months, I knew that I had not gone off the deep end. I had experienced God, and that changed everything.

A personal experience with God is evidence of his reality. Some might challenge this assertion, saying an experience with God could easily be an illusion or an emotional or psychological fantasy. But those who have genuinely experienced encounters similar to what Paul the apostle experienced on the Damascus road know better. They know it is real. Such experiences are one of many affirmations of Paul's statement: "Now that you belong to Christ, you are the true children of Abraham. You are his heirs, and now all the promises God gave to him belong to you" (Galatians 3:29).

It is true that we who are followers of Jesus and children of God must accept our personal relationship with God by faith. But that doesn't make the relationship any less real. As a Christ-follower you are one of "God's very own children, adopted into his family—calling him 'Father, dear Father.' For his Holy Spirit speaks to us deep in our hearts and tells us that we are God's children" (Romans 8:15-16).

Apart from an infinite personal Creator God we have no life or meaning.

If you have had a personal encounter with the Creator God through Jesus Christ, you know he is real. The evidence of a personal experience with God cannot necessarily be sufficient proof to others, but it can be one of many convincing arguments to the one who knows God personally.

Summary

Many philosophers have tried to exclude God from their explanations of human existence and the meaning to life. But apart from an infinite personal Creator God we have no life or meaning. Noted British atheist Bertrand Russell made this point perfectly clear when he declared it "nearly certain"

> that man is the product of causes which had no prevision of the end they were achieving; that his origin, his growth, his hopes and fears, his loves and his beliefs, are but the outcome of accidental collocations of atoms; that no fire, no heroism, no intensity of thought and feeling, can preserve an individual life beyond the grave; that all the labors of the ages, all the devotion, all the inspiration, all the noonday brightness of human genius, are destined to extinction in the vast death of the solar system, and that the whole temple of man's achievement must inevitably be buried beneath the debris of a universe in ruins.[9]

Either God is the "first cause" of life and of all things, or there is no lasting significance to our existence or to anything we accomplish. We and everything we do, as Russell says, will die in "a universe in ruins." To deny the existence of an infinite, personal God leaves us without hope, purpose, or meaning in life. It's as if we were all swept downstream in a swift river and must choose between climbing onto a rock or plunging over a waterfall. One option offers security and a solid grip on stable reality; the other ends with our hurtling into a void where nothing has meaning and nothing is true.[10] But the evidence surrounding our universe and life itself simply has too much specified complexity to deny the existence of our Intelligent Designer. That leaves us, as Paul said, "no excuse whatsoever for not knowing God" (Romans 1:20). And in knowing God and reflecting his image we find the joy and happiness he intended, both for this life and the one to come. Choosing to believe in God and having a relationship with him gives us a way to understand who we really are.

And that is the subject of our next chapter.

CHAPTER SIX

Discovering Your Identity

Imagine for a moment what it must have been like when the first man and woman were created. Adam, the first human, lived in the perfect paradise called the Garden of Eden. Everything was perfect. Grasses and flowers and animals of all kinds roaming, gamboling, and grazing under a canopy of clouds and sky…everything painted a breathtaking canvas of perfection and beauty.

Each new morning must have brought with it an ever-varying combination of forms, colors, textures, sounds, and movements that converged to bring pleasure to his senses. Musical birds and sparkling waterfalls filled the air. Lush tropical trees and plants grew delicious fruit whose taste and textures brought joy to the palate and satisfaction to the body. As this first human watched the sun go down, he no doubt gazed in awe as the multicolored clouds lit up the horizon in a silent but awe-inspiring fireworks display.

The perfect beauty of his world must have captivated his soul with pure rapture. In harmony with his environment as Adam was, each enchanted evening must have resulted in such satisfaction and contentment that he thought nothing could ever surpass it.

While we have no record that Adam complained about his condition in the pristine garden, something was in fact missing. God said, "It is not good for the man to be alone" (Genesis 2:18). Remember, this was a perfect world with no sin, and Adam had God as his friend and the unsurpassable beauty of his surroundings to enjoy. But God was about to add another dimension to Adam's reality.

Made for Relationship

Even though he had God, Adam was not yet complete. For deep within dwelled an aching aloneness, a sense of emotional disconnectedness and feeling of personal incompleteness because something was yet absent—a human relationship. Even in the perfect world of Eden before sin ever disrupted relationships, God declared that something wasn't good: "It is not good for the man to be alone" (Genesis 2:18). Human aloneness is not good.

So God caused Adam to sleep, and while he slept God formed another human. Imagine Adam's reaction when he awoke. Imagine how he might have gazed through softly waving palms to see a face so captivating that he thought he'd be content never to look at anything else again. He watches in rapt fascination as she emerges from a shroud of mist, gliding toward him with majestic elegance and grace. Her shape and form excite him like nothing ever has. As he reaches out to her he discovers that she is soft to the touch, and her fragrance fills his senses. He feels his heart beat faster, his breathing becomes deeper. He is in awe of this creature called woman. He has never experienced such beauty.

But he was intrigued by more than just her glorious face and form. There was a mystery to this attraction. Adam sensed an indefinable hunger to know more of this creature than what he could physically hold and caress and enjoy. And so did she. They were both drawn to a deeper intimacy than their physical senses could experience. Each of these first humans had a desire to know something about the other that they couldn't see with their eyes or touch with their physical bodies. They experienced a longing for an emotional connection, a bonding of the inner spirit, an intimate attachment of the soul. In short, they experienced a desire for a loving relationship. *For God had planted deep within them an identifying marker or distinguishing character of his own likeness—the capacity for loving relationships.* It is this God-created reality of loving relationships that removes human aloneness and makes you, you. It is your capacity for relationship that provides all the meaning, happiness, and joy you could ever hope to experience.

Your Mark of Personhood: God's Relational DNA

"In the beginning God created the heavens and the earth" (Genesis 1:1). Then God went on to say, "Let us make people in our image, to be like ourselves. They will be masters over all life...So God created people in his own image; God patterned them after himself; male and female he created them" (Genesis 1:26-27). So before there were humans, before Planet Earth or the universe or time as we know it, God existed eternally as a loving relational being.

He is a relational God by his very nature, three personalities blended in perfect harmony—Father, Son, and Holy Spirit. (More on the Trinity is covered in Truth Nine.) While he is the infinite one and we as humans are finite, we bear his relational DNA. We have inherited his relational ability to love another being. Scripture says, "Love comes from God...for God is love" (1 John 4:7-8).

Along with the ability to be relational—to love God and other beings besides ourselves—we have also inherited a number of other traits from God that are related to his relational nature. We have inherited his ability to communicate our thoughts, intents, and feelings to others. Scripture repeatedly uses the phrase "God said," showing us that relationships mean communication to others. The ability to express and enhance relationships by communicating is another way we reflect the image of God.

The basis of your true identity resides in the fact you are uniquely fashioned in God's image.

We have inherited his sense of value for human relationships and for life itself. God said, "Honor your father and mother...do not murder...do not commit adultery...do not steal...do not testify falsely...do not covet your neighbor's wife" (Deuteronomy 5:16-21). From God's giving of the law at Mount Sinai up through the early church and beyond, it was understood and taught that life is sacred at every stage. Promoting social justice, taking care of the poor, and defending human rights find their basis in each of us by the fact that we are purposely created in God's image. In his book *The Faith* Chuck Colson said it well: "When Christians today see life through God's eyes...we are compelled not only to care for the poor and vulnerable but to defend every human's God-given right."[1] That is because we were created in God's relational image with value, dignity, and worth.

We have inherited God's sense of satisfaction and joy in accomplishing things through relationships. After each creative act in Genesis, this relational God "saw that it was good" (Genesis 1:10). The Father, Son, and Holy Spirit found joy in their collective creative acts as the Master of the universe.

We inherited from the Master of the universe the charge to "be masters over all life" (Genesis 1:26). God told the first humans that in relationship with one another they were also to live in proper relationship with their home—Planet Earth. God said to be stewards of the earth and "to tend and care for it" (Genesis 2:15). So God instilled within his human creation an environmental responsibility to relate lovingly to the planet they inherited.

As you can see, God placed humans on a plateau above the rest of creation when he fashioned them in his relational image and likeness. To summarize, this Godlikeness bestowed upon the human race certain gifts and obligations:

- To love God and one another
- To effectively communicate
- To be creative
- To think logically
- To make moral decisions
- To defend the dignity, value, and worth of all human life, be the protector of peace and harmony among all people, and to preserve the unity and sanctity of marriage between a man and a woman and the family
- To be the steward of creation, and so on

It is this relational dimension with all its ramifications that distinguishes us as created in God's likeness and gives us special meaning. But this relational dimension does more than just set us apart from the rest of God's creation. It also defines who we are and gives us our sense of identity.

Discovering Who You Are

When you stop to think about it, you and I largely understand ourselves—our identity—in terms of relationships. We perceive ourselves—and others around us—as this person's son or daughter, that person's husband or wife, and someone else's mother or father, as "the McDowells' neighbor," "Sean's friend," or "Josh's pastor."

While human relationships may provide insight into your identity, the basis of your true identity resides in the fact that you are uniquely fashioned in God's image. Because sin caused us to be born alienated and disconnected from God, we have lost that instilled sense of personal identity. Even after becoming a Christian it does not automatically become easy to discover who we really are. Although I (Josh) trusted Christ and became a Christian as a university student, I didn't initially comprehend who I was. This was basically because I had very little, if any, experiential and emotional context in which to understand the true meaning of a loving relationship. My growing-up years were fraught with relational dysfunction, emotional pain, and chaos. Consequently, I didn't readily see myself as a distinct, one-of-a-kind person created to relate lovingly to God and others.

Yet each of us is an original. No other person is designed just like us. Just as no two snowflakes are ever alike, no two humans ever created are alike. We have similarities, of course. If you have a brother or sister, you can probably see the likeness that comes from being of the same family. Yet you also know that each of you is different. Parents can certainly attest that no two children are alike. Each of us, as a human child and as a child of God, has an original identity. You are a one-of-a-kind original. You have been given distinct and special qualities that make you relationally unique. God has placed deep within you special gifts, talents, passions, and a distinct personality that make you uniquely you.

Scripture recognizes our originality. One subtle but powerful indication of this is found in the familiar words penned by King Solomon: "Train up a child in the way he should go, even when he is old he will not depart from it" (Proverbs 22:6 NASB).

Unfortunately, this verse is often misunderstood, and misapplied, by those who are responsible for the training of young people. Some think it means, "Have family devotions, make sure kids attend church and youth group and a Christian school, and then when they are grown up, they will not depart from the faith."

The real emphasis of this verse, however, centers on the phrase "the way he [or she] should go." The writer is referring to the *child's* way, his or her leaning or bent. The root meanings of these words suggest guiding each child according to his or her own uniqueness. In other words, parents must discern exactly who their child is—his or her uniqueness, abilities, interests, and talents—and then draw out and develop that uniqueness. Train the child to be the unique person God relationally created him or her to be.

The same Hebrew word that is used in Proverbs 22 is translated "bend" in two psalms and refers to the bending of the archer's bow (see Psalm 11:2; 64:3). Today, with precision manufacturing, almost anyone can pick up a bow with a 45-pound draw weight and do a fair job of hitting the target. But in biblical days, nothing was standardized. All archers made their own bows, and each archer had to know the unique characteristics of his own bow if he hoped to hit anything with it.

God's Word is telling us that you have an inborn uniqueness that your parents and caregivers are to identify and train accordingly. In the *Ryrie Study Bible,* a note for Proverbs 22:6 explains that "'the way he should go' really means 'according to his way; that is, the child's habits and interests.' The instruction must take into account his individuality and inclinations, his personality, the unique way God created him, and must be in keeping with his physical and mental development."[2]

My (Sean's) parents understood this truth and guided me to understand my "bent"—those talents, gifts, inclinations, passions, and the distinctiveness that made me, me. My dad saw that I had an inclination toward playing basketball. I'm not a tall person; neither is my father. But as a young person Josh excelled at basketball, and he sensed I had the same talent. He encouraged me to pursue it, coaching me as I learned the game. And I eventually fulfilled my dream of being a point guard for Biola University.

My parents also picked up on my inquisitiveness. I wanted to know things; I enjoyed figuring out why this was true or that was true. And I enjoyed sharing what I was learning with others. Because they cultivated my natural inclinations in these directions, I ended up majoring in philosophy and theology and becoming an educator and speaker. All this resulted in my understanding who I am—the unique person God created in his own relational image.

What Is Your Unique Identity?

God has made you a special, one-of-a-kind person by giving you various skills and talents. And he has also placed within you certain personal preferences and a distinct personality that makes you a one-of-a-kind individual—a person designed to do things in ways only you can do. God has made you in his image like a complex snowflake, a unique person who stands out to him as his special and original creation.

God intends you to use the unique characteristics he gave you to relate not only to him but to others as well. "Just as our bodies have many parts," Paul said, "and each part has a special function, so it is with Christ's body. We are all parts of his one body, and each of us has different work to do. And since we are all one body in Christ, we belong to each other, and each of us needs all the others" (Romans 12:4-5).

There will never be another you. God has specially gifted you to fill a role—a purpose—that no one else can fill. You and I want to know our place in this world. God has crafted us specifically for that place that we—and only we—can fill.

You have unique characteristics with which to love and live for God in a way that only you are empowered to do. God needs you because there will never be another who can fill that place as you can. And he wants to exercise his love and life in and through you in a unique and original fashion. Paul declares,

> There are different ways God works in our lives, but it is the same God who does the work through all of us. A spiritual gift is given to each of us as a means of helping the entire church…It is the one and only Holy Spirit who distributes these gifts. He alone decides which gift each person should have (1 Corinthians 12:6-7,11).

Some aspects of your uniqueness are readily apparent. Your personal identification is distinctly yours. Your fingerprints are unique; your retina scans are distinct; your face and body are at least slightly different from those of anyone else who ever existed on the planet. But it's not always so easy to understand the distinctiveness with which God created you and what gifts the Holy Spirit has distributed to you.

You can learn to identify your distinctiveness by paying attention to how your mind works and what draws your interest. God has instilled within you certain *passions*: things you feel strongly about, things you're fervently interested in, things that give you a special sense of joy when you talk about them or pursue them. Those passions direct you to whom, where, and what God wants you to love in life…as only you can. Can you specifically identify your God-given passions?

Just as Mac and PC computers have different operating systems, God has given you distinctive built-in ways of processing information and making decisions. Do you tend to be emotional or rational? Reflective or outspoken? Creative or systematic? Artistic or mechanical? These tendencies, along with your passions and interests, make up your *distinct personality.* God's love is to be distinctly expressed through your distinct personality, as only you can express it.

If your parents understood that you were a one-of-a-kind individual and sought to train you up in "the way you should go," you have, no doubt, come a long way in identifying your personality type, talents, special gifts, and passions in life. But if you are like most people, you have only a partial understanding of who you are. You could probably use some help in figuring it out. Search "Bobb Biehl" on the web and check out his book *Why You Do What You Do.* Another excellent resource is *Discover Who You Are* by Jane A.G. Kise, David Stark, and Sandra Krebs Hirsh.*

One other thought about our personal identities. Understanding that we are God's children who have a special place in his body doesn't mean that unbelievers don't have talents or natural gifts. It doesn't mean that they can't come to understand themselves and their uniqueness to varying degrees. What it does mean, however, is that unless and until people come to know God as their Father through Christ, they will never understand their true place in this world. A non-Christian may exercise a talent or skill, but it will never be fully expressed as it was meant to be, or it will never bring maximum meaning to that life. God made us in his image, and when we live out his way, his truth, and his life we find both our true identity and experience pure joy because we are being what we are created to be. We are reflecting his image. Knowing who we are and living as God designed us provides a sense of meaning and purpose to life.

---

* *Why You Do What You Do* can be purchased online or through your local Christian bookstore. You can find *Discover Who You Are* and other Life Key resources at www.LifeKeys.com.

CHAPTER SEVEN

LIVING OUT YOUR
RELATIONAL IMAGE OF GOD

Knowing you are a relational being, created in God's image, is important. But how do you live that image out in relationship to others? As we stated earlier, reflecting the image of a relational God includes certain social responsibilities, moral and ethical choices, creativity, and so on. These responsibilities spring directly from the core characteristic that defines God best—love. "God is love," John says, "and all who live in love live in God, and God lives in them. And as we live in God, our love grows more perfect" (1 John 4:16-17). It is as if God wired into us a yearning to live out our relational nature, a yearning to love someone and have someone love us deeply enough to explore the depths of who we really are as people created in God's image.

The Relational Love Process

The relationships that are lasting and most meaningful are those in which we come to know another intimately and allow that person to know us equally. That is where the relational love process of knowing and being known comes in.

Know Others

One of the words Scripture uses for lasting intimacy is the Hebrew word *yada,* meaning "to know." It denotes a deep and intimate acquaintance. A 16-year-old girl sent me (Josh) one of the best definitions of intimacy I've seen. She wrote, "It is the capacity to be real with another person...no façade, no barriers." We all want to be real and be known. It's as if those around you had a sign hung around their necks reading, *Please know me!* In Jeremiah God uses this word to say to the prophet, "I knew you before I formed you in your mother's womb" (Jeremiah 1:5). God knew us intimately before we were born, and he wants to teach us to know others intimately.

Being made in God's image means we are complex and intricately designed. Therefore, it takes time to explore the relational depths of those you love—to discover their likes and dislikes, probe their interests and desires, and begin to uncover the wonders of who they are. As a person feels someone desires to truly know them and love them for who they are, they begin to experience relationship as God designed. And as you do, you will be replicating the DNA of God's image of love.

Be Known

King Solomon said that the Lord "offers his friendship to the godly" (Proverbs 3:32). Friendship in this verse is the Hebrew word *sod,* meaning vulnerable or transparent disclosure. In other words, God offers his friendship—a transparent disclosure of himself—to the godly. God wants us to know him intimately. The Lord said, "I want you to be merciful; I don't want your sacrifices. I want you to know God; that's more important than burnt offerings" (Hosea 6:6).

God is pleased to reveal himself to us, and he created us in his likeness to reveal ourselves to others. That is another dimension to experiencing deepened love relationships. It's not easy to open ourselves up and be vulnerable. It can be risky, and at times we may even get hurt. But it is a risk worth taking.

As you enter close relationships with others, it's important to let them get to know you for who you really are deep down. Let them know your dreams and aspirations, your fears and hesitations, your hopes and expectations. As you learn to "self-disclose" you will be reflecting a likeness of God, and you will experience a deeper love relationship with others.

Be Involved

King David wrote, "O LORD, you have examined my heart and know everything about me...Every moment you know where I am" (Psalm 139:1,3). The Hebrew word *sakan,* translated "know" here, means a caring involvement. God had much more than simply an informational knowing of David; he was caringly involved in David's life. God's DNA of relationships not only knows us and wants us to know him; he wants to be lovingly involved in our lives.

For us to do the same is to be involved in the lives of those we love. This means entering their world and becoming interested in what they're interested in. When you take a sincere interest in another and demonstrate you care, you are living out the image of God, and your relationship with the other person deepens.

When I (Sean) was around ten years old I was really into sports cars. I would cut out magazine pictures of cars like the Maserati, the Lamborghini, and the Ferrari Testarossa. I pinned them up on my bedroom wall and thought they were so cool.

My dad noticed my newfound interest, and one day he really surprised me. He had looked through the Yellow Pages and picked out some of the top sports car dealerships in Beverly Hills. Then he sent each car dealer a letter that said:

> I'm a desperate dad. I'll do anything to spend time with my son, and right now he's into sports cars. Would it be possible if I pulled him out of school and brought him up to your showroom so that we could take some test drives? I want to tell you up front, I'm not interested in buying a car.

Amazingly, he got positive replies from every dealer. He called and made appointments for us, and we drove up to Beverly Hills (a distance of some 150 miles) for a day in the sports car showrooms. And what a day it was! Dad waited in the showrooms while I went out on "test drives" with salesmen and "tried out" just about every big name car you can think of. As I came by the showroom in each car, I would wave to Dad—I was so proud.

And along with the test drives, I got posters, some of which were autographed by famous race car drivers. It was an incredible day. On the way home we discussed which cars we liked the best and went over all the flyers, books, and posters I had collected. Then Dad gently switched the subject and started talking to me about looking at all this in the light of our Christian worldview.

"You know, Sean," he said, "all these cars are fun, but they cost huge amounts of money. What we should be thinking about is what God has called us to value as a family." He then explained, "Let's look at what we did today in light of God's love for us… what Christ did on the cross…what he created us for." And with that beginning he was able to communicate to me as a ten-year-old one of the best lessons on materialism he could have possibly taught. He didn't make it preachy, but he did make the point about how we may like certain things and enjoy them, but their cost downgrades them to a very low category compared to importance of where we are as followers of Jesus.

I never forgot that lesson on materialism. But I'm convinced the lesson on what we value in life would have never stuck if my dad hadn't entered my world and demonstrated he loved me by focusing on my interests. The real lesson that day that has molded and shaped me as a father and husband is that I am to enter the life of my wife and family in order to love and be loved.

Talking About the Relational Context of Life

Everything that is around us and in us reflects the fact that we were made for relationship. You can talk about moral values or the creation around us—whatever it is, it is based in God's relationship with us.

Place God's Commands Within a Relational Context

Whenever you talk with someone about God's commands and rules, always put them within the context of his loving motivation to provide for us and protect us. This is important because so many people see his commands as restrictive and harsh. But the truth is, God's commands come from who he is and his desire to bless us. Discover the loving provision and protection behind his commands, and you will find the love that reflects his character. This is what we must teach.

God's commands are designed to bless us. For example, we are told not to steal from others nor lie or be a cheat (see Exodus 20:15-16). In other words, we are to live honest lives because God is true. "He is the Rock," Moses declared, "his works are perfect...a faithful God who does no wrong, upright and just is he" (Deuteronomy 32:4 NIV). His nature is true—he doesn't vary or deviate from the very essence of his being holy and righteous. The reason the writer of Hebrews said, "It is impossible for God to lie" (Hebrews 6:18) is that God cannot deny his own nature. And when we live honest lives we reflect God's true nature. By doing this we're protected from guilt and enjoy a clear conscience. We're protected from shame and enjoy a reputation of integrity. We're protected from ruined relationships and enjoy relationships based on trust.

When we place God's commands within a relational context... we can see that to be like him is for his glory and our benefit.

When my (Josh's) daughter Kelly was in fourth grade, several students in her class swiped an object off the teacher's desk while the teacher was out of the room. The children only wanted to play with the object, but it soon broke. Then they returned it to its previous place on the teacher's desk.

When the teacher discovered the damage, she asked one of Kelly's classmates what had happened. The girl yielded to the pressure of the group and lied. Then the teacher asked Kelly. Kelly explained matter-of-factly what had happened.

The next day I took Kelly out for breakfast at the Rong Branch Café, a local restaurant. I told her she'd done the right thing, in spite of any pressure or harassment she might get from her classmates.

"Honey," I then asked, "why is lying wrong?"

"Because the Bible says it's wrong," she answered.

"Why does the Bible say it's wrong?"

"Because God commanded it."

"Why did God command it?"

"I don't know," she admitted.

I took her hands in mine and locked eyes with her. "Because God is true. By his very nature he can't be dishonest. So what you did when you told the truth was to act like God. You reflected his nature." We went on and talked about the many benefits of being an honest person.

When we place God's commands within a relational context—that is, when we see ourselves as his creatures, related to him in love and designed to experience joy when we reflect his nature—we can see that to be like him is for his glory and our benefit. This enables us to avoid seeing his rules as restrictive or legalistic.

Place Your Own Instructions Within a Relational Context

As a parent you obviously don't need to give your children a reason or benefit for everything you instruct them to do. However, they need to understand that all your instructions and rules come out of your loving heart for them and a loving desire for their best interests.

Growing up I (Sean) remember at times how my dad or mom wouldn't always let me go everywhere I wanted to go or buy everything I wanted to buy. Of course I'd be disappointed and even at times complain or argue with them. As I think back, what stands out to me about those times is not the arguments or disappointment I felt, but their constant reminders of this one thing: They would say, "Sean, I hope you know it needs to be this way because I love you." That was the theme.

As a young person I certainly couldn't understand the depths of my parents' love. I understand it better now that I am a parent myself. But knowing they loved me and truly wanted my best kept me from making some costly mistakes. That doesn't mean I always listened. Like any kid, I made my share of poor choices. But knowing that my parents truly loved me was a powerful motivating force to take their wisdom to heart. None of us can be perfect parents, but we can be deeply loving parents. We can let our children know that what we do to correct them is because we love them.

Use the Fascinations of Nature to Praise God's Existence

Take advantage of our natural world to point to our Intelligent Designer God. You can do this with classmates, colleagues, friends, or family. Nature movies or a trip to the zoo can serve as great opportunities to wonder at the amazing design of God's world. You can pose questions like, "What does a rose tell us about God and what he likes?" or "Why did God make giraffes with such long necks?" We don't necessarily have to know all the answers in order to marvel at God's miraculous creation and praise him for it.

Some time ago the BBC produced a television series called *Planet Earth*. A lot of my (Sean's) friends were talking about it, so I decided to purchase the DVDs to see why all the commotion. I was completely blown away! The nature footage they captured was absolutely amazing. After I had shown a couple of episodes to our family, our young son, Scottie, started asking, "Can we watch *Planet Earth* tonight?"

In my favorite scene, a gigantic great white shark chases a seal. Sharks are swift and powerful; the seal is more agile. But despite its agility, the seal cannot escape earth's most feared predator. The chase ends when the shark explodes from the water and catches the seal in its jaws in midair. The slow-motion footage was worth the price of the entire series. Incredible!

My wife and I took the opportunity presented by the series to celebrate the powerful forces of God's creation with our son, using nature as a springboard to share a biblical worldview: "When I consider your heavens, the work of your fingers, the moon and the stars, which you have set in place, what is man that you are mindful of him, the son of man that you care for him?" (Psalm 8:3-4 NIV).

If you have an interest in astronomy, flowers, or gardening, or if you are fascinated with honeybees, ants, whales, or the hibernation of bears, you can use those interests to wonder aloud about the miracle of creation and what it might suggest about the nature of our Creator God. Physics and the study of gravity, light, atomic energy, or electricity are other fields rich in mystery that inspire wonder of the God of creation. You don't have to be a scientist or a botanist to see the natural world as a means to glorify God to those around you. Going on a hike and marveling at God's creation can be just as effective.

Use the Miracle of Birth to Praise God's Existence

Use the birth of a baby or remembering the day a person was born to marvel at the miracle of birth. King David said, "You made all the delicate, inner parts of my body and knit me together in my mother's womb. Thank you for making me so wonderfully complex! Your workmanship is marvelous—and how well I know it" (Psalm 139:13-14).

The fascinating aspects of our complex bodies can be used to praise God for this handiwork. You might remember from high school biology that the "double helix" shape of DNA resembles a twisted ladder. Each rung is a piece of your genetic code, and amazingly, every cell in your body contains a complete DNA blueprint for everything about you. The sequence of those rungs provides the pattern for the production of every building block of life. Not only that, but within each human being's reproductive cells lies the information that, when combined with genetic information from a mate, add up to the genetic pattern handed down to a child.

DNA, in other words, is what determines not only *who we are* but *what our children look like*. Use fascinating information like this to stand in awe of our Creator God.

Wonder aloud about "What would it be like to know everything there is to know?" "What does God look like?" "What if he has a favorite color?" "Why does he love us so much?" This exercise isn't meant to humanize God, but rather to help those around you understand that while God is infinite and beyond our comprehension on one hand, on the other he is an approachable, relational God who takes notice even of how many hairs grow on our heads.

Teach Your Kids the Basics of a Biblical Worldview

As a Christian educator I (Sean) am constantly thinking of simple ways to teach my students a biblical worldview. I explain to them that every worldview must answer three questions:

1. *Origin*—how did we get here?
2. *Predicament*—what went wrong?
3. *Resolution*—how do we fix it?

Since God created the world, everything was originally good (*origin*). But humans twist these good things and make them evil (*predicament*). God sent his son, Jesus, to die on the cross for our sins, so we could be restored in our relationship to him (*resolution*).

To apply this truth, I often ask my students a question such as "What gives human beings value?" The answer, of course, is that they are made in the image of God (*origin*). Then I ask, "How has this truth been twisted?" Answers include the false ideas that our value comes from our possessions, appearance, success, and so on (*predicament*). Then I ask, "How do we get back to seeing ourselves as God sees us?" (*resolution*). The answer, of course, is to replace the false ideas we accept from our culture with biblical truth. You can do this little exercise using anything God created, including art, sports, work, music, relationships, and more. By posing these questions on various issues you can help young people form a biblical worldview.

Summary

Because we believe the truth that a personal God exists and created us in his image, we can enjoy the benefits of his creation, especially loving relationships. Our ethics, morals, social and civic responsibilities, and the capacity to love and be loved come from the fact we were made in God's relational image. We find our true identity in our Creator. And as we live out who we are within the context of God's image and likeness of love, it brings pleasure to him and purpose, meaning, and joy to us.

TRUTH TWO

GOD'S WORD

CHAPTER EIGHT

WHY GOD GAVE
US HIS WORDS

When Sean was 12 years old and his sister Kelly was 14, I (Josh) wrote a book of 15 letters to them. The book cover was inscribed: "My precious son and daughter, here are the letters I promised. They're from my heart...Love, Dad." The first letter read in part:

> Dear Kelly...Dear Sean,
>
> If letters had arms to wrap around, they would be squeezing you right now with the world's biggest hug.
>
> For the past couple of years you both know I've crisscrossed America speaking, appearing on radio and TV and talking to young people about their sexuality. You've been with me on many of these trips.
>
> It really hurts when I listen to personal stories guys and girls have told me. My heart has been broken as they have talked about how their lives have been messed up because they didn't understand God's plan or know how to manage their sexuality.
>
> If there was ever a gift your mom and I want you, Kelly, and you, Sean, to have, it's the gift of sexual wholeness. And that gift can be yours if you make it through our world's minefield of teen sexual pressure without getting emotionally blown up. To help you win, I'm giving you this book. It's sort of a road map, drawn from the best insights, experiences, tips, and secrets I've been able to learn through 20 years of marriage to your mother...

Well, dear Kelly and dear Sean, here are my letters to you. WOW, do I ever love you both!

—Dad

P.S.—It's OK with me if you share these letters with some of your friends who might find them helpful.

Even though I (Sean) was only 12 at the time my father gave me this book of letters, it had a profound impact on my life. It was profound because it became the motivating factor in abstaining from sexual immorality. On the surface you might think I followed the guidelines for sexual purity because they were so explicitly laid out in a book for me. But that is not what impacted me so deeply. It was the fact that from a father's heart of love came guidelines to protect me from heartache and provide me maximum joy in my future relationships. Dad simply wanted me to experience what he had in life and marriage.

Letters from a Loving Heart

Your earthly father may not have written you a book, but your heavenly Father did. His book, called the Bible, is like letters from his heart to you. They have been written "so that your joy may be complete" (John 15:11 NIV). They are God's "road map" for you. They are his "secrets" on how you can make it through the world's "minefields" that threaten to cause you heartache and misery. The written Word of God comes from a Father's heart.

Every command and instruction from God comes out of his loving heart to provide for us and protect us.

"All Scripture is inspired by God and is useful to teach us what is true and to make us realize what is wrong in our lives. It straightens us out and teaches us to do what is right. It is God's way of preparing us in every way, fully equipped for every good thing God wants us to do" (2 Timothy 3:16-17). All the teachings of Scripture then—whether in the form of instruction, parable, admonition, precept, ordinance, or command—are intended to reveal who God really is and provide a detailed account of his ways. So when God says "avoid that attitude," "follow this way," "abstain from these actions," or "embrace these thoughts" he is not trying to restrict us from being happy. He is attempting to lead us to right living in relationship with him. That is what brings pleasure to him and happiness and joy to us.

Every command and instruction from God comes out of his loving heart to provide for us and protect us. As Moses told the nation of Israel,

Obey the LORD's commands and laws that I am giving you today *for your own good*...I am giving you the choice between a blessing and a curse! You will be blessed if you obey the commands of the LORD your God that I am giving you today. You will receive a curse if you reject the commands of the LORD your God and turn from his way (Deuteronomy 10:13; 11:26-28).

By commanding us to love him God is saying, in effect, "Devote yourself to knowing me intimately and open yourself to me fully so my ways will become your ways." God's design of humans is such that an intimate relationship with him is the only way they can succeed in living meaningful lives of joy. Moses understood this, and he begged God, "If you are pleased with me, teach me your ways so I may know you" (Exodus 33:13 NIV). Following God's ways leads to knowing him; knowing him leads to being and living like him; being and living like him leads to joy.

In other words, when we demonstrate our love for God by acting according to his ways, we enjoy blessing because God's ways reflect who he is—the ultimate good and perfect God. The closer we come to living like him, the closer we come to goodness and perfection. Being honest, for example, brings blessing because God is true. Staying sexually pure brings blessing because God is holy. Treating others justly brings blessing because God is just.

God's commands and instructions to act in certain ways flow out of who he is and how he himself acts. When we seek to know him intimately—love him—we can take on his ways and reap the benefits. The psalmist David said in Psalm 19 that the ways of the Lord revive the soul, make us wise, bring us joy, and give us insight for living. That is his loving provision. Life apart from him results in guilt, emotional distress, shame, loneliness, and disrupted relationships. That is what he wants to protect us from.

Thus, we can say the Bible is a perfectly right set of laws and guidelines that flow out of a perfectly right God to instruct us to live as God designed us to live. Therefore:

> We believe the truth that the Bible is
> God's revelation of himself to us, which
> declares his ways for us to follow.

It reveals a relational God, the God who "would speak to Moses face to face, as a man speaks to his friend" (Exodus 33:11). It is the revelation of "a God who is passionate about his relationship with you" (Exodus 34:14). And it is a revelation that, from the first words Moses penned in the book of Genesis to the last word John wrote in Revelation, reflects the loving heart of a God who wants us to be in right relationship with him so we can enjoy all the benefits that relationship offers.

To sum it up: Scripture is the means by which God has chosen to introduce and reveal himself to you so he can enjoy a relationship with you. God's Word—the record of all his ways—is given to you for a relational purpose: so you may know him and enjoy all the blessings of a relationship with your loving Creator.

Does It Matter If It's Reliable or Not?

Imagine a college-age group of Christians gathering for a Bible study. Listen to how the conversation turns as they begin to discuss the purpose of the Bible.

Chad, the small group leader, pulls up a chair and sits as he begins to address the dozen students gathered for the study.

"I'd like to start a new series," Chad begins. "What would you say to doing this study on 'How to Get the Most out of Your Bible'?" he asks as he holds up a study booklet. The group nods in approval.

"Okay, let me start by asking this question: What's the purpose of the Bible?" He looks around the room at the expectant faces. "How would you describe what it does for us?"

Moments pass. A few in the group seem to be thinking.

Finally Allen speaks up. "It's God's truth. It's the inspired Word of God."

Chad nods. "Okay, good. What else?"

"It's...it's the book of Christian teachings," Sara offered.

"It's the teachings of the Jewish religion too," Megan added. "The Old Testament is, anyway."

Several others in the group spoke up, offering other answers.

"All right," Chad said, nodding his approval. "Those are all good responses. But let me give you a little different description of the Bible and see what you think." He glanced down at his booklet as he read, "The Bible is God's instruction manual for living. It is our road map to heaven. It is God's love letter to us. It's the means we use to get to know him." He allowed the words to sink in for a moment, then held up his Bible in one hand and continued. "So if people don't study this book, they can't very well know him."

"What if we don't have all of the Bible?" Allen interrupted. "What if there's, like, missing books or chapters? Does that mean we can't know God?"

"Well—" Chad began, setting his Bible down on his lap.

"Yeah," Sara interjected. "What if God really gave 15 commandments, but we have only 10 of them?"

"Now, slow down," Chad said, holding his hand in the air as if trying to stop traffic. "Let's not get carried away."

"But Sara and Allen are right," Megan protested. "What if the people writing the Bible didn't put down everything God said…or like, maybe they got it all wrong or something. Does that mean we're all out of luck? Is that what you're saying?"

Chad sighed deeply and stared at the group, his expression frozen. Finally he said, "Tell you what, maybe this is a good time for pizza." He looked at the curious faces around the room. "I'll, uh…we'll come back to these questions some other time, okay?"

We can hardly blame Chad for being caught a little off guard. The questions these college students are asking might overwhelm even the most seasoned Bible teacher. But they're good questions—ones that must be answered if we expect to develop a deep, solid, and lasting understanding of the Bible. And they are questions that will inevitably confront each of us and our children in a postmodern society that considers religious truth something that can be determined subjectively.

If the Bible is just a helpful collection of nice thoughts, then it doesn't matter too much if parts have disappeared or been mistranslated over the years. If the Bible is merely another version of truth, then it makes little difference whether it is accurate. But if the Bible is what Chad claims—God's instruction manual for living, and the primary means by which we can know God—then it becomes extremely important to know whether it's reliable, whether it was recorded exactly as God gave it, and whether it's been accurately passed down to us. When we truly understand what the Bible is, then questions about its reliability become critically important. As Megan, the college student, asked, "What if the people writing the Bible didn't put down everything God said…or like, maybe they got it all wrong or something. Does that mean we're all out of luck?"

As it happens, Megan's question has already been answered in the Bible itself, in an incident that's recorded in the Old Testament.

When the Book of the Law Was Lost

The incident took place in Judah, during a period when a young man named Josiah reigned as king. At that time, the people of Judah had been worshipping idols for many years, and many of the old ways had been neglected or lost. But Josiah "began to seek the God of his ancestor David" (2 Chronicles 34:3). He decreed the destruction of the pagan idols and altars that dotted the land and began an effort to repair, restore, and reconsecrate the temple in Jerusalem.

One day, as Hilkiah the high priest was working amid the flurry of the temple restoration efforts, a long and ancient scroll was discovered. The priest's hands must have trembled as he rolled through the scroll, reading words that had been lost many years earlier. Recognizing its importance, Hilkiah conveyed the scroll to a man named Shaphan, the king's private secretary.

As Shaphan read from the scroll to Josiah, the king no doubt recognized the words. Even though he had never heard them before, much of what Shaphan read had been circulated for years by word of mouth, from parent to child and sage to student. Josiah, like Shaphan and Hilkiah, recognized this as "the Book of the Law of the LORD as it had been given through Moses" (2 Chronicles 34:14).

But soon Josiah's fascination turned to worry and then quickly to horror as Shaphan read:

> If you fully obey the LORD your God by keeping all the commands I am giving you today, the LORD your God will exalt you above all the nations of the world. You will experience all these blessings if you obey the LORD your God...
>
> *But* if you refuse to listen to the LORD your God and *do not obey* all the commands and laws I am giving you today...
>
> You will be cursed wherever you go...
>
> [with] curses, confusion, and disillusionment in everything you do, until at last you are completely destroyed (Deuteronomy 28:1-20).

When the king heard those words, he tore his clothes with his bare hands. "We have not been doing what this scroll says we must do" (2 Chronicles 34:21). He understood that, regardless of his good intentions, God had not been revealed to his people because they had been without the written revelation of God. Fearful for himself and his people, Josiah gathered the people together. He read to them from the lost scroll, and together they pledged to obey the Lord and his Word.

A Distorted Revelation Produces Distorted Results

The story of King Josiah emphasizes how dangerous it would be if God's Word were lost...or distorted, altered, or misrepresented to us through inaccurate copying over hundreds or thousands of years. Before the written word, God spoke directly to Moses, Abraham, and the prophets. God also revealed himself in the flesh and spoke to us through his Son, Jesus (see Hebrews 1:1-2). These revelations of God have been recorded in written form and preserved in the pages of Scripture. But if the facts and events of the Bible weren't carefully and truthfully recorded, then the Bible we have today is a distorted reflection of God's nature and character.

So knowing God and living in relationship with him are dependent on our receiving and possessing an accurate revelation of him. Unless the Bible is reliable, we have no assurance that its teachings we follow and obey are true at all. Imagine, for example, that God really did give Moses 15 commandments, and some scribe along the way decided to eliminate 5 of them. We would—at best—possess an incomplete picture of what God is like and what he requires of us. And at worst, as Josiah realized, we would be courting disaster, inviting "curses, confusion, and disillusionment in everything [we] do" (Deuteronomy 28:20).[1]

If we hope to enjoy the benefits of knowing God, we must be sure that we have a Bible that accurately represents what God inspired people to write on his behalf. Because if the Word of God was not accurately recorded and relayed to us, then we and our children, like Josiah and the nation of Judah, will be cheated in our efforts to know God and may be exposed to "curses, confusion, and disillusionment."

CHAPTER NINE

EVIDENCE THAT GOD'S
WORD IS RELIABLE

How can you be sure the Bible you read is what God actually said? Remember it was written thousands of years ago. How can you be sure it was copied correctly? Who is to say large passages haven't been left out or distorted by people adding their own ideas? Or is there evidence that the Bible we have today is a reliable reproduction of what God inspired his writers to write? Let's explore these questions.

God's Words Have Been Relayed Accurately

This God-inspired book called the Bible was written during a 1500-year span through more than 40 generations by more than 40 different authors from every walk of life— shepherds, soldiers, prophets, poets, monarchs, scholars, statesmen, masters, servants, tax collectors, fishermen, and tentmakers. Its God-breathed words were written in a variety of places: in the wilderness, in a palace, in a dungeon, on a hillside, in a prison, and in exile. It was penned on the continents of Asia, Africa, and Europe and was written in three languages: Hebrew, Aramaic, and Greek. It tells hundreds of stories, records hundreds of songs, and addresses hundreds of controversial subjects. Yet with all its variety of authors, origins, and content, it achieves a miraculous continuity of theme—God's redemption of his children and the restoration of all things to his original design.

Because of the redemptive and relational purpose of the Bible, God cannot allow it to be lost, twisted, or distorted. As Jesus said, "I assure you, until heaven and earth disappear, even the smallest detail of God's law will remain until its purpose is achieved"

(Matthew 5:18). He will permit nothing to impede his purpose. "Heaven and earth will disappear," Jesus said, "but my words will remain forever" (Matthew 24:35).

God is so passionate about his relationship with us that he has personally—and miraculously—provided the inspiration of his Word, supervised its transmission, and repeatedly reinforced its reliability so all those who have open eyes and open hearts may believe it with assurance and confidence. Nations have rejected it, tyrants have tried to stamp it out, heretics have tried to distort it, but the evidence for the Bible's reliability is sufficient to assure us and our kids that it has remained a true reflection of reality—of who God is—and that "it is stronger and more permanent than heaven and earth" (Luke 16:17).

It's not difficult to see the superintending work of God in the composition of the Old and New Testaments. Considering the process of writing and preserving manuscripts in ancient times, the fact we can be confident we have an accurate Bible is truly miraculous. None of the original manuscripts that God inspired authors to write—called autographs—is in existence today. What we read now are printed copies based on ancient handwritten copies of yet other copies of the original. This is because the Bible was composed and transmitted in an era before printing presses. All manuscripts had to be written by hand. Over time, the ink would fade, and the material it was written on would deteriorate. So if a document was to be preserved and passed down to the next generation, new copies would have to be made or the document would be lost forever. Of course, these copies were made just like the originals—by hand with fading ink on deteriorating materials.

But, you may rightly wonder, doesn't the making of hand-copied reproductions open up the whole transmission process to error? How do we know that a weary copier, blurry-eyed from lack of sleep, didn't skip a few critical words or leave out whole sections or misquote some key verses? Or what if, during the copying of Mark's Gospel some hundred years after he wrote it, some agenda-driven, meddling scribe added five chapters of his own or twisted around the things Jesus said or did? If the words God gave to Moses, David, Matthew, or Peter were later changed or carelessly copied, how could we be sure we are coming to know the one true God? How could we be confident that the commands we obey are a true reflection of God's nature and character? What if it's true, as some critics say, that the Bible is a collection of outdated writings that are riddled with inaccuracies and distortions? How can we be sure that the manuscripts available to us today are an accurate transmission of the originals?

God has not left us to wonder. He has miraculously supervised the transmission of his Word to ensure that it was relayed accurately from one generation to another.[*1]

---

* This chapter has been adapted from *Beyond Belief to Convictions*, chapter 8; *The New Evidence That Demands a Verdict*, chapters 3 and 4; and "Can the New Testament Be Trusted?" article by Sean McDowell. Please see these two McDowell books and the article at www.seanmcdowell.org for more details on the reliability of Scripture.

The Case of the Meticulous Scribes

One of the ways God ensured that his Word would be relayed accurately was by choosing, calling, and cultivating a nation of men and women who took the Book of the Law very seriously. God commanded and instilled in the Jewish people a great reverence for his Word. From their very first days as a nation, God told them, "Listen closely, Israel, to everything I say…Commit yourselves wholeheartedly to these commands I am giving you today. Repeat them again and again to your children. Talk about them when you are at home and when you are away on a journey, when you are lying down and when you are getting up again. Tie them to your hands as a reminder, and wear them on your forehead. Write them on the doorposts of your house and on your gates" (Deuteronomy 6:3,6-9).

That attitude toward the commands of God became such a part of the Jewish identity that a class of Jewish scholars called the *Sopherim,* from a Hebrew word meaning "scribes," arose between the fifth and third centuries BC. These custodians of the Hebrew Scriptures dedicated themselves to preserving carefully the ancient manuscripts and producing new copies when necessary.

The Sopherim were eclipsed by the Talmudic scribes, who guarded, interpreted, and commented on the sacred texts from AD 100–500. In turn, the Talmudic scribes were followed by the better-known Masoretic scribes (AD 500–900).

The zeal of the Masoretes surpassed that of even their most dedicated predecessors. They established detailed and stringent disciplines for copying a manuscript. Their rules were so rigorous that when a new copy was complete, they would give the reproduction equal authority to that of its parent because they were thoroughly convinced that they had an exact duplicate.

This was the class of people who, in the providence of God, were chosen to preserve the Old Testament text for centuries. A scribe would begin his day of transcribing by ceremonially washing his entire body. He would then garb himself in full Jewish dress before sitting at his desk. As he wrote, if he came to the Hebrew name of God, he could not begin writing the name with a quill newly dipped in ink for fear it would smear the page. Once he began writing the name of God, he could not stop or allow himself to be distracted; even if a king was to enter the room, the scribe was obligated to continue without interruption until he finished penning the holy name of the one true God.

The Masoretic guidelines for copying manuscripts also required the following:

- The scroll must be written on the skin of a clean animal.
- Each skin must contain a specified number of columns, equal throughout the entire book.

- The length of each column must extend no less than 48 lines or more than 60 lines.

- The column breadth must consist of exactly 30 letters.

- The space of a thread must appear between every consonant.

- The breadth of nine consonants had to be inserted between each section.

- A space of three lines had to appear between each book.

- The fifth book of Moses (Deuteronomy) had to conclude exactly with a full line.

- Nothing—not even the shortest word—could be copied from memory; it had to be copied letter by letter.

- The scribe must count the number of times each letter of the alphabet occurred in each book and compare it to the original.

- If a manuscript was found to contain even one mistake, it was discarded.[2]

God instilled in the Masoretes such a painstaking reverence for the Hebrew Scriptures to ensure the amazingly accurate transmission of the Book of the Law so you and I—and our children—would have an accurate revelation of God.

Until recently, however, we had no way of knowing just how amazing the preservation of the Old Testament has been. Before 1947, the oldest complete Hebrew manuscript dated to AD 900. But with the discovery of 223 manuscripts in caves on the west side of the Dead Sea, we now have Old Testament manuscripts that have been dated by paleographers at around 125 BC. These Dead Sea Scrolls, as they are called, are a thousand years older than any previously known manuscripts.[3]

But here's the exciting part: Once the Dead Sea Scrolls were translated and compared with modern versions, the Hebrew Bible proved to be identical, word for word, in more than 95 percent of the text. (The variation of 5 percent consisted mainly of spelling variations. For example, of the 166 words in Isaiah 53, only 17 letters were in question. Of those, 10 letters were a matter of spelling, and 4 were stylistic changes; the remaining 3 letters comprised the word *light,* which was added in verse 11).[4]

In other words, the greatest manuscript discovery of all time revealed that a thousand years of copying the Old Testament had produced only excruciatingly minor variations, none of which altered the clear meaning of the text or brought the manuscript's fundamental integrity into question.

The critics will still make their pronouncements in opposition to the evidence. However, the overwhelming weight of evidence affirms that God has preserved his Word and accurately relayed it through the centuries so that when you pick up an Old Testament today, you can be utterly confident that you are holding a well-preserved, fully reliable document.

The Case of the New Testament Text

As you know, the Hebrew scribes did not copy the manuscripts of the New Testament. There were several reasons. The official Jewish leadership did not endorse Christianity; the letters and histories circulated by the New Testament writers were not then thought of as official Scripture; and these documents were not written in the Hebrew language, but rather in forms of Greek and Aramaic. Thus, the same formal disciplines were not followed in the transmission of these writings from one generation to another. In the case of the New Testament, God did a new thing to ensure that the blessing of his Word would be preserved for us and our children.

Historians evaluate the textual reliability of ancient literature according to two standards: 1) the time interval between the original and the earliest copy; and 2) how many manuscript copies are available.

For example, virtually everything we know today about Julius Caesar's exploits in the Gallic Wars is derived from ten manuscript copies, the earliest of which dates to within 1000 years of the time *The Gallic Wars* was written. Our modern text of Livy's *History of Rome* relies on 1 partial manuscript and 19 much later copies that are dated from 400 to 1000 years *after* the original writing (see chart below).[5]

Textual Reliability Standards Applied to Classical Literature

Author	Book	Date written	Earliest copies	Time gap	Number of copies
Homer	*Iliad*	800 BC	c. 400 BC	c. 400 yrs.	643
Herodotus	*History*	480–425 BC	c. AD 900	c. 1350 yrs.	8
Thucydides	*History*	460–400 BC	c. AD 900	c. 1300 yrs.	8
Plato		400 BC	c. AD 900	c. 1300 yrs.	7
Demosthenes		300 BC	c. AD 1100	c. 1400 yrs.	200
Caesar	*Gallic Wars*	100–44 BC	c. AD 900	c. 1000 yrs.	10
Livy	*History of Rome*	59 BC–AD 17	fourth century (partial); mostly tenth century	c. 400 years c. 1000 years	1 partial 19 copies
Tacitus	*Annals*	AD 100	c. AD 1100	c. 1000 yrs.	20
Pliny Secundus	*Natural History*	AD 61–113	c. AD 850	c. 750 yrs.	7

By comparison, the text of Homer's *Iliad* is much more reliable. It is supported by 643 manuscript copies in existence today, with a mere 400-year time gap between the date of composition and the earliest of these copies.

The textual evidence for Livy and Homer are considered more than adequate for historians to use in validating the original, but this evidence pales in comparison to what God performed in the case of the New Testament text.

The New Testament Has No Equal

Using this accepted standard for evaluating the textual reliability of ancient writings, the New Testament stands alone. It has no equal. No other book of the ancient world can even approach the reliability of the New Testament. (See chart of "Textual Reliability Standards Applied to the Bible.")[6]

Nearly *25,000* manuscripts or fragments of manuscripts of the New Testament repose in the libraries and universities of the world. The earliest of these is a fragment of John's Gospel currently located in the John Rylands Library of Manchester, England; it has been dated to within *50 years* of the date when the apostle John penned the original![7]

Textual Reliability Standards Applied to the Bible

Author	Book	Date written	Earliest copies	Time gap	Number of copies
John	New Testament	AD 50–100	c. AD 130	50-plus years	Fragments
The rest of the New Testament authors			c. AD 200 (books)	100 years	
			c. AD 250 (most of New Testament)	150 years	
			c. AD 325 (complete New Testament)	225 years	5600-plus Greek manuscripts
			c. AD 366–384 (Latin Vulgate translation)	284 years	
			c. AD 400–500 (other translations)	400 years	19,000-plus translated manuscripts
			TOTALS	50–400 years	24,600-plus manuscripts

Since the time the original manuscripts were written—more than 1900 years ago—skeptics have tried to refute the Bible, infidels have tried to stamp it out, and dictators have tried to burn it. However, God's Word has not only prevailed, it has also proliferated. Voltaire, the noted eighteenth-century French skeptic, predicted that within a hundred years of his time Christianity would be but a footnote in history. Ironically, in 1828, 50 years after Voltaire's death, the Geneva Bible Society moved into his house and used his printing press to produce thousands of Bibles to distribute worldwide.

"People are like grass that dies away," Peter wrote, quoting Isaiah the prophet, "but the word of the Lord will last forever" (1 Peter 1:24-25).

No other book in history has been so widely distributed in so many languages. Distribution of the Bible reaches into the billions! According to the United Bible Society's 2008 report, in that year alone, member organizations had distributed 28.4 million complete Bibles and just under 300 million selections from the Bible.[8] They also report that the Bible or portions of the Bible have been translated into more than 2400 languages. And, amazingly, these languages represent the primary vehicle of communication for well over 90 percent of the world's population![9]

God's Word Has Been Recorded Exactly

We can be confident that the manuscripts of both the Old and New Testaments have been handed down over the centuries with precision and accuracy. In other words, we can be assured that what was written down initially is what we have today. But a more basic question arises. Were the words from God recorded exactly as he intended? When these inspired writers were recording historical events, were they chronologically close to those events so we can have confidence in the accuracy of what they wrote?

You see, many ancient writings adhered only loosely to the facts of the events they reported. Some highly regarded authors of the ancient world, for example, reported events that took place many years before they were born and in countries they had never visited. While their writing may be largely factual, historians admit that greater credibility must be granted to writers who were both geographically and chronologically close to the events they report.

Such careful inspiration and supervision of the Bible underlines God's purpose, that not a single piece of this revelation about himself or the human condition be left to chance or recorded incorrectly.

With that in mind, look at the loving care God took when he inspired the writing of the New Testament. The overwhelming weight of scholarship confirms that the accounts of Jesus' life, the history of the early church, and the letters that form the bulk of the New Testament were all written by men who were either eyewitnesses to the events they recorded or contemporaries of eyewitnesses. God selected Matthew, Mark, and John to write three of the four Gospels. These were men who could say such things as, "This report is from an eyewitness giving an accurate account" (John 19:35). He spoke through Luke the physician to record the third Gospel and the book of Acts. Luke, a meticulously careful writer, used as "source material the reports circulating among us from the early disciples and other eyewitnesses of what God [did] in fulfillment of his promises" (Luke 1:2).

God could have spoken through anyone, from anywhere, to write his words about Christ. But to give us additional confidence in the truth, he worked through eyewitnesses such as John, who said, "We are telling you about what we ourselves have actually seen and heard" (1 John 1:3). He worked through Peter, who declared, "We did not follow cunningly devised fables when we made known to you the power and coming of our Lord Jesus Christ, but were eyewitnesses of His majesty" (2 Peter 1:16 NKJV). And whom did he choose as his most prolific writer? The apostle Paul, whose dramatic conversion from persecutor of Christians to planter of churches made him perhaps the most credible witness of all!

But God didn't stop there. Those through whom he transmitted his inspired Word were also apostles. These men could rely on their own eyewitness experiences and they could appeal to the firsthand knowledge of their contemporaries, even their most severe opponents (see Acts 2:32; 3:15; 13:31; 1 Corinthians 15:3-8). They not only said, "Look, we saw this," or "We heard that," but they were also so confident in what they wrote as to say, in effect, "Check it out," "Ask around," and "You know it as well as I do!" Such challenges demonstrate a supreme confidence that the "God-breathed" Word was recorded exactly as God spoke it (2 Timothy 3:16 NIV).

Such careful inspiration and supervision of the Bible underlines God's purpose, that not a single piece of this revelation about himself or the human condition be left to chance or recorded incorrectly. Ample evidence exists to suggest that God was very selective in the people he chose to record his words—people who for the most part had firsthand knowledge of key events and who were credible channels to record exactly those truths he wanted us to know.*

God's Word Has Been Reinforced Externally

God did not stop working after he had brought about the development of the massive textual evidence for the reliability of his Word. He has since worked to reinforce the evidence through external means.

A routine criterion in examining the reliability of a historical document is whether *other* historical material confirms or denies the internal testimony of the document itself. Historians ask, "What sources, apart from the literature under examination, substantiate its accuracy and reliability?"

In all of history, the Bible is by far the most widely referenced and quoted book. For example, the New Testament alone is so extensively quoted in the ancient manuscripts

---

* A comprehensive treatment of the internal evidence test is covered in chapters 3, 4, and 21 of *The New Evidence That Demands a Verdict.*

of nonbiblical authors that all 27 books, from Matthew through Revelation, could be reconstructed virtually word for word from those sources.

The writings of early Christians like Eusebius (AD 339) in his *Ecclesiastical History III.39* and Irenaeus (AD 180) in his *Against Heresies III* reinforce the text of the apostle John's writings. Clement of Rome (AD 95), Ignatius (AD 70–110), Polycarp (AD 70–156), and Titian (AD 170) offer external confirmation of other New Testament accounts. Non-Christian historians such as the first-century Roman historian Tacitus (AD 55–117) and the Jewish historian Josephus (AD 37–100) confirm the substance of many scriptural accounts. These and other outside sources substantiate the accuracy of the biblical record like that of no other book in history.*[10]

These extrabiblical references, however, are not the only external evidences that support the Bible's reliability. The very stones cry out that God's Word is true. Over and over again through the centuries, the reliability of the Bible has been regularly and consistently supported by archaeology. Consider the following evidences recently published in the *Apologetics Study Bible for Students,* of which I (Sean) was the general editor.

Biblical archaeology. Until the late eighteenth century, the pursuit of biblical relics in the Near East was the work of amateur treasure hunters whose methods included grave robbing. The discovery of the Rosetta Stone in Egypt by Napoleon's army in 1799 changed everything. Biblical archaeology became the domain of respected archaeologists. The discovery of ancient ruins all across the Near East has shed new light on peoples and events mentioned in Scripture. We can now better understand the customs and lifestyles that are foreign to the modern mind.

Archaeology has also established the historicity of the people and events described in the Bible, yielding over 25,000 finds that either directly or indirectly relate to Scripture. Moreover, the historical existence of some 30 individuals named in the New Testament, and nearly 60 in the Old Testament, has been confirmed through archaeological and historical research. Only a small fraction of possible biblical sites have been excavated in the Holy Land, and much more could be published on existing excavations. Even so, the archaeological data we now possess clearly indicates that the Bible is historically reliable and is not the product of myth, superstition, or embellishment (John 3:12; 2 Peter 1:16; 1 John 1:1-2).

Ancient Corinth. Archaeological research conducted in Corinth from 1928 to 1947 uncovered two startling objects relating to Paul's epistles to the Corinthian and Roman churches. A Latin inscription dating to about AD 50 carved into an ancient sidewalk identifies Paul's co-laborer "Erastus" as the city treasurer (Romans 16:23).

---

* For more information on the confirmation of the Bible's reliability in extrabiblical sources, see chapters 3 and 4 of *The New Evidence That Demands a Verdict.*

The inscription says Erastus laid a portion of sidewalk at his own expense in appreciation for being elected as treasurer. Moreover, a stone platform used to hold public lectures, official business, and trials, and to render judgments, was unearthed in 1935. It was identified as the *bema* seat. *Bema* is the same Greek word Paul used to describe the "judgment" seat of Christ (2 Corinthians 5:10) at which all Christians must appear for their rewards (1 Corinthians 3:10-17).

Arch of Titus. When Jesus talked with his disciples on the Mount of Olives about the buildings of the temple, he said, "Do you see all these things? I tell you the truth, not one stone here will be left on another; every one will be thrown down!" (Matthew 24:2). The accuracy of Jesus' prophecy is demonstrated by the Arch of Titus, which was constructed as a victory memorial for Emperor Titus (AD 79–81) by his younger brother Emperor Domitian (AD 81–96). Located in Rome between the ancient Forum and the Coliseum, the marble arch depicts the transportation of spoils (the menorah and sacred trumpets) from the ransacked Jerusalem temple.

In addition to this important evidence, excavations at the lower street along the southwest corner of the Jerusalem temple mount in the 1970s revealed large stones that had been toppled from the heights by the Romans in their military campaign of AD 70. Today, none of the original building structures remain standing on the temple mount. The depictions and inscription on the Arch of Titus, as well as the rubble found at the temple mount in Jerusalem, provide historical verification for the fulfillment of Jesus' prediction that the Jewish temple would be utterly destroyed.

Babylonian Chronicles. The Babylonian Chronicles are a series of cuneiform tablets that describe important events transpiring between the eighth and third centuries BC. One particular chronicle covers the period between 605–594 BC, recording the military exploits of Babylonian King Nebuchadnezzar II (605–562 BC) and his invasion of Jerusalem (2 Kings 23). It recounts how in 605 BC Nebuchadnezzar was crowned king after the death of his father, Nabopolassar. The Chronicles say that by 599 BC Nebuchadnezzar's army advanced to Syria, continued westward to Judea, and arrived there in March 597 BC. Once there he invaded Jerusalem, took captive King Jehoiakim (609–597 BC), and crowned his replacement King Zedekiah (597–586 BC; 2 Kings 24:10-20).

Robert Koldewey discovered supporting evidence for these events in the Babylonian ration records (595 BC), for they document the amount of food rations given to Jehoiakim and his royal family while in captivity (2 Kings 24:8-16). Additionally, hastily inscribed shards known as the Lachish Letters record Israelites' desperate pleas in the hours immediately before Babylonian forces overwhelmed Israel's military outposts some 25 miles outside Jerusalem. These strong archaeological evidences support the biblical record describing Jerusalem's final days under siege by Nebuchadnezzar.

Balaam Inscription. The story of Balaam and his talking donkey (Numbers 22:

22-40) was viewed skeptically by critical scholars for many decades. It was even doubted that Balaam ever existed. This outlook began to change in 1967 when archaeologists collected a crumbled plaster Aramaic text in the rubble of an ancient building in Deir 'Alla (Jordan). The text contains 50 lines written in faded red and black ink. The inscription reads, "Warnings from the Book of Balaam the son of Beor. He was a seer of the gods" (Numbers 22:5; Joshua 24:9). Though the building in which the text was found dates back only to the eighth century BC (during the reign of King Uzziah; see Isaiah 6:1), the condition of the plaster and ink of the text itself indicates that it is most likely much older, dating to the time of the biblical Balaam.

In addition to Balaam, nearly 60 other Old Testament figures have been either historically or archaeologically identified. These include kings David (1 Samuel 16:13), Jehu (2 Kings 9:2), Omri (1 Kings 16:22), Uzziah (Isaiah 6:1), Jotham (2 Kings 15:7), Hezekiah (Isaiah 37:1), Jehoiachin (2 Chronicles 36:8), Shalmaneser V (2 Kings 17:3), Tiglath-pileser III (1 Chronicles 5:6), Sargon II (Isaiah 20:1), Sennacherib (Isaiah 36:1), Nebuchadnezzar (Daniel 2:1), Belshazzar (Daniel 5:1), Cyrus (Isaiah 45:1), and others.

Ebla Tablets. Discovered by Italian archaeologist Paolo Matthiae in 1976 at Tell Mardikh in Aleppo (Syria), the Ebla Tablets represent a royal archive of over 16,000 clay tablets. Dating from 2400 BC, the records give us a glimpse into the lifestyle, vocabulary, commerce, geography, and religion of the peoples who lived near Canaan (later called Israel) in the time immediately before Abraham, Isaac, and Jacob. Translations of several tablets by Giovanni Pettinato in his *Archives of Ebla: An Empire Inscribed in Clay* support the existence of biblical cities such as Sodom (Genesis 19:1), Zeboiim (Genesis 14:2,8), Admah (Genesis 10:19), Hazor (1 Kings 9:15), Megiddo (1 Chronicles 7:29), Canaan (Genesis 48:4), and Jerusalem (Jeremiah 1:15).

Further, the tablets include personal names likened to biblical persons such as Nahor (Genesis 11:22-25), Israel (Genesis 32:28), Eber (Genesis 10:21-25), Michael (Numbers 13:13) and Ishmael (Genesis 16:11). Regarding vocabulary, the tablets contain certain words similar to those used in the Bible such as *tehom*, which in Genesis 1:2 is translated as "the deep." In addition to these, the tablets provide information related to Hebrew literary style and religion, helping us to understand the civilizations in the region that became known as Israel.[11]

Repeatedly throughout history, the astounding accuracy of God's Word has been confirmed externally. This is very different from the Book of Mormon, for example, for which there is no external support. The external evidence for the Bible is an extremely rare phenomenon, and it makes the Bible unique compared to other religious writings of the world.

■

The evidence for the reliability of the Old and New Testaments is not only convincing and compelling, it is also a clear and praiseworthy indication of how God lovingly supervised its transmission so that he might preserve for us—and our children—all the blessings that come from knowing him and obeying his Word.

CHAPTER TEN

THE PROTECTION AND
PROVISION OF GOD'S WORD

Have you ever asked a teenager what they believe about biblical truth? We have posed questions like the one below to countless young people, represented here by Amber, a typical 16-year-old Christian from a solid Christian home. The responses have been consistently similar from both young and old alike. Observe the response.

"Is it wrong to engage in premarital sex?" we ask.

"Well, I believe it's wrong for me," Amber responds.

We probe further. "But do you believe the Bible teaches that premarital sex is wrong for everyone?"

Amber's eyes shift back and forth as she weighs her answer. "Well," she begins slowly, "I know it's wrong for me, and I have chosen not to have sex until I'm married. But I don't think I can judge other people on what they do."[1]

You see, it's not that Amber doesn't believe the Bible provides an accurate description of moral truth. She would say that's exactly what she believes. But she's like the majority of people today who have been conditioned to believe that moral and spiritual claims are true only *when they choose to believe them.* When people hold this view of truth, the meaning and power of God's Word in their lives is diminished to the point of having little effect.

The Two Models for Viewing Truth

In our culture there are two distinct models for knowing that something is true.

Each model affects how we see and apply God's Word. The two models actually represent two radically different and opposing worldviews.

- *Model #1:* Truth is defined by God for everyone; it is objective and universal. The truth is known through discovering God and his Word.

- *Model #2:* What is true is defined by the individual; it is subjective and situational. Truth is known through simply choosing to believe it.

The first model acknowledges that God—not humans—is central, that he is the source of all things, and that he rules over all. God is the repository of truth, the author and judge of all that is right and wrong.

The second model, on the other hand, places the individual in control of moral matters. Because the standard resides within the individual, it is particular to that specific person (subjective) and circumstance (situational). In other words, each person considers himself or herself the judge of whatever is true for him or her in any given circumstance.

The second model—a relativistic model—is the model most people use today. This personal, fluctuating view of truth is shaping and molding their worldview. It is the lens through which they view life's choices and the basis on which they make life's decisions.

According to this relativistic model, when someone acts immoral or unethical he or she is offending another person's "idea" of what is right or wrong. But when a person acts immoral or unethical using God as the model for what is true, he or she is going against God's Word, the standard of morality that reflects his character and nature. One model denies the relevance of what God has to say; the other sees God as the arbiter of what is right and wrong.

Paul Copan gives this example of truth versus relativism in his book *True for You, but Not for Me.*

> Imagine a multiple-car collision at a central intersection near you. Immediately after the accident all parties run into the intersection sharing their side of the story. One says, "You cut me off!" Another says, "I have the right of way!" And a third cries, "Don't you know that a red light means STOP?" Even pedestrians who saw the accident from the sidewalk put in their two cents about the facts. Then, perhaps, finally the perpetrator steps forward and confesses: "It was my fault. I reached to turn off my radio and lost control of the car."
>
> Despite all the post-accident deliberations, one thing is clear: an accident happened. And in a matter of time, the truth will be known. We believe there is an objective truth about the accident. Eventually, a description of the accident will surface that corresponds to reality.[2]

In other words, what happened in the accident actually happened. The truth did not depend on the drivers' version of truth or the bystanders' opinions. The truth was what conformed to reality, not what the people involved believed it to be. In the same way, the truth of God conforms to reality. It does not accommodate personal beliefs at variance with it. It is not subject to opinions or personal views of it. It is what it is, and either we conform and live in accordance with that absolute reality, or we substitute our own version of truth and live with the consequence of defying reality.

Like the people at the accident scene, we may not always know the truth immediately. But as believers in God, we don't make up a truth that's comfortable to us at the moment. We know objective truth exists—it's out there waiting to be discovered. And when it seems unclear to us, we seek to discover it. When making decisions we consider facts and weigh evidence. We do our best to arrive at truth, and then we live accordingly. But to a relativist, there is no objective truth. The relativist will argue that since everyone has a different viewpoint, as at the accident scene, the truth cannot be known for sure. In fact, strange as it seems, some would argue that we could not even be sure the accident happened in the first place![3]

The same principle applies when it comes to moral truth. Without reference to an objective standard, people struggle with the impossible challenge of trying to define truth or falsehood, right or wrong, good or evil. When we stray from the objective standard—the Word of God that reflects the nature and character of our Creator—and attempt to devise our own moral standards, the picture not only becomes indistinct and muddy, the relevance of Scripture and its positive benefits of protection and provision are lost.

God and His Word as Our Standard

The town of Sèvres, a suburb of Paris, hosts the headquarters of the International Bureau of Weights and Measures. This bureau establishes and ensures reliable standards for all physical measurements—mass, length, volume, and weight—throughout most of the industrialized world.

If you wanted to be absolutely certain that the millimeter divisions on your ruler were accurate, you would compare them against the bureau's linear standards. If you wanted to know whether the bottle of Coke in your refrigerator contained exactly two liters of liquid, you could check it against the bureau's volume measurements.

Now, suppose we had a dispute about a length of wood that was cut for you. We measured it with our meter stick and told you it was one meter long; you measured it with your own meter stick and pronounced that it was less than one meter. How could we determine who was right? We could appeal to the objective and universal standard in Sèvres, France. To determine the validity of our individual measurements, we need only refer to the original.

The relevance of God's Word as our standard for living provides both the means to know God for who he is, and the way or guidelines to live in a godly manner.

In a similar manner, we know a standard exists for settling claims about moral knowledge—a standard for right and wrong that exists outside, above, and beyond ourselves. That standard is the nature of God himself as revealed in the Scriptures. So the relevance of God's Word as our standard for living provides both the means to know God for who he is, and the way or guidelines to live in a godly manner—which results in God being honored and us living a life of joy. That is why choosing God's definition of what is right and wrong and living accordingly grants us the benefits of his protection and provision.[4]

Living Under the Protection and Provision of God

Some people react to God's laws negatively. They see his commands as constricting and biblical morality as confining. They don't see the benefits to a moral lifestyle. They fail to realize that God's commands, like those of a loving parent—"Don't touch the stove," "Look both ways before you cross the street," "Eat your vegetables"—are not meant to spoil our fun and make us miserable. God gave commands—"Flee sexual immorality"; "Husbands, love your wives"; "You shall not commit adultery"—and all the others because he wanted to protect us and provide for us. He didn't concoct those rules just to be a killjoy or to throw his weight around; he gave them because he knew some things we didn't. He knew, for example, that sexual immorality is a path, not to pleasure and fulfillment, but to emptiness and frustration.

Moses acknowledged this truth when he challenged the nation of Israel:

> Now, Israel, what does the LORD your God require from you, but to fear the LORD your God, to walk in all his ways and love him, and to serve the LORD your God with all your heart and with all your soul, and to keep the LORD's commandments and His statutes *which I am commanding you today for your good?* (Deuteronomy 10:12-13 NASB).

The relevance of God's Word to each of us is simply this—*it is for our good!* Looking down from an eternal, omniscient perspective, he can see things that we cannot. He's like a general directing soldiers from a helicopter. He can see the entire battlefield. He knows where the enemy is hiding and has set traps. From his superior viewpoint he can direct his troops to avoid the enemy and his traps. Every truth, every rule, and every guideline coming from God's Word issues from the loving heart and character of God for our own good.

As Bill Hybels writes:

> The Lord tells us specifically that His commands are never burdensome (1 John 5:3). By this, He doesn't necessarily mean they're easy to keep. Rather, He's telling us that they're never foolish. They are never unnecessary or purely arbitrary. He doesn't force us to observe meaningless formalities, nor does He impose rules that have no value.
>
> On the contrary, every guideline, every law, every imperative in the Bible was crafted in infinite wisdom. They were given not only to honor God, but to benefit us as well. The entire book of Deuteronomy, for example, is a testament to this truth. In that book Moses repeatedly states that God gave the commandments for our good and promises to bless us if we obey them.[5]

"I know the plans I have for you," God told the nation of Israel, "they are plans for good and not for disaster, to give you a future and a hope" (Jeremiah 29:11). He went on to express his desire for his children to have "one heart and mind to worship me forever, for their own good and for the good of all their descendents" (Jeremiah 32:39). Choosing God's way instead of wrong does not sap all the fun and excitement out of life; on the contrary, it accomplishes our good, because we were created to reflect his likeness and image. When we live godly lives—lives that reflect the character of God—we inevitably experience true joy. Paradoxically, joy doesn't come from seeking joy. As the title of C.S. Lewis' spiritual autobiography, *Surprised by Joy*, indicates, true joy comes from the last place critics of God's laws would think to look. It comes from seeking God and following his ways.

Words of Warning

In discussing the joy of God's protection and provision that results from knowing and following God's ways, we must take care not to give the impression that bad things do not happen to moral people, or that people who engage in immorality are never happy. Indeed, the prophet Jeremiah asked, "Why are the wicked so prosperous? Why are evil people so happy?" (Jeremiah 12:1), and King David confessed he had seen "proud and evil people thriving like mighty trees" (Psalm 37:35).

Living out God's ways does not mean that in the short term morality is always immediately rewarded and immorality is always immediately punished. Sin does promise immediate satisfaction, and it does often deliver pleasure for a period of time. More often than not, the rewards of morality and the consequence of sin will become apparent in this life. But not always. Some of these rewards and consequences may not be measured out until after this life is over.

We must also be careful not to communicate the impression that God's commands are true simply because they are beneficial. To illustrate this point, think back to when you were in the third or fourth grade. You were taught the multiplication tables. That knowledge has paid off many times over for you. It helps you complete your tax return and compare prices in the grocery store. You might say that you get something good from your relationship with the multiplication tables.

But 5 x 6 = 30 is not true *because* you get something good out of it. It is true because it is true, because it reflects certain laws—it reflects reality. The benefit you derive from having learned the multiplication tables is not what makes those facts true; they are true whether you benefit from them or not. But as you make use of the truth of the multiplication tables, you indeed gain benefit.

Similarly, those things that are true and right in God's Word are not so *because* of any benefit you may derive from them; they are true because they are true.

Seeing God's Protection

There was a young man we'll call Greg. He lived down the block from a family who had an in-ground swimming pool in their backyard. Greg had never gone swimming in their pool; he barely knew the people, and a high wooden fence enclosed the pool.

One dark evening when Greg knew his neighbors were away, he and his girlfriend sneaked behind the house, scaled the fence, and entered the pool area to go for a swim.

Greg threw off his shoes, climbed the ladder and, while his girlfriend was still taking off her shoes and socks, leaped off the end of the diving board.

He heard his girlfriend scream just before he lost consciousness. The pool held only a few feet of water; Greg's dive ended with a shallow splat of water and a sickening crunch of bones. His late-night dive paralyzed him from the neck down for the rest of his life.

Greg ignored the fence that his neighbors had erected around the pool. He probably assumed it was there only to keep people like him and his girlfriend from having fun. In reality, it was meant for the protection of Greg and people like him, and his disregard of that boundary cost him dearly. Similarly, when we disregard the moral boundaries God has erected for our benefit—to protect us from harm—the cost can be devastating.

Over 40 years ago Dr. S.I. McMillen wrote a brilliant book called *None of These Diseases.* He demonstrated how over two dozen divine commands or standards served to prevent such disorders as heart disease, cervical cancer, and arthritis long before the advent of modern medicine! McMillen wrote in the preface:

> When God led the Israelites out of afflicted Egypt, he promised them
> that if they would obey his statutes, he would put "none of these diseases"

upon them. God guaranteed a freedom from disease that modern medicine cannot duplicate.[6]

That doesn't mean if we always obey God we'll never get sick. But God's commandments do act as an umbrella. When you put up an umbrella, it shields you from the rain. But if you choose to move out from under that umbrella during a storm, you're bound to get wet. As long as you and I stay under the umbrella of God's commands, we'll be shielded from many consequences. However, if we step out from under that protective cover, we should not be surprised if we suffer the negative effects of sinful behavior.

Seeing God's Provision

So far, most of what we've written about the benefits of God's Word has emphasized how it protects us from evil. But protection is only one side of the coin. The other side is provision. Adhering to God's instructions not only protects us from the consequences of evil, it also provides positive benefits. To illustrate, years ago, I (Josh) went hiking in the Great Smoky Mountains National Park with my son and daughter. We set out in the morning to hike to the top of Clingmans Dome, the highest point in the park, a towering 6643 feet.

It was a long hike from our campsite, much longer than I had expected. We really got tired, but we plodded on. Sean started to complain, so did his sister. And their groans and complaints seemed to increase in volume and intensity with the altitude. I began to wonder if I was being cruel by pushing my kids too hard.

But eventually we reached the "dome," the bald spot at what seemed to be the top of the earth. We all gazed in wonder at the breathtaking vista. The magnificent view made us forget about our aching legs and throbbing lungs. Sean actually wrapped his arms around me and whispered, "Thanks, Dad. This is great." His sister joined us in an embrace.

That view—and the sense of accomplishment at having completed a taxing hike—turned complaints into appreciation. My insistence on completing the hike had provided us an experience no painted picture or HD program on the Smoky Mountains could match.

That sort of thing may be what the psalmist had in mind when he wrote, "He [God] makes me as surefooted as a deer, leading me safely along the mountain" (Psalm 18:33). Obedience to God's commands not only protects us from harm; it also allows God to provide for us, sometimes in breathtaking ways.

When Jesus said, "You will know the truth, and the truth will set you free" (John 8:32), he spoke not only of freedom *from* (freedom from things like disease, disillusionment, and disappointment), but also of freedom *to* (freedom to love and be loved, to trust, to laugh). Being obedient to God's Word does not mean giving up the pleasures of leisure or satisfaction or liberty; it means being free to enjoy *maximum* leisure, *maximum* satisfaction, and *maximum* liberty—in the way God intended. God's prohibitions and directives to us come out of a heart of love that in effect says, "Follow in my ways and your joy will be made complete." God always has our best interest at heart.

CHAPTER ELEVEN

LIVING UNDER GOD'S PROTECTION AND ENJOYING HIS PROVISIONS

M issouri is called the "Show-me State." And there is a little bit of that attitude in all of us. Most of us are interested in seeing how things work and knowing why they function as they do. Well, when God gives us instructions to act in a certain way, there is a clear picture of how our obedience results in protection from harm and a provision of blessing. There are countless examples we could give here, but chapter length will limit us to two.[1]

God's Word on Sexual Immorality

In biblical terms, sexual immorality is all sex that occurs outside of a marriage between one man and one woman (extramarital and premarital sex). Scripture states:

- "Abstain from...sexual immorality" (Acts 15:29).

- "Run away from sexual sin" (1 Corinthians 6:18).

- "We must not engage in sexual immorality" (1 Corinthians 10:8).

- "Among you there must not be even a hint of sexual immorality...because these are improper for God's holy people" (Ephesians 5:3 NIV).

- "God wants you to be holy, so you should keep clear of all sexual sin" (1 Thessalonians 4:3).

Sexual Immorality Violates God's Nature of Purity and Faithfulness

God's very nature is pure. "Everyone who has this hope [of glory] in him purifies himself, just as he [God] is pure" (1 John 3:3 NIV). Because we are to reflect his image and follow in his ways, we are commanded to "have nothing to do with sexual sin, impurity, lust, and shameful desires" (Colossians 3:5).

God's very nature is faithful. "Understand...that the LORD your God is indeed God," Moses told the Israelites. "He is the faithful God who keeps his covenant for a thousand generations" (Deuteronomy 7:9). Because we are to reflect God's image of faithfulness and follow in his ways, we are commanded to "give honor to marriage, and remain faithful to one another in marriage" (Hebrews 13:4). Faithfulness can, of course, be broken even *before* one is married. To engage in premarital sex is to connect with another in a way intended only for a covenant relationship, thus having no ground for a solid commitment to being faithful.

The Protection and Provision of Living Sexually Pure and Faithful

Living sexually pure lives and remaining faithful to a present or future marriage relationship results in the following benefits:

Protects from:	Provides for:
• guilt • unplanned pregnancy • sexually transmitted diseases • sexual insecurity • emotional distress	• spiritual rewards • optimum atmosphere for child raising • peace of mind • trust • true intimacy

Both of us (Josh and Sean) made a decision early on to wait until the loving commitment of marriage before expressing ourselves sexually. Because we and our wives entered our marriage relationships as pure and faithful, we have been protected from feelings of guilt and have enjoyed an uninterrupted relationship with God.

We have never had to go through the heartache of an unplanned pregnancy. And consequently, our children, conceived out of a loving married relationship, have had the opportunity to be raised by their biological mother and father.

We have been protected from the fear that any sexually transmitted disease might come into our marriage bed.

We have been protected from the sexual insecurity that can occur from being compared to past sexual lovers one's spouses may have had. And consequently, we have experienced the provision of trust in our relationship.

We have been protected from the emotional distress that premarital sex can bring and the feelings of betrayal that an extramarital affair can cause. As a result we have enjoyed relational intimacy with our wives unobstructed by breaches of trust or ghosts from the past. Reflecting God's character in terms of purity and faithfulness in our human relationships brings glory to God and blessings to us.

Not everyone has remained faithful prior to marriage or during marriage. It is important for people who have made these mistakes to know that God is a faithful and forgiving God who can restore broken hearts, broken emotions, and broken marriages. Michael Leahy, author of *Porn Nation,* is just one example of this kind of restoration. His marriage was completely destroyed through his addiction to pornography. When he hit rock bottom in his life, he turned to God. Through God's love, forgiveness, and healing power Michael was fully restored. Today he travels across the country speaking to college students about the dangers of pornography and the power of God's redemptive grace. Our faithful God is the God of new beginnings.

Examples of Mentoring Others in Purity and Faithfulness in Marriage

✓ **Celebrate anniversaries.** Wedding anniversaries are ideal times to let children and friends know how faithfulness and purity have protected and provided for you in the areas discussed above. This can include people who have suffered divorce but are now pursuing a faithful relationship and oneness in their marriage. Make your own anniversary a family celebration. Let others know how much marital fidelity means to you. Explain what the marriage commitment has done for your relationship. The more that people, especially members of your own family, see how faithfulness and purity have benefited your lives and theirs, the more impact it will have on them.

Don't underestimate the ability of younger children (six, five, or four years old, for example) to understand the principles of sexual purity and marital fidelity. You have an excellent opportunity to build a foundation for their sexual chastity by helping them understand the principles of faithfulness and purity. You can explain to them your faithfulness to your spouse by putting it in the form of promise-keeping. "I promised I would love your mother always, and that's what I am going to do because I love your mother more than anyone, and God would be disappointed in me if I broke my promise to her." You can explain marital fidelity to them by saying, "I live only with your father and with no one else because I love him so much and because God created a wife to love only one man in that way." Teach them early of your commitment to each other and how you are exclusively devoted to each other. Your modeling and teaching will pay off in a decade or so when their hormones start raging.

Pastors and youth workers, you can take advantage of your anniversary or that of a mature couple in your church. Have your spouse come into the youth group or adult small group for a faithfulness and purity celebration. Explain how those principles have brought provision and protection into the marriage.

✓ **Take full advantage of weddings.** Whether you are a youth worker, pastor, or parent, you can use a wedding to celebrate God's principle of faithfulness and purity. Make sure your children or friends understand its significance. Take time prior to and following the ceremony to emphasize the commitment the couple is making and their promise to be faithful for a lifetime. Get a copy of the marriage vows and read them together with your friends or younger children. Teenagers may not respond favorably to reading the vows together, but you can make it meaningful to a child or pre-teen. Weddings are an ideal time to reinforce God's way of love and sex within the marriage commitment—and how that reflects the relational character of God.

✓ **Use opportunities presented by TV, news, and current affairs.** Take advantage of some of the many opportunities to correct the warped portrayals of love and sex in the "entertainment" media and news. When you and your kids, for example, see something on television or in the movies that contradicts God's standard for sex, discuss the benefits of obeying God's command and the consequences of violating them. You may be surprised how insightful young people are in detecting the benefits and consequences of people's actions once they begin to see life through the lens of God and his commands. (One fine resource to guide you in such teaching is the book *Hollywood Worldviews* by Brian Godawa.)

God's Word on the Family

For century upon century, faithful Jews have begun their daily prayers by reciting the *shema,* the phrase Moses spoke to the Israelites after delivering the Ten Commandments to them:

"Hear, O Israel: The LORD our God, *the LORD is one*" (Deuteronomy 6:4 NIV).

Those words are sacred to a Jew. Those are the words, written in Hebrew on tiny slips of paper, that Orthodox Jews bind to their arms and foreheads and attach outside the doors of their homes in a little box or cylinder called a *mezuzah.*

The *shema* reveals the singularity of God. "See now," God says in his Word, "there is no god besides me" (Deuteronomy 32:39 NIV). "Understand that I alone am God," he declares, "There is no other God; there never has been and never will be" (Isaiah 43:10).

But the *shema* does not only refer to the singularity of God; it also testifies to his unity. Long before Jesus Christ was revealed to humans as the Son of God, long before the Holy Spirit was given to the church at Pentecost, God revealed himself as a mysterious unity. The Genesis account of creation reports that God said, "Let *us* make people in *our* image" (Genesis 1:26), yet "the LORD is one." The first book of Moses records God's reaction to Adam and Eve's sin, saying, "The people have become as we are, knowing everything, both good and evil" (Genesis 3:22), yet "the LORD is *one.*"

The Bible reports that God responded to the Tower of Babel by saying, "Come, let *us* go down and confuse their language so they will not understand each other" (Genesis 11:7 NIV), yet "the LORD is *one.*" The divine name *Elohim,* applied to God throughout the Pentateuch, is a plural in the Hebrew, yet "the LORD is *one.*"

Even in Old Testament times, the concept of a plural Godhead—what Christians now call the Trinity—existed. The oneness of God represents a perfect relationship of unity. The *shema* makes it clear that God is not a partnership. He is not a conglomeration. He is not a committee. He is a *unity:* "Hear, O Israel: The LORD our God, *the LORD is one*" (Deuteronomy 6:4 NIV).

God cannot be separated. He cannot be divided. His perfect oneness in loving relationship is not something he strives for; it is not even something he manufactures. It is something he *is.* "The Father and I are one," Jesus said. "Realize that the Father is in me, and I am in the Father" (John 10:30,38).

Divided Families Violate God's Character of Unity

Unity is part of God's nature and character. He is relationally one. And it is that unity that he wishes us to reflect in our marriages and family relationships. When the Bible says that "a man will leave his father and mother and be united to his wife, and they will become one flesh" (Genesis 2:24 NIV), it is saying that marriage should reflect God's nature of oneness and unity. God went on to explain and amplify this unity theme regarding marriage. Jesus, speaking specifically of the marriage commitment, added, "Since they are no longer two but one, let no one separate them" (Mark 10:8-9).

The Protection and Provision of United Families

When marriages and families are bound by unity and love, the relationship results in the following benefits:

Protects from:	Provides for:
• parental inattention	• parental involvement
• emotional insecurity	• emotional security
• relational problems	• healthy role models

It doesn't take vast university and government research studies to tell us that marital unfaithfulness and divorce have negative consequences to all concerned. In July 2009 *Time* magazine devoted its cover story to the decay of marriage in America. The story was entitled, "Unfaithfully Yours—Infidelity is eroding our most sacred institution." In the magazine's essay "Why Marriage Matters," author Caitlin Flanagan stated:

In the past 40 years, the face of the American family has changed profoundly. As sociologist Andrew J. Cherlin observes in a landmark new book called *The Marriage-Go-Round: The State of Marriage and the Family in America Today,* what is significant about contemporary American families, compared with those of other nations, is their combination of "frequent marriage, frequent divorce" and the high number of "short-term co-habiting relationships." Taken together, these forces "create a great turbulence in American family life, a family flux, a coming and going of partners on a scale seen nowhere else. There are more partners in the personal lives of Americans than in the lives of people of any other Western country."...

How much does this matter? More than words can say. There is no other single force causing as much measurable hardship and human misery in this country as the collapse of marriage. It hurts children, it reduces mothers' financial security, and it has landed with particular devastation on those who can bear it least: the nation's underclass.[2]

Flanagan goes on to talk about the need of both a mother's love *and* a father's love to mature in a healthy manner.

Few things hamper a child as much as not having a father at home. "As a feminist, I didn't want to believe it," says Maria Kefalas, a sociologist who studies marriage and family issues and co-authored a seminal book on low-income mothers called *Promises I Can Keep: Why Poor Women Put Motherhood Before Marriage.* "Women always tell me, 'I can be a mother and a father to a child,' but it's not true." Growing up without a father has a deep psychological effect on a child. "The mom may not need that man," Kefalas says, "but her children still do."[3]

Jesus had good reason to say, "Since they [a married couple] are no longer two but one, let no one separate them, for God has joined them together" (Matthew 19:6). A united marriage and family fosters feelings of consistency, permanence, and stability. It helps a child to know who they belong to, who belongs to them, who they can trust, and what their lives will be like tomorrow.

I (Josh) grew up in an alcoholic home. I knew what a divided and dysfunctional home was like. And even today I still suffer some of the emotional fallout of growing up in a home that was not unified.

I (Sean) grew up in a united home. I witnessed the devotion of a husband and wife as they loved each other in front of me and my sisters. And that united family legacy lives on in my life and that of my own family.

The greatest security you can give your children is the experiential knowledge that you love your spouse. You can tell a child you love them with all your heart and demonstrate that love day after day, and it will emotionally tell them he or she is lovable. But if you want to provide real security for your child, demonstrate how much you love your spouse.

When Sean was six years old, I (Josh) noticed he wasn't quite himself one day when he came home from school. I asked what was wrong.

"Aw, nothing, Dad," he said.

Sean and I have pretty good communication so I said, "Come on, share with me what you're feeling."

He hesitated, and then he asked, "Daddy, are you going to leave Mommy?"

I knew that question would come up someday. "What makes you ask that?" I inquired.

Three of his friends' dads had just divorced their mothers, Sean told me, and he was afraid I might do the same.

I sat down with Sean, looked him in the eye and said, "I want you to know one thing. I love your mother very much. I'm committed to her, and I'll never leave her. Period."

That little six-year-old breathed a sigh of relief, smiled at me, and said, "Thanks, Dad." At that moment he didn't need reinforcement of my love for him as much as he needed the security that comes from knowing that his mother and I love each other and are committed to a permanent relationship. The loving oneness of a marriage reflects the nature of God's unity, and it is that unbreakable bond of love that communicates security to this generation.

Examples for Parents of Mentoring Unity in the Family

✓ **Openly communicate your love to your spouse today.** Take advantage of every opportunity to let your children know how much you love your mate and make an effort to do that today. Be affectionate with each other around them. As we said above, the more you show them how much you are devoted to your mate, the more secure they will feel. Kisses, roses, special dates, favorite meals—there are a hundred and one ways to openly demonstrate before your children how you love each other. Your kids will love it when you involve them in helping plan a special meal or a surprise that demonstrates your love and appreciation for your spouse. Your kids' participation in helping you plan these things also increases their awareness of—and confidence in—your loving commitment to each other.

✓ **Pull out your wedding album.** You may be surprised at how fascinated your children are—even your teenagers—by the story and pictures of your wedding. Pull out the wedding photos and use them as a way to share your deep convictions about marriage, the vows you made to your spouse, and how that commitment stands today.

Sharing stories of your courtship and marriage—and how honoring marriage has resulted in God's protection and provision in your life—will reinforce your child's beliefs in God's way for marriage and family.

Examples for Parents and Others of Mentoring Unity

✓ **Make birthdays special.** Whether you are 5, 15, or 50, hearing about the details of the day you were born is always fascinating. Use that fascination to provide your child a greater sense of belonging. Emphasize to your children the fact that they came from the union of your love for your mate. Explain how they have inherited distinct characteristics and features from each of you. Explain to a friend how his or her being in the world has brought you meaning. The more that people gain a sense of their heritage or significance, the more unity they will feel with their family and friends.

✓ **Use opportunities presented by TV, news, and current affairs.** Use movies or news events of divorces or pending marriages as topics of discussion. Rather than condemning a person who has suffered a divorce, talk about the protection and provision they will be missing. If you know the person, discuss how you and your children or friends can be supportive and helpful. Using current events can be an ideal way to discuss the negative consequences of violating God's standard of unity in marriage and family and a good way to point out the positive rewards of living by his way.

Summary

God has given us his reliable Word that accurately reflects who he is (pure, faithful, a unity, and so on). Because he created us in his image, he provides instructions in his Word that show us how to conduct our lives in a way that reflects his nature. By following these instructions, we can live godly lives and enjoy the protection and provision he planned for us. This truth of God and his Word is another component in the building of a Christian worldview. The more we understand God's character and nature and how they are reflected in the commands and instructions found in his Word, the more we gain a perspective on life as God intended it.

■

For more on the character and nature of God and the protection and provision of living out his ways, we suggest that you obtain the book *Right from Wrong* by Josh McDowell and Bob Hostetler. Most of this chapter was derived from that work. *Right from Wrong* expands the ideas presented in this chapter by going into other qualities of God such as honesty, love, justice, mercy, respect, and self-control. If you are unable to find this book in a Christian bookstore, go online to www.josh.org and click on "resources."

To help you as a family, youth group, or adult group to solidify the meaning of God's Word, we have developed a Judeo-Christian Feast of Harvest, the Revelation Celebration, which is described in appendix B in this handbook. This feast is designed to enable you to enjoy a meal together that specifically focuses on celebrating the God of relationships. He has created us and given us a revelation of himself through his Spirit and the Word so we can experience an intimate relationship with him. Conducting this celebration meal will add relevance to your Christian worldview and instill that view into your friends and family.

TRUTH THREE

ORIGINAL SIN

CHAPTER TWELVE

THE FIRST
BROKEN RELATIONSHIP

Scottie, our firstborn son, was a precious bundle of love that Stephanie and I (Sean) cherished from day one. We did nothing but shower him with love and devotion. Even from his first movements in his mother's womb he was part of our family. When little Scottie joined our family we did everything we could to nurture him with love and model before him a giving and trusting relationship.

Yet despite all our loving efforts and with no influence from the outside culture, one day Scottie grabbed a toy from me and declared authoritatively, "Mine." Rather than enjoying a giving relationship with his father he declared his independence to be in charge of the toy exclusively. I wasn't surprised or appalled by his actions—in fact I chuckled inside. Knowing human nature, I had been expecting that at some point my son would exhibit self-centeredness.

If you have been around children very long, you too can testify that a child without any training has an independent streak that is "me-centered." From infancy there appears to be a struggle for control to get what we want when we want it. In one form or another this independent drive to be in charge lies behind every struggle for power, every prejudice, every conflict, and every abuse of relationship since the dawn of time. Why is this? Humans were created in the image of a triune God whose Persons are in harmonious relationship with one another. Yet how can the human race fashioned in the likeness of this perfect God be so self-centered from birth? The answer is found in the beginning, when sin originally entered the world.

The Perfect Circle of Relationships

Imagine spending a day with the first man and the first woman in perfect relationship with God. At sunrise Adam and Eve awaken refreshed and cheerful, without a trace of morning grumpiness. They hug and kiss each other, then march off to work in the garden. Though they apply themselves diligently to every task, they never tire. In fact they seem to find immense joy in tending and shaping their property and nourishing and guiding the creatures that fawn on them. When they grow hungry they pause and eat from the abundant food growing all about them. They quench their thirst from crystal streams. As evening approaches they leave their work, plunge into a clear lake and swim about for half an hour, then dry off by chasing through the cool woods unblighted by stickers or poison ivy. Reaching the blossom-covered bower that is their home, they sit drinking fresh juice from a coconut shell as they eagerly await the highlight of their day.

"Is he coming yet?" Eve asks, looking down the path through the forest.

"I don't hear him," Adam replies. "It may be a little early."

They sip and talk of plans for a grove of trees near the waterfall to the east. After a few minutes, Eve looks again toward the woods, her eyes bright with anticipation.

"I still don't see him," she says.

"Listen," replies Adam. "I think I hear something."

They both keep still and listen, and in moments the familiar, soft sound of movement through the grass is unmistakable.

"Oh, he's coming!" Eve cannot contain her excitement. She bounds joyfully up the path as Adam closes the distance behind her. They run to God like children to a father returning home at the end of a workday. And until sundown, the happy pair walks the paths of the garden and chats with their Creator as their souls within them burn with ecstatic joy.

While the details of this scene are fictional, it is a true picture of how Adam and Eve must have loved God and responded to him. They looked forward to his presence with all the anticipation of a lover. God loved them and delighted in them. Man and woman loved God and each other. The two had joined the Godhead's circle of relationship, and together they experienced its indescribable goodness. They felt the joy of freely giving of themselves to one another. They experienced the security of being accepted without conditions. They felt valued by the all-sufficient God who wanted to spend time with them. The praise and appreciation God must have given them for their excellent tending of the garden made them feel significant. And the affection and gratitude they all offered one another was expressive of a devoted relationship of love.

This perfect circle of loving relationship was God's ultimate intention for all humanity from creation forward. He intended Adam and Eve and all their descendants to be ecstatically happy in a loving relationship with him and each other forever. And in Eden, it all worked perfectly.[1]

What's in a Choice?

Obviously, somewhere along the way something went wrong. This world we live in is hardly the Garden of Eden. Far from delighting in God, many people today feel quite the opposite toward him. Some see God as something like a strict judge watching their every move with a stern, disapproving eye. Some find the idea of God so far-fetched that they don't even believe he exists. And even if he does exist, they think he is remote and uncaring—somewhere off in his distant heaven, leaving us to struggle alone with problems that don't seem to have handles in a world filled with every kind of evil. Many people actually want God to remain distant. In fact, this is one common motivation for atheism. Aldous Huxley, author of *Brave New World,* explained that he and his atheist friends desired a world without the meaning God could give it because such a world gave them "liberation from a certain system of morality. We objected to the morality because it interfered with our sexual freedom."[2]

Sociologist Christian Smith found in his research that most teenagers in the U.S. believe that "God is something like a combination Divine Butler and Cosmic Therapist: he is always on call, takes care of any problem that arises, professionally helps his people to feel better about themselves, and does not become too personally involved in the process."[3] Such views of God, which are so common today, are almost infinitely removed from the way Adam and Eve saw him in Genesis. They saw God as a being who loved them dearly, and they exulted in their close and intimate relationship with him. How did we humans move from intimacy with God in a perfect world to alienation from him in today's messed-up world?

Freedom to Trust

There is no hint in Scripture that continuing a perfect relationship between humans and God would be automatic. The relationship was based on an authentic love that was to be expressed freely and voluntarily. Therefore the close relationship involved a choice and was to bear the fruit of trust. Of course, God was all-powerful and could have created humans with no choice capacity at all. He could have manipulated their every move and made them conform to his every wish. But had he done this, the humans would not have been created in his own image. God is free to choose, and he gave humans that same capacity. Adam and Eve exercised that capacity to choose by joining God's circle of relationship to freely and voluntarily express their love to him and one another. God's relationship was devoid of any self-serving power plays, or desires to control another person, or ambitions of independence. It was a relationship that was other-focused. It was a relationship that chose to look for the best in the other and freely gave of oneself to please the other. When a person knows another and has voluntarily chosen to love him or her this way, it engenders an intimate and trusting relationship.

So, in the pristine perfection of the Garden, God offered Adam and Eve a tangible way of expressing their unselfish love and trust in him. He gave them a command not to eat of a certain fruit. And so there it was; they had a choice to make, a voluntary choice to believe God was acting unselfishly and had their best interest at heart, or that he was selfishly keeping something good from them. In this simple choice Adam and Eve were being asked to demonstrate they trusted that God was good and that he would not selfishly withhold things from them. To choose otherwise would be to destroy the loving relationship established between God and humans. And to sever that relationship meant becoming unplugged from the only true source of love and life itself. That, of course, would result in a disastrous outcome. ✎

God is passionate about us loving him and jealous if we turn away from him because he knows loving him is the only way for us to truly find joy and completeness.

So there was a risk within God's masterly plan to create humans in his relational image and likeness. The risk was that they could choose to reject such a relationship. Authentic love cannot be forced. God knew this, as well as the consequences if they rejected him. That is why the very hint of his created humans trying to satisfy their needs outside of him would produce jealousy. His first commandment says, "Do not worship any other god, for the LORD, whose name is Jealous, is a jealous God" (Exodus 34:14 NIV). The New Living Translation renders "a jealous God" as "a God who is passionate about his relationship with you."

God's jealousy is far from being selfish. He wanted Adam and Eve and all their descendants to worship him and him exclusively—but not because his pride is hurt if they don't or because he can't stand rejection. Rather, he is passionate about us loving him and jealous if we turn away from him because he knows loving him is the only way for us to truly find joy and completeness.

God is love, joy, peace, goodness, and everything needed to bring pure happiness and joy. "Whatever is good and perfect," James declares, "comes to us from God" (James 1:17). So when God told Adam and Eve to avoid that fruit, he was actually attempting to lead them to unselfish, other-focused living in relationship with him. That kind of relationship would bring great pleasure to him and deep happiness to them.

Separation from God

But as we all know, Adam and Eve chose another course. Satan, the enemy of God, entered the Garden of Eden and convinced the humans to make a choice that ruined God's intended relationship with humans and inflicted on the world untold agony and devastation. "Toward evening they heard the LORD God walking about in the garden, so they hid themselves among the trees. The LORD God called to Adam, 'Where are you?' He replied, 'I heard you, so I hid. I was afraid because I was naked'" (Genesis 3:8-10). Just a day before, Adam and Eve couldn't contain their excitement over the arrival of their Creator. On this particular evening, however, their reaction was altogether different. Fear had driven a wedge between humans and God, which is why they hid from him in shame. This fear and hiding was the result of their self-centered act, which is what we call sin. But Adam and Eve's disobedience involved more than simply eating from a "do not take" tree. It involved rejecting God as the source of what is right and true. That rebellion against God brought death to the relationship. Both the man and the woman were sent out of the Garden of Eden (see Genesis 3:23-24).

Their act resulted in more tragedy than just Adam and Eve's expulsion from the Garden. The consequences were dreadful and devastating, affecting the planet itself. Every plant and animal and every human born since that day became subject to pain, disease, decay, sorrow, and death (see Romans 8:20-22).

The entrance of sin drove life from the world. By sinning, Adam and Eve disrupted their relational connection to a perfect and holy God—who is life itself and from whom all life comes (see John 1:4; 5:26). Gone were their shared moments of intimacy and joy with their Father God. Gone were the thrills of laughter they enjoyed together. Gone was their close relationship.

Their sin brought into the world not only the living death of separation from God, but sin's fallout brought hunger, disease, hatred, and heartache that would end in their physical death and eternal separation from God. Sin and death reigned over the whole human race from that moment forward. Scripture states, "When Adam sinned, sin entered the entire human race. Adam's sin brought death, so death spread to everyone, for everyone sinned" (Romans 5:12).

Think of the worst that can happen. What is the greatest tragedy of life? What saps all the joy out of living? The answer is death. In death there is no hope, there is no physical existence, there is no joy of any kind. Death is humanity's greatest curse, for it is the absence of the God of all life and goodness.

"The wages of sin," Scripture states, "is death" (Romans 6:23). And there is nothing we humans can do in and of ourselves to reverse the payoff of sin. The apostle Paul said we are "utterly helpless" (Romans 5:6).

When Goodness Is No Good

The general population of the U.S. believes that "good people go to heaven when they die."[4] They believe that if you and I improve ourselves over time, our good deeds will outweigh our bad ones, tipping the balance in our favor and earning entrance into heaven. The thinking is that God will grade us on the curve and let us again live with him in a perfect heaven and earth.

What this belief fails to take into account is the complete truth about death. Death is more than what happens when you stop breathing and they bury you. Even as we humans breathe and walk about on the face of the planet, we are already dead spiritually. Dead people have no ability to save themselves, good works, or no good works. They have no ability to do anything—they are dead! Doing good works no more means we're spiritually alive than the rigor mortis spasms of a corpse means it's physically alive. Scripture tells us plainly, "Salvation is not a reward for the good things we have done" (Ephesians 2:9). Strict adherence to God's law won't even help. "The law of Moses could not save us," Paul said, "because of our sinful nature" (Romans 8:3). There is absolutely nothing we can do on our own to solve our sin problem because we are all dead spiritually and will soon be dead physically.

The boundary of trust that God drew was crossed with the first humans. His command that displayed human obedience was violated. The self-centered choice of Adam and Eve brought death and a helpless dilemma for the entire human race.

To summarize what we've said up to now:

> We believe the truth that God created humans in his image to relate to him lovingly, but that relationship was destroyed because of original sin. Sin was passed to the entire human race, and consequently all are born spiritually dead and utterly helpless to gain favor with God.

As a result of sin and death the universe is in a state of entropy—moving from order to disorder. Everything is dying, and no amount of human ingenuity or technology or medical advances can permanently reverse the inevitable doom of us all. That is, nothing apart from a miraculous intervention by God.

There are, however, those who would say that humans are born naturally good. And in time the evolutionary process will work out and the best and strongest of human nature will survive. To some, the problems of humans have a natural explanation with natural solutions. Yet Scripture paints another story, a story that records the fact that human sin has consequences. This is the subject of the next chapter.

CHAPTER THIRTEEN

EVIDENCE THAT SIN HAS CONSEQUENCES

Today, as we write these words, some of the headlines in the local newspaper read:

- North and South Korea Fight at Sea
- Bombing Kills 24
- Cities Blacked Out
- Sniper Executed
- Ex-astronaut Guilty
- Bomb Scare at RTA
- County Engineer Dies at 49[1]

The problem of sin in the world isn't a sociological, economic, or intellectual problem; it is a spiritual or heart problem.

Every newspaper and every online news source around the globe today is full of headlines and stories like these, telling of the earth's population caught up in greed, distrust, robberies, conflict, killings, war, destruction, and death.

Could this really be the result of self-centered humans choosing to disregard God and his ways? Marxists blame capitalism and the unequal distribution of wealth for much of the evil of the world. Secular humanists blame religion. And certain forms of Buddhism say all evil in the world is simply an illusion. But Jesus said it's not outside circumstances that causes evil in the world, he said that "from the heart come evil thoughts, murder, adultery, all other sexual immorality, theft, lying, and slander" (Matthew 15:19).

The problem of sin in the world isn't a sociological, economic, or intellectual problem; it is a spiritual or heart problem. All of us have hearts that are naturally in rebellion against God and his purposes for the world.

You may need no further evidence other than your life's observations and the daily news to confirm that sin results in negative consequences. But if that isn't enough, thousands of years of recorded history of a particular family of people serves as a living testimony to the consequences of original sin. This accurate historic record is documented in the Hebrew Bible, the Old Testament. God has given us the accurate stories of his people, the children of Israel, that demonstrate how living in relationship with him brings blessing, and choosing a self-centered path (sin) brings negative consequences. Following are but a small sampling of headlines drawn from the pages of Scripture.

Resentment and Jealousy Produce Murder
From Genesis 4

Cain was the first child of Adam and Eve. He became a farmer. Abel was the couple's second son. He became a sheepherder.

As the boys grew to manhood, both brought offerings before God. Cain brought produce and Abel brought choice lambs. God accepted the offerings of Abel, but not of Cain. And Cain was furious.

"'Why are you so angry?' the LORD asked him. 'Why do you look so dejected? You will be accepted if you respond in the right way. But if you refuse to respond correctly, then watch out! Sin is waiting to attack and destroy you, and you must subdue it'" (Genesis 4:6-7).

If Adam and Eve learned anything from their own sin they would have surely shared it with their boys. You would think they must have stressed to their sons that a Godlike relationship is based on an unselfish focus for another and a trust that God is good—his ways are always best for them. But Cain obviously didn't get it. Because when God said, in effect, "Believe that my ways are right and follow them, and they will work for you because I have your best interest at heart," Cain responded in anger.

Cain rejected God's warning that sin was waiting to attack and destroy him. When he refused to lovingly relate to God, his resentment and jealousy drove him to murder his brother, Abel. This historically documented story illustrates that sin results in negative consequences.

Lust, Rape, and Mass Killings
From Genesis 34

Jacob was the son of Isaac, the grandson of Abraham. He, along with his large family, settled outside to the town of Shechem in Canaan. The town was named after its prince, Shechem.

One day Dinah, Jacob's daughter, was visiting some friends in the area. Prince Shechem saw Dinah and just had to have her. To the horror of Dinah, he forced himself on her and raped her.

The prince decided he wanted Dinah for his wife and started negotiations with Jacob through his own father. In fact, the proposal was that the men of Shechem take all of Jacob's daughters for marriage and Jacob's sons take all daughters of Shechem for marriage.

Jacob's sons counteroffered. They proposed that if the men of Shechem got circumcised, the exchange deal would be acceptable. Shechem agreed and the entire male population of the town got circumcised. But this was nothing but a ploy by the sons of Jacob. They had revenge in mind.

Three days after the circumcisions, when the men were still sore and less than agile, Jacob's sons slaughtered every man in town. Then they "seized all the flocks and herds and donkeys—everything they could lay their hands on, both inside the town and outside in the fields. They also took all the women and children and wealth of every kind" (Genesis 34:28-29). But after the mass killings, Jacob was so fearful of retaliation from the neighboring cities that he moved his entire family out of the area.

A woman was sexually abused because a man wanted what he wanted. Lust is about selfishly taking, not giving. Shechem's lust was a self-centered, brutal act of aggression that resulted in a tragic domino effect, breeding retaliatory sins in its wake and leaving a trail of tragedy. Lies and deception, death and destruction, women becoming widows, children becoming orphans, families being ripped apart and displaced. This historically documented story illustrates that sin results in negative consequences.

A Lust for Power Leads to Slavery
From Exodus 1

Soon after the debacle in Shechem, God changed Jacob's name to *Israel*. And eventually Israel moved his family to Egypt. In a few generations the children of Israel populated much of the land. This explosive growth concerned the new king of Egypt. "He told his people, 'These Israelites are becoming a threat to us because there are so many of them. We must find a way to put an end to this. If we don't and if war breaks out, they will join our enemies and fight against us'" (Exodus 1:9-10).

The lust for power and keeping it drove the Egyptian king to a brutal solution: slavery. This lustful thirst for power forced free men and women into chains and bondage. But even during their captivity the children of Israel continued to multiply. Afraid of an uprising by the masses, the king had an idea to keep the Israelites to a manageable minimum. He called for the murdering of all the newborn male population of the Israelites. But it didn't work. God's people continued to multiply.

Eventually, a baby would miraculously be saved from the male killings and grow to become the deliverer of Israel. Moses would lead his people out of slavery in Egypt and march them toward God's Promised Land.

A total disregard for others and a rejection of God's way of respecting and honoring his creation is self-centered and sinful. A lust for power caused an entire nation of people to suffer the brutality of enslavement. This sinful appetite for dominance resulted in physical pain, emotional suffering, and the loss of human dignity. This historically documented story illustrates that sin results in negative consequences.

The Price of Sin

God had given his words to Moses on Mount Sinai, and Moses relayed them to the children of Israel.

> Now, Israel, what does the LORD your God require of you? He requires you to fear him, to live according to his will, to love and worship him with all your heart and soul, and to obey the LORD's commands and laws that I am giving you today for your own good (Deuteronomy 10:12-13).

So there are definite benefits in living in relationship with God. But as we've seen in the illustrations above, there are negative consequences to sin. In fact, God warned the children of Israel repeatedly.

> If you refuse to listen to the LORD your God and do not obey all the commands and laws I am giving you today…[you will experience] curses, confusion, and disillusionment in everything you do, until at last you are completely destroyed for doing evil and forsaking me (Deuteronomy 28:15-20).

The price of sin is high. The Old Testament has this common theme woven throughout. Scripture tells of a people who at times walk in the ways of God. They live out godly relationships and reap the benefits of joy and happiness. Then we learn that they sin—they act self-centered and fail to trust in God and his ways. Throughout the history of the nation, this turning away from God accelerates, and in spite of the warnings of several prophets, the people do not repent, and they refuse to turn back to

God. Consequently "disaster came upon the nation of Israel because the people worshiped other gods, sinning against the LORD their God, who had brought them safely out of their slavery in Egypt" (2 Kings 17:7). The result is always the same: pain and suffering, heartache and ruin, destruction and death. Death ultimately is the wages of sin, just as God proclaimed to Adam and Eve. History records it; we see it all around us; we even experience some of it in our own lives.

We implied earlier that we need go no further than the mirror to see the effects of original sin. The apostle Paul made the case "that all people, whether Jews or Gentiles, are under the power of sin" (Romans 3:9). He then went on to quote from the Old Testament, saying, "No one is good—not even one. No one has real understanding; no one is seeking God. All have turned away from God; all have gone wrong. No one does good, not even one" (Romans 3:10-12).

The McDowell family, your family, and each of us personally suffer the fallout of our own sins. The Old Testament stories may give us clear examples, but each of us has personal examples of the negative consequences of sin in our lives. The sins of a sharp tongue, an explosive temper, lust, jealousy, greed, family neglect, are the sins that bring us and those around us heartache and pain. Big or small, committed in secret or in the open, we all must admit that we struggle with the issue of sin.

But we do have a choice. Just as Adam and Eve were free to choose God's way or their own way, we too can make moral choices that affect our everyday lives. God has not left us without instructions in making these choices. He has provided us with a formula for turning our back on sin, choosing him, and making right choices in life. The question is how we make those right choices.

CHAPTER FOURTEEN

CHOOSING RIGHT
FROM WRONG

Satan's disguise was perfect. Serpents were wise and subtle, and the innocent Eve would not suspect a thing if such a creature started a conversation with her. He slipped into the Garden of Eden and approached the woman.

"What is it with this relationship between you and God?" he asked Eve. "Look at you—it's all about what he wants. But what about what you want? He's robbing you of your true identity as a real person." The creature rolled his eyes upward. "That God of yours has fooled you into thinking that listening to him is in your best interest. But how can you think it's in your best interest to never be free enough to make your own decisions? He's not even allowing you to decide what is good for you to eat."

"Oh, it's not like that at all," answered Eve. "He gives us the run of this garden, we have plenty of delicious food to eat, and he doesn't tell us to do anything except what makes us happy." She paused to wrap an ivy tendril around an oak limb. "Why should we want anything different?"

"But he did forbid you to eat one fruit, did he not?" replied the serpent. "Why can't you eat that sweet-smelling, bright, juicy morsel hanging on that tree right there?" he pointed to the thick, leafy tree in the center of the garden, its branches heavy with glistening orbs of fruit.

"Well, you're right. God did tell us not to eat that fruit," said the woman. "He said if we ate it we would die."

"Ah, but I happen to know better," replied Satan. "That fruit won't kill you. Do you want to know the real reason God forbids it?" He leaned close to her ear and lowered his voice to little more than a whisper. "It will make you equal to him, and he doesn't want rivals. He wants to keep you ignorant so he can control you. If you really want to be like God, you must be independent enough to call your own shots and eat what you want to eat. Let him know that you won't be kept down any longer. Get an identity of your own—take control of your own destiny. Be your own person. Do your own thing."

The more Eve listened to the smooth-talking serpent, the more God's warning faded and his words became hazy. They didn't seem to make sense any more. Maybe that snake was right; maybe God didn't have her best interest at heart. Maybe she needed to break free of God to become her own person. With her heart racing, she reached out and gingerly touched the fruit. Nothing happened. She touched it again, tentatively closing her fingers around it. Nothing happened. Then she gripped it firmly, pulled it from the tree, and took a quick bite before she could change her mind. Immediately she ran to Adam and managed to cajole him into eating it with her.[1]

Obviously the infamous encounter between Satan and Eve recounted in Genesis 3 has been greatly amplified here. But we believe this expansion of the story provides telling insights that help us understand the nature of Satan's temptation and Eve's fatal decision. That decision has had a catastrophic effect on the human race and the entire universe from that time forward. In fact, your own concept of right and wrong and how you make moral decisions has been distorted by the aftermath of Eve's decision. No matter how close your relationship with God may be right now, you still must struggle with making right moral choices. Knowledge of what is good no longer comes naturally. It now requires a deliberate process of spiritual discipline to keep God in the center of each decision.

> *God and God alone is the arbiter of what is right and what is wrong.*

What was the real sin that Adam and Eve committed that day? Was it that they didn't love God enough to do what he asked them to do? Was it that they failed to be "other-focused" in their relationship with God? Or, was it that they didn't trust God enough to believe that the prohibition of the fruit was for their own good? All those things are part of the picture. What is central to all of them is that of independence—self-sovereignty. Eve felt she had the right to choose for herself whether or not she should eat the fruit. She chose to be relationally independent of God and his concerns.

The serpent was right on one count. When he told Eve that in making her choice she would become a god of her own, he hit the nail on the head. From that moment on, she would take on the godlike option of choosing for herself what was right and wrong. But what he didn't tell her is that no mere human could ever accurately determine right or wrong for herself. God and God alone is the arbiter of what is right and what is wrong. He is the absolute standard of rightness, and everything moral flows from his innate nature. When Adam, Eve, or anyone else decides that they alone know what is right for them, they are in effect worshipping the god of self. Right, godly choices that bring fulfillment and joy to our lives are those that relationally align with the person and character of a holy, righteous God. He and he alone establishes the boundaries of right and wrong—which, by the way, are always in our best interest.

The Four "Cs" of Right Choices

There is a relational process of making right moral choices that, if followed, will bring God's protection and provision in life every time. We have distilled this process into an easy-to-remember formula that we call the "4-Cs." Each time you and I are confronted with a moral choice we can follow this process.

1. Consider the Choice

In a single day each of us makes literally scores of choices. Most of them are almost automatic. We choose what time to get up in the morning, what clothes to wear, what to eat, what route to take to work or school, where to park, and so on. We take little time considering these choices.

But when it comes to considering moral choices, we need to pause and realize we are at a crossroads. The choices we make—to be less than honest, to advance a flirtation to the next level, to enhance our score by "borrowing" someone else's answers, or to show mercy to someone—are often made without considering the gravity of what we are really doing. To make right moral choices, we must first pause long enough to remind ourselves that we are facing an opportunity for a right or wrong decision.

2. Compare the Choice to God

Eve seemed to pause long enough to realize she was about to make a right or wrong choice. But she failed to compare her decision to God. That is what godly relationship does—it focuses on the desires of the other. But the serpent told her she would become just like God, independent enough to know both good and evil without regard to him. Eve was convinced. "The fruit looked so fresh and delicious, and it would make her so wise! So she ate some of the fruit" (Genesis 3:6).

What Eve failed to do, like many of us, was to take God into consideration and compare her attitude and action to him, which would have meant looking at the choice in relation to the commands that emanate from his nature. This, of course, would have required that she believe that God was her absolute standard for right—not herself. When we choose to obey God we in are in effect telling him, "I love you enough to place your interests first in my life. You are the sovereign God whose character and nature defines what is right for me."

When we pause to consider our choice and then compare our attitude or action to God's character and commands, it changes everything. Let's say, for example, you've been paid a sum of cash on a business deal with a friend. By not reporting the payment on your income tax return you'll save $1000. You know that some might call that cheating, but you wonder if under the circumstances it would be justified.

For one thing, you think the government gets more than its fair share from you. Besides, those spendthrifts in Washington spend money in all kinds of ways that you consider wasteful and immoral. And their irresponsible spending causes costs to rise, forcing you into debt in order to keep up. In a sense they owe you that $1000 for all they are doing to you. It's not like you're cheating your friend. He's getting his share of the money. Anyway, you know that a lot of other Christians don't report all their income either. So it's really not that big of a deal.

When we justify our actions or attitudes based on what *we* think is right, we are, as we say, rationalizing. To rationalize is to convince ourselves with "rational lies" that an action is right when it's actually in opposition to God's character. We are actually usurping God's role as the sovereign arbiter, based on his character and nature, of what is right or wrong. God's Word says:

> Do not steal.
>
> Do not lie.
>
> Do not deceive one another…
>
> Do not defraud your neighbor or rob him (Leviticus 19:11-13 NIV).

God's commands to be honest come out of his nature, and his nature is absolute truth. His actions do not deviate from his character of integrity. God always fulfills his promises and does what he says he will do. When we compare ourselves to him we are admitting that he is sovereign; he is the one who defines what is right and what is wrong regarding honesty and every other moral action. When we make our moral decision in light of the character of God, our choice becomes crystal clear—we are to, in this example, commit to being honest with the U.S. government.

3. Commit to God's Way

Committing to God's way is easier said than done. It means we have to admit we are not the ruler over our lives—God is. The present-day concept of deciding what is "right for you" appeals to so many people because it puts us in charge. It permits us to justify our attitudes and actions regardless of how they compare to God's nature and character. Giving ourselves the capacity to decide our own morality feels independent and empowering. And it has the added advantage of making us feel we're being moral because we're not being judgmental. We allow everyone to make his or her own moral decisions without judging their choices. What could be fairer than that?

To think this way is simply to fool ourselves with more "rational lies." But even when we see through our rationalizations and recognize that what we want to do may be self-serving, we still find it hard to commit to God's way. What we want to do fights with what we ought to do because we are plagued with a sin nature that wants what it wants when it wants it. That is why Paul said to "put to death the sinful, earthly things lurking within you" (Colossians 3:5). We must turn our backs on the appetites and desires that don't measure up to our holy God. Those attitudes and actions are not pleasing to him. When we deny our self-serving ways and commit to following him, we are loving him. And in response he gives us the power to walk in his ways. And then finally we can…

4. Count on God's Protection and Provision

When we humbly admit God's sovereignty and lovingly seek to please him, not only can we begin to see clearly the distinctions between right and wrong; we can also begin to count on God's protection and provision.

This doesn't mean that everything will be rosy; in fact, God says bluntly that we may sometimes suffer for righteousness' sake. But even such suffering has rewards. Living according to God's way brings many spiritual blessings, like freedom from guilt, a clear conscience, and the joy of God's smile upon our lives.

We can also enjoy many physical, emotional, psychological, and relational benefits when we commit to God's ways. Of course, God's protection and provision should not be the primary motivation for obeying God; we should obey him simply because we love him, trust him, and want to be like him. But the practical and spiritual benefits of obeying certainly provide powerful encouragement for choosing right and rejecting wrong.

Adam and Eve failed to go through the 4-Cs process. They didn't consider the choice, compare it to God, commit to his way, and count on his protection and provision. Today we all suffer the consequences of their poor choice.

God has made a way to redeem us from eternal consequences, which we will cover in the next section. But as followers of Christ we still need to learn how to resist our natural tendency to decide for ourselves what is right or wrong and choose God's way (*consider, compare, commit,* and *count*). And when we do we can experience the joy that results with being in a loving relationship with God and following his ways.

CHAPTER FIFTEEN

PRACTICAL EXAMPLES OF HOW TO MAKE RIGHT CHOICES

Trusting in Christ to redeem us does protect us from the permanent consequences of sin (eternal death and separation from God) and provides us with eternal life with Christ and all our loved ones who have equally trusted in Christ. But that eternal salvation will not protect us from the negative consequences of making wrong choices here on earth. As Christians there are guidelines to follow and a process of making godly choices that we have called the "4-Cs." To help understand this process better we have created two "case studies" that give practical examples of the 4-Cs process. Discuss these with your family and friends and make the 4-Cs process a pattern of life.

Case Study #1: Honesty
"Your Loss Is My Gain"

Terry had bought a fan at the local hardware store. The first time he plugged the device in and tried to turn it on, it would not work. He took the screw out of the casing, took the casing off, and looked inside to see if he could spot any problem in the wiring. He was not a mechanic and knew nothing about electricity, so without touching any of the mechanisms or wiring he simply replaced the casing. He took the fan back to the store and asked for a replacement or a refund.

"I'm sorry, sir," the supervisor said. "We just can't replace a fan that has been damaged this way. It is clear that this screw has been tampered with. That indicates internal tampering, which no doubt caused the electrical short."

"I'm telling you," Terry persisted, "I didn't tamper with anything! It wouldn't work the first time I tried it."

"There is nothing more I can do," the supervisor responded. "We can repair the fan, but there will be a service charge."

"Forget it," Terry angrily retorted and stormed out of the hardware store.

A few weeks later, Terry was checking out at the same hardware store after purchasing $50 or so worth of various items. As he walked to his car he looked at his receipt and recounted the change the clerk gave him. The clerk had undercharged him by $10. What should Terry do? What would you do?

Consider the choice. It would be easy for Terry simply to disregard the clerical error and go on his way without another thought. Especially since the clerk's error would seem to balance the cheating he had suffered earlier from the same store. But there is a choice to be made here, and it is important for Terry to pause and consider the choice. Either he can a) go back inside and return the $10 he received in error, or b) keep them as partial repayment for the money he lost when the store cheated him.

Compare it to God. Terry's natural impulse is to keep the money. But he needs to stop and think how that choice compares with God's character. He could ask himself, *If this store had cheated Jesus and then later had accidentally given him too much change, what would he have done?* Terry must remember that God's very nature is true. Regardless of the circumstance, God does not deviate from his character, which is the standard of all rightness. Out of God's character of absolute truth comes the principle of honesty, which includes not cheating someone out of something that belongs to him. Comparing his options to God means Terry must return the $10 to the hardware store.

Commit to God's ways. Now Terry must make a decision, but he has a problem. Under ordinary circumstances he would return the money, but he figures his present situation is a special case. The hardware store has cheated him out of the cost of a fan repair. So really, keeping the $10 mistake helps to settle the score. So Terry convinces himself that he is justified in keeping the extra money. He pockets it and goes on his way.

Is Terry right? Or is he rationalizing? He wants to be honest, but in this situation does the store's apparent greed outweigh the need to return the undercharge? Let's look at Scripture to see what Terry gained or lost by the choice he made.

Count on God's protection and provision. What does Terry gain in justifying his action? Well, it seems that he has gained two things: He is $10 richer, and he has the satisfaction of knowing a greedy hardware store didn't get away with cheating him.

What did Terry lose by his action?

Scripture says, "Don't repay evil for evil…Instead, pay them back with a blessing. That is what God wants you to do, and he will bless you for it…Remember, it is better to suffer for doing good, if that is what God wants, than to suffer for doing wrong" (1 Peter 3:9,17).

- According to Peter's principle, paying the money back would have brought a blessing to Terry. It would also have provided him a clear conscience and protection from guilt. Terry lost out on those blessings. "Choose a good reputation over great riches, for being held in high esteem is better than having silver or gold" (Proverbs 22:1).

- Paying the money back provides a reputation of integrity and protects from shame. Terry lost out on that.

King David said that the righteous "keep their promises even when it hurts" (Psalm 15:4). Paul says it's better to be cheated than to cheat. He told the Corinthians, "Why not just accept the injustice and leave it at that? Why not let yourselves be cheated?" (1 Corinthians 6:7). Even though Terry believed the hardware store had done him wrong, and the $10 error could have helped pay for their misdeed, in the long term, God's way of integrity brings honor to him and blessing to us.

Case Study #2: Mercy
"What Goes Around Comes Around"

Geena, a bank loan officer, was grocery shopping on her day off. As she was loading her trunk with groceries in the parking lot, a woman put a bad scrape in Geena's car with a cart.

"Excuse me, ma'am," Geena said, "you just put a big scratch in my car with that cart."

"You shouldn't have parked so close to the cart return," the woman replied. "It's your problem, not mine."

"Now wait a minute," Geena responded. "I want this taken care of. Please give me your insurance information."

"I'm out of here," came the reply. "My insurance won't cover that." And she walked quickly to her car and drove off. In her frustration, Geena failed to write down the woman's license plate number.

A week later Geena was on the job at her bank processing a car loan application that was on the borderline of being approved. The bank manager told Geena it was her call. The applicant came in to determine whether she was approved for the car loan. When she sat down in front of Geena's desk, Geena was surprised to see it was the same woman who had put the scratch in her car. The woman, however, didn't recognize Geena.

Consider the choice. It would be very tempting to deny the "car scratcher" the loan. The woman had been discourteous and irresponsible in not repairing the damage she had caused to Geena's car. Geena had a choice to consider—show mercy, forgive the woman, and approve the loan or give her a taste of her own medicine. What should Geena do? What would you do?

Compare it to God. "This is what the LORD Almighty says: Judge fairly and honestly, and show mercy and kindness to one another" (Zechariah 7:9). Mercy is right and a virtue because it comes from the very nature of God. As Micah declared, he is one who "delight[s] to show mercy" (Micah 7:18 NIV). King David said that God's "mercy endures forever" (Psalm 107:1 NKJV). Paul noted that "God is so rich in mercy" (Ephesians 2:4).

If Geena is to reflect God's nature of mercy, she must show mercy.

Commit to God's ways. Geena has a problem. Showing mercy to this woman would, in effect, be rewarding an irresponsible person who showed no mercy on her. The interesting thing is that the car scratcher doesn't even recognize Geena and doesn't know she offended her. So Geena could deny the loan and no one would be the wiser.

Geena chose to approve the loan. What did she gain by showing mercy?

Count on God's protection and provision. Jesus promised, "If you give, you will receive...Whatever measure you use in giving—large or small—it will be used to measure what is given back to you" (Luke 6:38).

- By showing mercy Geena can count on God to protect her from want. "If you forgive those who sin against you, your heavenly Father will forgive you" (Matthew 6:14).

- Showing mercy protects us from God's judgment and provides for forgiveness. It's relatively easy to show mercy on the merciful. But it requires a commitment to God's ways to show mercy on the undeserving. But Jesus said, "Blessed are the merciful, for they will be shown mercy" (Matthew 5:7 NIV).

We are born in sin, and even though God forgives us of our wrongdoing we are still faced with the desires of the sin nature. The 4-Cs process is a means of training ourselves to resist the natural impulse to follow our nature and commit instead to God's ways. Paul said, "I discipline my body like an athlete, training it to do what it should" (1 Corinthians 9:27). And as we do we can count on God's protection and provision.

SUMMARY OF PART II

God's Truth Declaration:
I am the God of Creation—The God of Relationships

- *We believe the truth* that an infinite, personal God exists, and that there is sufficient evidence to allow us to believe that truth with confidence.

  God's existence is relevant to us specifically because we were created in his likeness. That likeness gives us the capacity for loving relationships.

  When we explore our relational capacity to know and be known, we discover our true identity as a child of a real and relational God. This discovery allows us to know who we are.

- *We believe the truth* that the Bible is God's revelation of himself to us, which in turn discloses his character to us. From his character emanate his ways, which, the Bible declares, are the pattern for us to follow in all our actions.

  Because the Bible has been reliably passed down from one generation to another we can believe with confidence that it reflects an accurate revelation of God and his truth.

  When we follow God's ways and live out the truths of Scripture we can experience God's protection and provision and live the life of joy that he meant for us to live.

- *We believe the truth* that God created humans to relate to him lovingly, but that relationship was destroyed because of original sin.

  Sin was passed to the entire human race, and consequently all are born spiritually dead and utterly helpless to gain favor with God. We can believe this truth with confidence because historically we see the devastating consequences of sin.

  Our sin nature prods us to follow our own ways. When we resist our sin nature, compare our attitudes and actions to God, and commit to his ways, he empowers us to make godly choices. Right choices will enable us to enjoy God's provision and protection in life.

The Christian faith puts forth the truth that a relational Creator God exists, that he reveals himself through his reliable Word, and that sin has destroyed the God/human relationship. If that were where the human story ended, it would be tragic beyond words. But the story doesn't end there. In part III we lay out what we believe about the solution to the great human dilemma of sin and death: *the truth of the incarnation.*

PART III

THE UNSHAKABLE TRUTH OF GOD'S INCARNATION

God came to earth in human form.

■

Jesus' death atones for our sin.

■

Justification before God is by grace through faith in Jesus Christ.

■

Our joy is made complete as we are conformed to the image of Christ.

God Became Human

CHAPTER SIXTEEN

WE REJECTED GOD—
GOD ACCEPTED US

N ow you build a house out of these blocks, Joslin," the second-grade teacher demanded, tapping her foot ominously and holding a ruler threateningly in her right hand. Mrs. Lenard had me (Josh) sit down at the small table of blocks to teach me a lesson—to use my right hand.

I was born left-handed, but my teacher was trying with all her might to make me switch to being a right-hander. When I reached out with my left hand, she smacked it with the ruler and said, "Stop—think it through. Do it with your right hand." I was terrified and confused. I was only doing what came naturally, but I was severely punished for it. This experience significantly affected how I saw myself. I began to think I was defective, a factory reject.

The trauma of this experience also caused me to develop a speech impediment. Whenever I became frightened, anxious, or tired—usually at school—I stuttered. My stuttering was a great embarrassment to me. In the fifth grade I was told to memorize and recite the Gettysburg Address. I was so nervous when I stood up that I began to stutter. In front of the entire class, my teacher demanded, "Say it! Say it! Stop stuttering, and say it!" Mortified in front of my friends, I ran out of the classroom crying.

Because my parents' education had stopped at the second grade, they had never learned good grammar. As a result, I usually mangled the language. If my English teachers emphasized correct grammar, it never got through to me. Somehow I got by. But when I entered college, my down-home grammar caught up with me, and I again became the object of ridicule. I was embarrassed to speak up in class. One day in freshman English, the professor asked me, "Where's Bob?" I said, "He doesn't feel good." In front of everyone, the professor corrected me: "Mr. McDowell, you mean 'Bob doesn't feel *well*.'" I looked at her perplexed, wondering what the big deal was. To me it seemed just as well to say "good"! Experiences like these further solidified my perception that I was an inferior human being and a totally unacceptable person.

Accepting the Unacceptable

Adam and Eve must have felt that way as well after they sinned. At first they had experienced a wonderful love relationship with God in the perfect Garden of Eden. There was no hunger, greed, fear, or pain because God's holy presence produced nothing but goodness. But after they sinned, they were banished from the garden.

We rejected God yet he still accepted us.

They were no longer innocent—instead they were guilty. They no longer delighted in God—instead they felt fear and shame. Rather than basking in God's favor and enjoying his provisions, they worked the cursed ground and sweated to make ends meet. Their sin had left them feeling alone and unacceptable.

But how did God feel? Was he angry and vindictive? Did he never again want anything to do with the human creation that had rebelled against him?

Instead of anger, God felt grief and sadness. From one generation after another his cherished humans lived a life of sin and rebellion and "it broke his heart" (Genesis 6:6).

Imagine God as he watches in grief and sadness while your own generation sins and suffers the consequences of those sins. He was there when you were born into the very world where he and the first human couple once walked in perfect relationship. And instead of rejecting you, he accepts you in spite of your sin. He longs to relate to you and me and those around us as intimately as he once did to them. He wants to take pleasure in us. He wants to see in our eyes the delight that only his life and love can bring. But that's not possible, because our sin has separated us from the life that is found in him, from the moment we were conceived. While his heart accepts us without condition, his holiness cannot embrace our life of selfishness. For each of us have followed in Adam and Eve's footsteps, becoming his *enemy* by repeatedly and selfishly choosing our own sinful ways instead of his holy ways.

So what did God do? He took the initiative. We are the ones who desperately need him, but we didn't seek him out. We are the ones who should have been crying out for help. Yet the all-sufficient Lord, who "has no needs...[but] gives life and breath to everything, and...satisfies every need there is" *wants you and wants me* (Acts 17:25). We rejected him yet he still accepted us. He wants to relate to us—to enjoy and delight and take pleasure in a personal relationship with us. He wants to complete our joy.

So God entered our world to cancel the curse of sin and death that has power over us. He "became human and lived here on earth among us" (John 1:14). "Because God's children are human beings—made of flesh and blood—Jesus also became flesh and blood by being born in human form. For only as a human being could he die, and only by dying could he break the power of the Devil, who had the power of death" (Hebrews 2:14). "God's secret plan has now been revealed to us; it is a plan centered on Christ" (Ephesians 1:9). Only the Son of the living God could wrench the power of death out of the hand of our archenemy, Satan, so God could be reconnected to his children in a personal, one-on-one relationship.

The incarnation is the miracle of God's Son taking on human form.

> We believe the truth of the incarnation (God becoming human), in which God accepted us without condition and sent Jesus Christ, born of the Virgin Mary, to redeem us and restore us to a relationship with him.

The incarnation says, "You may have turned away from me, but I'm not turning away from you. You are so important to me that I will go to extraordinary lengths to have a personal relationship with you. I'll enter your world and become human like you to save you from death and eternal aloneness without me." Faced with the issue of restoring a relationship with humans, God did not merely send a prophet or even an angel to declare his truth of his unconditional acceptance of us; he sent the ultimate gift—himself!

CHAPTER SEVENTEEN

EVIDENCE THAT GOD BECAME HUMAN TO REDEEM US

December 25 is a date celebrated by billions of people all over the world each year. It commemorates a birthday that people have been recognizing for centuries. Thousands of songs are sung annually in festive celebration. Re-enactments of a lowly birth in a manger are performed. And millions hear the reading "she brought forth her firstborn son, and wrapped him in swaddling clothes, and laid him in a manger; because there was no room for them in the inn" (Luke 2:7 KJV).

We celebrate the birth of Jesus Christ year after year. We proclaim the miraculous incarnation of God taking on human form. We preach about a God full of love and acceptance, who entered our world to save us from eternal death. And though the Scripture says God "became human and lived here on earth among us" (John 1:14), how can we really know if God actually showed up to demonstrate his acceptance and love for us?

God has given us a way to identify this person of history as truly being the Son of God.

That question may sound cynical, but the reality is, God himself wants to assure us that he actually came to earth to redeem us. That is why he had an angel declare to shepherds, "I bring you good news of great joy for everyone! The Savior—yes, the Messiah, the Lord—has been born tonight in Bethlehem, the city of David!" (Luke 2:10-11). God wanted to assure those living at the time that Mary's baby was actually the Son of God—the Supreme Being that came to redeem them. God wants us to believe with confidence that his Son born 2000 years ago is our redeemer as well.

God gave Mary a sign she would give birth to the God-man. God gave the shepherds a sign that the Savior had been born in a manger. He gave the "wise men" a sign that the son of Mary was in fact the King of kings. And he has given us a sign. He has given us a way to identify this person of history as truly being the Son of God "who takes away the sin of the world!" (John 1:29).

Jesus of Nazareth, born in Bethlehem of Judea some 2000 years ago, is the person of history who claimed to be God's Son. His claim was exclusive. No other but the Incarnate One could redeem the human race. In fact, he made that truth central to all he said and did. It was crucial that this claim be true, because only the Son of God could solve the problem of sin and death. He made believing in him as the Incarnate One the pivotal point. Jesus told his skeptics, "You are of this world; I am not. That is why I said that you will die in your sins; for unless you believe that I am who I say I am, you will die in your sins" (John 8:23-24). "I am the way, the truth, and the life," Jesus said. "No one can come to the Father except through me" (John 14:6). But if Jesus wasn't the true Son of God, then his offer of salvation was a sham and a lie. It is absolutely vital that his claim to deity be valid if we are to trust him to be our salvation.

Lord, Liar, or Lunatic?

Some say Jesus Christ's claim to deity is not really the important thing here. They suggest it is the *teachings* of Jesus that are really important—love your neighbor, feed the hungry, make this planet a better place, and so on. So they point to Jesus as a great moral teacher and discount his claim to deity. But anyone who said the things that Jesus said about himself could not be a great moral teacher. C.S. Lewis, professor at Cambridge University and once an agnostic, understood this issue clearly. He writes:

> I am trying here to prevent anyone saying the really foolish thing that people often say about Him: "I'm ready to accept Jesus as a great moral teacher, but I don't accept His claim to be God." That is the one thing we must not say. A man who was merely a man and said the sort of things Jesus said would not be a great moral teacher. He would either be a lunatic—on a level with the man who says he is a poached egg—or else he would be the Devil of Hell. You must make your choice. Either this man was, and is, the Son of God: or else a madman or something worse.

Then Lewis adds:

> You can shut Him up for a fool, you can spit at Him and kill Him as a demon, or you can fall at His feet and call Him Lord and God. But let us not come up with any patronizing nonsense about his being a great human teacher. He has not left that open to us. He did not intend to.[1]

Jesus' claim to be God (Deity) leaves us with two alternatives: either his claim is true or it is false. And if his claim is false we are left with two added options (see diagram).

Jesus' Claims to Be God[2]

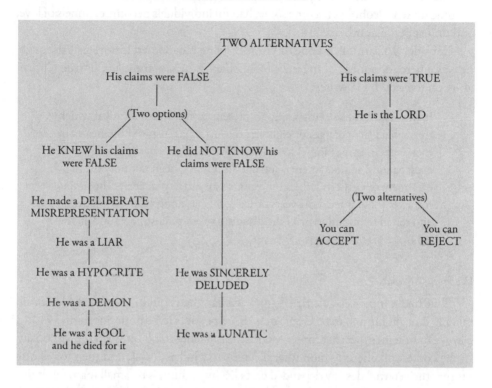

First, let's consider the alternative that Jesus' claim to be God *was* false. This would give us two options, he either knew it was false, or he didn't know it was false.

Was Jesus a Liar?

If, when Jesus made his claims, he knew that he was not God, then he was lying and deliberately deceiving his followers. But if he was a liar, then he was also a hypocrite because he taught others to be honest whatever the cost. Worse than that, if he was lying, he was a demon because he told others to trust him for their eternal destiny. If he couldn't back up his claims and knew it, then he was unspeakably evil for deceiving his followers with such a false hope. Last, he would also be a fool because his claims to being God led to his crucifixion—claims he could have backed away from to save himself even at the last minute.

How could Jesus ever be considered a great moral teacher if he really wasn't Deity?

This means he would be knowingly misleading people about the most important issue of his teachings—believing in him as the Son of God.

To conclude that Jesus was a deliberate liar doesn't coincide with what we know either of him or of the results of his life and teachings. Wherever Jesus has been proclaimed, we see lives change for the good, nations change for the better, thieves become honest, alcoholics become sober, hateful individuals become channels of love, and unjust persons embrace justice.

Consider William Lecky, one of Great Britain's most noted historians. Although he was a fierce opponent of organized Christianity, he saw the effect of true Christianity on the world. He writes:

> It was reserved for Christianity to present to the world an ideal which through all the changes of eighteen centuries has inspired the hearts of men with an impassioned love; has shown itself capable of acting on all ages, nations, temperaments, and conditions; has been not only the highest pattern of virtue, but the strongest incentive to its practice...The simple record of these three short years of active life has done more to regenerate and soften mankind than all the disquisitions of philosophers and all the exhortations of moralists.[3]

Was Jesus a Lunatic?

If we find it inconceivable that Jesus was a liar, then couldn't he actually have mistakenly thought himself to be God? After all, it's possible to be both sincere and wrong. But we must remember that for someone to mistakenly think himself God, especially in the context of a fiercely monotheistic culture as Judaism was, and then to tell others that their eternal destiny depended on believing in him, is no small matter. It is the delusional ravings of an outright lunatic. Is it possible that Jesus Christ was deranged?

Today we would treat someone who believes himself to be God the same way we would treat someone who believes he is Napoleon. We would see him as deluded and self-deceived. We would lock him up so he wouldn't hurt himself or anyone else. Yet in Jesus we don't observe the abnormalities and imbalance that go along with such derangement. If he was insane, his poise and composure were nothing short of amazing.

Eminent psychiatric pioneers Arthur Noyes and Lawrence Kolb, in their *Modern Clinical Psychiatry* text, describe the schizophrenic as a person who is more autistic than realistic. The schizophrenic desires to escape from the world of reality. Let's face it— for a mere man to claim to be God would certainly be a retreat from reality.

In light of other things we know about Jesus, it's hard to imagine he was mentally disturbed. Here is a man who spoke the most profound words ever recorded. His instructions have liberated many people from mental bondage. Clark Pinnock, professor emeritus of systematic theology at McMaster Divinity College, asks, "Was he deluded about his greatness, a paranoid, an unintentional deceiver, a schizophrenic? Again, the skill and depth of his teaching support the case only for his total mental soundness. If only we were as sane as he!"[4]

Psychologist Gary R. Collins explains that Jesus

> was loving but didn't let his compassion immobilize him; he didn't have a bloated ego, even though he was often surrounded by adoring crowds; he maintained balance despite an often demanding lifestyle; he always knew what he was doing and where he was going; he cared deeply about people, including women and children, who weren't seen as important back then; he was able to accept people while not merely winking at their sin; he responded to individuals based on where they were at and what they uniquely needed. All in all, I just don't see signs that Jesus was suffering from any known mental illness…He was much healthier than anyone else I know—including me![5]

Was Jesus Lord?

As we can see, it would be very difficult for anyone to conclude that Jesus was a liar or a lunatic. The only remaining alternative is that he was—and is— the Christ, the Son of God, as he claimed. Yet in spite of the logic and evidence, many people cannot seem to bring themselves to accept this conclusion.

In his book *The Da Vinci Code,* Dan Brown claims, "By officially endorsing Jesus as the Son of God, Constantine turned Jesus into a deity who existed beyond the scope of the human world, an entity whose power was unchallengeable."[6] The novel propagates the idea that Christ's deity was invented at the Council of Nicaea. This simply was not the case.

The New Testament itself provides the earliest evidence for the belief that Jesus is divine. Since these documents were composed in the first century, just decades after the events surrounding Jesus, they predate the Council of Nicaea by more than two centuries. While they were written by different people for a variety of purposes, one unmistakable theme they share is that Christ is God.

The ante-Nicene fathers were early Christian writers who lived after the close of the New Testament period (c. 100), yet before the Council of Nicaea (325). They provide additional support that Jesus was considered divine long before the Council of Nicaea. They include men such as Justin Martyr, Ignatius, and Irenaeus. There is no doubt that they understood Jesus to be divine. Consider some quotes from their ancient works:

Ignatius of Antioch (AD 110): "God incarnate…God Himself appearing in the form of man."[7]

Justin Martyr (AD 100–165): "Being the First-begotten Word of God, is even God."[8]

Irenaeus (AD 177): "The Father is God and the Son is God; for He who is born of God is God."[9]

Probably the most convincing evidence that Jesus was considered divine before Nicaea comes from non-Christian writers. The Greek satirist Lucian of Samosata (c. AD 170), the Roman philosopher Celsus (c. 177), and the Roman governor Pliny the Younger (c. 112) make it clear that early Christians understood Jesus as divine. Pliny persecuted Christians because of their belief that Jesus was divine. Pliny acknowledged, "They had met regularly before dawn on a fixed day to chant verses alternately among themselves in honour of Christ as if to a god."[10]

Given these facts, in addition to many more, the authors of *Reinventing Jesus* conclude: "To suggest that Constantine had the ability—or even the inclination—to manipulate the council into believing what it did not already embrace is, at best, a silly notion."[11] The evidence is clear: Jesus was believed to be divine long before the Council of Nicaea.

The issue with these three alternatives concerning Jesus is not which is possible. Obviously all three are possible. Rather, the question is, "Which is most probable?" We cannot, as so many people want to do, put Jesus on the shelf merely as a great moral teacher or a prophet. That is not a valid option. He is a liar, a lunatic, or Lord and God. We must make a choice. Our decision about Jesus must be more than an idle intellectual exercise. As the apostle John wrote, "These are written so that you may believe that Jesus is the Messiah, the Son of God, and"—more important—"that by believing in him you will have life" (John 20:31).[12]

Jesus *Did* Claim to Be God

There are some today who would even say Jesus never really claimed to be the Son of God—he only said he was the Son of man, implying he wasn't making a claim to deity. But these people are simply wrong. Jesus *did* claim to be the Son of God. He made his identity central to his message.

According to the New Testament record, Jesus repeatedly made it clear that he was the unique Son of God, an assertion that did not go unnoticed by the religious leaders of his day. In fact, that claim was the very reason they tried to discredit him and, eventually, the reason they put him to death: "The Jewish leaders tried all the more to kill him. In addition to disobeying the Sabbath rules, he had spoken of God as his Father, thereby making himself equal with God" (John 5:18).

On more than one occasion, Jesus' clear assertion of his own deity caused his fellow Jews to want to stone him. Once, when he told the Jewish leaders, "Your father Abraham rejoiced at the thought of seeing my day; he saw it and was glad," his listeners became indignant: "'You are not yet fifty years old,' the Jews said to him, 'and you have seen Abraham!'

"'I tell you the truth,' Jesus answered, 'before Abraham was born, I am!' At this, they picked up stones to stone him, but Jesus hid himself, slipping away from the temple grounds" (John 8:56-59 NIV). On another occasion, when Jesus said that he was one with the Father, the Jewish leaders again picked up stones to kill him (see John 10:30-31).

When Jesus asked why they wanted to kill him, they retorted, "for blasphemy, because you, a mere man, *have made yourself God*" (John 10:33).

Yet another time, Jesus told a paralyzed man, "My son, your sins are forgiven" and again the religious leaders reacted with outrage. "What?" they said. "This is blasphemy! *Who but God* can forgive sins!" (Mark 2:5-7).

In the final days prior to Jesus death, he made it clear—even to the Sanhedrin (the Jewish high council)—just who he was: "The high priest asked him, 'Are you the Messiah, the Son of the blessed God?' Jesus said, 'I am...'" In response to the proclamation, they "condemned him to death" (Mark 14:61-64).

All that Jesus said and did pointed to his identity as the Deity and the Messiah, and all of it pointed to the purpose for which he came to earth. If he is not who he claimed to be, then his teachings are either the rantings of a lunatic who sincerely *thought* he was God (but wasn't) or the words of a liar who *knew* he wasn't God (but said he was).

But we can be confident in the truth—that he is Lord! He is the incarnate Son of the one and only God of the universe, the one who said, "I am the LORD, and there is no other" and "Do not worship any other gods besides me" (Isaiah 45:6; Exodus 20:3).

Given the three options considered above, it is fully reasonable to conclude that Jesus is Lord. But we have much more evidence of his deity than this. We will provide some of that evidence here and the rest of it in chapters 21 and 25.

Jesus Was Born of a Virgin

Long before there was even the written Word, before anyone had heard of the Messiah, God erected in the Garden of Eden a signpost that pointed directly to the means by which his Son would be born. When God cursed the serpent who tempted Eve, he said to it, "I will put enmity between you and the woman, and between your seed and her seed; he shall bruise you on the head, and you shall bruise him on the heel" (Genesis 3:15 NASB). This verse is prophetic, for the offspring of the woman is, of course, Christ. The words "you and the *woman*" stand out as both unique and prophetic, for a critical reason we will now explore.

It is highly significant that Genesis 3:15 refers specifically to the offspring of the woman and not of the man. The natural process of conceiving and giving birth involves the ovum of a woman and the sperm of a man. The ovum and the sperm are the "seeds" from the two sexes that are necessary for human birth. When God promised the serpent that he would be crushed by the seed of the woman, he referred to a *supernatural* process: Satan would be defeated by a person conceived from the seed of a woman only, without the usual requirement of the seed of a man.

Scripture foretold that same supernatural process again, 700 years before God was born as a child, when the prophet Isaiah said, "The LORD himself will choose the sign. Look! The virgin will conceive a child! She will give birth to a son and will call him Immanuel— 'God is with us'" (Isaiah 7:14).

What striking words: "The *virgin* will *conceive.*" In the course of nature, virgins don't conceive. Conception requires fertilization of the female's ovum (egg) by the male's gamete (sperm) to form a new cell, called a zygote. The zygote must then implant itself in the lining of the uterus. That single cell possesses a complete set of chromosomes containing genetic information, half of which comes from the father and half from the mother.

But God, speaking to the serpent, and again through the prophet Isaiah, promised something that human history had never seen before (nor has it since): A child would be born outside the natural process of conception. Instead, the Holy Spirit of God himself would form, in the dark ocean of a virgin's womb, a child of divine origin. This person would bear a unique identity because the infinite God would be his father and a finite human virgin would be his mother—thus the God-man would be born. From that miraculous moment of conception, that God-human fetus would develop from a single cell into sixty trillion cells and would be brought into the world as Immanuel, "God is with us"! (See Isaiah 7:14; Matthew 1:23.)

If that really happened—if the historical Jesus truly was born to a virgin—it would provide compelling evidence for his deity. If Jesus was conceived apart from the natural process of conception, then we have powerful corroborating evidence to support his claims to deity. We can see that the Genesis record and Isaiah's prophecy point to a virgin birth for the Messiah, but is there evidence that what had been promised in these passages actually came to pass? Is there any reliable way to investigate the circumstances of Jesus' birth?

The Accounts of the Event

Let's begin with the historical record. Seven centuries after Isaiah's prophecy, Matthew reported the extraordinary circumstances of the birth of a child called Jesus of Nazareth. He wrote,

> This is how Jesus the Messiah was born. His mother, Mary, was engaged to be married to Joseph. But while she was still a virgin, she became pregnant by the Holy Spirit...All of this happened to fulfill the Lord's message through his prophet. "Look! The virgin will conceive a child! She will give birth to a son, and he will be called Immanuel (meaning, God is with us)" (Matthew 1:18, 22-23).

The Gospel of Luke, the careful historian whose writings have been repeatedly supported by archaeology, records the appearance of the angel Gabriel to Mary and his announcement that she would give birth to the Messiah. Mary answered with a question: "But how can I have a baby? I am a virgin." Gabriel replied, "The Holy Spirit will come upon you, and the power of the Most High will overshadow you. So the baby born to you will be holy, and he will be called the Son of God" (Luke 1:34-35).

These two historical accounts give us a record of the event of the virgin birth, but they give us no evidence to assure us the event actually occurred. As we continue to look at the record, however, evidences begin to appear, and these evidences give us confidence that the overall account is true.

Reactions of Jesus' Contemporaries

Among the most significant of these evidences are those contained in the accounts of how the people of Jesus' hometown, Nazareth, reacted to him after he began his public ministry.

On one occasion, after he had taught in the synagogue, the people he had grown up with said, "'He's just the carpenter, the son of Mary'...They were deeply offended and refused to believe in him" (Mark 6:3). The label "son of Mary" was an unambiguous insult in a society that called children by the name of their fathers—except, of course, in the case of children whose paternity was doubted.

At another time, Jesus' opponents threw a sharply pointed barb at him when they said, "*We* were not born out of wedlock!" (John 8:41).

The insult and the reference to Jesus as the "son of Mary" imply that it was common knowledge in Jesus' hometown that he had been conceived before Mary's wedding to—and without the help of—Joseph.

In other words, it seems very likely that the circumstances of Jesus' miraculous birth—to a virgin—caused him to be labeled as an illegitimate child in the society of his day. Thus, as a direct result of the unusual circumstances of his birth, he not only accepted the robe of humanity but undoubtedly endured cruel taunts on the playground of his childhood and coarse comments from critics as an adult. When Jesus made claim of deity, the people ridiculed him and scoffed, "We were not born out of wedlock! Our true Father is God himself" (John 8:41).

In an irony of unbelief, the evidence of his divine *glory* became a smear on his human reputation. This irony persisted in some of the vehemently anti-Christian writings of Jewish rabbis in the years following his death. The rabbis invented a story that cast Jesus as the illegitimate son of a Roman soldier named Panthera, "unintentionally admitting that Jesus was not born of an ordinary marriage," as the third-century theologian and biblical scholar Origen put it.[13]

These insults hurled at Jesus give us evidence that his hometown people knew he was not Joseph's son. This gives us a leg up in believing in the virgin birth, but it is not a clincher. How do we know these insulters were not right? How do we judge whether the birth was indeed miraculous or whether Mary was lying and Joseph was deceived? For answers let's look first at Mary's story and then at Matthew's account of Jesus' birth.

The Responses of Mary and Joseph

When Mary turned up pregnant, why would she have insisted that she was a virgin? She knew that such a story would certainly be too wild to believe; why didn't she come up with a story more believable? She could have concocted an excuse to make herself look innocent of any wrongdoing, or at least to put all or part of the blame on someone else. She could have claimed she was raped, or she could have claimed Joseph pressured her into yielding to his desire. Joseph would have known better, but no one else would have. But instead of a rational explanation that would fit the known laws of nature, she tells people that she is pregnant by God's Holy Spirit. Why would she say such a thing when it is so certain to be the least believable of explanations? Only one reason makes sense. It was true.

Now let's look at her pregnancy from her fiancé Joseph's point of view. Here is what Matthew tells us about Joseph's reaction:

> This is how Jesus the Messiah was born. His mother, Mary, was engaged to be married to Joseph. But before the marriage took place, while she was still a virgin, she became pregnant through the power of the Holy Spirit. Joseph, her fiancé, was a good man and did not want to disgrace her publicly, so he decided to break the engagement quietly.
>
> As he considered this, an angel of the Lord appeared to him in a dream. "Joseph, son of David," the angel said, "do not be afraid to take Mary as

your wife. For the child within her was conceived by the Holy Spirit"…
When Joseph woke up, he did as the angel of the Lord commanded and
took Mary as his wife (Matthew 1:18-20,24 NLT).

As you can see, Joseph knew all about the birds and the bees. He knew how babies
were made, and he had not had sex with his fiancée. So when Mary turned up pregnant, he was naturally convinced that she had committed fornication. So he resolved
to do what any man would—call off the engagement. Matthew's account, however,
tells us that an angel told Joseph the truth about Mary's pregnancy. And based on that
communication he believed and went on with the wedding.

Think about what this tells us. Joseph would have been the hardest man on the
planet to convince of Mary's story that she was a virgin. He was the man most closely
affected. He was the man who would, for the rest of his life, be ridiculed for marrying
an unfaithful, pregnant woman who was bearing another man's child. He would have
to endure the contempt of the men in the town, who would forever look on him as a
cuckold, too stupid not to believe Mary's wild story about God making her pregnant.
He would have to endure the humiliation of being married to a shamed woman and
raising the child of her adultery.

Yet it's clear that Joseph was not stupid and made his decision fully aware of its implications. The fact that he first did not believe Mary and resolved to break the engagement, just as any man would, shows us he was not stupid. It shows us he knew full well
the implications of violating social expectations about purity and the sanctity of marriage. A good and prudent man, as Matthew calls him, would be well aware of how
marrying Mary would mar his reputation for the rest of his life. So why would he go
on and marry the girl? Only one reason makes any sense at all. He knew the truth. He
actually received a message from an angel, and that message delivered to him was the
absolute truth. Mary was a virgin who was bearing in her womb the Son of God.

The fact that Joseph believed this truth, knew the lifelong consequences, and yet
did the right thing and took under his protective wing the Son of God and his earthly
mother is what makes this man one of the great heroes of the Bible.

The evidence for the virgin birth not only points to the conclusion that Jesus
of Nazareth is who he claimed to be; it also shows how much he identified with us.
Though he was God, he humbled himself and willingly endured the sneers and scorn
of those who didn't believe in him. The evidence of Christ's deity through the miracle of the virgin birth is just one of the truths God has given us to reinforce that he
accepted us in spite of our sin and sent the one and only person who could redeem
us.[14]

CHAPTER EIGHTEEN

What God's Unconditional Acceptance Produces

It was time for the big season to start. I (Sean) was 12 and ready to play Little League baseball. Prior to the first game my dad, Josh, got an idea about how to teach me—and my teammates—an important lesson. He bought 12 coupons good for ice cream sundaes at a local restaurant and took them to my coach.

"Coach, these are for the kids," he said.

"Good," the coach said with a big smile. "This is great. I wish more dads took an interest like this. I'll take them for sundaes after our first win."

"No, Coach," Josh said quickly. "I want you to take them for sundaes after their first *loss.*"

My coach looked at my dad strangely. What Dad was saying wasn't computing with the coach's concept of winning, losing, and rewards for good play. So Dad proceeded to explain his thinking.

"Coach, I don't know about you, but as I raise my kids I don't want to acknowledge their success as much as their effort. And I don't want to acknowledge their effort as much as their being created in the image of God. I believe my son is created in the image of God and that he has infinite value, dignity, and worth. None of these things have anything to do with playing baseball. If he never played baseball an inning in his life, I would love and accept him just as much."

My coach looked at Josh for a long moment. Finally, all he could muster was, "That's weird!" But he agreed to use the coupons as Dad instructed.

The season started and our team won their first few games. But we lost the third or fourth game, and the coach was true to his word. He gave each player an ice cream sundae coupon and we all went out to "celebrate" our loss.

Of course, my teammates and I certainly appreciated the sundaes. But there was an even greater benefit to my dad's generosity. Over the next two weeks three of the kids on my team came up and thanked him for the special treat. One of my teammates, a boy named Jesse, came up to Dad and said, "Thanks a lot for the ice cream sundaes, Mr. McDowell. Wow! It doesn't matter to you if we win or not—you love us anyway." The lesson I learned so powerfully that day was that my dad accepted me no matter what.

God's Acceptance Is Even "Weirder"

A father rewarding his son and the baseball team when they lose a game may be weird. But God's acceptance of us is even weirder. The apostle Paul said, "You were [God's] enemies, separated from him by your evil thoughts and actions" (Colossians 1:21). We as humans didn't just lose a sports game. We rejected God's ways and his love and brought evil into his perfect world of absolute good. Yet Jesus came to die for us "while we were still his enemies" (Romans 5:10). It's not just that we were undeserving—we were rebels against God. And since we were dead spiritually we couldn't do anything to change our enemy status. If we were so undeserving and enemies of God, what kind of acceptance is it that motivated him to come to earth to die for us?

There is perhaps nothing that brings greater joy to the human heart than for another person to know all your faults and failures and, despite them, love you for being you.

We can say that "God so loved the world that he gave his only Son" (John 3:16), and of course that is true. God's love caused him to accept us even when we didn't deserve it. But it was a unique kind of acceptance that finds its roots only in God. It was a love that accepted you and me without any conditions whatsoever. God was motivated by a love that embraced us for exactly who we were—undeserving rebellious sinners.

God coming to earth isn't based on anything you have done or could do in the future. It is purely the result of his grace. Every other religion in the world teaches that human effort is required to attain some type of "salvation." But what some religions call salvation is essentially escape from evil with no prospect of joy. Buddhists explain that a person must go through countless cycles of reincarnation to reach what is called nirvana, which is essentially a state of personal oblivion. Islam teaches Muslims that they must work very hard to qualify for rewards that Allah may choose to give them.

Mormons declare that grace is obtained only after a person does all he or she can do to receive salvation.

But Christianity teaches that humans are helpless and can do nothing to merit salvation. It is God who takes the initiative to reach out to his enemies. "God saved you by his special favor when you believed. And you can't take credit for this; it is a gift from God. Salvation is not a reward for the good things we have done, so none of us can boast about it" (Ephesians 2:8-9). We state it again for emphasis: His grace was extended to us while we were gripped by death—sinners by birth and enemies of God. "When we were utterly helpless, Christ came at just the right time...God showed his great love for us by sending Christ to die for us while we were still sinners" (Romans 5:6,8). "Can we boast, then, that we have done anything to be accepted by God? No, because our acquittal is not based on our good deeds" (Romans 3:27). Regardless of all you've done—or haven't done—he offers grace. *God accepts you* completely without any conditions, and in spite of your sin he provides a way back to him. That is more than weird!

God coming to earth in human form is about turning the paradise lost of Genesis into the paradise regained of Revelation, even though none of us deserves it. It is about abolishing our death sentence even though we have done nothing to warrant eternal life in relationship with God. "Life itself was in him," John said, "and this life gives light to everyone" (John 1:4). Yet the basis of receiving such life is nothing we can do; it is strictly a gift from God.

The relational meaning of the incarnation is that you and I are unconditionally loved and accepted. There is perhaps nothing that brings greater joy to the human heart than for another person to know all your faults and failures and, despite them, love you for being you.

When Josh gave me (Sean) and my team ice cream sundaes after we lost our first baseball game, his gift said, "I know you messed up and didn't really play that well, but despite your failure I love you." My dad looked beyond my failures in playing baseball and loved me for being me. And how much more does God know us for all that we are, including our faults, failures, and sin—yet he accepts us without conditions. Bill and Gloria Gaither nailed it when they wrote the song "I Am Loved." In that song they say, "The one who knows me best loves me most."[1]

Accepted in Spite of Our Weaknesses

After I (Josh) became a Christian, I transferred to Wheaton College, a Christian school. The more I grew in my faith, the more I struggled over the challenge to give myself entirely to God. I resisted the challenge because I thought he might want me to go into Christian ministry, which meant only one thing to me—public speaking. At that time my poor grammar and stuttering problem I mentioned earlier were still very evident. As a result, it seemed to me that giving "everything" to God was giving him very little he could use.

Finally I said, "God, I don't think I have any speaking talents or other gifts you can use in ministry. I stutter when I'm scared, and I speak horrible English. I have all these limitations, so you surely don't want me in ministry. But if you can take these limitations and glorify yourself, then I will serve you the rest of my life with every breath I breathe."

God accepted all of me, regardless of my limitations. And because he accepted me without any conditions, I could give him myself without reservation. And amazingly he did something with my limitations. I truly believe I am living a supernatural life because I am living beyond my human limitations.

I have now been privileged to speak about Christ to millions of people in over half the countries of the world. I am humbled when I realize how many have been reached through the writings in my books. After all these years, I still struggle a little with my grammar when I speak and write. Every time I address a crowd or begin work on a book, I am aware of both my weakness and the grace of God. He accepts me for who I am, weakness and all, and I couldn't be happier. Webster says joy is "the emotion evoked by well-being, success or good fortune or by the prospects of possessing what one desires." God's unconditional acceptance of us, warts and all, evokes a deep joy that is hard to explain. While it takes the pressure off to perform, it creates a motivation to do our best. And when we do mess up, we are not condemned. The freedom of being accepted without conditions produces a relationship that is secure.

Acceptance Without Conditions
Creates a Secure Relationship

When someone accepts you for who you are, it gives you a sense of security. Since that kind of relationship is not based upon performance, it creates a natural vulnerability where you open up and trust another. Unconditional acceptance is the foundation of a healthy relationship because it engenders a security that gives you confidence that, no matter what happens, you'll be loved.

The incarnation is a reflection of the Godlike acceptance that produces a secure relationship. We see this in Jesus dying for us while we were sinners and enemies of God. But we also see it in how he interacted with others. Take, for example, the Samaritan woman in John 4. She had three strikes against her socially: 1) She was a woman, who was inferior to men in that culture; 2) she was a Samaritan, a race of people despised by the Jews; and 3) she was immoral, living with a man who was not her husband. While Jesus exposed her sin, he engaged her in conversation without judgment or condemnation. As a result, the woman welcomed the truth when Jesus shared it, and her life was changed.

The Pharisees of his day criticized Jesus for fraternizing with "tax collectors and many other notorious 'sinners'" (Matthew 9:11). Jesus replied, "Healthy people don't need a doctor—sick people do" (verse 12). How does a doctor respond to a person who comes to him or her with an illness or injury? Can you imagine a doctor condemning the poor patient for being sick? "How stupid can you be? If you had been paying better attention, you wouldn't have hit your thumb with the hammer." No, the physician accepts the patient right where he or she is and focuses on providing the comfort and healing needed.

This is how the Incarnate One connects with us when we are in pain, trouble, or crisis. He doesn't condemn us or criticize us, even though we may be in the wrong. God does not condone or overlook our sin either; it must be dealt with on his terms. But he loves us for who we are and accepts us at the point of our failure. And when we embrace such love and acceptance from God it gives us the joy of a secure relationship so we can say like Paul, "I am convinced that nothing can ever separate us from his love" (Romans 8:38).

Acceptance That Identifies with Us Creates an Intimate Relationship

Jesus not only accepts us for who we are, he identifies with all that we feel. He knows what we are going through, no matter what it is, and he understands it like no other. And that creates a bond and intimacy like nothing else can.

Remember, he experienced life as a human baby, child, teenager, and man. He suffered embarrassment, humiliation, and rejection. As God, Christ understood his creation perfectly. But by becoming a human being, he let us know how intimately and completely he identifies with us —and with all we experience.

Yes, God loved us and sent his Son in the form of a human being to die for us so we can have a relationship with him. But some tend to focus so exclusively on that central truth that they miss the full significance of how intimate he wants that relationship to be.

Because Christ took on human form, we can know that he affirms us in our weaknesses, pain, and temptations. He wanted me (Josh) to know that he identified with my humiliation as the son of the town drunk and with my sense of aloneness. He wants you to know that he identifies with your feelings of rejection when your child is not chosen for the basketball team or when you're overlooked for a job promotion. He identified with you as you were teased cruelly by classmates or shunned by associates or "friends." He can identify with what you feel when you are betrayed by a girlfriend or boyfriend, a co-worker, or a spouse.

Think of it: He is the all-sufficient Lord, yet when he was born to Mary he became as dependent as you were when you were a baby. He was the one who fashioned the human body, yet like you he had to learn to walk. He was the preexistent Word, yet he had to learn to speak, just as you did. He created clouds and rivers and lakes, yet he got thirsty. He endured the taunts of those who knew only part of his family's story. He must have felt the almost unbearable weight of grief when his earthly father, Joseph, died. He suffered not only the physical torture of the cross as he died for you but also the anguish of being rejected, humiliated, denied, abandoned, and even betrayed by his closest friends. Why did he willingly go through all that?

Because he wants you to know that he understands. He suffered like a human being, and he wants to affirm you in your suffering. The writer of Hebrews tells us that Christ "has gone through suffering and temptation...[and] is able to help us when we are being tempted...[He] understands our weaknesses, for he faced all of the same temptations we do, yet he did not sin. So let us come boldly...and we will find grace to help us when we need it" (Hebrews 2:18; 4:15-16). There is nothing you have experienced that God in Christ does not understand firsthand! He, like you, has experienced

- rejection—by his own people
- abandonment—by his own disciples
- misunderstanding—by his own followers
- ridicule—at his own trial
- betrayal—by a close friend
- criticism—by the religious leaders of his day[2]

But that's not all. He has also experienced human achievement and victories. He knows what it's like to feel loved and accepted. He knows the joy of completing a job well done. He has heard the voice of his Father say, "This is My beloved Son, in whom I am well pleased" (Matthew 17:5 NKJV). He has also known the joy of fulfilling his Father's will and the victory of conquering what no one has ever conquered: death.

He has experienced all the ups—and downs—of human existence. He's "been there, done that"—wherever you have been. The incarnation is Jesus' way of saying, "No matter what emotion you may be feeling, no matter what experience you may be enduring, I can identify with what you're going through and I'm here for you." This is the relational relevance of the incarnation.

CHAPTER NINETEEN

HOW TO ACCEPT OTHERS AS GOD ACCEPTS US

G od's coming to earth says to each of us, "Regardless of your sin I will give my life
to redeem you." That kind of unconditional acceptance is the basis for a relationship with God that is both intimate and secure. But that Godlike acceptance isn't
just for God to express to us—he wants us to express that same kind of acceptance toward others.

Paul the apostle exhorts us to "accept each other
just as Christ has accepted you; then God will be
glorified" (Romans 15:7). God did not wait until we
were believing right or living right before he invited
us into a relationship with him; he gave himself for
us "while we were still sinners" (Romans 5:8). That
is a key message Jesus was conveying in the story of
the prodigal son in Luke 15. It was the response of
the Father—a response of unconditional acceptance.
Yes, the son came back home...but only to ask to live

> *If we are to live out
> Godlike acceptance in
> our lives, we must learn
> to accept others for who
> they are, no matter what.*

as a servant, not as a son. The father, however, was "filled with love and compassion,
he ran to his son, embraced him, and kissed him" (Luke 15:20). The father broke the
custom of the day, took the initiative toward the wayward boy, and unconditionally
received him with all the rights of sonship. That is true, Godlike acceptance.

If we are to live out Godlike acceptance in our own lives, we must learn to accept others for who they are, no matter what. Then God will be glorified, and others will experience a relational connection that reflects Christ's connection to us. And that kind of connection will foster the joy of secure relationships and will help us to pass on our faith to others.

Acceptance Involves Making Yourself Available to Others

Accepting others as Christ accepts us means we must take the time to be *with* people.

The pressure was on. The book deadline was fast approaching, and I (Josh) needed to focus on writing and editing. Although the memory of this experience takes me back more than 30 years, I recall it vividly. I was right in the middle of editing a chapter when two-year-old Sean wandered in.

"Want to play, Daddy?" he chirped expectantly.

As an experienced parent (we had already been through the two-year-old stage with Kelly), I should have realized that Sean really wanted only a hug, a pat, and a minute or two to show me the new ball he was carrying. But I was working on an "important" chapter and felt I just didn't have even two minutes to spare.

"Son, how about playing a little later?" I replied. "I'm right in the middle of a chapter."

Sean didn't know what a chapter was, but he got the message. Daddy was too busy, and he'd have to leave now. He trotted off without complaining, and I returned to my manuscript. But my relief was short-lived. Dottie soon came in and sat down for a "little chat."

She began, "Honey, Sean just told me you were too busy to play with him. I know that this book is important, but I'd like to point something out."

"What is that?" I asked rather impatiently, because now my wife was keeping me from my all-important project.

"Honey, I think you have to realize that you are always going to have writing to do, and you are always going to have deadlines. Your whole life will be researching and doing similar projects. But you're not always going to have a two-year-old son who wants to sit on your lap and ask you questions and show you his new ball."

"I think I hear what you're saying," I said, "and you make a lot of sense as usual. But right now I've got to finish this chapter."

"All right, Josh," she said. "But please think about it. You know, if we spend time with our kids now, they will spend time with us later."

I did think about it, and the more I thought, the more Dottie's gentle words were like a knife slicing me to the core. She was right. I would always have deadlines to meet, contracts to fulfill, phone calls to answer, people to see, and trips to take. But my children would only be children for a short time. Soon the years would sweep by. Would I have any more time for them next year than I did this year?

I knew what the answer would be if I didn't change my ways. Quietly, without any big speeches or fanfare, I made a decision. I took Sean out in the yard and tossed the ball with him for a while. Ever since, I have tried to place my children ahead of my contracts, deadlines, and the clamor of a world that wants me to get back to them ASAP. And it has paid off.

I (Sean) have often been the beneficiary of Josh's decision. I don't remember that day when my dad didn't take time with me. I was too young to remember it. But I do remember my dad doing his best to plan his speaking schedule around my basketball games and working hard to be involved in my life, as well as the lives of my sisters. The older I get, the more I appreciate the sacrifice my father paid to build a relationship with me—especially now that I have my own family. He refused to sacrifice his family on the altar of success, fame, or popularity. This doesn't mean it wasn't hard, at times, having a father who was so busy and who traveled so much. I missed him often—badly. What got me through was knowing how passionately he loved us kids, as well as my mom's unwavering commitment to our family and to God's call on my father's life.

To demonstrate that you accept a child, a spouse, or a loved one for who they are involves taking the time to be there for them when they need you.

Acceptance Involves Entering Another's World

I (Josh) remember talking to one father who told me that he had taken time to spend it with his son, but he now regretted it. The son and father did not maintain a good relationship, and he saw the time with his son as a big failure. "What did you do together?" I asked.

"Well, I love to golf," he said, "so I took him golfing and it was a disaster."

"Does your son like to golf?" I inquired.

"No, but I do," he responded.

The Incarnate One stepped into our world; he did not demand that we enter his. He came to us and accepted us in order to deal with *our* problem. We too must enter the world of others and focus on *their* interests and issues if they are going to sense we love and accept them. You can't do this without truly coming to know the other person. If people you care about could verbalize this deep longing to be loved for who they are, it might sound like this: "I long for you to take thought of me and enter my world—to show an interest in what I do and what I like, to care about my dreams and aspirations. But it doesn't help me if you enter my world just because I want you to; it has meaning if you do it only because *you* want to, because you truly love and accept me for who I am."

Dottie, who is my (Sean's) mother, tells a story of what her own mother did to enter her world and accept her imaginative spirit when she was a little girl. She tells it in her own words:

> As a little girl, my hero was Peter Pan. Just hearing the story took my breath away. I spent much of my playtime living and reliving each scene, and I couldn't get enough of it. Each time I dreamed about the boy who could fly, I felt inspired and energized.
>
> I remember clearly the day I wandered down into our basement when I was about five years old. I spotted a box of Ivory Snow, a popular laundry detergent in those days, next to my mother's washing machine. In my well-developed imagination, each handful of soap flakes looked like the pixie dust that Tinker Bell sprinkled on Wendy, Michael, and John to enable them to fly. Thrilled at the prospect, I decided to relive the Tinker Bell scene. I'll never forget the exhilaration I felt as I took handfuls of "pixie dust" and sprinkled them generously throughout the entire basement. It was a magical moment in my young life.
>
> When I was done, everything in the basement was covered with soap. When my mom discovered what I had done, she listened to my explanation, lovingly understood my childish fantasy, and recognized how much the experience meant to me. Instead of reacting in anger or frustration at the mess I had created, she laughed with me and encouraged me to repeat the whole story of Peter Pan to her. Later, still in a lighthearted mood, we cleaned up the enormous mess together.
>
> What did this experience communicate to me? It assured me that my mom accepted me and my wild imagination. She unselfishly chose to encourage my childish dreams and that made me feel accepted. I shall never forget it!
>
> Even as an adult my mother would dream my dreams with me, wanting to know every detail and delighting in every interest that I pursued. Mom is with the Lord now. But her interest in knowing the details of my pursuits communicates that she accepted me for who I am. And it has taught me how to demonstrate acceptance of my husband, children, and those around me.

Acceptance Involves Accepting the Faults of Others

We all have the need for others to accept us for who we are, "warts and all." Genuine acceptance is able to separate the person from his or her behavior, just as Christ loves and accepts us in spite of our sin.

At its core, the need for acceptance may sound something like this: "Please allow me to make mistakes, and love me anyway. I know I'm not perfect, but I need you to look beyond my failures and imperfection and love me for who I am. I always need ten times more positive feedback than constructive criticism."

When someone you love does something different from how you would do it or makes a costly mistake, acceptance will focus on the person you love, not the difference or the failure. Godlike acceptance says: "Even if nothing about you changed, I would love you anyway"; "I want to know how you're feeling, because how you feel is important to me"; "I'm so proud of how you handled that situation"; "What happened to the car in the fender-bender isn't important—I'm just glad you're all right, because you are the one who matters to me."

After a disagreement or a clash of wills, it's likely that your acceptance needs to be expressed again. This might take the form of fixing a person a favorite meal, sending a bouquet of flowers, or any outward expression that communicates, "We may not always see eye to eye, but I always love you."[1]

As a teacher, I (Sean) would sometimes ask my freshman students to write journals. I will never forget the words of one young girl as she wrote about her relationship with her parents. She said, "If my parents were more understanding and forgiving, I think I would get in less trouble." In other words, understanding expresses care, love, and relationship, and reaching out in relationship causes the other person to reciprocate by loving in return, which means wanting to please. This is why Solomon said, "Good understanding wins favor" (Proverbs 13:15 NIV). The more we take the time to understand another person, the more accepted he or she feels. The Incarnate One who entered our world and accepted us without condition is our perfect role model.

Celebrating the Incarnation at Christmas

The Christmas season provides rich opportunities each year to focus on the awesome truth of the incarnation— "God wants to have a relationship with you!" Here are some practical ways to accomplish that goal.

✓ **While trimming the tree.** Some people say that the Christmas tree tradition began when Martin Luther, struck by the beauty of a forest of starlit fir trees, brought one indoors and decorated it with candles to remind his children of God's creation. When you and your family are trimming your Christmas tree, you can have this conversation:

Ask, "What can the lights on the tree tell us about the meaning of Christmas?" After fielding questions, turn off the Christmas lights on the tree and say, "This is what all of us are like without Jesus—empty bulbs without light or life." Turn on the lights and say, "This is what all of us are like when we make a relational connection to God.

He gives life and light to all who believe in Christ as their Savior. When you see the Christmas tree lit up, think of the true meaning of Christmas—that God sent his Son to earth because he wants so very much to have a relationship with you."

Ask, "What can the evergreen tree tell us about the meaning of Christmas?" After the answers and discussion say, "You know that the leaves of other trees turn brown and die in the fall. But the evergreen tree never turns brown. Its leaves remain green year round. Before Christ was in our lives, we were like other trees. We could never live forever. But because of Christ we have the promise of eternal life. When you see the evergreen tree, remember that Christ came so that you can remain alive forever if you have a relationship with him."

✓ **On singing or hearing Christmas music.** Christmas music is an excellent tool to reinforce the meaning of the incarnation. When the word *Immanuel* is used in a song, ask what the word means. Explain that Christ was called Immanuel, meaning "God is with us," because Jesus is God who came to live with us. And why did Jesus come to earth? He came to offer himself as a sacrifice so we could have a relationship with God.

When hearing "Silent Night," ask, "What does it mean that Jesus was a 'holy infant so tender and mild'?" This phrase gives you the opportunity to point out that Jesus was the "holy infant" because his birth father was not Joseph but rather the Holy God of the universe. Thus, Jesus was born of a virgin, with God as his birth father.

When hearing "Angels We Have Heard on High," ask, "Why did the angels sing 'Gloria in excelsis deo'?" Explain that the phrase means "Glory to God in the highest" and explain that the angels sang it because it was a most glorious day when God became a human being as part of his wonderful plan to restore us to a relationship with him.

✓ **When "decking the halls."** Young people generally love Christmas and all the decoration that accompanies the season. They may not, however, give much thought to the deeper reasons for decorating with garlands, tinsel, and other decorations. Use the time of decorating your home or youth-group meeting place or church to emphasize the purpose of the decorations. "We decorate our homes and buildings to express how very thankful we are that God did what he did in sending Christ to earth so we can enjoy a relationship with God."

✓ **Write a Christmas card to Jesus.** Christmas cards are used primarily to express holiday wishes and sentiments to one another. But you can also use cards to teach young people the relational meaning of Christmas. Ask them to write a card to Jesus, expressing their thankfulness for his becoming human and for what he says to them through the incarnation.

The basic message of the card should be, *"Thank you for accepting me unconditionally."* Ask the kids to express in their own words how they feel about God's accepting them regardless of whether they are rich or poor, good-looking or plain, popular or not, smart or ordinary, successful or not. Suggest: "First, tell Jesus that you know that he sees and knows everything you do and think (good or bad), yet he accepts you just the way you are. And then tell Jesus how that makes you feel. Thank him for accepting you without any conditions."[2]

CHRIST'S ATONEMENT FOR SIN

CHAPTER TWENTY

THE HIGH PRICE OF FORGIVENESS

I (Sean) grew up in the small mountain town of Julian, California. Most of my shopping was done at the general store in town. That is where I got candy, school supplies, crafts, and so on. My parents had dropped me, two of my school friends, and Katie, my five-year-old sister, off to do some shopping while they sat in the car. When we came out of the store, Katie had a handful of lapel pins and colorful craft pencils. As we walked to the car she handed them to my two friends and said, "Here, I bought these things for you."

We got in the car and Josh and Dottie looked at each other in a strange way. Dottie then got out and asked Katie to join her. My parents had sensed something was up because they hadn't given Katie any money to buy things. Within minutes I found out that my sister was a shoplifter!

My dad and mom conferred with each other for a moment. Then Dottie collected the stolen goods, took her little thief by the hand, and walked her right back into the store.

There are laws against shoplifting in California. Stealing is punishable by fines and jail time. Of course, I wasn't too worried. I figured with Katie returning the stolen stash and giving an apology, she'd be forgiven and go free.

But what if the store owner was really ticked at Katie? What if he refused to forgive and pressed charges? I figured the courts would then demand justice of my sister, and she would face the consequences—jail time. And I would have a convict for a sister.

Of course, that didn't happen. Forgiveness was offered, and Katie was set free of the consequences of stealing.

But what about the higher court of heaven? Can God just say, "Sure, you sinned, but that's okay, forget it—I'll forgive you and we'll be friends"? The reality is that God by nature is holy. He can't just overlook sin. The Bible says of God, "Your eyes are too pure to look on evil; you cannot tolerate wrong" (Habakkuk 1:13 NIV). God is so holy that he "cannot allow sin in any form" (Habakkuk 1:13). So by his very nature he is unable to have a relationship with those infected with sin.

Therefore, even though he is "rich in mercy" (Ephesians 2:4), sin separates us from him. And that separation is a big deal because sin has caused a dreadful consequence: death. The apostle Paul said we "were dead, doomed forever because of [our] many sins" (Ephesians 2:1). Dead people can't accept forgiveness even when it's offered. They can't accept anything, because they're dead. So that presents quite a dilemma. In order for God to forgive us he had to address our sin. And to do that he put in place an amazing and miraculous plan. One that carried with it a very high price.

A Sacrifice Is Needed

They had traveled for three days. The young boy couldn't remember ever being on such a long journey with his father. It was exciting.

When his father saw their destination in the distance, he told his two servants, "'The boy and I will travel a little farther. We will worship there, and then we will come right back.' Abraham placed the wood for the burnt offering on Isaac's shoulders, while he himself carried the knife and the fire" (Genesis 22:5-6).

Isaac knew about burnt offerings, and he knew that something was missing from his father's preparations. "'We have the wood and the fire,' said the boy, 'but where is the lamb for the sacrifice?'" (verse 7). Isaac had been taught that there was a price to be paid to obtain forgiveness. A living, breathing creature had to die as a blood sacrifice.

You know the story. Abraham placed his son on the altar to sacrifice him as God had told him. But just as he lifted his knife to sacrifice his son to God, "the angel of the LORD shouted to him from heaven, 'Abraham! Abraham!...Lay down the knife,' the angel said. 'Do not hurt the boy in any way, for now I know that you truly fear God. You have not withheld even your beloved son from me.' Then Abraham looked up and saw a ram caught by its horns in a bush. So he took the ram and *sacrificed it* as a burnt offering on the altar *in place of his son*" (Genesis 22:11-13).

Accepting a Substitute

Abraham, like all of us, had sinned and was dead spiritually and separated from God. But in this dramatic example, God was showing him that he had a miraculous plan in place by which Abraham and the rest of us could be brought back to spiritual life in exchange for another life. A blood sacrifice would be made in our place and, in a real sense, purchase our resurrection to a new life in relationship with God.

But this "life-for-a-life" exchange was very specific. Scripture tells us that "the Lord called to Moses from the Tabernacle and said to him, 'Give the following instruction to the people of Israel. When you present an animal as an offering to the Lord...it must be a male with no defects...Lay your hand on the animal's head, and the Lord *will accept its death in your place* to purify you, making you right with him'" (Leviticus 1:1-4 NLT).

The priests were then instructed to offer the sacrifice before God in place of—or as a substitute—to atone for the person's sin. The ram sacrificed before God was offered *in place* of Isaac. The priests offered burnt offerings and sin offerings to God so the Lord would "accept its death *in your place.*" People were guilty of the sins, but the animal without defects became a holy sacrifice that God accepted. The death of the holy animal substituted for the death of the sinner.

However, the annual sacrifices were not God's permanent solution to our dilemma of sin and death. They were only a symbol of what was to come. In order for the consequences of sin (death) to be reversed so we could be made alive to God, a more powerful and perfect sacrifice had to be made.

The Perfect Redeeming Sacrifice of Christ

Since we were born dead spiritually, sin has all of us enslaved. The apostle Paul said, "I am sold into slavery, with sin as my master" (Romans 7:14). Paul said he was a prisoner to sin and declared, "What a wretched man I am! Who will rescue me from this body of death?" (Romans 7:24 NIV). He then answers his own question: "Thanks be to God—through Jesus Christ our Lord" (Romans 7:25 NIV).

"God so loved the world that he gave his only Son" (John 3:16), and in doing so "God made Christ, who never sinned [the holy Lamb of God without defects] to be the offering for our sin" (2 Corinthians 5:21). It was Jesus, the God-man, who had to be sacrificed "for only as a human being could he die, and only by dying could he break the power of the Devil, who had the power of death" (Hebrews 2:14).

> It is Jesus' death on the cross that atones for your sins.

Our freedom from the enslavement of sin and death was through the redeeming act of Christ as our sacrifice. It was "redemption that came by Christ Jesus. God presented him as a sacrifice of atonement" (Romans 3:24-25 NIV). Redemption in this verse is a commercial term. It is a reference to the high price paid to purchase a slave in that day—a price so high that it not only purchased the slave, but also purchased the legal paperwork to buy the slave completely out of slavery. This redemptive price brought total freedom so the person would never again be sold back into slavery. Redemption is the act of Christ freeing us from slavery to sin and death.

There it is! God's miraculous and merciful redemptive plan to set us free of our sins and bring us back to life in relationship with him. "God is so rich in mercy, and he loved us so very much, that even while we were dead because of our sins, he gave us life when he raised Christ from the dead" (Ephesians 2:4-5). The blood sacrifices of bulls and goats were not sufficient or powerful enough for a just God to cancel our death sentence. You see, a sacrificial death was just part of the redemptive plan. The sacrifice also had to rise to life again so that we too could be brought back to life.

It is an amazing miracle. Even though the "wages of sin is death" (Romans 6:23), "God paid a ransom [your wages]…And the ransom he paid was not mere gold or silver. He paid for you with the precious lifeblood of Christ, the sinless, spotless Lamb of God" (1 Peter 1:18-19). It is Jesus' death on the cross that atones for your sins. He became your sacrifice for sin. His death substitutes for your death, and then his resurrection to life is your resurrection to new life in him. So because of his atoning sacrifice you can be set free, forgiven of your sins, and escape eternal banishment from the presence of God. "For Christ died for sin, once for all, the righteous for the unrighteous, to bring you to God" (1 Peter 3:18 NIV).

Just as the priests of old took the sin offering into the holy tabernacle and made a sacrifice to God to redeem the people, "so Christ has now become the High Priest over all good things that have come. He has entered that great, perfect sanctuary in heaven, not made by human hands and not part of this created world. Once for all time he took blood into that Most Holy Place, but not the blood of goats and calves. He took his own blood, and with it he secured our salvation forever" (Hebrews 9:11-12).

The book of Hebrews gives us a clear picture of Jesus, our great High Priest, sprinkling his own blood in the temple before his Father God "to remove the power of sin forever by his sacrificial death for us" (Hebrews 9:26). What the priests of the Old Testament did as they sacrificed animals year after year in order to atone for sin was a continuing, ritualistic picture foreshadowing the real sacrifice to come. The true sacrifice was completed in Jesus' final act as High Priest when he "offered himself to God as one sacrifice for sins, good for all time. Then he sat down at the place of highest honor at God's right hand" (Hebrews 10:12).

Therefore:

> We believe the truth that Jesus, as the sinless Son of God, atoned for our sin through his death on the cross. And the offering of his blood as a sacrifice for sin redeems us so we are forgiven—set free—and raises us to new life in him.

Some would say that Jesus' death as the "spotless Lamb of God" satisfies the demands of both God's holiness and his justice. His holiness is satisfied because Jesus was sinless—a perfect sacrifice without sin. His justice is satisfied in that Christ's death paid our "wages of sin" which is death. There are various views on the doctrine of atonement, with substitutionary atonement the most widely accepted by Protestant and evangelical churches. That is, God's perfect justice demanded that the penalty for sin be paid, and Christ stepped in and paid it. Others see his sacrifice more as a ransom. That is, when we sin we become enslaved to Satan. Christ ransoms us by saying, in effect, "Take me instead." And Satan jumped at the offer. Biblically speaking, both views are true.

While there is some disagreement over the distinction as to whether Christ "suffered for us" or whether he was "punished instead of us," there is common agreement that through Jesus' death we are redeemed—forgiven of our sin, raised to new life, and reconciled to God. "God made Christ, who never sinned, to be the offering for our sin, so that we could be made right with God through Christ" (2 Corinthians 5:21). This was a very high price for God to pay, but he considered you and me worth it.

CHAPTER TWENTY-ONE

EVIDENCE THAT JESUS WAS GOD'S PERFECT SACRIFICE

When you are put on the justice scales of God, there is only one thing that can outweigh your sin. It isn't your good deeds, a life of penance, or even the sacrifice of your own life. The only thing that will cancel out your sin and satisfy the justice scales of a holy God is a pure and holy sacrifice.

God told the children of Israel, "I, the LORD your God, am holy" (Leviticus 19:2). And he made it clear that the sacrificial offerings to him had to be pure and without defects, offered up to him by holy priests. When these conditions were met he would accept the offering as a substitute for their sin and his justice scales were satisfied.

God wants us to feel confident in our faith that Jesus of Nazareth is the holy Lamb of God. That is why he has given us such clear signs.

The book of Hebrews tells us that not only did Jesus die for us, but he "is the kind of high priest we need because he is holy and blameless, unstained by sin...He does not need to offer sacrifices every day like the other high priests...Jesus did this once for all when he sacrificed himself on the cross...[God's] Son has been made perfect forever" (Hebrews 7:26-28).

If the Jesus of history born in Bethlehem some 2000 years ago was truly God's Son, then it is clear that he was the perfect sacrifice and holy high priest needed to secure our salvation. And God wants us to feel confident in our faith that Jesus of Nazareth is the holy Lamb of God. That is why he has given us such clear signs.

First, God gave John the Baptist a clear sign to identify Jesus as God's Son. John saw Jesus coming toward him the day after he baptized him and said,

> "Look! There is the Lamb of God who takes away the sin of the world!"... Then John said, "I saw the Holy Spirit descending like a dove from heaven and resting upon him. I didn't know he was the one, but when God sent me to baptize with water, he told me, 'When you see the Holy Spirit descending and resting upon someone...he is the one who baptizes with the Holy Spirit.' I saw this happen to Jesus, so I testify that he is the Son of God [the Chosen One of God]" (John 1:29-34).

Just as God gave John a way to identify Jesus as "the Chosen One of God," he has also given us clear and indisputable means to identify his Son through what are called *messianic prophecies*. It is a clear means of knowing with certainty that we can be forgiven by God—because the Jesus of the Bible is our perfect sacrifice.

Messianic Prophecies Fulfilled in One Person

Imagine agreeing over the phone to meet a distant business acquaintance—someone you've never met in person—at a large business convention.

"How will I know you?" you ask.

"Well," your associate says, "I'll be carrying a briefcase."

"That helps," you reply, "but a lot of people will probably be carrying briefcases. What color is yours?"

"Black."

"That might narrow it down some," you say, "but not enough."

"I'm a redhead," your associate offers.

"That helps," you answer. *Redhead carrying a black briefcase. Still might not be specific enough.* "What will you be wearing?"

"A blue blazer. How's that?"

"That's better. But just to be sure, can you wear red tennis shoes?"

"Very funny," your associate replies. "I'll just make sure I'm wearing a name tag with my name in big bold letters."

"That should do it," you answer. *I'll just look for a redhead carrying a black briefcase and wearing a blue blazer with a name tag.* "I should be able to recognize you from a distance, and your name on the tag will seal it."[1]

Identifying the Deity

Now imagine God, several millennia ago, devising the plan to send his only Son to earth to be born as a human infant. If we could have spoken down the corridors of time, we might have asked, "How will we know him? How will we recognize him as the Messiah, the holy Lamb of God—your acceptable sacrifice for sin?"

God might have responded, "I will cause him to be born as an Israelite, a descendant of Abraham (Genesis 22:18; Galatians 3:16)."

"But," we might have protested, "Abraham's descendants will be as numerous as the stars!"

"Then I will narrow it down to only half of Abraham's lineage, and make him a descendant of Isaac, not Ishmael (Genesis 21:12; Luke 3:23-34)."

"That will help, but isn't that still an awful lot of people?"

"Let him be born from Jacob's line, then, eliminating half of Isaac's lineage (Numbers 24:17; Luke 3:23-34)."

"But—"

"I will be more specific. Jacob will have twelve sons; I will bring forth the Messiah from the tribe of Judah (Genesis 49:10; Luke 3:23-33)."

"Won't that still be a lot of people? We still may not recognize him when he comes."

"Don't worry! Look for him in the family line of Jesse (Isaiah 11:1; Luke 3:23-32). *And* from the house and lineage of Jesse's youngest son, David (Jeremiah 23:5; Luke 3:23-31). And then I will tell you *where* he will be born: Bethlehem, a tiny town in the area called Judah (Micah 5:2; Matthew 2:1)."

"But how will we know which person born there is your Son?"

"He will be preceded by a messenger who will prepare the way and announce his advent (Isaiah 40:3; Matthew 3:1-2). He will begin his ministry in Galilee (Isaiah 9:1; Matthew 4:12-17) and will teach in parables (Psalm 78:2; Matthew 13:34-35), performing many miracles (Isaiah 35:5-6; Matthew 9:35)."

"Okay, that should help a lot."

"Oh," God might have responded, "I'm just getting warmed up. He will ride into the city of Jerusalem on a donkey (Zechariah 9:9; Matthew 21:2; Luke 19:35-37) and will appear suddenly and forcefully at the temple courts and zealously 'clean house' (Psalm 69:9; Malachi 3:1; John 2:15-16). Why, in *one day* I will fulfill no fewer than *29* specific prophecies spoken at least 500 years earlier about him! Listen to this:

1. He will be betrayed by a friend (Psalm 41:9; Matthew 26:49).

2. The price of his betrayal will be 30 pieces of silver (Zechariah 11:12; Matthew 26:15).

3. His betrayal money will be cast to the floor of my temple (Zechariah 11:13; Matthew 27:5).

4. His betrayal money will be used to buy the potter's field (Zechariah 11:13; Matthew 27:7).

5. He will be forsaken and deserted by his disciples (Zechariah 13:7; Mark 14:50).

6. He will be accused by false witnesses (Psalm 35:11; Matthew 26:59-60).

7. He will be silent before his accusers (Isaiah 53:7; Matthew 27:12).

8. He will be wounded and bruised (Isaiah 53:5; Matthew 27:26).

9. He will be hated without a cause (Psalm 69:4; John 15:25).

10. He will be struck and spit on (Isaiah 50:6; Matthew 26:67).

11. He will be mocked, ridiculed, and rejected (Isaiah 53:3; Matthew 27:27-31; and John 7:5,48).

12. He will collapse from weakness (Psalm 109:24-25; Luke 23:26).

13. He will be taunted with specific words (Psalm 22:6-8; Matthew 27:39-43).

14. People will shake their heads at him (Psalm 109:25; Matthew 27:39).

15. People will stare at him (Psalm 22:17; Luke 23:35).

16. He will be executed among 'sinners' (Isaiah 53:12; Matthew 27:38).

17. His hands and feet will be pierced (Psalm 22:16; Luke 23:33).

18. He will pray for his persecutors (Isaiah 53:12; Luke 23:34).

19. His friends and family will stand afar off and watch (Psalm 38:11; Luke 23:49).

20. His garments will be divided up and awarded by the casting of lots (Psalm 22:18; John 19:23-24).

21. He will thirst (Psalm 69:21; John 19:28).

22. He will be given gall and vinegar (Psalm 69:21; Matthew 27:34).

23. He will commit himself to God (Psalm 31:5; Luke 23:46).

24. His bones will be left unbroken (Psalm 34:20; John 19:33).

25. His heart will rupture (Psalm 22:14; John 19:34).

26. His side will be pierced (Zechariah 12:10; John 19:34).

27. Darkness will come over the land at midday (Amos 8:9; Matthew 27:45).

28. He will be buried in a rich man's tomb (Isaiah 53:9; Matthew 27:57-60).

29. He will die 483 years after the declaration of Artaxerxes to rebuild the temple in 444 BC (Daniel 9:24).[2]

"As a final testimony, on the third day after his death, he will be raised from the dead (Psalm 16:10; Acts 2:31), ascend to heaven (Psalm 68:18; Acts 1:9), and be seated at the right hand of God in full majesty and authority (Psalm 110:1; Hebrews 1:3)."

What extraordinary lengths God went to in order to help us identify and recognize his only begotten Son! Jesus fulfilled 60 major Old Testament prophecies (with about 270 additional ramifications)—all of which were made more than 400 years before his birth. This makes a compelling case for Jesus being the one and only person to "take away the sin of the world."

The Probability Factor

Of course Jesus was not the only Jew to be born into the tribe of Judah, in the city of Bethlehem, and be buried in a rich man's tomb. So is it possible to believe that the details of Jesus' life just *happened* to coincide with all those Old Testament prophecies?

To answer that question, we need only turn to the science of statistics and probabilities. Professor Peter W. Stoner, in an analysis that was carefully reviewed and pronounced to be sound by the American Scientific Affiliation, states that the probability of just *eight* prophecies being fulfilled in one person is 1 in 10^{17} (that's 1 in 100,000,000,000,000,000).[3]

To get just a little idea of that number, assume you were to take 100,000,000,000, 000,000 silver dollars and spread them across the state of Texas. That many silver dollars would not only cover the entire state but also pile up two feet deep! Now, take one more silver dollar, mark it with a big red X, toss it into that pile, and stir the whole pile thoroughly.

Then blindfold yourself, and starting at El Paso on the western border, walk the length and breadth of that enormous state, from Amarillo in the panhandle to Laredo on the Rio Grande all the way to Galveston on the Gulf of Mexico, stooping just once along the way to pick up a single silver dollar out of that two-foot-deep pile. Then take off your blindfold, and look at the silver dollar in your hand. What are the chances that you would have picked the marked coin out of that pile of silver dollars the size of the Lone Star State? *The same chances that one person could have fulfilled just eight messianic prophecies in one lifetime.*[4]

In other words, it is nearly nonsensical to imagine that eight Old Testament prophecies about the Messiah could have come true in one man by chance—let alone the *60* major prophecies that were fulfilled in Jesus of Nazareth—unless, of course, he *is* (as he himself claimed) "the glory of the only Son of the Father" (John 1:14).

God gave us these prophecies so we could be confident in the truth that Jesus truly is God's perfect atonement for our sins. Because of Christ's death on the cross we can be set free—forgiven—of wages of death and have eternal life with God. That truth causes us to join in with the angels as they sing, "Worthy is the Lamb, who was slain, to receive power and wealth and wisdom and strength and honor and glory and praise!" (Revelation 5:12 NIV).

CHAPTER TWENTY-TWO

THE TRUE MEANING OF LOVE

The cross fell into the hole with a loud thud, sending shock waves of agony through Jesus' legs and arms. Prior to being nailed to the cross he had been beaten almost beyond recognition. Now he hung there on the tree in excruciating pain. Soldiers below him gambled for his clothes. Religious leaders mocked him. He pushed himself up from his nail-pierced feet, scraping against the rough-hewn cross, in his attempts to get deep breaths. Each time he did this, pain shot up his legs. But he finally managed to draw enough breath to speak: "Father, forgive these people, because they don't know what they are doing" (Luke 23:34). That kind of love is so amazing it defies our understanding.

The crowd laughed and jeered at the powerful Creator of the universe, who appeared to hang helpless on the cross. "'He saved others,' they said, 'let him save himself if he is really God's Chosen One, the Messiah'" (Luke 23:35).

Two guilty and convicted criminals were crucified on either side of Jesus. One of them scoffed, "'So you're the Messiah, are you? Prove it by saving yourself—and us, too, while you're at it!' But the other criminal protested, 'Don't you fear God even when you are dying? We deserve to die for our evil deeds, but this man hasn't done anything wrong.' Then he said, 'Jesus, remember me when you come into your Kingdom.'"

"And Jesus replied, 'I assure you, today you will be with me in paradise'" (Luke 23:39-43). Though guilty and dying alone, this criminal who deserved his punishment experienced the forgiving love of the Savior.

You Are Loved and Forgiven

The criminal hanging there beside Jesus was as good as dead. So are you. Like that dying criminal, you are guilty of sin as charged. Your sin stands between you and a holy God without hope of forgiveness. You are dead to him with no ability in yourself to change your death status. That is, unless Christ remembers you as he did the criminal crucified beside him.

It was a Saturday morning. I (Josh) was 11 years old. I dressed before dawn and hurriedly got my morning chores done before the workmen arrived.

A team of men had been working for days to jack up a small house on my parents' farm, preparing it to be moved to a new location. My grown brother, Wilmont, was having it moved over the objections of my father. Wilmont had been engaged in a bitter feud with my dad, which had escalated into an all-out war for half of the family farm. Having successfully sued my father, Wilmont had arrived that morning with a sheriff, a deputy, and a court order authorizing him to move the house.

I, however, was trying hard to stay out of the family conflict. I hated to see my dad and brother fight, but that was between them. Today I just wanted to savor the excitement of watching an entire house being towed down the road, a spectacle more entertaining to an eleven-year-old mind than a traveling circus.

Then, just as the tractors were being attached to the house, my father, drunk as usual, began yelling at Wilmont. The sheriff moved quickly toward the staggering man to prevent an ugly scene.

You and I were on the mind and within the heart of a loving God the day Jesus sacrificed himself on the cross.

But it was too late for that. My brother, expecting something like this, had arranged for numerous families from our small farming community to be on hand to provide moral support for him. Many of them began chanting obscenities at my father as the sheriff restrained the old man.

I watched in horror, my excitement turning to embarrassment. Frightened by the escalating conflict and humiliated to see our family's feud played out in full view of my friends and neighbors, I ran from the shameful scene and into our nearby barn. Slamming the barn door behind me, I scrambled into the corn bin and buried myself up to my neck in corn.

Dark, quiet, and alone, my shame slowly turned to anger. I was angry that my father's drinking brought such division to my home. I was angry that he was rarely sober. And I was angry that he had caused such pain to my mother's life. But more than anything, I felt alone.

I lay there in the corn for what must have been hours. No one came looking for me. No one seemed to even notice that I was gone. I felt forgotten.

It's not hard to feel alone even in a world full of busyness and activity. But I really wasn't forgotten in that corn bin. And neither are you in your loneliest moments. Though a sinner by birth, deserving nothing except your sentence of death, your holy and blameless Creator spreads his arms the width of the cross and says, "I love you and you are forgiven."

The Meaning of Love

As alone as you may feel at times in life, you are not forgotten by God. You and I were on the mind and within the heart of a loving God the day Jesus sacrificed himself on the cross. If you have trusted in Jesus as your Savior as the dying criminal did, your wages of sin are freely forgiven. You now have a place waiting in paradise with him forever.

"God showed how much he loved us by sending his only Son into the world so that we might have eternal life through him. This is real love. It is not that we loved God, but that he loved us" (1 John 4:9-10). The high price for your forgiveness was worth the sacrifice to God. Even when you were an enemy of God, separated and alone, he loved you. He saw your need, identified with your pain of death, and sacrificed himself so you might be forgiven of your sins and be raised to new life in relationship with him forever. That is the true meaning of Christ's atoning sacrifice for you.

It is hard to comprehend that Christ would love each of us that much. The great songwriter and preacher Charles Wesley couldn't comprehend it either and penned the words to "And Can It Be?"

> And can it be that I should gain
> An interest in the Savior's blood?
> Died He for me, who caused His pain—
> For me, who Him to death pursued?
> *Amazing love! how can it be*
> *That Thou, my God, shouldst die for me?*
>
> He left His Father's throne above,
> So free, so infinite His grace—
> Emptied Himself of all but love,
> And bled for Adam's helpless race:
> 'Tis mercy all, immense and free,
> For O my God, it found out me!

No condemnation now I dread;
Jesus, and all in Him, is mine;
Alive in Him, my living Head,
And clothed in righteousness divine,
Bold I approach th' eternal throne,
And claim the crown, through
   Christ my own.[1]

CHAPTER TWENTY-THREE

How to Love Others
As God Loves Us

We know what real love is because Christ gave up his life for us. And so we also ought to give up our lives for our Christian brothers and sisters" (1 John 3:16). Yes, "God so loved the world that he [sacrificially] gave his only Son" (John 3:16). But are we commanded to actually live out that kind of love to those around us? How can our human love for others ever match to his infinite love? Our efforts to love don't compare to God's love any more than a preschooler's coloring book compares to God's multicolored sunset or a hand-molded vase by a pottery maker compares to God's delicate crafting of a newborn baby. Yet his love stands as a pattern to follow, for by walking in his footprints of love we find our purpose and true joy in living. Let's look at two dimensions of Godlike love and see what it does. And by doing so we can see how God completes our joy as we love as he loves.

Real Love Sacrifices

A sacrificial love gives whether it gets anything in return or not. "Observe how Christ loved us," Paul stated, "He didn't love in order to get something from us but to give everything of himself to us" (Ephesians 5:2 MSG). "Love...doesn't think about itself" (1 Corinthians 13:4,5 GWT). God wants us to love others like he loves us, and that means sacrificing something. Perhaps we don't literally sacrifice our physical life, but it does mean loving and living unselfishly. That may mean giving up our comforts for another, giving freely of our time, and, giving unselfishly of our possessions. That is how we demonstrate a Godlike love to others.

Real Love Sacrifices Comfort

When Stephanie and I (Sean) had our first child, we didn't realize all it would mean to love and care for our bundle of joy. Scottie was a healthy and active baby. I knew I would enjoy feeding and rocking him and even singing to him. And I did. But I guess I just didn't realize it was such a 24/7 proposition. Stephanie and I would alternate caring for Scottie at night. So at times I found myself up at two o'clock in the morning attending to the needs of a crying baby. Sometimes at four o'clock Stephanie or I walked a crying Scottie during some of his stomachaches. It was uncomfortable losing valuable sleep and dragging off to work the next day. As a young married couple we missed going out at night with friends because we had to stay home with our baby. However, we gave up some of our past comforts willingly and in a strange way, joyfully, because we loved our little boy. That's what sacrificial love does.

> *The big payoff for enduring the discomforts of sacrificial love is joy— some on this earth and the rest in eternity.*

Max Lucado, in his book entitled *3:16: The Numbers of Hope,* tells of a father who loved his son sacrificially.

> I know a father who, out of love for his son, spends each night in a recliner, never sleeping more than a couple of consecutive hours. A car accident paralyzed the teenager. To maintain the boy's circulation, therapists massage his limbs every few hours. At night the father takes the place of the therapists. Though he's worked all day and will work again the next, he sets the alarm to wake himself every other hour until sunrise.[1]

A sacrificial love forgoes personal comforts to give of ourselves freely. We shouldn't love others sacrificially with personal gain in mind, but let me (Josh) tell you something surprising. Spending sleepless nights with a baby, traveling long hours to get home for a child's basketball game, enduring some of the struggles of a boy's teen years and all the ongoing, smaller yet tedious and grinding sacrifices of raising a child definitely have a payoff. The sacrifices Dottie and I made to raise Sean to adulthood have produced more joy than I can explain. A father could not be more proud of a son than I am. I won't embarrass him here by citing all his qualities as a son, a husband, a father, a speaker, and an educator. But my life has been worth living just to be married to the most wonderful woman in the world and to watch a baby boy and three baby girls grow up to become people who are sacrificially loving God, their families, and the world around them. God's gift of my family has made my joy complete. Love your family sacrificially, and that kind of joy can be yours as well.

The smaller sacrifices of life can at times be more difficult than the big sacrifices. But don't be discouraged that loving another unselfishly causes some personal and temporary discomfort. The planting of sacrificial love in another person reaps a harvest of joy. Give of yourself without thought of a return, accept the trials and discomforts that come with unselfish sacrifice, and God will give back more than you can ever imagine. The apostle Peter said, "Be truly glad! There is wonderful joy ahead, even though it is necessary for you to endure many trials for a while" (1 Peter 1:6). The big payoff for enduring the discomforts of sacrificial love is joy—some on this earth and the rest in eternity.

Real Love Sacrifices Possessions

After the apostle John told us to "give up our lives for our brothers and sisters," he went on to say, "If someone has enough money to live well and sees a brother or sister in need but shows no compassion—how can God's love be in that person?" (1 John 3:17 NLT). "Pure and lasting religion in the sight of God our Father," Jesus stated, "means that we must care for orphans and widows in their troubles, and refuse to let the world corrupt us" (James 1:27). A sacrificial love means giving of our possessions to others.

We don't have to be wealthy in the world's eyes to give of our possessions. And the gift doesn't have to be of Bill Gates proportions in order to mean something. When the widow woman dropped two pennies in the temple collection box, Jesus said, "I assure you, this poor widow has given more than all the others have given. For they gave a tiny part of their surplus, but she, poor as she is, has given everything she has" (Mark 12:43). Giving isn't as important as giving sacrificially.

God doesn't ask for just ten percent of your possessions; he asks that you give him your all—and when you do that, your possessions are included. Jesus said "you must love the Lord your God with *all* your heart, *all* your soul, and *all* your mind...[and] love your neighbor as yourself" (Matthew 22:37-39). "Give your bodies to God," Paul admonishes, "Let them be a living and holy sacrifice—the kind he will accept. When you think of what he has done for you, is this too much to ask?" (Romans 12:1). There is a worldview that considers ownership of property and the accumulation of wealth to be what makes the world economy work. Putting number one first enables you to get enough to give to others. Jesus had a different perspective on ownership and wealth. He said, "Foxes have dens to live in, and birds have nests, but I, the Son of Man, have no home of my own, not even a place to lay my head" (Matthew 8:20).

This doesn't mean home ownership or gaining wealth is wrong, it simply means everything we have actually belongs to God in the first place. Possession is more a matter of stewardship than ownership. He has given all of us certain possessions, and he wants us to be good stewards of those possessions by using them to meet the needs of others. That is why Scripture says, "You should look not only to your own interests, but also to the interests of others" (Philippians 2:4 NIV).

In his book *The Faith,* Chuck Colson challenges us to see the world of possessions through God's eyes:

> As we see the world through God's eyes, we actually do put others' needs ahead of ours. This is why, when the great novelist Flannery O'Connor was asked by one of her correspondents how he could experience God's love, her reply was, "Give alms." She meant do something for the poor, for those in need, which in fact is one of the most telling marks of Christian holiness, as the apostle James reminds us (1:27; 2:17).
>
> When we care for God's favorites, the poor, who include the destitute, the widowed, the fatherless, the sick, prisoners, and anyone suffering injustice, we plunge immediately into the cosmic battle that's always raging between good and evil. We choose sides. Once on God's side, we come to understand God's point of view and position ourselves to experience God's love and friendship in a whole new way.[2]

Christ's kind of love—a sacrificial love—is love in action that includes giving to others of what God has given you.

Real Love Sacrifices Time

We both have done our share of traveling and speaking to young people. And if there is one thing we hear consistently from today's kids, it's this, "I have a problem with my dad—he won't spend time with me." It's not that these kids don't need their mothers—they do. But their perception is, "My mom's there for me, but my dad is just not there. And when he is home it's like he's not really there, you know?"

What we sense kids are saying is that love is spelled T-I-M-E. In fact, we all spell love that way. When someone says they love us but don't take the time to be with us, their declaration of love rings untrue. Dads who don't spend time with their kids often make up for it by bringing home elaborate and expensive gifts. But what we want from those we love is not gifts; we want their time. We don't want more stuff; we want the person. Philosopher and poet Ralph Waldo Emerson is credited with saying that a gift is an excuse for not giving yourself. Gifts are important, but they don't replace the ultimate gift of our time.

Some people try to get around the need to spend time with their loved ones by saying it's not the quantity of time that counts but the "quality of the time" that is important.

One of the biggest myths going today is the myth of "quality time." Of course we all want quality moments with our families. But you don't get them by appointment or on some kind of schedule. You get quality moments by spending larger quantities of time with your family. Out of the quantity needs to come the quality. We must have both!

One of the biggest advantages of quantity time spent with your children is that you are able to serve as a role model for them. Whenever you run an errand, try to take one of your kids with you. Otherwise, you might miss an opportunity to model for them. It's when they are with us, their parents or grandparents, that they can see how we respond to the world: how we act when another driver cuts us off or when a pushy sales clerk or a slow waitress irritates us. Our kids learn more about living their life when they are with us, watching us, and experiencing our reactions to others than they can learn in any classroom or from any textbook.

Another myth we fall victim to is the one that says, "It's the big moments that count." You might call them the "Disney World experiences"—those major excursions that take all day or all week and usually cost a lot of money. For parents, these "big moments" include trips to the amusement park, movie theater, or zoo; for youth leaders, activities such as ski trips or youth camp or big vacations. But the truth is, your kids may remember the "big moments." Yet it's the consistent small day-in and day-out moments that will truly mold them. It's not that the big events are wrong or harmful; we plan big events with our own kids and they have created some amazing memories. But big events can never replace the consistent little moments of just *being with* them.

There is more to being with a person than simply being in their physical presence. You can spend time around a person and still not *be with* them. To be with a person means you focus on them and their interests to let them know you really love and care for them.

Jeff Myers, president of Passing the Baton International, stresses the importance of knowing how to ask questions to engage a person and let them know you're there *with* them. Jeff says:

> My goal in asking questions is not for an opportunity to give instruction,
> but to help my students solve problems for themselves.
>> "What do you think about that?"
>> "Why is that happening?"
>> "What took place?"[3]

Based on Jeff's approach, here are some suggested questions you can ask your kids when you're taking time to be with them.

- Let's share our favorite color, food, music, sport, vacation spot, and so on. Now let's think about this—why do we like some of the same things and yet have some other interests that are different? (This focuses on individual uniqueness as well as family connections.)

- Describe your most embarrassing moment, happiest moment, saddest moment. Now why did you feel that way? What was happening then?

- If you could ask God one question, what would it be?

Author Mary DeMuth has some great questions that can bridge to truly being "with" a person.* She suggests asking:

- What one thing would you like to change about yourself? Why?

- Describe the perfect day. What would you do? What would you see?

- If you could give your best friend any gift what would it be? Why?

Sacrificing your time to demonstrate a Christlike love requires a relational mindset. Consistently focusing your attention on the interests of another will convince him or her to believe, "I'm really loved."

Real Love Affirms

Because Jesus suffered torture and death for us, we know we are recipients of his sacrificial love. But when we go to him in prayer and pour out our grief over the loss of a loved one, our hurt over a betrayal by a "friend," or our feeling of being abandoned by a colleague, how does God respond? He responds with an affirming love. Christ's sacrificial love, which motivated him to come to earth and live with us, enabled him to experience the same kind of losses and hurts we have experienced. Therefore we have confidence that he understands. He is with us in these hurts, saying, "I hurt for you. I know you are hurting and I'll be there for you." Christ's kind of love—an affirming love—is our pattern to be there for those who are suffering or struggling with the problems of life—and also for being happy with them when their life is going great.

Every day we encounter situations that enable us to model affirming love. Consider the following common situations: Your spouse arrives home from a trip to the store and confesses to a minor accident that bent the fender of the car. How do you respond?

Your 14-year-old daughter, a B-plus student, brings home a report card with three Cs and a D. What is the first thing you will say to her?

Your friend calls in frustration, saying he got into a fight with his supervisor and got fired today. What do you say to him?

---

* For more great questions by Mary DeMuth, go to www.marydemuth.com and click on "free stuff."

These trying situations, and countless others like them, reflect life in a world of difficulties and struggles. Humans make mistakes. Kids have problems. Friends get hurt. People get into trouble. Sometimes these incidents are genuine crises: a life-threatening disease or injury, the breakup of a serious relationship, the death of a friend or relative, an unplanned pregnancy, and so on. But most of the time, they are the relatively minor disappointments, losses, conflicts, and hurts of everyday life. Dealing with difficulties goes with the territory of living life as a human.

At these moments people are not in need of a pep talk, a lecture, or a fix-it plan. They need someone to identify with their pain and feel bad with them. Scripture tells us that "when others are happy, be happy with them. If they are sad, share their sorrow" (Romans 12:15). That is what an affirming love does. It impels you to identify with a person's situation, whether happy or sad, and to be there for them.

For years, I (Josh) didn't grasp the truth of an affirming love. Whenever Dottie came to me with a problem that she was struggling with, especially one that had caused her hurt, I would try to fix it. I wouldn't address her pain; rather I would address the problem that *caused* the pain.

One day Dottie came home from a meeting at school very hurt over what some mothers had said about one of our kids. In the past when she shared a problem like that with me, I would leap on the situation and say something like, "Honey, don't let it get to you. Here's what you need to do." Then I would outline a plan to fix the problem. It may have been a good plan, but it didn't address the pain Dottie felt at the moment. But on this particular occasion, I finally got it right. I simply put my arms around her and said, "Honey, I'm so sorry that you had to hear those words, and I hurt for you." That was it—no fix-it plan, no corrective measures outlined, just a heartfelt expression that identified with her pain.

Amazingly, it worked. Dottie felt affirmed and understood, and that was all she needed at the moment. A few days later she came back to me and asked what I thought she could do to address those critical comments about the family member. My fix-it plan was then welcomed.

We don't have to understand exactly what a person is going through in order to give them affirming love. A friend of ours found this out the hard way.

Once when his wife was at a very low point emotionally, he, in an effort to help her, said, "Honey, I know just what you're going through." She snapped back angrily, "No you don't! How dare you say you know what I'm going through?" My friend was speechless, but his wife was right. To share another person's sorrow does not mean that we necessarily know what he or she is going through. We cannot always participate in another person's unique experience. Rather, it means that because we know our friend is hurting, we *hurt* with that person. Our love causes us to identify with the one we love who is feeling pain. My friend should have said, "Honey, what you're going

Living out an affirming love brings healing to the pain of another and deepens your relationship with that person.

through must be tough, and I want you to know that I hurt because you hurt."

That's how we can identify with people's sorrow and pain without giving the impression that we know exactly how they feel—which they know is not true. Consider using words similar to these when your loved one is struggling and hurting. "What you're going through must really hurt you, and I want to let you know that I hurt for you. And I'll be here with you." Living out an affirming love brings healing to the pain of another and deepens your relationship with that person. Such a demonstration of love also pleases God, and he gives you the joy of being his minister of comfort. Paul tells us that Jesus "is the source of every mercy and the God who comforts us. He comforts us in all our troubles so that we can comfort others. When others are troubled, we will be able to give them the same comfort God has given us" (2 Corinthians 1:3-4). Loving others as Christ loves us ministers to others, brings us joy, and gives God honor.

■

Because of Christ's atoning sacrifice, we can be forgiven. Jesus loved us sacrificially, which is why he was willing to come to earth, live with us, and give himself up as our perfect sacrifice. The incarnation—God taking the form of a human—also enabled Jesus to experience what we have experienced and be there for us with an affirming love. Christ demonstrated real love for us, and he wants to love others that way through us. When we accept God's sacrificial and affirming love and in turn love others with this same sacrificial and affirming love, we are living out the truth of Christ's real love.

JUSTIFICATION
THROUGH FAITH

CHAPTER TWENTY-FOUR

WHAT MAKES US
RIGHT BEFORE GOD?

The crowd was silent. You could have heard a pin drop. I (Josh) had walked down into the audience and asked one of the deacons of the church sitting near the front this question: "How are you saved—how have you gained a relationship with Christ?" He answered without hesitation, "By faith—I am saved by faith." I looked at the entire congregation and then to him and said, "No, you're not. No one is ever saved by faith!" That is when the crowd went deathly silent and a chill swept over the auditorium. I went on to explain my statement before the crowd branded me with a capital "H" for heretic.

The truth is none of us is saved by faith. If we could be saved by faith, then Jesus didn't have to die for us. We could have saved ourselves simply by an exercise of faith.

Here's the question: Does faith and faith alone have any power? An entire generation is growing up today believing so. Many think that their choice to believe something has, in fact, the power to make that belief into their own truth. They seem to think if you believe something hard enough and sincerely enough, it will be the truth that will work for you.

But when it comes to truth about your salvation, there is only one power that can change your separated and lost status before God. Your faith has no power to save. Rather, it is the *object* of your faith that has the power to save, namely Jesus Christ—because Jesus, Son of the Almighty God, is the one who died for you and rose again to purchase your salvation. "It is by grace you have been saved, through faith—and this is not from yourselves, it is the gift of God" (Ephesians 2:8 NIV).

In Scripture, faith is never presented as the power that justifies or makes us right with God; rather, faith is the arm that reaches out to receive the saving grace of God. It is Jesus and Jesus only who has the power to forgive and raise us from death to life. That is why we are not saved *for* believing, but *through* believing in Jesus. If Jesus is not the Messiah, the Son of God who died on the cross for your sins, then your faith is absolutely "worthless."

The Absolute Necessity of Being Justified

Born dead spiritually, we can do nothing to gain favor with God. As we stated earlier, it is sin that continues to enslave all of us to a "life of death." But through faith in Christ we can be set free from a life of slavery to sin. Yet we still have a problem. We are still human beings tainted by sin. How can a holy God be in relationship with unholy and imperfect humans? God is so holy, as we indicated earlier, he "cannot allow sin in any form" (Habakkuk 1:13). But God had a solution. Redemption (purchasing us out of a life of slavery) also includes justification (being declared righteous before God).

By placing our faith in Jesus we are redeemed—purchased out of slavery; and justified—declared righteous before God.

As Paul explained it, "No one can ever be made right in God's sight by doing what his law commands, for the more we know God's law, the clearer it becomes that we aren't obeying it. But now God has shown us a different way of being right in his sight...We are made right in God's sight when we trust in Jesus Christ [place our faith in him] to take away our sins...God in his gracious kindness [grace] declares us not guilty" (Romans 3:20-24). So by placing our faith in Jesus we are redeemed—purchased out of slavery; and justified—declared righteous before God.

When God declares that we are right before him, he is establishing us as his people; he sets us apart from a life of continual sin. This set-apart life is called *sanctification.* Paul began his letter to the church in Corinth by addressing it "to those sanctified in Christ Jesus and called to be holy" (1 Corinthians 1:2 NIV). While being justified is a "declared righteous" state that comes into being instantly, sanctification is the process of continually being conformed to Christlikeness, as some churches teach; other churches emphasize sanctification as a separate instantaneous work followed by continued growth in holiness. Whichever emphasis you or your church makes, we are in right standing before God due to being redeemed, justified, and sanctified.

King David had sinned and sought forgiveness before God. He prayed, "Purify me from my sins, and I will be clean; wash me, and I will be whiter than snow" (Psalm

51:7). David was praying for an unobstructed relationship with a holy God. But how could David enjoy a redeemed, justified, and sanctified relationship with God prior to Christ's death? Jesus had not been born into the world yet. On the surface it would seem that David, having lived centuries prior to Christ's redeeming and justifying sacrifice, had no avenue by which to be cleansed and purified.

The answer is that the power of Christ's death and resurrection not only reaches forward in time to free us from sin today, it also reaches back in time to cover all those born prior to Jesus' sacrificial death (see Romans 3:25-26). Our righteousness before God is made possible through our trust in Jesus, because he solves our sin problem past, present, and future. Because of Christ's atoning death, we too can claim the promise God made to Israel: "No matter how deep the stain of your sins, I can remove it. I can make you as clean as freshly fallen snow. Even if you are stained as red as crimson, I can make you as white as wool" (Isaiah 1:18).

So is there nothing we can say to God or do for God that would merit our redemption? Is there nothing we can do to earn our justification? Is there nothing we can leverage to acquire sanctification? Paul asked and answered those questions when he wrote:

> Can we boast then, that we have done anything to be accepted by God? No, because our acquittal is not based on our good deeds. It is based on our faith [in Jesus]. So we are made right with God through faith and not by obeying the law (Romans 3:27-28).

Performance-based people who want to earn what they get may find salvation by grace through faith hard to grasp, or at least hard to accept. But there is no human requirement to obtain God's offer of a relationship except to freely accept it. It is a gift based upon the requirements fulfilled by Jesus. That is why when speaking of salvation Paul said, "It does not depend on the man who wills or the man who runs, but on God who has mercy" (Romans 9:16 NASB).

Therefore:

We believe the truth that being justified before God and cleansed of our sins is a result of God's grace through faith alone in Jesus as our sacrifice for sin.

Christ atoned for our sin by his death on the cross. When we place our faith in him as our substitute, we are redeemed and justified before God. We are set apart as his holy people. Not by what we have done, but because of what Christ has done. "Abraham believed God, and God counted him as righteous because of his faith. When people work, their wages are not a gift, but something they have earned. But people are counted as righteous not because of their work, but because of their faith in God who forgives sinners" (Romans 4:3-4 NLT).

CHAPTER TWENTY-FIVE

EVIDENCE THAT CHRIST
HAS THE POWER TO SAVE US

H er brother had been dead for four days. So Martha pointed out the obvious when her friend told the men to open up the tomb. "'Lord, by now the smell will be terrible...' Jesus responded, 'Didn't I tell you that you will see God's glory if you believe?'" (John 11:39-40).

Is the implication here that if Martha believed hard enough her brother, Lazarus, would be raised from the dead? Does believing have that kind of power? Not at all. There is no power in the act of believing in and of itself. The power of our faith resides in the object of what is believed. Unless Jesus was truly the Son of God all the believing in the world could not have raised Lazarus from the dead, and no amount of faith in Christ will save us if Jesus isn't truly the God-man. We cannot be redeemed and justified before God, given the gift of eternal life, unless Jesus is who he claimed to be—the Son of God, the acceptable

> *Jesus clearly intended his miracles to be understood as a validation of his identity as God's Son.*

sacrifice before God. It is important therefore to our confidence in salvation that we know with certainty that Jesus is indeed God in the flesh.

We have already discussed two reasons why we can have such a confident faith that Jesus is the Christ: He was virgin born, and he fulfilled all the messianic prophecies. But there is yet another piece of evidence to buttress our assurance. Jesus himself pointed out that his actions, like his miracle to raise Lazarus from the dead, were evidences that he is God's Son.

The Miracles of Christ

The following verses give us examples of how Jesus himself asserted that his miracles provided proof of his identity as the Son of God:

> I have a greater witness than John [the Baptist]—my teachings and my miracles. They have been assigned to me by the Father, and they testify that the Father has sent me (John 5:36).

> The miracles I do in my Father's name speak for me (John 10:25 NIV).

> Even though you do not believe me, believe the miracles, that you may know and understand that the Father is in me, and I in the Father (John 10:38 NIV).

Jesus clearly intended his miracles to be understood as a validation of his identity as God's Son. After his ascension his followers also pointed to his miracles as proofs of his identity. As the apostle Peter said on the Day of Pentecost, "God publically endorsed Jesus of Nazareth by doing wonderful miracles, wonders, and signs through him, as you well know" (Acts 2:22). The apostle John, pointing to Christ's identity as God, reports that Jesus did many other "miraculous signs" that weren't even recorded for us (John 20:30).

The most important miracle Jesus performed was rising from the dead. For if he had not conquered death, "your faith is useless, and you are still under condemnation for your sins" (1 Corinthians 15:17). We will devote two full chapters to his resurrection later in this book.

Imagine Walking with Jesus

Imagine being one of Jesus' disciples walking along beside him on a sunny Sabbath afternoon. You have just exited the temple, where religious leaders have accused Jesus of being possessed by a demon. They were so angry that they had come close to stoning him before you made your escape.

Walking briskly, you pass a blind beggar sitting cross-legged on the street. You proceed some distance before you realize that Jesus has not kept pace with you and his other disciples. You look back and see the Master gazing at the man, who is somewhat of a fixture in the area because he frequently begs at this spot. Though few know the beggar's name, most know his circumstances; he has been blind since birth.

You turn with the disciples, and tentatively, you approach the pair—the beggar and the teacher—wondering why Jesus has stopped here. One of Jesus' companions, always impetuous and eager to please, blurts out a question. "Teacher, why was this man born blind? Was it a result of his own sins or those of his parents?" (John 9:2)

Jesus, with characteristic kindness, plants his knees in the dirt beside the man and answers, more to him than to the questioner, "It was not because of his sins or his parents' sins…He was born blind so the power of God could be seen in him" (John 9:3).

The strangeness of Jesus' words echoes off the stone walls of the buildings that surround the scene. He explains that this man's eyes—which have never seen his mother's smile, never beheld the dazzling white marble of Herod's Temple reflecting the rays of the sun, never watched waves of wind wafting through the golden grain of a wheat field, never gazed on the face of a blushing young girl in love—have been dark all these years so the power of God can be seen in them today!

You and the others watch, your attention riveted on the man who has lived in darkness and the man who has called himself the light of the world. Jesus spits in the dust, not once but several times. No one speaks as he forms a mud pack in his carpenter's hands and patiently, tenderly, spreads the mud over the blind man's eyes.

Jesus speaks, "Go and wash in the pool of Siloam" (John 9:7). What happens next defies natural explanation; it even exceeds the comprehension of twenty-first-century medical science. When the man obeys Jesus and washes the mud from his eyes, he can see!

In an instant of time, one of the most complex organs in the human body is mended. Without a scalpel to gingerly remove the probable cause—a congenital cataract that had clouded the man's lenses—without a tiny suction tube to clear the clouded, jellylike orbs of vitreous humor, the man's eyes are healed. There was no laser surgery to reattach the retinas. There was no highly sophisticated serum applied to the complex layer of light-sensing cells at the back of the eyes that allowed 7 million cones and 125 million rods to once more send their coded messages of light to the brain via the millions of fibers that comprise the optic nerve. And there was no prescribed therapy for the permanent amblyopia inside the man's eyes—the underdevelopment of the visual system resulting from decades of disuse.[1]

Twenty centuries later, such congenital blindness is still often irreparable, even if the surgery is performed by the most skilled surgeons in the most advanced operating room of the best hospital in the world. But Jesus, the Galilean carpenter, performed it in an instant, using mud and his own saliva as his only tools.

As fascinating as this healing is—and it's just one among the many miracles Jesus performed—it should not be surprising. Though the task of removing cataracts, reattaching retinas, and reconstructing the ultrasensitive machinery of the human eye is a highly specialized and still-evolving field of modern medicine, it was no great feat for Jesus of Nazareth—because he is Creator God, the architect of the human eye.

"I Believe!"

The healing of the man who had been born blind was more than simply miraculous to those who first heard about it—to some, it was disturbing. When the news got to the Pharisees, it caused a stir: "Some of the Pharisees said, 'This man Jesus is not from God, for he is working on the Sabbath.' Others said, 'But how could an ordinary sinner do such miraculous signs?' So there was a deep division of opinion among them" (John 9:16).

The healing of the man born blind was mind-boggling to Jesus' critics. Many of the Pharisees had already rejected him as the Messiah. He had not measured up to their political and religious expectations. The kingdom he was proclaiming called for humility, repentance, servanthood, and devotion to the person of God. They expected the Messiah to insist on devotion to a body of rabbinical rules and regulations in order to purify the people for their national destiny. So they wanted nothing to do with Jesus' relational brand of religion. Yet his miracles presented them with a major dilemma. How could they accept a man who did not share their nationalistic ambitions; and yet how could they reject a man who exhibited such astounding powers?

First, the Pharisees decided to investigate. They called for the healed man to come before them to explain what had happened. Then they called for his parents to confirm that he in fact had been born blind. Finally, they brought the man back again for cross-examination, hoping to resolve the dilemma.

The truth is, their investigation was not really open and objective, because they could not bring themselves to believe what the miracle clearly indicated: that Jesus was more than a man. And yet, they could not explain how a mere man—a man they presumed to be a sinner like themselves—could perform such a miracle (see John 9:17-22). To their questions, the formerly blind man replied, "I don't know whether he is a sinner...But I know this: I was blind, and now I can see!...Never since the world began has anyone been able to open the eyes of someone born blind. If this man were not from God, he couldn't do it" (John 9:25, 32-33).

John's account concludes the story:

> When Jesus heard what had happened, he found the man and said, "Do you believe in the Son of Man?"
>
> The man answered, "Who is he, sir, because I would like to." [Remember, this man had no idea what Jesus looked like; he had never seen him before.]
>
> "You have seen him," Jesus said, "and he is speaking to you!"
>
> "Yes, Lord," the man said, "I believe!" And he worshiped Jesus (John 9:35-38).

The man who had been born blind had no trouble seeing the truth because the Truth was standing before him. This man who could work miracles was more than merely human. "I was blind, and now I can see!" the healed man said, citing the evidence that would soon convince him. "If this man were not from God, he couldn't do it." But Jesus *did* do it; he had the power to perform this and other miraculous works because he was the Chosen One (see John 1:1). His power simply reflected his identity.

Who else but God has the mastery Jesus demonstrated over the human body, weather, gravity, and even death itself? Who else but God's Son could do these things?[2]

- calm a storm (see Matthew 8)
- make a mute person speak (see Matthew 9)
- feed 5000 people with five loaves and two fish (see Matthew 14)
- cast out demons (see Mark 5)
- walk on water (see Mark 6)
- bring sight to the blind (see Mark 10)
- curse a fig tree (see Mark 11)
- foretell the future (see Mark 14)
- heal a paralyzed man (see Luke 5)
- raise a boy from the dead (see Luke 7)
- heal incurable hemorrhaging (see Luke 8)
- cleanse lepers (see Luke 17)
- turn water into wine (see John 2)
- make the lame walk (see John 5)
- forgive sin (see John 8)
- raise a man from the dead (see John 11)

■

The miracles of Jesus provide convincing evidences that Jesus was the perfect Lamb of God who sacrificed himself so you and I might be redeemed and justified before God. Jesus said, "Believe that I am in the Father and the Father is in me. Or at least believe because of what you have seen me do" (John 14:11). When we place our faith in Jesus, we can be confident that he is the One who God accepts as a sacrifice on our behalf. Being declared righteous in spite of our sins means "there is no condemnation for those who belong to Christ Jesus. For the power of the life-giving Spirit has freed you through Christ Jesus from the power of sin that leads to death" (Romans 8:1-2). Your death sentence has been commuted, and you are a child of God!

CHAPTER TWENTY-SIX

The Joy of Salvation

Imagine being transported to a great courtroom. Almighty God sits as Judge behind a towering desk; the prosecution table is to his left and the defense table is on his right. You identify Satan standing at the prosecution table, while a frightened-looking man sits alone at the defense table. The court clerk proclaims loudly, "Case #8032666." The Great Judge responds, "Proceed."

"Your...*Honor,*" Satan sneers at the judge as he motions toward the cowering defendant. "I know I don't have to tell you all the sins the accused has committed. His sins of adultery alone are enough to convict him, not to mention his heritage from Adam. Exhibit A details the times and dates the accused lusted after women—65,243 times. To make matters worse, the lines marked in red on the chart show the occasions when the man's lust led him to actual adultery. For example, in July 19—"

"All right, all right," the man interrupts. "That's enough."

"How do you plead?" the Judge asks.

"Not guilty, Your Honor, because I do have a defense."

"Proceed," the Judge says with a nod.

"It really wasn't my fault," the man begins. "My secretary was a lonely woman, and what I did was out of a heart of compassion. You see, she was abused by her husband, and someone had to comfort her. I was there, and—"

"Immaterial!" Satan shouts. "It doesn't matter why, Your Honor. The simple fact that he committed the deed is all that counts. His so-called reasons are mere excuses. This man's a sinner." He lifts a ream of paper into the air and shakes it. "And your law says, 'The soul who sins will die'" (Ezekiel 18:4 NASB).

"I...I may be a sinner, but...I have another defense, Your Honor," the accused stammers.

"Proceed," the Judge states.

"I know you are fair and just," he replies. "So I offer here all the good I have done throughout my life as a defense." Three men entered, carrying large notebooks filled with paper. "I have compiled my noble deeds of kindness. I have recorded how I helped my fellow humans, gave some of my time and considerable sums of money to ease the suffering of others. Furthermore, I faithfully loved my second wife." The man smiles proudly. "So, you see, my good deeds are many while my adulteries are few—by comparison, at least. Clearly the good far outweighs what little bad I've done."

"Immaterial!" Satan shouts. He faces the man. "It doesn't matter how much good you've done, you're still a sinner. That's all this court needs to know. And all sinners are *mine*!"

"No, I'm not!" the man objects.

"Oh yes, you are," Satan retorts. "Let's look at the heritage issue. Are you a son of Adam?"

"Of course," the man answers. "All humans are. What's that got to do with anything?"

"Everything!" Satan snaps. He speaks to the Judge without taking his eyes off the man. "Your Honor, I appeal to the eternal words of the court: 'Sin entered the world through one man, and death through sin, and in this way death came to all men, because all sinned'" (Romans 5:12 NIV). He points to the man. "Good deeds can't erase your sin, Mister, and nothing you can do will commute your death sentence!"

Satan turns to the Judge, an expression of smug satisfaction on his face. "I rest my case, Your Honor. You have no alternative but to administer justice and hand down a sentence of death."

"So it is written," the Great Judge states, certainty and sadness mingling in his voice. "The wages of sin is death" (Romans 6:23). He bangs the gavel on his desk, and two demon guards enter and drag the man from the courtroom, slumped and sobbing bitterly. Satan follows, hissing at him all the way.

Suddenly you are ushered to the defense table, and you lower your head in shame at what you fear will be revealed.

The Judge reads from a sheet in front of him. "Case number 2308777." He looks at you and says, "How do *you* plead?"

"Not guilty, Your Honor," you answer.

"So entered," says the Great Judge. "The prosecution may make its case."

Satan strides forward, cocky, arrogant, his pitiless countenance exuding contempt and disdain. "So you think you're innocent," he sneers. "I happen to know otherwise. I have a long record of all your sins, and they are legion." Satan proceeds to list your sins, one after the other—pride, envy, lust, greed, bursts of uncontrolled anger, hatred, selfishness—giving example after example of your worst sins. You hang your head in shame as the list goes on and on. Finally he stops, looks at the Great Judge, and says, "And Your Honor, these are things the defendant did in only one year." Turning to you he says, "Shall I continue, or do you want to change your plea?"

"I stand by my plea," you say.

Satan cackles in fiendish derision. "What kind of fool are you? You have no defense! According to the law, your birth as a sinner warrants your death. And to top that off, your list of sins would sink a battleship. You may as well quit wasting the court's time. You have no possible defense, and it's an outrage that you even pretend to be innocent."

You stand and reply, "It's true, I have no right to plead innocent. I would stand before this holy court condemned by my very nature and guilty in thought and deed of all you accuse me of. Except for one thing."

"And just what could that one thing possibly be?" replies Satan, his voice dripping with snide contempt.

You swallow hard, drop to your knees, gaze up at the Judge, and cry out, "Mercy, Your Honor." At that moment a figure you had somehow failed to notice stands up beside the Great Judge and makes his way toward you. He gives you a nod and a smile, indicating that you should continue. You clear your throat, stand to your feet, and continue. "I have sinned. I have been a slave to sin and death."

"Now you're talking my language," Satan chimes in.

"And there is no question I deserve death," you continue. "But I claim the blood of my dear Savior Jesus Christ, which has cleansed me from my sins and wiped all guilt away." By this time the figure from behind the Judge's bench has made his way to your side. He speaks.

"It is true—this human is guilty of death." At that point Satan breaks out in applause. The Great Judge raises his hand. "Silence!" he demands.

"Death is the payment for sin," the figure at your side continues. "And I have made that payment myself."

"Objection!" Satan screams out.

"Overruled!" The word booms out in the mighty voice of the Great Judge. You feel a hand gently squeeze your shoulder. You look up and see that it is Jesus who stands beside you.

"It is true," Jesus states, his voice strong and confident. "I, God the Son, have paid the debt of sin on this human's behalf." Then Jesus looks at you as he continues. "And you, my child, have placed your complete trust in me as your defense."

"Preposterous!" Satan screams at the Great Judge. "You can't allow this kind of double-talk. Who's in charge here anyway? The law must rule—'The soul who sins will die.'" Satan turns toward Jesus and glares. "The defendant sinned, thus it is the human who is deserving of death, not you." Satan jabs his pointing finger at Jesus. "So it's the defendant who must die."

Jesus addresses the Great Judge, saying, "The prosecution is making my case for me, Your Honor. He is absolutely right—I was not deserving of death, and thus I was a perfect substitute for my client."

"This is crazy…outrageous! Unfair! It's…it's not legal," Satan bellows.

"Apparently the prosecution has forgotten your infallible words, Your Honor," Jesus responds. "If the court please, I will refresh his memory by asking my client to read from your holy writings." Jesus hands you God's holy words and points to a passage. He smiles assurance at you and whispers, "Read it loud and with confidence." You clear your throat again and read. "'God put into effect a different plan to save me. He sent his own Son in a human body like mine, except that mine is sinful. God destroyed sin's control over me by giving his Son as a sacrifice for my sins'" (Romans 8:3 paraphrased).

"No. No. No!" Satan yells out beating the table with his fist. "That's not fair. That's mercy, and I can't stand mercy. Besides, that's not what this court is about. Your Honor, you are a just Judge, and I know you will insist on justice. In fact, I demand justice!"

Jesus looks up at the Great Judge and says, "Justice has been done, Your Honor. Sin was committed, and my death as God the Son paid the penalty for it. Now that justice has been served, this court has every right to extend mercy and exonerate this human. My dear friend here is legally innocent because I have taken all sins committed upon myself and suffered the penalty. Is that not true, Father?"

"It is written in my eternal Word," the Judge began. He looks straight at you as he continues. "'You are made right in my sight when you trust in my Son, Jesus Christ, to take away your sins'" (see Romans 3:22). "And your testimony here is that you have done that, correct?"

"Right!" you say without hesitation.

"No! No! No! No!" Satan screams. "This wretch is a sinner through and through. I've shown you the evidence. The human has fallen short of your standards of rightness. Far short! I insist payment of the wage—eternal death for this child of Adam."

The Judge lifts his hand and says, "Silence in my court! The payment of death has been made. The sins of this human are abolished; they are cast as far as the east is from the west. And this child of Adam is now a child of God. It is written, 'Yet, now, I in my gracious kindness declare you,' he looks directly into your eyes, 'not guilty. I have done this through Christ Jesus, who has freed you by taking away your sins'" (see Romans 3:24).

You feel the arm of your defender wrap around your shoulder as he pulls you to him. You look into his face. He smiles and gives you a wink of assurance.

The Great Judge continues to read. "'I sent Jesus to take the punishment for your sins and to satisfy my anger against you. You are made right with me when you believe that Jesus shed his blood, sacrificing his life for you'" (see Romans 3:25).

"Not fair or just! Not fair or just!" Satan screeches.

The Judge raises his hand to bring silence again and says. "'I am entirely fair and just in this present time when I declare this sinner to be right in my sight because [this child of mine] believes in Jesus'" (see Romans 3:26).

With that the Great Judge pounds his gavel thunderously on the great judgment desk and declares, "This person is justified by my grace through faith in Jesus. Case dismissed!"

■

The essence of this fictional illustration is absolutely true. The telling passages from Romans 3, while personalized within the context of our story, are not fiction at all, but direct scriptural quotes. The majority of people may believe their good deeds will persuade God to give them a place in heaven. The reality is, your death sentence, your wages of sin, is commuted and you are redeemed and justified before God through your faith alone in Christ. And just as important, because of Christ's sacrifice and your faith in him, your status as a son or daughter of Adam has changed. You are now a child of God.

Your Joy Made Complete

"Long ago, even before he made the world, God loved us and chose us in Christ to be holy and without fault in his eyes. His unchanging plan has always been to adopt us into his own family by bringing us to himself through Jesus Christ. And this gave him great pleasure" (Ephesians 1:4-5). You were born dead. You were alone, abandoned, and without love because of sin. You were afraid, disconnected, and without a true family connection. But now, if you have trusted in Jesus, you have a real family and you are somebody special. The apostle Paul said that "God has sent the Spirit of his Son into our hearts prompting us to call out, 'Abba, Father [or Daddy]'" (Galatians 4:6 NLT).

As a result of being justified before God, his Holy Spirit enters our lives and we are adopted into his family. We not only receive his eternal life and can call God our Daddy, but "since we are his children, we will share his treasures—for everything God gives to his Son, Christ, is ours too" (Romans 8:17).

We have been freed from sin, received peace of mind and heart, released from guilt, given a reason for living, and provided hope of eternal life with him.

Chosen, redeemed, justified, sanctified, adopted into a family, given eternal life, and willed an eternal inheritance! What more could we ask?

King David spoke of this, describing the happiness of an undeserving sinner who is declared to be righteous:

> Oh, what joy for those whose disobedience is forgiven, whose sins are put out of sight. Yes, what joy for those whose sin is no longer counted against them by the Lord (Romans 4:6-8).

In effect Jesus is saying to you, "I have come to earth, demonstrated my love by giving my life for you, and I ask you to trust in me as your only solution to life, 'so that my joy may be in you and that your joy may be complete'" (John 15:11 NIV). "He [Christ] himself gives life and breath to everything, and he satisfies every need there is" (Acts 17:25). Your completion, your total joy and happiness, is found in a relationship with God as your Daddy. He didn't have to save you. But by his grace he grants you an adoptive relationship—and all of us who have placed our faith in Jesus. We have been freed from sin, received peace of mind and heart, released from guilt, given a reason for living, and provided hope of eternal life with him. "We've been given a brand-new life and have everything to live for, including a future in heaven—and the future starts now!" (1 Peter 1:3-4 MSG).

One of the Greatest Joys of My Life

From the age of 11, when I (Josh) left that corn bin feeling abandoned, alone, and angry, I was determined to find happiness. I have explained how my quest to find it took me through religion, education, and prestige, only to be disappointed at each turn. But God was faithful to me. I didn't love him, but he loved me. I could sense Jesus at the door of my heart pleading, "Look, I have been standing at your door and constantly knocking. If you hear me calling and will open the door I will come in" (paraphrased from Revelation 3:20). I was in my second year at the university and I was keeping that door shut and bolted. I didn't care if Jesus did walk on water or turn water into wine. I didn't want any party pooper spoiling my fun. I couldn't think of any faster way to ruin my good times. I called them good times, but I was really miserable. I was a walking battlefield. My mind was telling me that Christianity was true, but my will was resisting it with all the energy it could muster.

Then there was the pride problem. At that time the thought of becoming a Christian shattered my ego. I had just proved that all my previous thinking had been wrong and my friends had been right. Every time I got around those enthusiastic Christians, the inner conflict would boil over. If you've ever been in the company of happy people when you are miserable, you know how their joy can get under your skin. Sometimes I would literally get up, leave the group, and run right out of the student union. It came to the point where I would go to bed at ten o'clock at night but wouldn't get to sleep until four in the morning. I couldn't let go of the problem. I had to do something before it drove me out of my mind.

It was at that point that I took a step of intelligent faith. I turned my back on my old life and placed my trust in Jesus as my sacrifice for sin—my Savior. And I can say with Paul, "How differently I think about him [Jesus] now! What this means is that those who become Christians become new persons. They are not the same anymore, for the old life is gone. A new life has begun!" (2 Corinthians 5:16-17).

For me, one aspect of this new life was peace—the relief from my restlessness. Before I trusted Christ, I always had to be occupied. I had to be over at my girlfriend's place, at a party, at the student union, or running around with friends. I'd walk across the campus with my mind in a whirlwind of conflicts. I was always bouncing off the walls. I'd sit down and try to study or cogitate but couldn't do it. But after I turned my life over to Jesus, a kind of mental peace settled over me. Don't misunderstand; I don't mean all conflicts ceased. What I found in this relationship with Jesus wasn't so much the absence of conflict as the ability to cope with it. I wouldn't trade that for anything in the world.

Another area that began to change for the better was related to my bad temper. I used to blow my stack if anyone just looked at me cross-eyed. I still have the scars from a fight in which I almost killed a man in my first year at the university. My temper was such a part of me that I didn't consciously seek to change it. But one day I encountered a crisis that should have set me off, only to find that I stayed calm and collected. My temper was gone! It wasn't my doing; Jesus had given me a new life. That doesn't mean I was perfect. I went 14 years without losing my temper, but when I did blow it, I'm afraid I made up for all those times I didn't.

Jesus changed me in another way. My old life consisted of hatred. I had a heavy load of hatred weighing me down. It sapped the joy out of my life. It didn't show outwardly, but it kept grinding away inwardly and made life miserable. I was ticked off with people, with things, with issues. I was insecure. Every time I met anyone different from me, that person became a threat, and I reacted with some level of hatred.

But I hated one man more than anyone else in the world...and that was my father. I was mortified that he was the town alcoholic. If you're from a small town and one of your parents is an alcoholic, you know what I mean. Everybody knows. My high school friends would make jokes about my father's drinking. They didn't think it bothered me because I fell in with the joking and laughed with them. I was laughing on the outside, but let me tell you, I was crying on the inside. I would go to the barn and find my mother beaten so badly by my father that she couldn't get up, lying in the manure behind the cows. That tore me up as a kid. When we had friends over, I would take my drunken father out to the barn, tie him up, and park his car behind the silo. I was ashamed of anyone seeing him that way. We would tell our guests he'd had to go somewhere. I don't think anyone could hate a person more than I hated my father.

About five months after I placed my faith in Christ, a love from God entered my life so powerfully that it took that hatred, turned it upside down, and emptied it out. In its place God gave me love and joy. I was able to look my father squarely in the eyes and say, "Dad, I love you." And I really meant it. After some of the things I'd done to him, that really shook him up.

After I transferred to a private university, a serious car accident put me in the hospital. When I was moved home to recover, my father came to visit me. Remarkably, he was sober that day. But he seemed uneasy, pacing about the room. Then he blurted out, "Son, how can you love a father like me?" I answered, "Dad, six months ago I despised you." Then I shared with him the story of my research and conclusions about Jesus Christ. I told him, "I have placed my trust in Christ, received God's forgiveness, invited him into my life, and he has changed me. I can't explain it all, Dad, but God has taken away my hatred and replaced it with the capacity to love. I love you and accept you just the way you are."

We talked for almost an hour, and then I received one of the greatest joys of my life. This man who was my father, this man who knew me too well for me to pull the wool over his eyes, looked at me and said, "Son, if God can do in my life what I've seen him do in yours, then I want to give him the opportunity. I want to trust him as my Savior and Lord."

Usually after a person places their trust in Christ, the changes in his or her life occur over a period of days, weeks, months, or even years. In my own life the change took about six to eighteen months, and there are still changes taking place. But the life of my father changed right before my eyes. It was as if God reached down and flipped on the light switch. Never before or since have I seen such a dramatic change. My father touched an alcoholic beverage only once after that day. He got it as far as his lips before thrusting it away. Forever. I can come to only one conclusion: A relationship with Jesus Christ changes lives, and that makes our joy complete.[1]

CHAPTER TWENTY-SEVEN

EXPLAINING HOW TO HAVE A RELATIONSHIP WITH GOD

God went to extraordinary lengths to form a relationship with you. He left heaven, died a torturous death, and rose again to raise you to new life in him. Again, he did all this because "he is a God who is passionate about his relationship with you" (Exodus 34:14).

So, if you do not have that relationship and want to find it, what steps should you take? Here is a simple presentation of the gospel story that you can use as a guide to establishing a relationship with God—or to lead someone you know into that relationship.

1. Can you really know God personally?

- God does *love* you. "This is real love. It is not that we loved God, but that he loved us" (1 John 4:10).

- God has a *plan* for you to know him personally. "Now this is eternal life: that they may know you, the only true God, and Jesus Christ, whom you have sent" (John 17:3 NIV).

- God has a *future* for you. "You can claim the promise God made to the children of Israel when he said, 'I know the plans I have for you,' declares the LORD, 'plans for welfare and not for calamity to give you a future and a hope'" (Jeremiah 29:11 NASB).

2. What prevents us from knowing God personally?

- Humans are *sinful.* "All have sinned and fall short of the glory of God" (Romans 3:23 NIV).

  Although we were created to have a relationship with God, because of our self-centeredness, we choose to go our own independent way in disobedience to him. This self-will, characterized by an attitude of active rebellion or passive indifference, is an evidence of what the Bible calls sin.

- Humans are *separated.* "The wages of sin is death" (Romans 6:23). The death Paul speaks of here is not mere physical death, but spiritual separation from God. It means that "those who do not know God and do not obey the gospel of our Lord Jesus…will be punished with everlasting destruction and shut out from the presence of the Lord" (2 Thessalonians 1:8-9 NIV).

  This sin, which is manifested in each of our individual lives, separates us from experiencing God's love and from an intimate relationship with him. Such separation brings both earthly turmoil and eternal consequences.

3. God provided a way to bridge this separation.

Jesus Christ, God's Son, is God's *only* provision for our sin. Through him alone we can know God personally and experience his love.

- *Christ died in our place.* "God sent Jesus to take the punishment for our sins and to satisfy God's anger against us" (Romans 3:25).

- *Christ rose from the dead.* "Christ died for our sins…He was buried, and he was raised from the dead on the third day, as the Scriptures said. He was seen by Peter and then by the twelve apostles. After that, he was seen by more than five hundred" (1 Corinthians 15:3-6).

- *Christ is the only way to God.* Jesus said, "I am the way, the truth, and the life. No one can come to the Father except through me" (John 14:6).

But…

4. It is not enough just to know these truths.

- We must individually *receive* Jesus Christ as Savior and Lord; then we can know God personally and experience his love. "To all who received him, to those who believed in his name, he gave the right to become children of God" (John 1:12 NIV).

- We receive Christ through faith, placing our trust in him, his power and authority. "It is by grace you have been saved, through faith—and this not from yourselves, it is the gift of God—not by works, so that no one can boast" (Ephesians 2:8,9 NIV).

- We receive Christ by accepting his personal invitation. He says, "Look! Here I stand at the door and knock. If you hear me calling and open the door, I will come in" (Revelation 3:20).

And…

5. When we receive Christ, we are changed.

- When we receive him by faith, as an act of our will, we experience a new life. "He died for everyone so that those who receive his new life will no longer live to please themselves. Instead, they will live to please Christ" (2 Corinthians 5:15).

  Just to agree intellectually that Jesus Christ is the Son of God and that he died on the cross for our sins does not qualify as faith. Faith requires a serious renouncing of one's previous ways and a trust in God to direct the future. Mere intellectual belief is not adequate to have Christ come into your life. Nor is it enough to have an emotional religious experience. Receiving Christ involves turning to God from self (repentance) and trusting Christ to come into our lives to forgive us of our sins and to make us what he wants us to be.

6. The Bible promises eternal life to all who receive Christ.

- When we receive him, we are assured of eternal life in heaven and joy here on earth. "God has given us eternal life, and this life is in his Son. He who has the Son has life; he who does not have the Son of God does not have life. I write these things to you who believe in the name of the Son of God so that you may know that you have eternal life" (1 John 5:11-13 NIV).

If you have not yet trusted in Christ by faith, you can do so right now. The words of the following prayer are not magical; they are simply a suggestion to enable you to express a sincere desire to turn from self to God:

> *"Lord Jesus, I believe that you are who you claim to be, and I want to know you personally. Thank you for dying on the cross for my sins. I accept your forgiveness and place my trust in you as my Savior and Lord. Come into my heart and make me the person you created me to be. In your name. Amen."*

A New Beginning

If you just now placed your trust in Jesus, or if you have just led someone to trust him for salvation, you or your acquaintance has embarked on a new beginning. "Those who become Christians become new persons. They are not the same anymore, for the old life is gone. A new life has begun!" (2 Corinthians 5:17). What does this mean?

- You have *recognized* that you had a problem. You had sinned against God and had gone your own way.

- You have *realized* that Jesus is your only solution. You asked God to forgive you of your sins. You turned away from your old life and turned to Jesus as your only hope of a relationship with God.

- You have *responded* to Jesus in faith, placing your trust in him as your Savior—the one who took your place.

- You have *relied* upon Jesus to raise you from death to life. In faith you reached out and received his gift of eternal life, and you now have an adopted relationship in God's family.*

What's next? The remaining chapters of this book explain your purpose and mission as a transformed follower of Christ. God does have a plan for your life and mine.

Leading a Person to Jesus

One of the keys to leading a person to Christ or nurturing someone to spiritual health is developing a relationship with that person. Since you will have established a relationship with the person to whom you present the gospel message, you will find it's good to have another effective tool in your arsenal. There is no better way to show an example of what it means to be a Christian than your own testimony. A testimony is a simple sharing of what Christ has done in your life. It can be a powerful tool if developed properly. Scripture tells us, "They have defeated him [Satan] because of the blood of the Lamb and because of their testimony" (Revelation 12:11). It is not difficult to develop your own story in a way that can be concisely and effectively shared. Here are some guidelines.

How to Prepare Your Personal Testimony

Before you begin, ask God to give you wisdom and guidance in coming up with an effective presentation. Then you can use the following three-point outline as a framework for putting together your own personal story.

---

* Hundreds of thousands of people have been led to a personal relationship with God through the simple presentation of the gospel given to you above. This presentation is drawn from a booklet entitled *Would You Like to Know God Personally?* published by New Life Publications, a ministry of Campus Crusade for Christ. You can order quantities of that booklet by going online to www.campuscrusade.com/nlp_outreach_tools.htm.

✓ **My life before knowing Christ.**

    a. Make your first sentence interesting and attention-getting.

    b. Include the good elements of your life before Christ (for example, good person, athlete, achievements, moral, generous, church attender, and so on).

    c. Identify one key problem (for example, lack of joy, lack of purpose, pride, wrong priorities) that characterized your life before you became a Christ-follower.

    d. Show how this problem affected your life.

    OR if you had a childhood conversion, describe your "early years."

    e. Tell of how you were provided for as a child (for example, physical needs of food and shelter were provided for by your parents or guardians).

    f. Tell of how your need for a personal relationship with God was made evident (for example, "at the age of _____ I became aware of my spiritual need to know God").

✓ **How I came to Christ.**

    a. Be specific.

    b. Avoid confusing statements (for example, "I went forward," "I marked a card"). Also avoid "Christianese" (for example, "I was redeemed by the propitiatory, substitutionary death of the Lamb," and so on).

    c. Talk about Christ and his work (that is, actually give a gospel presentation within your testimony).

✓ **My life since I trusted Christ.**

    a. Describe how life has changed since you accepted Christ (for example, what problem he has helped you with, how he has affected your actions and attitudes, and so on).

    b. Tell how Christ dealt with your problem or, if yours was an early childhood conversion, give one positive benefit of following Christ (for example, joy, peace, hope of eternal life, no fear of death, forgiveness of sin, purposeful life).

    c. Be honest, positive, and realistic (for example, "Not all of my problems in this life have been eliminated").

    d. Include an appeal to know God personally.

    e. Close with a strong, impelling conclusion.

✓ **Avoid:**

- Clichés that are meaningless to the non-Christian, such as "blessings," "born again," "praise God," "conversion," "redeemed," "glorious," and so on.

- Vague generalities about what has happened in your life. Be specific.

- Being critical of any churches, denominations, or individuals.

- Employing too many overused catchwords such as "fantastic," "exciting," "awesome," and so on.

- Preaching. Just share your experience.

To further help develop your own testimony we have provided two examples of what a testimony might sound like.

Testimony example #1: *Early childhood conversion.*

(My life before Christ) I had parents who genuinely loved me and cared for me as a child. Even though they were never rich, they always provided for my most basic needs of food, clothing, shelter, and love. Along with providing for my physical needs, my parents also made me aware of my need for a spiritual life.

(How I met Christ) When I was six years old, my father and I attended a funeral service. As we were walking through the cemetery grounds, I asked him a basic question I think we all ask some time or another. That question was, "Dad, where do you go when you die?" My father answered that question by using the Bible and showing me that there are two possible destinations for us after death...heaven and hell. He also explained that the Bible was written that we might know for certain that we can have eternal life...or heaven (1 John 5:13). Dad told me that heaven was the benefit given by God for those who would become Christ-followers. He said that following Christ was as simple as depending on Christ to guide my life instead of myself.

(Since I met Christ) Since I've become a Christ-follower, I have never feared death because Christ has promised that as his follower I will live forever with him in heaven. Don't get me wrong, my life isn't perfect; I still face many of the same problems you do. But the assurance of eternal life gives me a peace and confidence in which to face these problems.

If you don't mind, I would like to share with you how you too can have a personal relationship with God and have the certainty of eternal life.

Testimony example #2: *Later-life conversion.*

(My life before Christ) At age 20 I realized that I was putting up a front—looking good on the outside but hitting a lot of peaks and valleys on the inside. I spent a lot of time searching for a personal relationship that would last, but I was disappointed time after time until I found it in friendship with Jesus Christ.

(How I met Christ) When I gave my life to Jesus Christ, I began to understand that true, meaningful relationships begin with a relationship with God. I didn't know how to find that relationship until a friend explained it to me. He said that God loved me and sent His Son to pay the penalty for my sin so I could have a personal relationship with God. Because my friend cared enough for me to tell me the truth, I asked Jesus Christ into my life.

(Since I met Christ) My Christian faith has helped me put my priorities in order. Since I made God number one and keep his priorities in my life, I have found a new understanding of what it means to have a friend who cares about you. Jesus has become my best friend, and that has helped me be a better friend to others.

Additional opportunities for leading a person to Christ may be found in celebration of the Judeo-Christian Passover meal, the Redemption Celebration, outlined in appendix A of this book. As we mentioned earlier, we have included detailed instructions for preparing this meal and conducting the celebration. The celebration includes an opportunity for participants, even your children, to place their trust in Christ as Savior.

TRUTH SEVEN

LIVING THE TRANSFORMED LIFE

CHAPTER TWENTY-EIGHT

Understanding Your Purpose

Carl is hungry all the time. He is obsessed with eating. He thinks of nothing except keeping his stomach full. You see, Carl is a caterpillar, and as a caterpillar he will shed his skin four or five times in order to make room for the steady supply of leaves his insatiable appetite demands. In fact, he will increase his weight ten-thousand-fold in less than 20 days. His gluttonous appetite will cause tremendous damage to crops and the economy of humans. There is nothing of lasting value or worth to say about Carl the caterpillar.

But something marvelous is about to happen to Carl. Deep inside something calls him to stop eating and yield to a process of being fully encapsulated by a mysterious substance that hardens around him.

Many days pass, and then it happens. Carl bursts out of his cocoon. He has undergone a radical change called metamorphosis. He is now a new creature with new habits and a whole new look...because Carl the caterpillar, obsessed only with fulfilling his gluttonous appetite, has been transformed into a beautiful butterfly. He no longer crawls about with a ravenous appetite that destroys crops. He now soars through the air, flying from plant to plant, pollinating flowers to enhance the beauty of his world.[1]

> *Our transformation changes us from self-seeking creatures to godlike beings.*

Our Metamorphosis to Be like Christ

"Those who live only to satisfy their own sinful desires," Paul the apostle says, "will harvest the consequences of decay and death" (Galatians 6:8). Like Carl the caterpillar, "their god is their appetite, they brag about shameful things, and all they think about is this life here on earth" (Philippians 3:19).

But deep within our souls a voice is heard. It is the voice of God that calls us out of sin and death so a miraculous metamorphosis can take place. For "those who become Christians become new persons. They are not the same anymore, for the old life is gone. A new life has begun! All this newness of life is from God, who brought us back to himself through what Christ did" (2 Corinthians 5:17-18).

Our transformation changes us from self-seeking creatures to godlike beings. "God knew his people in advance," Paul declared, "and he chose them to become like his Son" (Romans 8:29). Even though sin broke our relationship with God and we crawled about fulfilling our own sinful appetites, because of Christ our Godlikeness is restored, as "we, who with unveiled faces all reflect the Lord's glory, are being transformed into his likeness with ever-increasing glory, which comes from the Lord, who is the Spirit" (2 Corinthians 3:18 NIV).

"You must display a new nature," Scripture says, "because you are a new person, created in God's likeness—righteous, holy, and true" (Ephesians 4:23). As redeemed, justified, sanctified, and adopted children of God, "his divine power gives us everything we need for living a godly life...And by that same mighty power...he has promised... that you will share in his divine nature" (2 Peter 1:3-4). When God raises us to new life he imparts his DNA to us so we can be a living replica of Christ. That is the root meaning of Christian— "Little Christ."

"God loved us and chose us in Christ to be holy and without fault in his eyes. His unchanging plan has always been to adopt us into his own family by bringing us to himself through Jesus Christ. And this gave him great pleasure" (Ephesians 1:4-5). Just as we humans take pleasure in our children looking and acting like us, so our heavenly Father exults to see each of us transformed into a new person who is becoming more and more like his Son.

I (Sean) will never forget the birth of our first child. It had been a long day, and when Stephanie told me it was time to take her to the hospital I was both excited and a little scared. I would be a father. That was going to be a new and frightening experience all rolled into one.

Then little Scottie was delivered. And I was a proud father. I have to admit that as I looked at him I searched for any resemblance he might have to Stephanie or me. Did he have my nose or Stephanie's eyes? Did he have my color hair, or was the shape of his face like Stephanie's? For some reason I wanted my offspring to have a resemblance to me and his mother.

By the time Scottie was one year old, it was clear. He was the physical image of what his father had been at that age. In fact, when I pulled out both my baby pictures and those of Josh, my dad, we found that little Scottie resembled two generations of McDowells. In the future when our ancestors look at these photos of the three of us at that age, it will be difficult to distinguish who was who because we three looked so alike. There was something about having a child that looked like me that felt honoring. And it filled me with joy.

So it is with God. He is honored when we live in relationship with him and begin to look like him and act like him. That is our purpose, to live in relationship with him and reflect his likeness. When God said, "Let us make people in our image, to be like ourselves" (Genesis 1:26), he was designing each of us to live and enjoy life as he did. God in effect was saying, "become intimate with me and through our close relationship you will experience the true joy of living, for you will bear the fruit of my nature— love, joy, peace, patience, kindness, goodness, faithfulness, gentleness and self-control, and that will make me proud and give me honor" (see Galatians 5:22-23). It pleases God to see us resemble him. In fact, that defines our purpose in life.

Why Are We Here?

Our purpose in life is to honor our Creator God by living in relationship with him and out of that relationship becoming more and more like him. God created us to bring glory to himself. And we glorify God—reflect honorably upon him—as we live in devoted love of him, desiring to please him. "Whatever you eat or drink or whatever you do," Paul said, "you must do all for the glory of God" (1 Corinthians 10:31).

You and I begin to fulfill our purpose when we begin to live out the Godlike life he designed for us. He created us to relate to him and enjoy all the blessings that come from being godly. As we said before, acting according to God's ways brings blessing because all that is defined as perfectly right and good is derived from his nature (see James 1:17). Therefore:

> We believe the truth that followers of Christ are meant to live in relationship with God and be transformed into the likeness of Christ, which defines our very purpose for living—to honor and glorify God.

We were created to live contented lives of joy. We were made to know the gratifying joy of being accepted, approved of, and appreciated, with the ability to freely love and be loved. We were designed to experience fulfillment and satisfaction beyond measure, contentment and peace beyond understanding, and complete joy. And that kind of meaningful life comes only from living in fellowship with God and being conformed to his image. When we come into relationship with God, it begins a process of change that allows his divine nature to permeate our lives. And as we live out that Godlike nature we fulfill the very reason we are here.

CHAPTER TWENTY-NINE

EVIDENCES OF
A CHANGED LIFE

Hypocrites—the church is full of hypocrites." You have probably heard more than one person say that. Today perhaps more than ever, one of the justifiable criticisms of Christianity is that those who call themselves Christians don't live much differently than non-Christians. People may wear the name and want the benefits, but many have not submitted to God for the process of transformation.

How can we tell the difference? How can we know who is really Christian and who is not? Jesus gives us a simple measure by which we can identify false prophets or false Christians: "You can detect them by the way they act, just as you can identify a tree by its fruit" (Matthew 7:16). The same criteria can be used to identify authentic Christians as well. One who has submitted to God's redeeming love will inevitably show evidence of a changed life. My (Josh's) life is a testimony to the fact that God changes lives. My father is living proof that a drunk can be transformed into a godly person.

> *Multiplied millions of lives over the course of history stand out as a testimony to the God of redemption who changes lives.*

Multiplied millions of lives over the course of history speak out as a testimony to the God of redemption who changes lives. There are not enough books to hold the stories. If you have placed your faith in Christ, you are living proof that a "metamorphosis" has taken place—you, a child of God, have been redeemed and are being continually transformed into the image of Christ. Use your testimony as a way to honor God and give him pleasure. Whenever you have an opportunity to tell others how God has changed you, take it. The more you display his godly nature and tell others of God's love and mercy, the more it honors him and fills him with joy.

Following are just a few stories of people who are living proof that God changes lives.

A New York Gang Leader

After David Wilkerson shared the gospel message to a large crowd in New York City he stated, "God's here! God's in this room. And he's come especially for you. If you want your life changed, now is the time." Then he shouted with authority: "Stand up! Those who will receive Jesus Christ and be changed—stand up! Come forward!"

Nicky Cruz, a member of the Mau Maus, a New York gang, was seated in the auditorium. His life was full of hatred, violence, and crime of all kind, and he was miserable. He desperately needed a life change.

He felt one of his gang members beside him stand to his feet. "Boys, I'm going up. Who's with me?" he said.

Nicky stood to his feet as well. He turned to the gang and waved them on with his hand. "Let's go." There was a spontaneous movement out of the chairs and toward the front. More than 25 of the Mau Maus gang responded. Behind Nicky about 25 boys from other gangs followed their example.

"I wanted to be a follower of Jesus Christ at that moment," Nicky explained later. "I was happy at the choice I was making, yet I was crying. Something was taking place in my life that I had absolutely no control over…and I was happy about it."

That night Nicky Cruz trusted Christ as his Savior and his life was radically changed. He quit the gang and his life of violence and crime. He started sharing his testimony with his former gang members and friends. He shared his story with the rest of the world in a book entitled *Run Baby Run,* which was read by countless thousands. A movie based on the book ministered to yet many more thousands. Nicky Cruz serves as a walking testimony of God's transforming power. Jesus said his followers were the light of the world and urged them to let their light shine "like a city on a mountain, glowing in the night for all to see…In the same way, let your good deeds shine out for all to see, so that everyone will praise your heavenly Father" (Matthew 5:14-16). Tens of thousands of young people have come to know Christ as a result of the testimony of Nicky Cruz, a life that was changed from darkness to light.

An Addict and Alcoholic

Rich was an angry man with a violent temper, addicted to drugs and alcohol. He shares his own story:

I grew up on the west side of Cleveland. I was thirteen when I first joined the Milford gang. That's when I started to drink and take drugs. By the time I was fourteen I had graduated to more serious drugs. Stealing, fighting, dealing drugs, and taking them myself was all I knew.

That summer a buddy of mine gave me a book entitled *Run Baby Run* by Nicky Cruz. It was about how Cruz, a member of a New York street gang, became a Christian. His story had a real impact on me, but it would be fifteen years before the message of Jesus took root. Drugs, alcohol, and my stormy temper would haunt me into my forties.

I wasn't good at relationships. I was in my late twenties and already into my second marriage. The new marriage wasn't going too well. Laura, my second wife, was also into drinking and drugs. She had two twin boys, Tim and Tom, who were around eight years old when I married Laura. I wasn't a very good dad to those kids. I was away from home most of the time—at work or drinking—and when I was home I yelled a lot.

While driving home from a night of drinking and doing drugs, I came to the end of my rope. Life had no meaning. I couldn't keep a love relationship; I wasn't a good father; drugs and drinking brought no satisfaction anymore. So what was the point of even living?

The Nicky Cruz story came back to me, and I started praying. When I got home I began reading the Bible. The twins had been attending church, and that had an impact on me. I went to Laura and said, "Why don't we stop going to the bars, start going to church like the boys are, and try to turn our lives around?" Laura said she'd be willing to try.

I'm not really sure why I wanted to go to church, because I didn't have a high regard for church people. They were a judgmental bunch. All I got from church people was condemnation and Scripture verses thrown at me. My life was already going up in flames, so I didn't need more condemnation. And when your house is in flames you don't want someone on your front lawn quoting scriptures; you want a fireman with a water hose. Yet for some reason, I felt that I needed to go to church. I guess what I was hoping for was that somewhere out there I might find a church with a hose that gushed with love and acceptance. Maybe in the back of my mind I figured that was probably too much to ask, given my experience with church people. But I was going to give it a try anyway. What did I have to lose?

When I walked into church I was greeted by a lady in a pretty flowered dress. With a smile that stretched from ear to ear, she greeted me sweetly, saying, "Hello, welcome to Grace Church." We chatted for a minute. She was so bubbly and happy, I figured this must be some kind of cult congregation. I thought no one could be that happy at a regular church.

She then introduced me to her husband and said, "Tom will take you to the Stoner's class." Stoner's class! Were these guys really going to get stoned in a church meeting? As it turned out, Stoner was the last name of the small group leader. I was a long-haired, skinny, burned-out addict. And they could see that. Yet these people accepted me for who I was, without judgment or condemnation.

In the past, most people had told me that my problem was drugs and alcohol. But the reality was that these things were my "solution." These church people knew that too. They saw that my problem was being alone and disconnected. I was looking for a sense of meaning and belonging. They saw that I was trying to solve things by joining a gang and getting into drugs and alcohol. But I didn't find what I was really looking for. Those things were an attempt to drown out my problem—the hurt and aloneness of my miserable existence. My solution wasn't a solution at all.

For the first time in my life I met real people who loved me for being me. *I* didn't even love me, and so I was sort of shocked that these people could really care about me. And they were so doggone happy it almost bugged me. They loved life; it had meaning to them, and I began to really crave what these people had.

Over time I learned who Jesus really was, what he did for me, and how he was the real solution to my messed-up life. Laura struggled. She said she couldn't make it without her old life. And one day she up and moved out without warning. The marriage I hoped could be salvaged was permanently broken. The twins were now stuck with me, their stepdad.

Two years later the pastor introduced me to Pam, a Christian woman. I guess he believed I had a shot at making a relationship work since Christ would be the head of it. I fell in love with Pam, and while it's not all been a bed of roses since, life after finding Christ has been more than I could ever have dreamed. The twins went off to college, and we adopted three children. A broken and shattered life was transformed into a loving marriage, a loving home, and a family that is reaching out to give hope and light to others.

—Rich Bucha

Today Rich is a leader in his church. He leads a recovery group that guides men and women with a dependency into recovery. He is also writing a book and is the happy father of his three adopted children. He's still married to Pam, and she also is an active leader in the church, participating in small group discipleship and outreach events.

The transformation of this family is nothing short of extraordinary. Here was a man on the verge of suicide—an alcoholic and drug user with two broken marriages.

His life's trajectory was destined to plunge him into heartache and ruin. But thanks to the transforming power of God's Holy Spirit, Rich and his new family are now living lives that are truly extraordinary.[1]

A Searching Physicist

A graduate student shares a story of his quest for life's answers:

> After two years of graduate studies at Stanford University, I went to work as a research physicist, studying the upper atmosphere of the earth…I became acquainted with the wonders of this universe—I also discovered that humans had real problems on their hands with weapons of mass destruction. Life kept slipping by…I was not happy at all…I faced a strong possibility of becoming an alcoholic.
>
> I began searching for answers to my unhappy life. I studied Buddhism, Confucianism, Taoism, and Zen. I was intrigued by the possibility of Nirvana…I wanted to die, but the thought of what awaited me after death kept me from suicide…
>
> Then some Christian friends appeared on the scene. I asked these new friends the same kinds of questions I had asked science and philosophy and psychology. I was surprised when they gave me satisfying answers. These friends led me to place my trust in Jesus Christ as a solution to my unhappy and unfulfilled life.
>
> The following days and weeks after I trusted Christ saw miracle after miracle of God's working in my life. The Bible is a supernatural book to me. Old problems and desires have faded away. For the first time I feel complete as a human being. After years of study and reading, which led me no place, I have begun to build a new understanding of reality on the foundation of the Solid Rock, Jesus Christ.
>
> —Lambert Dolphin Jr.

A Medical Scientist

Dr. Francis Collins is one of this country's leading geneticists and former head of the Human Genome Project. During his medical residency, this budding medical professional was shocked by the serenity of some of his mortally ill patients. As an agnostic, he would listen intently while someone with an incurable brain tumor would calmly say, "Well, I guess it won't be long before I see my husband and my dear Savior." He would observe others in dreadful pain say things like, "I know this hurts a lot, but when I think how much more Jesus suffered for me, I can't really complain."

Time after time he saw patients and families of patients face tragedy with a sense of gratitude, courage, and optimism. It was the display of God's grace in the lives of those facing death that drew Dr. Collins to search for the source of such peace. Someone gave him the book *Mere Christianity* by C.S. Lewis. And he began to read it.

The argument Lewis made for God on the evidence of the moral law had a profound impact on Collins. That evidence convinced his mind there was a God. But it was the eternal hope of the suffering believers that attracted his heart. As a result this brilliant scientist gave his heart and mind to Jesus Christ.[2]

A "Super Spiritual" Churchgoer

Jeff Bogue shares how, as a seminary student, his "super spirituality" was exposed as a fake.

During summer break from seminar I got a job in the inner city of Philadelphia. The job involved working with physically, sexually, and emotionally abused kids that had been removed from their homes. They were now living in a group home environment. I drove out to Philadelphia and settled into my new job, interacting with several other college students who, like me, were there working for the summer.

I met this guy named Steve. To put it mildly, Steve was a freak of nature. When I first looked at him, I could not believe what I saw. Both ears were pierced and he had rings hanging from them. Tattoos covered his arms, and his hair hung past his shoulders—all things I had been taught were sure signs of a *liberal*. I, on the other hand, considered myself a super spiritual person. My hair was short, there were no unnecessary holes in my body, and my skin was never marred with anything other than an occasional sunburn.

So Jeff the "super spiritual" and Steve "the liberal" had to work together. I knew it would be hard, but somehow I had to find a way to get along with this freak, because we would be working side by side all summer. I tried to make polite conversation, but I was convinced that Steve and I really had nothing in common. This was going to be a tough summer.

One day, Steve invited me to go to a Bible study with him. I must tell you I had about as much interest in studying the Bible with Steve as I had in hanging out with him—none. However, also working at the center was a really attractive blonde girl that I wanted to impress. I had learned that girls like her were impressed if you were spiritual enough to attend Bible studies and prayer meetings. So I agreed to go to the Bible study with Steve. It was to take place in someone's apartment.

I walked into the Bible study, and all the participants were like Steve: long-haired, ear-pierced, tattooed freaks! I was definitely the odd man out. But that night I experienced something radical. All of these long-haired, ear-pierced, tattooed freaks loved Jesus. The meeting wasn't just to get together and listen to U2; they actually read the Bible to get to know its author.

When they sang worship songs, they seemed to be singing directly to God; I sang them because they were in style. When they read the Bible and meditated on it, they seemed to be doing it to get to know God intimately; I memorized it to take tests and to impress people with my knowledge. When they prayed aloud they seemed to be talking to their dearest friend; when I prayed aloud I was making a point to the people around me.

I remember thinking, *With these guys it's not about following a certain set of rules, it's about loving a certain person.* I started meeting with them more and more. There was something about them that I sensed was authentic and real, and I was drawn to them. Instead of just going to church, they were about being the church. Instead of focusing on being "super spiritual," they focused on a loving relationship with Jesus that affected every aspect of their lives.

I started to change my view about Steve and his friends. I had intense conversations with them that lasted until the wee hours of the morning. I found their authenticity and openness to God so winsome and appealing. The God they talked about seemed different than the God I believed in. They were passionately pursuing an intimate relationship with him—a closeness with God I never knew was possible.

I had just enough spiritual intuition to know that I couldn't fake what Steve and his friends had. But it wasn't as simple as yielding to God and admitting I didn't have what it took to be a spiritual person. To do this would be like exposing me as a spiritual infant who needed God and others to mature. To me that felt like starting at the bottom. And to think of being led by a group of freakish people that my church and college consider totally unacceptable was out of the question. But these guys had turned my world upside down. I was having a crisis of faith. I didn't quite know how to cope with this new reality of what being spiritual really meant. I was in a quandary because these guys had a connection with God that was so real and mine seemed so fake.

Then came a moment of clarity. I was walking around a soccer field one evening at around nine o'clock. It was summertime and still light outside. I often went to the soccer field to run and exercise. I had my Bible with me, and as the sun was setting I sat down in the soccer field and prayed. "God, I want what those guys have. I don't even really know what it is. I want it but I'm also afraid of how it is going to affect my life. Would you show yourself to me so I can know you for who you really are?"

I opened my Bible and began to read the story of Jesus walking on the water. Then it happened. Somehow, God interacted with me on a deep level. I began to realize that either Jesus walked on the water or he didn't. Either this whole religion thing is real, or it is all fake. I thought, only God could overcome and suspend the laws of nature to perform such a miracle. So either Jesus is who he claimed to be or he isn't. Either that water walking account is true, and he is the God of the universe and the One that I should submit to and trust in as my Savior, or the whole thing is one big lie made up from the beginning.

That night I sensed God spoke to me, saying, "Jeff, you have to choose. Trust in me for who I am and let me take your ordinary life and transform it into an extraordinary life, or forsake the God of your mother and father and walk away from me forever." I saw the gravity and the far-reaching impact of that choice. It was an either/or decision. No halfway choice would do.

At that moment, it was as if I could hear Steve saying, "Trying to make it on your own, Jeff, may feel right at first. But it is a lonely road. It not only pushes God away, it pushes people away from you as well, people that really love you. Yeah, it's humiliating to admit you need God and other people. Truth is, you've already found that living a self-sufficient life doesn't really give you the security you're looking for." Steve was right. The verse I was taught came to me: "If we confess our sins to him, he is faithful and just to forgive us and to cleanse us from every wrong" (1 John 1:9). That night I made a choice to trust in Christ and know him for who he is, and it changed my life forever.[3]

—Pastor Jeff Bogue

An Imprisoned Thief

Pacing back and forth in his prison cell, Leo D'Arcangelo was deeply disturbed—who wouldn't be, facing what was ahead of him?

As a boy of 11, he had snatched a lady's handbag. That was the start.

Five years of stealing followed, before his first arrest at 16 in a Philadelphia department store. After being put on probation, he started mainlining heroin. Then began the seemingly endless set of arrests and finally jail time.

As he paced his jail cell, he noticed these few lines crudely scrawled on the wall:

When you come to the end of your journey and this trouble is racked in your mind, and there seems no other way out than by just mourning, turn to Jesus, for it is Him that you must find.

The verse started him thinking. *This is the end of my journey. What have I got to show for it? Nothing except a lousy past and a worse future.*

He cried out, "Jesus, I need your help. I've made a mess of my life, and this is the end of the journey. Jesus, if you can change my life please do it. Help me make tomorrow different."

For the first time Leo felt something besides despair. He felt free even though he was imprisoned.

Released two years later, Leo earned his high school diploma and then went on to graduate from West Chester State College and the Reformed Episcopal Seminary in Philadelphia. Leo was changed. He became active in prison work, leading others to the same spiritual freedom he had found in Christ.

■

They overcame him [Satan] by the blood of the Lamb and by the word of their testimony (Revelation 12:11 NIV).

We put no confidence in human effort. Instead, we boast about what Christ Jesus has done for us (Philippians 3:3).

I am not ashamed of this Good News about Christ. It is the power of God at work, saving everyone who believes (Romans 1:16).

CHAPTER THIRTY

SEEING YOURSELF
AS GOD SEES YOU

Don't be so hard on the young man," I (Josh) said as I pulled my colleague over to one side. "You need to extend a little grace to Don."

Don, my new assistant, came from a difficult family background and had some issues to deal with. And, I admitted, those issues were playing out in his lackluster performance. But my colleague thought that was no excuse for Don to be "mouthing off" to him and shooting hoops instead of packing up for my next trip.

"Do you know who Don reminds me of?" I asked my colleague.

"No, who?" he responded.

"Don reminds me of *me* at that age. I had a tough childhood, and even though I was a Christian there were some unhealthy patterns that stayed with me a while." My friend began nodding in agreement. "I needed some mature people around me," I continued, "to extend grace and help me correct some of those unhealthy patterns. That's what Don needs too."

Even though God imparts his new nature to us, it requires a process to live it out. And we need others around us to administer grace sometimes to help us in the process of correcting our unhealthy patterns—or you might say, help us unravel our grave clothes.

An Instant New Life, Yet a Process to Live It

The man approached the grave of his dead friend. He had missed the funeral that was conducted four days prior. The body was actually entombed in a cave with a massive stone rolled across its entrance.

"Roll the stone aside," the man commanded to those with him. He then raised his head toward heaven, said a prayer, and shouted, "Lazarus, come out!" At that moment his dead friend came to life, raised at the call of Jesus of Nazareth.

Lazarus had been wrapped in a linen burial shroud soaked in spices to help preserve his corpse. With the spices now dried, the linen was hardened. At Jesus' word, new life went right through the hardened grave clothes and into the body, and Lazarus hobbled out of the tomb wrapped like a mummy.

Outside the tomb, Lazarus no longer needed his grave clothes. They were definitely an impediment to a body that was now alive. So Jesus told Lazarus' family and friends, "Unwrap him and let him go!" (John 11:44). With the help of his friends and family, Lazarus was unwrapped and set free to experience a brand-new life.

Notice that the grave clothes did not fall off Lazarus the moment Jesus called out to him. There was a *process* involved in getting him unwrapped after he had come to life again. When we become Christians, Christ gives us new life. It is as if he calls to us, "Come out! Come out of your old, dead existence. Come out and enjoy the new life I have given you." Christ is the initiator of the new life. And it is his power that activates the transformation process of becoming more and more like him. "You have stripped off your old evil nature and all its wicked deeds," Paul says. "In its place you have clothed yourselves with a brand-new nature." But notice how Paul refers to the process when he concludes that your brand-new nature "is continually being renewed as you learn more and more about Christ, who created this new nature within you" (Colossians 3:9-10).

Like Lazarus, we emerge from the tomb of our past shrouded in grave clothes. We may be bound by the negative influences of our family of origin, our old friends, and the old life we used to live. Christ's invitation to new life penetrates the grave clothes—the things that bind us—and new life begins. But we may still be hobbled by the wrappings. We may instantly be alive with Christ's nature within us, but it takes a process of time and spiritual growth for that nature to be lived out to maturity. Paul talked about being built up so "we will be mature and full grown in the Lord, measuring up to the full stature of Christ…becoming more and more in every way like Christ" (Ephesians 4:13,15).

Jesus could have chosen to have Lazarus burst out of his grave clothes in a display of power. But he didn't. He chose to involve the people in Lazarus' life. It was as if Jesus said to Lazarus' friends and family, "You unwrap him! You be part of the process of releasing him from the grave clothes! You help him in the transformation process!" Jesus does the same with us. He continues the process of transformation by bringing others into our lives who love us enough to extend grace to us, teach us, and mentor us in the process of becoming more and more like him.

Paul said, "I'm sure that God, who began the good work within you, will continue

his work until it is finally finished on that day when
Christ Jesus comes back again" (Philippians 1:6). The
work has begun in us, but it must be continued day
in and day out as God's nature is unleashed through
our attitudes and actions. Peter said, "As we know
Jesus better, his divine power gives us everything we
need for living a godly life" (2 Peter 1:3).

There is a very important principle here about
the transformation process of becoming more and
more like Christ. As new followers of Christ we *do*
live differently from our old lives. But the doing isn't what continually transforms us.
It is living in relationship with Christ and his nature, which is being imparted and
empowered by the Holy Spirit, that continually transforms us. *So the process isn't so
much in learning to do all the right things perfectly as it is learning who Christ is and acting according to our new nature.*

> *Living a Christlike life is
> about discovering the new
> person we already are in
> relationship with Christ
> and acting accordingly.*

Discover Who You Already Are

The transformation process isn't about becoming a new person by just doing right;
we are to discover the new person we have become in Christ and act accordingly. There
is a very important distinction.

A lot of new Christians are urged to start immediately *doing* things in order to acti-
vate the process of becoming like Christ. Well-meaning mentors challenge new converts
to study the Bible, memorize verses, attend church as often as possible, witness to others,
and replace old, sinful habits with patterns of godly living. These are all important things
to do in order to be rooted in the faith. In fact, we can't actually discover who Christ is
and the power of God's truth without prayer and the study of God's Word. But we must
realize that spiritual or studious activity isn't what continually transforms us.

Living a Christlike life is about *discovering the new person we already are in relationship with Christ and acting accordingly.* It's about interacting with and relating to
Christ so the grace and power of God's Spirit is appropriated within us. Studying the
Bible, attending church, and sharing our faith do not cause God to regard us as more
redeemed, justified, sanctified, or adopted more as his child. He *already* sees us in these
ways because they define who we really are. So we don't *do* our way into becoming
God's adopted children; we don't *do* things to cause his divine nature to dwell within
us. We are not changed from the outside in; we are changed from the inside out. As
we live in relationship with Christ, we can start behaving according to our new nature
and do those things that God's children do—act like Christ.

I (Josh) have a good friend who became a Christian in his early twenties.

Well-meaning Christian leaders got him involved in personal Bible study right away to help him start growing in his faith. They loaded him down with materials that challenged him to scrutinize portions of Scripture in order to discover promises to claim, sins to avoid, and commands to obey. It was a very thorough study project, and he dived into it wholeheartedly, spending hours and hours each week digging through the Bible to see what he had to do.

But after only a few weeks he told me he was worn out. He was so busy digging out verses in order to "grow" that he had missed the whole point of his exercise. So he changed his focus. He turned his attention to getting to know the God of the Bible personally, the God who had so marvelously saved him. His pursuit led him back into the Word, but his motivation was completely different. Instead of diving into its pages to *become* someone, he scoured the Word to find the heart of the One who had *made* him someone and sought a deeper relationship with him.

Today my friend is one of the most knowledgeable men of the Word I know. More importantly, he is more intimately in touch with the God of the Word than most Christian leaders. He learned early that living like Christ is primarily a matter of getting to know Jesus better because "his divine power has given us everything we need for living a godly life" (2 Peter 1:3). We should read, memorize, and meditate on the Bible primarily to get in touch with God's heart. The more we know God's heart, the more we know who we are in him, which will naturally result in acting like him.

How the Most Important Person in Your Life Sees You

The truest statements about your transformed relationship with God are what God says about you in his Word. The Bible is where God opens his heart about who you are and how he sees you. If what you think or feel about yourself does not line up with how the Bible describes you, you are making yourself the victim of a case of mistaken identity.

It has been said that our self-concept is largely determined by what we believe the most important person in our lives thinks about us. If my (Josh's) wife tells me I'm a loving husband, I'll tend to believe her, because she is the most important woman in my life. And if she thinks that about me, I believe her. If my (Sean's) father tells me I'm a caring son, I'll tend to believe him, because he is the most important man in my life.

So when God tells you there are certain things about you that are true, what should you do? If he is the most important person in your life, then your self-concept—how you think and feel about yourself—will conform to his view. The ongoing change of your life in Christ is inextricably linked to how confidently you believe the truth of what God says about you.

Thirty-four-year-old Scott became a Christian in college, but he has lived under a dark cloud of guilt over his past sins ever since. As a teenager, Scott was involved in sexual immorality. After he trusted Christ, he changed his lifestyle because he knew immorality was wrong according to Scripture. But Scott could not escape the sense that God still condemned him for his past sin. He felt like a second-class Christian; he felt that God would never trust him with an important ministry because of his teenage promiscuity. As a result he felt defeated most of the time.

Scripture declares that "now there is no condemnation for those who belong to Christ Jesus" (Romans 8:1). Who has the accurate picture of Scott's true identity: Scott, who sees himself as condemned and of little value? Or God, who has forgiven Scott for his sin and no longer condemns him? God, of course! We see God's heart concerning Scott's sin in Romans 8:1. Scott is forgiven, cleansed. Scott's inaccurate sense of himself began to change only as he believed the truth of what God said of him in that scripture passage.

Apart from the Word of God, we will have great difficulty understanding how God sees us. It is like the man who had a friend who loved jigsaw puzzles. When the friend's birthday came around, the man bought two large puzzles as gifts. But as a joke, he switched the box tops on the two puzzles. The fellow who received the gift became totally frustrated as he tried to put the first puzzle together. Using the picture on the box top as a guide, he could not make any sense of the pieces inside. He found the second puzzle just as difficult, until his friend revealed the prank.

We experience similar frustration in understanding our position in Christ when we look at the wrong "box top." If you regard your feelings, judgments, and personal experiences as the criteria for determining who we are, you will struggle to put together your true identity in Christ. Our picture to go by is the Word of God. The more you are in tune with God's picture, the easier the pieces of your life will fit together to resemble that picture.

There are certain things that are true of you from the moment you trust Christ as Savior and Lord. The first two chapters of Ephesians provide a concentrated look at your attributes as a new creation in Christ. Below we have listed the many benefits of transformation that describe your position in Christ. Remember, these statements from God's Word are *already* true of you because you are in Christ. They are part of your basic identity apart from how you might perform from time to time. This list shows how the most important person in your life sees you. The list is written in the first person so that you can read the blessings as your own. We suggest that you reread this list from Ephesians often to help you see yourself clearly as God sees you.

- I am blessed with every spiritual blessing (1:3).

- I was chosen before the creation of the world to be holy and blameless in God's sight (1:4).

- I was chosen to be adopted as his child through Christ (1:5).
- I have redemption through his blood (1:7).
- I am forgiven (1:7).
- I have received an eternal inheritance from God (1:11).
- I am identified as God's own by receiving the Holy Spirit (1:13).

Because of your position in Christ, great things are true of you. Paul understood that Christians' lives would be stronger, brighter, more effective, and more joyful if they would accept and internalize the truth about ourselves in Christ. He therefore prayed that "your hearts will be flooded with light so that you can understand the wonderful future he has promised to those he called. I want you to realize what a rich and glorious inheritance he has given to his people. I pray that you will begin to understand the incredible greatness of his power for us who believe him" (Ephesians 1:18-19). God really does want you to see yourself as he sees you.

Paul goes on to describe Christ's resurrection and ascension to the right hand of the Father (see Ephesians 1:20-23). He adds that you were raised with Christ and seated with him next to the Father (see Ephesians 2:6). Then in chapter 2 he continues with more descriptions of the believer as seen from God's perspective. Again, we have paraphrased these statements in the first person.

- I am alive in Christ (2:5).
- I am seated with Christ in the heavenly realms (2:6).
- I am an example of God's grace (2:7).
- I am saved by his grace (2:8).
- I am God's masterpiece (2:10).
- I belong to Christ (2:13).
- I have direct access to God through the Spirit (2:18).

In addition to this concentrated dose in Ephesians 1 and 2, God's Word abounds with many other descriptions of how God sees you. Here is a broader list of statements drawn in part from Neil Anderson's book *Victory Over the Darkness* that reflect your transformed life in Christ. Read these statements aloud to yourself as often as possible. Meditate on these truths during the week so that God can use them to shed the spotlight on who you really are in him.[1]

- I have peace with God (Romans 5:1).
- I am a child of God (John 1:12).

- I am indwelled by the Holy Spirit (1 Corinthians 3:16).
- I have access to God's wisdom (James 1:5).
- I am helped by God (Hebrews 4:16).
- I am reconciled to God (Romans 5:11).
- I am not condemned by God (Romans 8:1).
- I am justified (Romans 5:1).
- I have Christ's righteousness (Romans 5:19; 2 Corinthians 5:21).
- I am his ambassador (2 Corinthians 5:20).
- I am completely forgiven (Colossians 1:14).
- I am tenderly loved by God (Jeremiah 31:3).
- I am the sweet fragrance of Christ to God (2 Corinthians 2:15).
- I am a temple in which God dwells (1 Corinthians 3:16).
- I am blameless and beyond reproach (Colossians 1:22).
- I am the salt of the earth (Matthew 5:13).
- I am the light of the world (Matthew 5:14).
- I am a branch on Christ's vine (John 15:1,5).
- I am Christ's friend (John 15:15).
- I am chosen by Christ to bear fruit (John 15:16).
- I am a joint heir with Christ, sharing his inheritance with him (Romans 8:17).
- I am united to the Lord, one spirit with him (1 Corinthians 6:17).
- I am a member of Christ's body (1 Corinthians 12:27).
- I am a saint (Ephesians 1:1).
- I am hidden with Christ in God (Colossians 3:3).
- I am chosen by God, holy and dearly loved (Colossians 3:12).
- I am a child of the light (1 Thessalonians 5:5).
- I am a holy partaker of God's heavenly calling (Hebrews 3:1).
- I am sanctified (Hebrews 2:11).
- I am one of God's living stones, being built up in Christ as a spiritual house (1 Peter 2:5).
- I am a member of a chosen race, a royal priesthood, a holy nation, a people for God's own possession (1 Peter 2:9-10).

- I am firmly rooted and built up in Christ (Colossians 2:7).

- I am born of God, and the evil one cannot touch me (1 John 5:18).

- I have the mind of Christ (1 Corinthians 2:16).

- I may approach God with boldness, freedom, and confidence (Ephesians 3:12).

- I have been rescued from Satan's domain and transferred into the kingdom of Christ (Colossians 1:13).

- I have been made complete in Christ (Colossians 2:10).

- I have been given a spirit of power, love, and self-discipline (2 Timothy 1:7).

- I have been given great and precious promises by God (2 Peter 1:4).

- My needs are met by God (Philippians 4:19).

Can you see more clearly from this list what it means to be a new creation in Christ? One of the keys to your transformed relationship with God is to acknowledge that something very good happened to you when you trusted Christ. In Paul's words, you have "clothed yourselves with a brand-new nature that is continually being renewed as you learn more and more about Christ, who created this new nature within you" (Colossians 3:10).

You are not primarily what your parents, spouse, or friends say you are, even though many of them may be Christians. You are not what your negative emotions or condemned feelings may say you are. And you are certainly not what the godless culture says you are. You are who God says you are—nothing more, nothing less. The more you review, recite, and internalize the verbal picture God paints of you in Scripture, the better positioned you are to grow like that picture.[2]

CHAPTER THIRTY-ONE

LIVING OUT
A CHANGED LIFE

Prior to mechanically powered tractors, plowing the land for farming was done with horses or oxen. But harnessing two oxen separately made it very difficult to plow because the oxen would not pull in unison. This made it nearly impossible to plow a straight furrow. So a yoke was employed. A yoke was usually made of wood and consisted of a strong crossbar that spanned the backs of both animals. Extending downward from the bar were two U-shaped loops that fitted around the oxen's necks. The yoke actually bonded them together so they would walk side by side in step and pull the plow in unison.

Prior to receiving God's divine nature, we could not walk in step with Christ. We were not yoked together with him, and we could not accomplish God's purpose. As Paul the apostle said, "No matter which way I turn, I can't make myself do right... When I want to do good, I don't. And when I try not to do wrong, I do it anyway" (Romans 7:18-19). What he needed, as all of us need, was God's imparted nature as a yoke enabling him to walk together in unison with Christ.

Jesus extends this invitation to each of us: "Take my yoke upon you. Let me teach you, because I am humble and gentle, and you will find rest for your souls. For my yoke fits perfectly, and the burden I give you is light" (Matthew 11:29-30). When we are harnessed in Christ's yoke, he will teach us how to be motivated like him, think like him, and act like him. He wants us to know what his true nature is like and live it out yoked with him. But if we don't really know the characteristics of his nature and how it is to be acted out, it will be difficult for us to reflect it.

The Nature of God Defined

Moses had gotten his instructions. While he was on Mount Sinai, God had provided exacting details for how sacrifices were to be offered. God's instructions were to be carried out to the letter.

On the first day of presenting the sin offering, burnt offering, and peace offering, Aaron's sons, Nadab and Abihu, who were the priests officiating at the sacrifices, put coals of fire in their incense burners in a way that was in direct contradiction to God's commands. "So fire blazed forth from the LORD's presence and burned them up...Then Moses said to Aaron, 'This is what the LORD meant when he said, "I will show myself holy among those who are near me. I will be glorified before all the people"'" (Leviticus 10:2-3). That day the children of Israel got a clear understanding that their God was a holy God.

God's holiness could not tolerate sin, and he consumed the offenders with fire. Holiness is the fundamental descriptor of who God is. He is holy, and anything or anyone who is out of character with him is impure and unholy.

Some people have trouble grasping the concept of holiness. What does it really mean to say God is holy? God's holiness is reflected in his absolute perfection of goodness and righteousness. There is no imperfection of character or motive in God; he is the holiest of the holy, the purest of the pure.

To be holy is to be set apart from the unclean. A blemish or imperfection would mar anything holy, and it would therefore become impure. For example, if you had an absolutely pure glass of water, you would say it is unadulterated—without impurities. But if a dirty sliver of wood dropped into your glass, your water would become adulterated. Since a foreign substance had entered the water, it would be considered unclean and impure. To be holy is to be set apart from the unclean and impure things of life.

No one compares to God's absolute holiness. When God spoke of himself as "I Am Who I Am" (Exodus 3:14) he was defining himself by himself. He separated himself from all others because there was no other purer being he could compare himself to. Yet God said to his people, "You must be holy because I, the LORD your God, am holy" (Leviticus 19:2). Paul the apostle wrote, "God has called us to be holy, not to live impure lives" (1 Thessalonians 4:7). The very essence of God's nature is holy, and humans created in his likeness are designed to be holy too. We obviously cannot be holy in the absolute sense as God is, yet he does require us to be holy. So the question is, what exactly does holiness look like in the lives of fallen people who cannot be perfectly pure as God is perfectly pure?

If you were to crystallize the essence of what holiness looked like in a person's life it could be summed up in perhaps two words: "Godlike love." John, a disciple of Jesus, wrote, "God is love, and all who live in love live in God, and God lives in them. And as we live in God, our love grows more perfect. So we will not be afraid on the day of judgment, but we can face him with confidence because we are like Christ here in this world" (1 John 4:16-17).

John was very conscious of God's holy judgment when he wrote this. God is holy, and his holiness will ultimately consume everything that is unholy. But he said that when love lives in us and we live in love, we don't need to fear judgment "because we are like Christ here in this world." The divine nature of God's holiness is imputed to us. That is, since we as sinners lack holiness on our own, when we submit to him he shares his holiness with us. By that sharing he sets us apart and consecrates us as his holy people (Ephesians 3).

A practical aspect of this setting apart is a Godlike love. And when we receive his holy nature we receive this pure love. Because we are redeemed, justified, sanctified, and adopted into God's family, we are holy in our standing with God. That enables us to live his love out in relationship to others. So, one of the clear expressions of God's holiness in our lives is loving as God loves.

Defining Godlike Love

A lot of people know that God is love and that we are to love others as he does, but they lack a concise definition as to what Godlike love is. In 1 Corinthians, the apostle Paul gives a good description of what love does and does not do. "Love is patient and kind. Love is *not jealous* or *boastful* or *proud* or *rude*. Love does not demand its own way. Love is not irritable, and it keeps no record of when it has been wronged. It is never glad about injustice but rejoices whenever the truth wins out" (1 Corinthians 13:4-6).

Paul also wrote that "love does no wrong to anyone" (Romans 13:10). Instead, we are to treat all people as we would like to be treated. Remember the Golden Rule? "Do for others what you would like them to do for you" (Matthew 7:12). Paul put it this way: "Each of you should look not only to your own interests, but also to the interests of others" (Philippians 2:4 NIV).

> *Love is making the security, happiness, and welfare of another person as important as your own.*

When Jesus was asked to identify the most important commandment, he said it was to love God and "love your neighbor as yourself" (Matthew 22:39). Paul gave us a specific application of this principle when he told husbands "to love their wives as they love their own bodies...No one hates his own body but lovingly cares for it" (Ephesians 5:28-29). Loving like this is one way of living out the holiness of God.

Drawing from these verses and others similar, we can derive a concise definition of pure Godlike love. *Love is making the security, happiness, and welfare of another person as important as your own.* This is Godlike love, a pure love that protects the loved one from harm and provides for his or her good. Godlike love is giving and trusting, unselfish and sacrificial, secure and safe, loyal and forever. And because its priority is to protect and provide for the loved one, Godlike love will not do things that are harmful to the security, happiness, and welfare of another person.

What Godlike Love Looks Like

His time on earth was coming to an end. Jesus had spent the last few years pouring his life and teachings into his followers. Just hours before his death he met with them to celebrate Passover, and Scripture says, "He now showed the disciples the full extent of his love" (John 13:1).

"He got up from the table, took off his robe, wrapped a towel around his waist, and…began to wash the disciples' feet" (John 13:4-5). When he was finished he asked his disciples, "Do you understand what I was doing? You call me 'Teacher' and 'Lord,' and you are right, because it is true. And since I, the Lord and Teacher, have washed your feet, you ought to wash each other's feet. I have given you an example to follow. Do as I have done to you…That is the path of blessing" (John 13:12-17).

Jesus had just taken on the role of a servant to wash the feet of his followers. And within that context he issues a new commandment: "A new command I give you: Love one another. As I have loved you, so you must love one another. By this all men will know that you are my disciples, if you love one another" (John 13:34-35 NIV).

This was huge. God had written out Ten Commandments on tablets of stone for all to read and follow. Now Jesus was dictating the eleventh commandment to his disciples. You can't get much bigger than a commandment coming straight from the mouth of God. And this one command would be the mark of a true Christian. This "love one another as I have loved you" would be the universal identifier—the distinguishing brand—of Jesus' disciples. Loving as Christ loved would be a clear expression of God's holiness.

If Jesus had done nothing more than simply pronounce the command, these disciples might have raised the question, *Well, if we are to love each other like he loves us, just how has he loved us? What does that look like?* Jesus illustrated the command with a demonstration so they would see, firsthand, that to love another is to serve him. A few hours later, they would see love stretched out on the cross, dying in their stead.

Following Jesus' death and resurrection, God inspired the disciples and apostles to write out specific instructions to show what Christlike love looks like in our lives. Many of these instructions appear in the "one another" passages of Scripture. At least 35 times in the New Testament, we see a recurring word pattern—an action verb followed by the words "one another." These admonitions give us practical examples of how to love as Jesus loved. We know, for example, the nature of Jesus' love was gentle, humble, and forgiving. Scripture admonishes us to live out those characteristics of Christ by being gentle to one another (Ephesians 4:2), being humble toward one another (1 Peter 5:5), and forgiving one another (Colossians 3:13). By identifying these "one another" passages, we get a much clearer picture of how Christ wants us to live out his divine nature of love in our lives. Consider the following list in light of *"love is making the security, happiness, and welfare of another person as important as your own."*

The "One Anothers" of Scripture

1. Love one another (John 13:34).
2. Accept one another (Romans 15:7).
3. Forgive one another (Ephesians 4:32; Colossians 3:13).
4. Be gentle to one another (Ephesians 4:2).
5. Be clothed in humility toward one another (1 Peter 5:5).
6. Weep with one another (Romans 12:15).
7. Live in harmony with one another (Romans 12:16).
8. Don't judge one another (Romans 14:13).
9. Be patient with one another (Ephesians 4:2).
10. Admonish one another (Colossians 3:16).
11. Greet one another (Romans 16:16).
12. Wait for one another (1 Corinthians 11:33).
13. Care for one another (1 Corinthians 12:25).
14. Serve one another (Galatians 5:13).
15. Be kind to one another (Ephesians 4:32).
16. Be devoted to one another (Romans 12:10).
17. Be compassionate toward one another (Ephesians 4:32).
18. Encourage one another (1 Thessalonians 5:11).
19. Submit to one another (Ephesians 5:21).
20. Make allowances for one another (Colossians 3:13).
21. Stimulate love in one another (Hebrews 10:24).
22. Offer hospitality to one another (1 Peter 4:9).
23. Minister gifts to one another (1 Peter 4:10).
24. Rejoice with one another (Romans 12:15; 1 Corinthians 12:26).

25. Don't slander one another (James 4:11).

26. Don't grumble against one another (James 5:9).

27. Confess your sins to one another (James 5:16).

28. Pray for one another (James 5:16).

29. Fellowship with one another (1 John 1:7).

30. Don't be puffed up against one another (1 Corinthians 4:6).

31. Carry one another's burdens (Galatians 6:2).

32. Honor one another (Romans 12:10).

33. Depend on one another (Romans 12:5 AMP).

34. Prefer one another (Romans 12:10).

35. Comfort one another (2 Corinthians 1:4).

Living Out the "One Anothers"

In the last chapter we talked about how we could feel bound by the "grave clothes" of our old life—things like the negative influences of our family of origin, old friends, old habits, and so on. For me (Josh), living out Christ's holiness through loving others was not easy. I still needed to shed some of those grave clothes that clung to me after my conversion.

Because I grew up in the home of an alcoholic, I developed a pattern of behavior that made me what psychologists call a "rescuer." Each time I saw my father try to hurt my mom, I would step in and try to prevent her from being hurt. This became a lifelong psychological and emotional pattern for me. I always tried to rescue hurting, struggling people.

When I became a Christian I continued this unhealthy behavioral pattern, but I didn't realize it was unhealthy. Each time I saw someone hurting, my compulsion kicked in. But I didn't know it was a compulsion; I thought it was compassion. I thought I was exhibiting Godlike love. Take the "one another" scripture that says we are to "bear one another's burdens, and thereby fulfill the law of Christ" (Galatians 6:2 NASB). Because of my rescuer compulsion I felt emotionally responsible to solve the person's problem by removing whatever burden they had. I thought I was fulfilling the "law of Christ" and making the security, happiness, and welfare of the other as important as my own. In reality, I was doing myself harm and in most cases doing the person a disservice, all because I was seeing God's love through the baggage or grave clothes of my rescuing dysfunction.

It took the help of others more wise and spiritual than I to help unwrap my grave clothes. Through wise and spiritual counsel, I learned that bearing another person's burden doesn't mean taking responsibility for that person's problem or hurt. It means coming alongside and gently helping a person lift the load. Bearing the burdens of others doesn't mean taking responsibility *for* their problem; it means being responsible *to* them—to comfort, encourage, and support them in their pain or difficulties.

It was God's Word that ultimately brought me around. Yes, Galatians 6:2 tells us that we are to "bear one another's burdens." The key to my turnaround was the passage I discovered just three more verses down the page. Galatians 6:5 declares, "Each one will bear his own load" (NASB).

Now, this may sound confusing at first, but it comes together when you consider that there is an important difference between a "burden" and a "load." The Greek word for "burden" is a word that means "boulder," a large rock that is too heavy to carry alone. We all face situations that bear down heavily on us, and we need someone to come alongside and share our burden. The situation causing the burden could be an injury, an illness, the death of a loved one, or the loss of a job, for example.

The Greek word for "load" is different, however; it refers to a military knapsack, the supply pack a soldier would carry into the field. It represents something each of us is responsible to carry. It's yours, it's assigned to you, and bearing it is your responsibility alone. It's the idea Paul was conveying when he said, "Each of us will have to give a personal account to God" (Romans 14:12).

We all have personal responsibilities, and when we fail in our responsibilities—by using poor judgment or making wrong choices or harboring bad attitudes—we must face up to the consequences. To step in and remove the natural and corrective consequences of people's irresponsible behavior may rob them of valuable lessons—lessons which may be critical for their continued growth and maturity.

I can't possibly express how valuable this revelation from God's Word has been to me. When I realized that loving others as Christ loved didn't mean I was responsible *for* other people, then I was set free to be responsible *to* others—and particularly to those who were hurting. I then began looking for opportunities to allow his comfort, encouragement, and support to flow through me to others because I knew that in doing this I was loving others as Christ loves me.

The apostle Paul challenges us to "be diligent [in]…accurately handling the word of truth" (2 Timothy 2:15 NASB). As we understand accurately from Scripture how God wants us to love and what that looks like in our lives, we can "fulfill the law of Christ," which is to love others as he has loved us.

Take time this week to *do* one or more "one anothers" of Scripture. With a servant's heart and in a spirit of sacrifice, make someone's security, happiness, and welfare as important as your own. As you do this you will be expressing your transformed, Christlike nature.

We close with Paul's admonition:

Since God chose you to be the holy people whom he loves, you must clothe yourselves with tenderhearted mercy, kindness, humility, gentleness, and patience. You must make allowance for each other's faults and forgive the person who offends you. Remember, the Lord forgave you, so you must forgive others. And the most important piece of clothing you must wear is love. Love is what binds us all together in perfect harmony. And let the peace that comes from Christ rule in your hearts. For as members of one body you are all called to live in peace. And always be thankful (Colossians 3:12-15).

SUMMARY OF PART III

God's Truth Declaration:
I Am God Incarnate—The God of Redemption

- *We believe the truth* that God became human. And when we examine the evidence that Jesus is the God-man we can believe this truth with confidence.

  Jesus Christ's coming to earth demonstrates to us that even though we are sinners, God accepts us without condition.

  When we accept others as God accepts us, we form secure and intimate relationships.

- *We believe the truth* that Christ's death on the cross is an atonement for our sin so that we may be redeemed by God. We can believe this with confidence because there is sufficient evidence to establish the truth that Jesus is God's Son—a perfect and acceptable sacrifice.

  Christ's sacrificial death is relevant to us specifically because it demonstrates Christ's love for us and enables God to forgive us our sins.

  Christ's sacrificial death also defines what real love is, a love we are to demonstrate to others. And when we do this we experience the joy of lasting love relationships.

- *We believe the truth* that being justified before God and completely forgiven of sin is by God's grace through faith alone in Jesus.

Because there is sufficient evidence that Christ is the Son of God, we can believe with confidence that our justification is secure.

When we experience a relationship with God, being redeemed, justified, sanctified, and adopted as his child, we are changed from dead to alive and have joyful expectation of eternal life.

- *We believe the truth* that our relationship with God transforms us into a new person.

We can believe this truth with confidence as we see our life being consistently changed into the image of God's Son.

As we are conformed to the image of God, we discover our purpose for living—to honor God by being and living like Christ. We can know why we are here.

The Christian faith demonstrates the truth that God entered our world to regain an intimate relationship with us. He mercifully raises us from death to life by his grace through faith in Jesus, and is continually conforming us more and more to the image of his Son—which fulfills our purpose in life.

But as amazing and miraculous as that is, the story doesn't end here. In part IV we will discover the truth of God's *re-creation*—his mission to involve us in restoring all things back to a perfect world without sin.

THE UNSHAKABLE TRUTH OF GOD'S RE-CREATION

Our faith is real because of Christ's resurrection.

■

We experience God through three persons in one—
God the Father, God the Son, God the Holy Spirit.

■

Jesus came to establish his kingdom.

■

We have a kingdom mission.

■

We inherit Jesus' kingdom when he returns to earth.

TRUTH EIGHT

JESUS' BODILY RESURRECTION

CHAPTER THIRTY-TWO

THE HISTORICAL NECESSITY OF CHRIST'S RESURRECTION

She stood a few feet away sobbing as her son hung there, nailed to a rugged cross. John stood beside Mary, trying to comfort her. Moments later Jesus took one last breath and said, 'It is finished!' Then he bowed his head and gave up his spirit" (John 19:30).

Joseph of Arimathea and a few women lowered Jesus' lifeless body from the cross and prepared him for burial. After placing their dead Messiah in the tomb, they rolled the large stone over the entrance to seal him away for good, or so many thought.

Imagine a conversation between two observers of Jesus' ministry immediately after his death.

"I thought this Messiah Movement was going to last," Hamon says dryly.

"Yeah, me too," agrees Benjamin. "I wonder what his disciples are going to do now?"

"Oh, I think it'll be difficult," Hamon responds, "but they can still keep things going."

"How?" Benjamin asks skeptically. "Without their Messiah they don't have a message!"

"Sure they do," Hamon argues. "Of course, since Jesus is dead he can't marshal an army to overthrow the Romans, but his disciples can still propagate all his great teachings."

The two men ponder for a moment. Finally Benjamin says thoughtfully, "Yeah, they've lost their charismatic speaker and miracle worker, but they still have a lot of

If Jesus did not break the power of death over his own body by rising to life, he could not enter the Most Holy Place, offer his blood on our behalf, and cancel our death sentence.

solid teaching, especially if they'll key on his 'love your neighbor as yourself' theme. That should keep things going. Maybe they'll be just fine."

If Jesus came to earth just to offer a "love your neighbor" message, Hamon and Benjamin might have a good point. But that was not Jesus' primary mission. Far more than the fate of Jesus' teachings or an earthly Messiah Movement hung on the cross that day. The fate of the entire human race hung with him.

What was the fate of the entire human race? As Paul explains, "Adam's sin brought death, so death spread to everyone" (Romans 5:12). Jesus, as the Holy Lamb of God, was the perfect sacrifice for sin. His death was an atoning necessity if Adam's race was to survive the death that sin imposed on it. No other sacrifice would do. As we have explained, there was also the need of a holy and blameless High Priest to offer the blood of the Holy Lamb on the altar before God. For if Jesus did not break the power of death over his own body by rising to life, he could not enter the Most Holy Place, offer his blood on our behalf, and cancel our death sentence (see Hebrews 9:11-12). Jesus' bodily resurrection was a historical necessity.

"Because God's children are human beings—made of flesh and blood—Jesus also became flesh and blood by being born in human form. For only as a human being could he die, and only by dying could he break the power of the Devil, who had the power of death" (Hebrews 2:14). Jesus had to rise physically, bodily, from the dead "so that he could be our merciful and faithful High Priest before God. He then could offer a sacrifice that would take away the sins of the people" (Hebrews 2:17). That is why Paul the apostle was so emphatic about the bodily resurrection of Jesus being the foundation of our faith. He said, "If Christ has not been raised, then all our preaching is useless, and your faith is useless" (1 Corinthians 15:14 NLT). Jesus' promise to forgive us of our sins and be the atoning sacrifice that would allow us to have a relationship with God was based, not only upon his death, but also upon his resurrection.

"If Christ has not been raised...then your faith is useless, and you are still under condemnation for your sins...[and] we are the most miserable people in the world... But the fact is that Christ has been raised from the dead" (1 Corinthians 15:17,19-20). It is a historical reality that Jesus' body was raised to new life. And because of that, we have new life. "God is so rich in mercy, and he loved us so very much, that even while we were dead because of our sins, he gave us life when he raised Christ from the dead" (Ephesians 2:4-5).

Therefore:

> We believe the truth that Jesus died
> on the cross as a sacrifice for our sins
> and on the third day bodily rose to life
> again in order to transform our lives
> and secure our eternal salvation.

By the resurrection of Christ, God took an apparently disastrous Friday and turned it into Good Friday. The resurrection shows us clearly that death has no power over the righteous Son of the sovereign God. Jesus broke the power of death by rising from the grave, and in doing so he pierced the kingdom of darkness with a penetrating light. What seemed to be the destruction of Christ, throwing the human race into a hopeless situation, proved to be the very means of the hope of eternal life.

Even Gerd Lüdemann, an atheist scholar who has criticized Christianity for its supernatural claims, admits to the importance of Jesus' resurrection to the Christian faith. He states, "The resurrection of Jesus is the central point of the Christian religion...Evidently everything quite simply depends on the event of the resurrection of Jesus."[1] Lüdemann is right about that—everything does depend on the event of the resurrection. Christ's sacrificial death for our atonement would have been meaningless without his bodily resurrection.

Unless Jesus literally did rise from the dead, his promise of forgiven sins and an eternal relationship with God is nothing but a fantasy, a false hope. Jesus' death was an atoning necessity and his resurrection a historic necessity if our salvation is to mean anything at all.

CHAPTER THIRTY-THREE

EVIDENCE THAT JESUS LITERALLY ROSE FROM THE DEAD

Mr. McDowell,

I cannot fully agree with you. Christ's sacrificial death *is not* meaningless without his bodily resurrection. A sacrifice like that could never be meaningless.

Laura

The young woman who wrote this, even though a committed Christian, is missing the key point many people overlook about Christ's resurrection. Of course, it was the apostle Paul, not a McDowell, who said "our preaching is useless and so is your faith" if Christ has not risen from the dead (1 Corinthians 15:14 NIV). He said this because Jesus would have been less than deity if he could not conquer death. And he would not have been able to present his atoning blood before God without his bodily resurrection. Christ's redemptive act wasn't just in dying. Christ's redemptive act was both dying *and* offering his blood before God in a resurrected bodily form.

If we are not confident that Jesus literally rose from the grave to atone for our sins, our faith for salvation is on shaky ground. But the good news is that Christ's bodily resurrection is a historical fact. We have ample reason to believe that this pivotal event is factually true, and this gives us ample reason for great confidence in our hope of eternal salvation. As we consider some of these evidences for Christ's resurrection, allow them to solidify and firm up your faith as never before.

The Empty Tomb

It was early in the morning on the first day of the week when several women approached the tomb where Jesus had been buried. Jesus had been placed in the tomb late on Friday, which was the beginning of the Sabbath. Because of strict rules forbidding certain kinds of activities on the Sabbath, the women had not fully completed anointing the body of Jesus. Therefore, they had returned to complete the task.

But as they approached the tomb, they experienced a huge shock. The stone in front of the tomb was rolled away, and after looking inside they discovered that Jesus' body was gone. As they gaped, stunned and bewildered, two men appeared dressed in clothes that gleamed like lightning and said:

> "Why are you looking in a tomb for someone who is alive? He isn't here! He has risen from the dead! Don't you remember what he told you back in Galilee, that the Son of Man must be betrayed into the hands of sinful men and be crucified, and that he would rise again the third day?" Then they remembered that he had said this. So they rushed back to tell his eleven disciples—and everyone else—what had happened. The women who went to the tomb were Mary Magdalene, Joanna, Mary the mother of James, and several others. They told the apostles what had happened, but the story sounded like nonsense, so they didn't believe it (Luke 24:5-11).

As much as Jesus' disciples must have wanted to believe that the Messiah rose from the dead, they didn't. The women's report was simply too incredible—too good to be true. But soon they would see for themselves. Shortly afterward when the disciples were meeting together, Jesus appeared. "As he spoke, he held out his hands for them to see, and he showed them his side" (John 20:20). But Thomas, one of Jesus' disciples, wasn't at the meeting. When the others told him what they had seen with their own eyes he said, "I won't believe it unless I see the nail wounds in his hands, put my fingers into them, and place my hand into the wound in his side" (John 20:25).

Eight days later Jesus showed up again at a meeting of the disciples, and this time Thomas was there. Jesus offered to let the doubting man put his fingers in the wounds in his hand and side and said, "'Don't be faithless any longer. Believe!' 'My Lord and my God!' Thomas exclaimed" (John 20:27-28). The evidence was clear even to this man who insisted on empirical evidence—Jesus had risen from the dead!

Neither the friends of Christianity nor its foes could deny the stark fact that three days after Jesus was buried, his tomb was empty. The many who saw him after his resurrection knew why: They had direct, empirical, physical proof that he was alive. It is significant that after the resurrection, these suddenly emboldened disciples of Christ did not go off to Athens or Rome to preach that he had been resurrected; they went right back to the city of Jerusalem to proclaim it. That fact is highly significant because if what they were claiming was false, their message would have been easily disproved. The resurrection claim could not have been maintained for a moment in Jerusalem, the city where Jesus had been killed and buried, if the tomb had not been empty.

Philosopher Stephen Davis observes:

> Early Christian proclamation of the resurrection of Jesus in Jerusalem would have been psychologically and apologetically impossible without safe evidence of an empty tomb...in other words, without safe and agreed-upon evidence of an empty tomb, the apostles' claims would have been subject to massive falsification by the simple presentation of the body.[1]

Both Jewish and Roman sources and traditions acknowledge an empty tomb. These sources range from the Jewish historian Josephus to a fifth-century compilation of Jewish writing that satirized Jesus' life, called the *Toledoth Jeshu*. Author Dr. Paul Maier calls such acknowledgments "positive evidence from a hostile source, which is the strongest kind of historical evidence. In essence, this means that if a source admits a fact decidedly *not* in its favor, then that fact is genuine."[2]

One of the most compelling evidences for the truth of the empty tomb story is the fact that it records women as the first discoverers of the empty tomb. In first-century Palestine, women had a low status as citizens or legal witnesses. Except in rare circumstances, Jewish law precluded women from giving testimony in a court of law. Why would those who wanted to advance Christianity have contrived a story that embarrassed the disciples — the essential proponents of the new faith—by having them flee during the crucifixion and yet have women courageously approaching the tomb and providing the first testimony to its vacancy? Such a story would not have served the purpose of advancing the cause. Common sense tells us that the only reason the women were reported as the first witnesses was because it was the truth. Dr. Paul Maier accurately observes that "if the resurrection accounts had been manufactured... women would *never* have been included in the story, at least, not as first witnesses."[3]

The empty tomb of Jesus stands as a clear witness that, as the angel said, "He isn't here! He has risen from the dead" (Luke 24:6).

While the fact of the empty tomb is historically undeniable, there have been various alternative theories offered as explanations for why it was empty, as well as for the other phenomenal events in the days and weeks after Jesus' death. These theories attempt to explain these events without resorting to Jesus' bodily resurrection as the answer. We will cover six such theories here.*

---

* A more exhaustive treatment of Christ's resurrection can be found in our book entitled *Evidence for the Resurrection*, published by Regal Books.

The Stolen-Body Theory

The evidence of an empty tomb following the crucifixion and burial of Jesus does not by itself prove that he rose from the dead. Yet it does require explanation. One explanation that was offered within hours of the empty tomb's discovery was the theory that the disciples of Jesus had stolen the body. Matthew reports:

> Some of the men who had been guarding the tomb went to the leading priests and told them what had happened. A meeting of all the religious leaders was called, and they decided to bribe the soldiers. They told the soldiers, "You must say, 'Jesus' disciples came during the night while we were sleeping, and they stole his body.' If the governor hears about it, we'll stand up for you and everything will be all right." So the guards accepted the bribe and said what they were told to say. Their story spread widely among the Jews, and they still tell it today (Matthew 28:11-15).

The possibility that Jesus' tomb was empty because the disciples stole his body may seem plausible at first glance. However, the most cursory consideration will quickly show that the stolen-body theory creates more problems than it solves. For example:

- It was the Roman guards who were bribed into accusing the disciples of stealing the body. If the guards were sleeping, how could they have known whether the disciples—or anyone—stole the body? Sleeping sentinels can't reliably report what happened while they slept.

- Roman soldiers were executed for sleeping on guard duty (which explains Matthew's report of the religious leaders promising to protect the guards, saying, "If the governor hears about it, we'll stand up for you and everything will be all right"). How plausible is it that all the guards at the tomb would have decided to take a nap, knowing it could cost them their lives?

- Even if the Roman guards had slept, consider what it would have taken for thieves to remove the body from the tomb. The circular stone used to seal the tomb would have weighed between one and two tons! Thieves would have had to sneak past the guards, roll the large stone up a grooved incline, enter the dark tomb, and exit with the body...all without waking a single member of the detachment!

The notion that the disciples stole the body while the Roman guards slept more than strains the bounds of believability.

The Case of the Stolen Body

The detachment of Roman soldiers is not the only problem with the stolen-body theory. It's also difficult to imagine the followers of Jesus as being capable of pulling off such a feat. Consider this:

- It would have taken considerable bravery—even outright daring—to go up against a detachment of Roman soldiers whether they were asleep or awake. Yet the historical record shows that in the days following the death of Jesus the disciples were a depressed and cowardly group. They ran away at the first sign of trouble, denied any association with Jesus, and cowered behind locked doors—hardly the picture of a group that would risk arrest to steal their dead teacher's body (see Mark 14:50; Luke 22:54-62; John 20:19).

- One of the first witnesses on the scene of the empty tomb reported that the linen wrappings from Jesus' body were still present, and the grave cloth that had covered his head was neatly folded and arranged on the burial slab (see John 20:5-8). Can you imagine grave robbers taking the time to meticulously unwrap the body and neatly arrange the cloth on the stone slab? On the contrary, if the body had been stolen, the burial wrappings would certainly have been removed with the body.

- According to the historical accounts, the disciples were skeptical when they heard the news of the empty tomb. From all indications, they were not expecting an empty tomb, much less plotting to steal Jesus away.

- Why would a group of men who had run and hidden when Jesus was alive suddenly and courageously decide to steal his body and begin propagating a story that would certainly bring on them the very treatment (arrest, beatings, even death) they had fled just three days earlier?

Yet propagating the story of Jesus' resurrection is exactly what these disciples did. The historical record asserts that mere weeks after the death of Jesus, his followers were publicly preaching the news of his resurrection. During the week of Pentecost, in fact, thousands were "baptized and added to the church" as a result of this preaching (Acts 2:41).

|||||||||||||||||||||||||||||||||||||||||||||||||||||||||||||||||||||||||||||||||||||||||||||||||||||

You can be sure that if Jesus' body hadn't been resurrected, the religious and political leaders of the day could have quickly and effectively quashed the rising sect of Christianity by locating Christ's corpse and wheeling it through the streets of Jerusalem.

|||||||||||||||||||||||||||||||||||||||||||||||||||||||||||||||||||||||||||||||||||||||||||||||||||||

Such preaching must have driven the Jewish leaders to the point of utter consternation. The fact they could do nothing to disprove the resurrection further attests to its truth. You can be sure that if Jesus' body hadn't been resurrected, the religious and political leaders of the day could have quickly and effectively quashed the rising sect of Christianity by locating Christ's corpse and wheeling it through the streets of Jerusalem. This would have been undeniable evidence that the resurrection was a hoax. It would have destroyed Christianity practically before it started. But that never happened, which further bolsters the case for Jesus' resurrection.

The enemies of Jesus had every reason to produce his body. On the other hand it is implausible to believe that the followers of Jesus could or would have stolen his body. It seems clear that subscribing to the stolen-body theory means climbing a mountain of implausibilities. In short, while "the difficulties of belief may be great," as noted author George Hanson points out in *The Resurrection and the Life*, "the absurdities of unbelief are greater."[4]

But if the disciples did not steal the body of Jesus from his tomb, where did it go?

The Swoon Theory

Some people have tried to explain the empty tomb by suggesting that Jesus never really died. The swoon theory, as it has come to be called, supposes that Jesus was indeed nailed to the cross and suffered tremendous pain and loss of blood. But when he was removed from the cross, he wasn't quite dead; he was merely in shock.

Some proponents of this view even cite the New Testament record for evidence, showing that even "Pilate couldn't believe that Jesus was already dead" (Mark 15:44). They surmise that the disciples—aided by Joseph of Arimathea—took down the still-living Jesus from the cross and laid him in the tomb. (Hugh J. Schonfield, author of the bestseller *The Passover Plot,* even suggested that Jesus *planned* all this!)

Then—so the theory goes—Jesus, aided by the cool air of the tomb, by the reviving effects of the burial spices he was wrapped in, and by the many hours of quiet rest in the tomb, rose from his own burial slab, cast off his shroud, and left the tomb. When he met his disciples, they mistakenly thought he had risen from the dead...when, in fact, it was nothing more than a surprising resuscitation.

But the swoon theory has several fatal flaws.

The "Death Certificate"

Jesus had undergone a vicious beating. It was typical for Romans to use an instrument known as a *flagrum,* which often ripped the victim's back to shreds (as a result of this scourging many prisoners died before they could be executed). Jesus was then nailed by his hands and feet to a cross.

Then, because the next day was the beginning of the Jewish Passover and Jewish law did not allow them to leave a victim hanging on the cross overnight, the religious leaders asked Pilate to hasten death by ordering that the prisoners' legs be broken (see Deuteronomy 21:22-23; John 19:31). This action usually resulted in death by asphyxiation, as the victim, unable to push up on his feet to relieve the constriction caused by the weight of his body on his lungs and breathing passages, slowly suffocated.

When the crucifixion detail came to break the legs of Jesus, however, they discovered he was already dead. Nonetheless, to be sure, "one of the soldiers...pierced his side with a spear, and blood and water flowed out" (John 19:34). Soon thereafter, when Joseph of Arimathea requested custody of the body, the Roman governor expressed surprise that Jesus was already dead and demanded confirmation. *Only after receiving a firsthand report* did Pilate release the body into the hands of Joseph, thus fully verifying the fact that Jesus was dead before he was buried.

We not only have the scriptural account of Jesus' death by crucifixion, we also have extrabiblical evidence from first-century historians. Biblical scholar John Dominic Crossan writes, "Jesus' death by execution under Pontius Pilate is as sure as anything historical can ever be. For if no follower of Jesus had written anything for one hundred years after his crucifixion, we would still know about him, from two authors not among his supporters. Their names are Flavius Josephus and Cornelius Tacitus."[5] Neither the people most directly involved with Jesus' death nor the writers who reported it believed Jesus merely swooned. They knew he was dead.

The Grave Cloths

Jesus' followers prepared his body according to Jewish burial customs. Nicodemus provided "about seventy-five pounds of embalming ointment made from myrrh and aloes. Together [Nicodemus and Joseph] wrapped Jesus' body in a long linen cloth with the spices" (John 19:39-40).

The custom was to wrap the body tightly from the armpits to the ankles, layering the spices—often of a sticky, gummy consistency—between the wrappings. The spices served the dual purpose of preserving the body and acting as an adhesive for the grave cloths. The head was also wrapped in a turban-style cloth.

The historical records report that when the empty tomb was discovered on the first day of the week, the witnesses on the scene saw "the linen wrappings lying there, while the cloth that had covered Jesus' head was folded up and lying to the side" (John 20:6-7).

Accepting the swoon theory would require us to believe that Jesus, having suffered the unspeakable torture of scourging and crucifixion, awoke in a dark tomb, and with his arms bound to his side within the wrappings maneuvered himself out of the tightly wound cloths and spices, folded the cloth, laid it on the burial slab, and exited the tomb...naked.

Nineteenth-century theologian David Strauss was one of the most bitter of all opponents of the supernatural elements in the Gospels and a man whose works did much to destroy faith in Christ. Despite all of his vicious criticisms and firm denials of anything involving the miraculous, Strauss said this about the theory that Jesus revived from a swoon:

> It is impossible that a being who has been stolen half-dead out of the sepulcher, who crept about weak and ill, wanting medical treatment...could have given to the disciples the impression that he was a Conqueror over death and the grave, the Prince of Life, an impression which lay at the bottom of their future ministry.[6]

The Stone

Not only was Jesus tightly encased in burial cloths and spices, he was also buried in a rock tomb whose entrance was blocked by a stone weighing as much as one to two tons.

Let's assume Jesus had been taken from the cross in a "swoon," and the cold, damp tomb had revived him sometime later. Let's also assume that he managed to extricate himself from the hardened encasement of his burial clothes. We must next assume that once free of those constraints, he managed—from the inside of a tomb designed to be opened only from the outside—to roll a two-ton circular stone up the slotted incline (a difficult job for several men), while somehow propping the stone to prevent it from rolling down again and closing the tomb. All this had to be done by a man who, hours before, had been flogged, pierced with a crown of thorns, hanged on a cross by nails through his hands and feet, and stabbed in the ribs with a Roman spear. And it had to be done quietly enough to escape the notice of the soldiers who were guarding the tomb, allowing him to slip away unnoticed.

The Appearances

On the same day that Jesus was supposedly resuscitated in a cold, damp, dark tomb, unwrapped himself from the grave cloths, rolled a two-ton stone uphill, and sneaked by Roman sentinels guarding the tomb, he also walked more than seven miles from Jerusalem to Emmaus.

Luke 24 records Jesus' appearance to two of his followers, who were on the road to Emmaus, a seven-mile trek from Jerusalem. They didn't recognize Jesus until they reached their destination and invited him to eat with them. When he broke the bread in his customary way, "their eyes were opened, and they recognized him" (Luke 24:31).

Walking seven miles to Emmaus is hardly the kind of activity you would expect from a man who had been removed from an executioner's cross and had lain in a tomb for more than 36 hours. And somehow the two men he was walking with failed to notice that his skin was punctured, bruised, and shredded.

Yet the appearance of Jesus on the road to Emmaus is only the first in a string of appearances (within days of his brutal experience on the cross) that convinced Jesus' followers that he had defeated death and risen from the dead. The apostle Paul gives us yet another record of Christ's appearing after the resurrection:

> I passed on to you what was most important and what had also been passed on to me—that Christ died for our sins, just as the Scriptures said. He was buried, and he was raised from the dead on the third day, as the Scriptures said. He was seen by Peter and then by the twelve apostles. After that, he was seen by more than five hundred of his followers at one time, most of whom are still alive, though some have died by now. Then he was seen by James and later by all the apostles (1 Corinthians 15:3-7).

In these verses, Paul appeals to his audience's knowledge of the fact that Christ had been seen by more than 500 people at one time. Paul reminds them that most of these people were still alive and could be questioned. This statement is as strong evidence as anyone could hope to find for something that happened 2000 years ago.

Author C.H. Dodd has observed, "There can hardly be any purpose in mentioning the fact that most of the five hundred are still alive, unless Paul is saying, in effect, 'The witnesses are there to be questioned.'"[7]

This is why apologist William Lane Craig claims that "it is nearly indisputable that this appearance took place."[8] So soon after the event, Paul could never have claimed that Jesus had appeared to 500 witnesses if the event had not actually occurred.

If each of these 500 people were to testify in a courtroom for only six minutes each, including cross-examination, you would have an amazing 50 hours of firsthand eyewitness testimony. Add to this the testimony of the many other eyewitnesses, and you could well have the largest and most lopsided trial in history.[9]

The Ascension

If Jesus revived from a deathlike swoon, there is no reason to believe that he later ascended into heaven, as Mark and Luke record. But if Christ didn't ascend, where did he go? Is it reasonable to believe that Jesus withdrew from his followers to live out the rest of his life in seclusion and die in obscurity?

Such a theory would necessitate the belief that while the young church was preaching the news of Christ's resurrection, Jesus himself lived in some solitary retreat, unknown even to his closest followers, while his absence perpetuated the legend of

Christianity. This scenario would make Jesus Christ—whose teachings extolled the highest standards of morality—the greatest deceiver of all time and his resurrection the greatest hoax in history.

That would require believing that Jesus knowingly pursued an insane course of action: contriving his own resurrection to gain a renown he would never witness or enjoy.[10]

The Relocated Body Theory

This theory suggests that Jesus did not rise from the dead, but his body was temporarily stored in the tomb of Joseph of Arimathea on Friday night before being relocated to a criminal's tomb. Thus, the disciples mistakenly believed he was resurrected. This hypothesis has gained a considerable following on the Internet.

The "relocation hypothesis" gains support from the fact that reburial was common in ancient Palestine. But it's important to note that the reburial procedures of the Jews differed significantly from the theory proposed here. The Jewish tradition was to bury a body for one year, and then after the flesh deteriorated and only bones remained, they would remove the bones and place them in an ossuary—a "bone box" that was then buried.

The problem for this theory of the relocation of the body of Jesus is the complete lack of historical support, either in biblical or nonbiblical sources. None of the Gospel accounts suggest that the body of Jesus was reburied. The white-robed messenger at the tomb clearly undermines this view when he said, "He isn't here! He has been raised from the dead!" (Mark 16:6).

The relocation theory actually faces even a more significant problem. Dr. Michael Licona observes:

> At best, even if the reburial hypothesis were true, all it accounts for is the empty tomb. And interestingly, the empty tomb didn't convince any of the disciples—possibly with the exception of John—that Jesus had returned from the dead. It was the appearance of Jesus that convinced them, and the reburial theory can't account for these.[11]

If the body of Jesus was simply relocated, why didn't someone uncover the body when the disciples began proclaiming the resurrection? The Jewish leaders could have produced the body and stopped Christianity in its tracks. Some have suggested that by this time the body of Jesus would be unrecognizable, but given the climate of Palestine, the body would have been recognizable for a considerable amount of time. The relocation theory simply isn't plausible.[12]

The Hallucination Theory

There are only so many ways to explain the empty tomb. If the body wasn't stolen and hidden away, if Jesus didn't swoon and then resuscitate, and if his body wasn't relocated, what else could possibly have happened? Another explanation that has been offered is the hallucination theory.

This theory suggests that those who "saw" Jesus Christ after his death and burial were actually hallucinating. They may have *thought* they saw Jesus alive, but such appearances were the results of hallucination or the power of suggestion.

Hallucinations do occur. People are often mistaken, even deluded, about the things they see or experience. However, there are certain patterns to the experience of delusions and hallucinations. They are highly individualized and extremely subjective. It is exceedingly rare for two persons to experience the same hallucinations simultaneously.

The accounts of Jesus' resurrection appearances do not bear the marks of a hallucination. They occurred at disparate times. The witnesses were not expecting an appearance and were often puzzled or skeptical at first (see Luke 24:16; John 20:14,24-25). Most appearances were to groups of people (see Mark 16:14-18; John 21:1-24; 1 Corinthians 15:6). Jesus appeared at least ten different times following his resurrection:

1. to Mary of Magdala (Mark 16:9; John 20:11-18)

2. to the women returning from the tomb (Matthew 28:9-10)

3. to Peter (Luke 24:34; 1 Corinthians 15:5)

4. to two followers on the road to Emmaus (Luke 24:13-33)

5. to the disciples and a number of others (Luke 24:36-43)

6. to the disciples, including Thomas (John 20:26-29)

7. to seven disciples by the Sea of Galilee (John 21:1-23)

8. to more than five hundred followers (1 Corinthians 15:6)

9. to James, his brother (1 Corinthians 15:7)

10. to the eleven disciples at his ascension (Acts 1:4-9)

Another factor that argues against the hallucination theory is the record of Jesus' invitations to verify his flesh-and-blood presence with them:

> "Look at my hands. Look at my feet. You can see that it's really me. Touch me and make sure that I am not a ghost, because ghosts don't have bodies, as you see that I do!"...Then he asked them, "Do you have anything here to eat?" They gave him a piece of broiled fish, and he ate it as they watched (Luke 24:39-43).

The people who saw Jesus were not the kind of people most likely to suffer delusions. They were a skeptical bunch, who were often slow to believe. When the women came to the apostles that Sunday morning with the first news of the empty tomb, "the story sounded like nonsense, so they didn't believe it" (Luke 24:11). Peter and John's first reaction was to race to the site themselves to see with their own eyes what the women had reported. And Thomas could not have been the victim of wishful thinking. "I won't believe it," he vowed, "unless I see the nail wounds in his hands, put my fingers into them, and place my hand into the wound in his side" (John 20:25).

The hallucination theory—like the other theories—doesn't stack up against the historical record. Like the other attempts to explain the resurrection, it seems to require more faith than it does to believe the testimony of the eyewitnesses: that "during the forty days after his crucifixion, [Jesus] appeared to the apostles from time to time and proved to them in many ways that he was actually alive" (Acts 1:3).[13]

The Spiritual Resurrection Theory

This theory claims that Christ's body decayed in the grave and his real resurrection was spiritual. Jehovah's Witnesses espouse a form of this theory. Rather than believing that Jesus' body decayed in the grave, however, they believe that God destroyed the body in the tomb and that Jesus rose in an immaterial body. Both of these "spiritual resurrection" theories have insurmountable problems.

First, to have any meaning, a resurrection must entail the physical. In the view of Palestinian Judaism, a spiritual resurrection without the physical body would not be a resurrection at all. Dan Cohn-Sherbok, a Jewish rabbi and visiting professor at Cambridge, observed:

> Either Jesus was physically resurrected or he wasn't. It's as simple as that. The Gospel account of the empty tomb and the disciples' recognition of the risen Christ point to such a historical conception of the resurrection event. To them it would make no sense that in some spiritual—as opposed to physical sense—Jesus' body was revivified.[14]

British scholar N.T. Wright has demonstrated that although there were various conceptions of the afterlife in first-century Judaism, "resurrection" had a particular meaning. Wright explains:

> However wide that spectrum may have been and however many positions different Jews may have taken upon it, "resurrection" always denotes *one position within* that spectrum. "Resurrection" was not a term for "life after death" in general. It always meant reembodiment.[15]

Wright also demonstrates that "there is no evidence for Jews…using the word *resurrection* to denote something essentially nonconcrete."[16] If Jesus had been raised in an immaterial body, the disciples would not have described it as a *resurrection*.

Jesus himself completely demolished the spiritual-resurrection theory. When his startled disciples thought they were seeing a spirit, Jesus admonished them: "See My hands and My feet, that it is I Myself, touch Me and see; for a spirit does not have flesh and bones as you see that I have" (Luke 24:39 NASB). Later, Christ ate fish with his followers, further demonstrating his flesh-and-bone mode of existence. Matthew records that when they met Jesus they took hold of his feet and worshipped him (see Matthew 28:9). You don't grab the legs of a spirit! Some have argued that Jesus temporarily manifested himself in a physical body so the disciples would recognize him. While this is a creative response, it is arbitrary, and what is worse, it would involve deception on Jesus' part, which is clearly inconsistent with his character and nature.

Paul also demolishes the spiritual-resurrection theory in his discussion of the resurrection body in 1 Corinthians 15:29-58. As a former Pharisee, Paul firmly believed in a physical resurrection. Basing his theology on the resurrection of Christ, Paul argues that we too will be physically raised someday. While resurrected bodies are physically different from our current bodies, the difference involves enhancement; they are nonetheless thoroughly physical.

Some have disagreed with this interpretation of this passage, basing their argument on Paul's claim in 1 Corinthians 15:44 that "it is sown a *natural* body, it is raised a *spiritual* body." "See," they claim, "Paul believed in an immaterial resurrection!" What this objection fails to consider is that the word *spiritual,* in this context, does not connote *immaterial.* We often refer to the Bible as a "spiritual" book, yet we clearly don't mean that it is immaterial!

Michael Licona did a fairly exhaustive historical investigation of the Greek terms translated "natural" and "spiritual" in 1 Corinthians 15:44. After searching ancient texts from the eighth century BC through the third century AD he concluded, "Although I did not look at all of the 846 occurrences, I viewed most. I failed to find a single reference where *psuchikon* [the word translated *natural* in 15:44] possessed a meaning of 'physical' or 'material.'"[17] It is simply false to say that Paul was contrasting a physical body with a nonphysical body. Stephen Davis warns:

> We should not be misled by Paul's use of the term "spiritual body." He is not using this term to signify a body "formed out of spirit" or made of "spiritual matter," whatever that might mean, but rather a body that has been glorified or transformed by God and is now fully dominated by the power of the Holy Spirit.[18]

A good example of this is when Paul speaks of "those who are spiritual" in 1 Corinthians 2:15. He clearly did not mean invisible, immaterial people with no physical body; he meant those who are guided by the power of the Holy Spirit.

Others object to a physical resurrection because in 1 Corinthians 15:50 Paul says that "flesh and blood cannot inherit the kingdom of God." "See," they say, "Jesus' body had to be immaterial so he could be in heaven!" Theologian Norman Geisler responds to this assertion: "The phrase, 'flesh and blood,' in this context apparently means *mortal* flesh and blood, that is, a mere human being."[19] His interpretation is supported throughout Scripture. For example, in Matthew 16:17 Jesus says, "Blessed are you, Simon Barjona, because *flesh and blood* did not reveal this to you, but My Father who is in heaven" (NASB).

The spiritual-resurrection theory completely ignores our two principles of research. The facts of the case don't even begin to fit the theory, and they are forced into a preconceived conclusion about what happened.[20]

The Mystery-Religion Theory

"Nothing in Christianity is original" is one of the most memorable lines from the runaway bestseller *The Da Vinci Code.* In the late nineteenth and early twentieth centuries many scholars believed that the central claims of Christianity had been plagiarized from Greco-Roman mystery religions. Jesus was considered another "dying and rising" god in the tradition of Osiris, Mithras, Adonis, and Dionysus.

While this theory has experienced a surprising resurgence on the Internet and in popular-level books, it faces near universal rejection by contemporary scholars. Here's why.

Although parallels between Jesus and the mystery religions may appear striking on the surface, they collapse under scrutiny. Osiris, for instance, is considered by many to be a dying and rising god from ancient Egypt. According to the myth, Osiris was killed by Seth and resuscitated by Isis. But rather than returning to the world in a resurrected body, Osiris became king of the underworld—hardly a parallel to the historical resurrection of Jesus. This is one of numerous reasons why Paul Rhodes Eddy and Greg Boyd, authors of *The Jesus Legend,* conclude that "the differences between Christianity and the mystery religions are far more profound than any similarities. While there certainly are parallel *terms* used in early Christianity and the mystery religions, there is little evidence for parallel *concepts.*"[21]

Unlike the accounts of the historical Jesus, there is no evidence for the reliability of any of the alleged parallel stories in the mystery religions. Jesus of Nazareth ate, slept, performed miracles, died, and returned to life. These accounts are supported by a reliable historical record. In contrast, the dying and rising gods of the mystery religions were timeless myths repeated annually with the changing seasons.

The most recent scholarly treatise on dying and rising gods was written by T.N.D. Mettinger, professor at Lund University. In *The Riddle of Resurrection,* Mettinger grants the existence of the myths of dying and rising gods in the ancient world, which, he admits, is a minority view. Yet his conclusion puts the nail in the coffin of the copycat theory:

> There is, as far as I am aware, no prima facie evidence that the death and resurrection of Jesus is a mythological construct, drawing on the myths and rites of the dying and rising gods of the surrounding world. While studied with profit against the background of Jewish resurrection belief, the faith in the death and resurrection of Jesus retains its unique character in the history of religions. The riddle remains.[22]

The Reality of the Risen Lord

The reality of Jesus' resurrection had a profound impact on the disciples. They were transformed from cringing cowards who hid themselves away to bold preachers, most of whom suffered persecution and gave their lives for their risen Lord. This sudden bravery and boldness is an enormous change that demands explanation. Let's examine this transformation more closely and consider its implications.

When the authorities captured Jesus in the Garden of Gethsemane, the Bible tells us that "all the disciples left him and fled" (Matthew 26:56; see Mark 14:50). During Christ's trial, Peter went out and denied three times that he even knew Jesus (see Mark 14:66-72; John 18:15-27). After Christ was crucified, the fearful disciples hid themselves in an upper room and locked the doors (see John 20:19). These disciples were skeptical when they first heard about the empty tomb. One of them refused to believe until he personally touched Jesus' wounds. And two disciples on the road to Emmaus doubted even as they talked personally to Jesus.

But within days something happened to utterly change this group of cowardly followers into a bold band of enthusiasts who were willing to face a life of suffering for the cause of Christ.[23] What was it? What transformed these disappointed followers into true believers? Only one explanation makes sense. It was the reality of the risen Christ. And in the days to follow they openly proclaimed this good news in Jerusalem, Judea, and Samaria, and eventually to the ends of the earth.

That truth is for us as well. Like those early disciples, we can also trust the eternal salvation we have in the risen Christ because we have ample evidence to show us that the record of what he did for us is absolutely true.

So, dear brothers and sisters, we can boldly enter heaven's Most Holy Place because of the blood of Jesus. This is the new, life-giving way that Christ has opened up for us through the sacred curtain, by means of his death for us. And since we have a great High Priest who rules over God's people, let us go right into the presence of God, with true hearts fully trusting him (Hebrews 10:19-22).

CHAPTER THIRTY-FOUR

Overcoming the Fear of Death

Sixty-five-year-old Thelma sat in the waiting room fidgeting with the magazine in her lap. Her husband of over 48 years chatted quietly with a patient next to him, who was also waiting to see the doctor.

"Mrs. Milner?" the nurse called, "The doctor will see you now." Thelma and her husband made their way to an examination room.

"Good to see you again, Thelma," the doctor said in a cheery voice as he entered. "You too, Mr. Milner." The doctor made his way to a chair and opened the file folder in his hand.

"Well, there is no easy way to say this, Thelma," the doctor said in a serious tone. "The tests confirm you are in the first stages of Alzheimer's disease."

Thelma's hand instinctively went to her mouth as she let out a slight groan. Her husband grimaced as he placed his arm around his stunned wife.

For the next 15 years, one of the longest cases ever, Thelma's family watched as her body, mind, and all traces of her memory were ravaged. A once beautiful and vibrant woman was reduced to nothing more than skin and bones. Finally, unable to eat, speak, or respond to the voice and touch of loved ones, Thelma gasped her last breath and was gone, leaving behind a grieving family.

Like the Milner family, all of us will at some point suffer the loss of a loved one. The emptiness and suffering from such a death is real, and at times it feels almost unbearable. While the comfort from loved ones and the passing of time dulls the pain, the reality is that death is an inevitable shadow that robs people of the ones they love.

It is understandable that death is a scary thought, even to many Christians. Job described it as "the king of terrors" (Job 18:14). Most of us avoid talking about death, and even when we do talk about it, we use euphemisms to soften or disguise the harsh reality. We prefer terms such as "pass away," "go to sleep," or "go to be with the Lord."

Why, exactly, do we fear death? There are at least five reasons.

1. *Death is mysterious and unknown.* It is normal to fear the unknown. There is often a great deal of apprehension because we don't know exactly what to expect. And death poses the greatest of all unknowns.

2. *We have to face death alone.* If we could join together and face the unknown mysteries of death in a group, perhaps it would be easier to bear the thought of it. But we cannot. We must travel alone into that dark night.

3. *We are separated from our loved ones.* Like the Milner family, death robs us of the ones closest to us. And some may even question whether we will ever meet them again.

4. *Our personal hopes and dreams will not be realized.* When we die, our goals die with us. We cannot continue to build our dreams. Death ends the best of our plans.

5. *Death is unavoidable.* Even with today's scientific advances that extend the length of our lives, all of us will die. No one can escape the inevitability of death.[1]

While all of this is true, there is still a significant consolation. As Christians we can experience freedom from the fear of death. The relevance of Jesus' bodily resurrection is not only that our sins are atoned for, but that we will also live again. So will our loved one if he or she has placed their trust in Christ.

Freedom from Fear Because Death Has Been Conquered

When Jesus' close friends Mary and Martha lost their brother, he told them, "I am the resurrection and the life. Those who believe in me, even though they die like everyone else, will live again. They are given eternal life for believing in me and will never perish" (John 11:25-26). Because Jesus is our resurrected Lord, we will be God's resurrected children. God "has made all of this plain to us by the coming of Christ Jesus, our Savior, who broke the power of death and showed us the way of everlasting life" (2 Timothy 1:10).

Yes, death is inevitable and so we all must die. But death isn't permanent for those who have trusted Christ. "Everyone dies because all of us are related to Adam, the first man. But all who are related to Christ, the other man, will be given new life. But there is an order to this resurrection: Christ was raised first; then when Christ comes back, all his people will be raised" (1 Corinthians 15:22-23).

Although we are redeemed, justified, sanctified, and adopted as God's children in this life, we have yet to gain the full rights of our adoption. Paul said that "what we suffer now is nothing compared to the glory he will reveal to us later...for we long for our bodies to be released from sin and suffering. We,

Not only are we forgiven of our sins and made right with God, but we also inherit a body that will live forever.

too, wait with eager hope for the day when God will give us our full rights as his adopted children, including the new bodies he has promised us. We were given this hope when we were saved" (Romans 8:18,23-24 NLT). That is the added relevance of Christ's resurrection. Not only are we forgiven of our sins and made right with God, but we also inherit a body that will live forever. This means that one day we will experience glorification.

New bodies. Bodies that won't suffer pain, endure hardships, or wear out. That is our future inheritance. "Someone may ask, 'How will the dead be raised? What kind of bodies will they have?'...Our earthly bodies, which die and decay, will be different when they are resurrected, for they will never die. Our bodies now disappoint us, but when they are raised, they will be full of glory. They are weak now, but when they are raised, they will be full of power. They are natural bodies now, but when they are raised, they will be spiritual bodies...Every human being has an earthly body just like Adam's, but our heavenly bodies will be just like Christ's" (1 Corinthians 15:35,42-44,48).

That is certainly a truth we can embrace and look forward to. Peter called it our "priceless inheritance." "Now we live with a wonderful expectation because Jesus Christ rose again from the dead. For God has reserved a priceless inheritance for his children. It is kept in heaven for you, pure and undefiled, beyond the reach of change and decay" (1 Peter 1:3-4). This priceless inheritance is a state of being in which each of us will be given "full rights" to a glorified, heavenly body to live where "there will be no more death or sorrow or crying or pain" (Revelation 21:4). This means we will have perfect bodies in a perfect world. Yet for that to come about, Paul said, "our perishable earthly bodies must be transformed into heavenly bodies that will never die" (1 Corinthians 15:53). And that can, and will, happen to the redeemed because Jesus rose from the grave.

This promise is as exciting as anything we read in the Bible. It elates us; it gives us hope; it stimulates the imagination. And it excites our natural curiosity. When does that eternal life begin? When do we get our resurrected bodies? Do our loved ones in Christ have them already? Do we get the "new bodies he has promised us" immediately upon our own death? Or do we have to wait in the grave or somewhere else until Christ returns in order to get a resurrection body?

The Timing of Our Resurrection

Jesus said, "There are many rooms in my Father's home, and I am going to prepare a place for you. If this were not so, I would tell you plainly. When everything is ready, I will come and get you, so that you will always be with me where I am" (John 14:2-3). This passage makes it clear that Jesus plans to come back to get his followers. Paul the apostle said that Christ "has become the first of a great harvest of those who will be raised to life again" (1 Corinthians 15:20). Jesus is the first one to receive a spiritual body, and all those who trust in him are next in line to get theirs. "Christ was raised first; then when Christ comes back, all his people will be raised" (1 Corinthians 15:23).

Scripture makes clear there is an order or timing to the resurrection of believers. "Let me tell you a wonderful secret God has revealed to us," Paul says. "Not all of us will die, but we will all be transformed. It will happen in a moment, in the blinking of an eye, when the last trumpet is blown. For when the trumpet sounds, the Christians who have died will be raised with transformed bodies. And then we who are living will be transformed so that we will never die" (1 Corinthians 15:51-52; also see 1 Thessalonians 4:13-18). The order is clear: Christ was raised first and he ascended into heaven. When he returns, the dead in Christ will be raised with new bodies, and those Christians who remain alive will receive their new bodies as well.

This naturally raises another question: "If we don't get our spiritual bodies until Jesus returns, are God's children existing consciously without bodies? And if so, where?" Some say that Christians who have died are simply "asleep" and will remain in an unconscious state until the return of Christ. Since Paul makes reference to those "who have fallen asleep in him" (1 Thessalonians 4:14 NIV), and other such passages use a similar language (see 1 Thessalonians 5:10; Matthew 9:24; John 11:11), some believe we go into what they call a "soul sleep." They say that those in Christ who are "sleeping" will be awakened at the resurrection and receive new bodies.

However, most evangelicals consider the "fallen asleep" phrases in Scripture as euphemisms for death that describe the body's outward appearance. The physical body is "sleeping" until the resurrection, while our nonphysical souls enjoy a conscious existence with the Lord. The Old Testament declares, "You were made from dust, and to the dust you will return" (Genesis 3:19) and "For then the dust will return to the earth, and the spirit will return to God who gave it" (Ecclesiastes 12:7).

But is this actually a conscious spirit existence with God even before we are bodily resurrected? Yes. Jesus told the dying thief on the cross, "I assure you, today you will be with me in paradise" (Luke 23:43). Obviously, the thief wouldn't be getting his spiritual body until Christ returned, yet Jesus said that the man would be with him. Paul said he preferred "to be absent from the body and to be at home with the Lord" (2 Corinthians 5:8 NASB). All the references in Revelation to humans prior to the resurrection of the dead depict them as conscious souls.

As these passages indicate, when Christians die they enter into what theologians refer to as an "intermediate state." This is considered a transitional existence spanning the period between a believer's death and Christ's return when all who are dead will be bodily resurrected. This moment of resurrection when the spirit is reunited with a transformed body is often referred to as "going to heaven." But as we will discuss in later chapters, there is a difference between an intermediate heaven and the eternal heaven (see chapters 26 and 27).

If our souls are with the Lord in an intermediate heaven prior to the resurrection of the dead, do we function as physical human beings during that time? These are issues that Scripture simply doesn't address. Yet theologians such as Randy Alcorn have ventured to say:

> Given the consistent physical description of the intermediate Heaven and those who dwell there, it seems possible—though this is certainly debatable—that between our earthly life and our bodily resurrection, God may grant us some physical form that will allow us to function as human beings while in that unnatural state "between bodies," awaiting our resurrection.[2]

Because He Lives

Because of Christ's resurrection and the promises he has made to us, our fear of death can be lifted. Because he lives...

- *The mystery of death is revealed.* Yes, death is mysterious and unknown, but after the resurrection of Jesus, we know something about it that we could not have known before. It is not permanent. Christ went through it, and he blazed a trail we can follow. Some of the mystery has been removed because we now have footprints to follow that we know will lead us into new life.

- *We don't have to face death alone.* Although from our perspective it may seem that we have to go through death alone, we now know this is an illusion. The death and resurrection of Jesus shows that this promise is not empty. Christ has actually stepped into the darkness of death and awaits us there with the light of life to lead us safely through.

- *We are not permanently separated from our loved ones.* The resurrection calms this fear as well. Because God has conquered death through Jesus Christ, our loving relationships will continue after death. Death may separate us temporarily from our loved ones, but the resurrection of Christ will bring us back together.

- *Our personal hopes and dreams have a future.* The resurrection also does away with this fear. In fact, it would be accurate to say that in heaven all our hopes and dreams will be fulfilled.

- *Death is unavoidable, yet it is a transition to eternal life.* It's true that death is inevitable and no one can escape it. But because of Christ's resurrection, death is simply the passage to our eternal home in heaven.[3]

While there may not be answers to all our questions, the resurrection of Christ answers the most pressing ones. Above all, this one thing is certain: We are guaranteed a "priceless inheritance" that includes a resurrected spiritual body that will live forever with the Lord and our loved ones. That is possible because Jesus conquered death and rose from the grave. While we may not have all our questions answered about our future bodies and home in heaven, by Christ's resurrection God has revealed a taste of what it will be like. Paul says:

> The wisdom we speak of is the secret wisdom of God…That is what the Scriptures means when they say,
> "No eye has seen, no ear has heard, and no mind has imagined what God has prepared for those who love him."
> But we know these things because God has revealed them to us by his Spirit, and his Spirit searches out everything and shows us even God's deep secrets (1 Corinthians 2:7,9-10).

In the scriptures we have explored in this chapter, God has revealed to us, his adopted children, a taste of what an eternal relationship with him will be like. He has revealed himself through his Spirit and his Word in order that, as Jesus said, "My joy may be in you and that your joy may be complete" (John 15:11 NIV). As a loving father and mother desire to fill their child with anticipation of a vacation or trip to Disney World, so our heavenly Father wants to see our hearts filled with joy of what awaits us. He wants us to sense the joy of what heaven and eternity will be like. He wants us to anticipate living with him eternally in a place where there is no sin or heartache.

One day Jesus will conquer death to bring you and your loved ones into a place of completed joy beyond compare. At that point death will be "swallowed up in victory" (1 Corinthians 15:54). As a Christian, your resurrection is an assured reality. Because of Christ's resurrection, your eternal relationship with God and with your loved ones in heaven is guaranteed. You are destined for an eternal future of bliss. Anticipate what is to come and be excited!

CHAPTER THIRTY-FIVE

LIVING BODILY ON EARTH
WITH OUR HEARTS IN HEAVEN

If you have trusted in Christ as your Redeemer, your bodily resurrection is assured and you will live forever in God's presence. But how is your anticipation of that future life to affect your life now? Paul says, "Since you have been raised to new life with Christ, set your sights on the realities of heaven, where Christ sits at God's right hand in the place of honor and power. Let heaven fill your thoughts. Do not think only about things down here on earth" (Colossians 3:1-2).

How are we to take this scripture? How are we to fill our thoughts with anticipation of a perfect life in heaven when we have so many things to do, places to go, obligations to fulfill? Your life and ours are consumed with earthly concerns. What am I going to eat today? How am I going to pay all these bills? When am I going to get another raise? Who am I going to marry? How do I keep this marriage together? When are we going to have kids? Who's watching the kids? What are they getting into, anyway?

Our minds are flooded with a million things at once, most of them about earthly things—college, marriage, raising a family, retirement. Yet Jesus said, "Don't store up treasures here on earth, where they can be eaten by moths and get rusty...store your treasures in heaven...Wherever your treasure is, there your heart and thoughts will also be...So I tell you, don't worry about everyday life—whether you have enough food, drink, and clothes...Why be like the pagans who are so deeply concerned about these things? Your heavenly Father already knows all your needs, and he will give you all you need from day to day if you live for him and make the Kingdom of God your primary concern" (Matthew 6:19-21,25,32-33).

What does all that really mean? How do we live in anticipation of the resurrection and not make this life such a big priority?

Focusing Our Hearts in the Right Place

I (Sean) remember how my thought process and entire life changed after meeting this stunning girl named Stephanie. Yes, I was struck by her beauty, but it was more than that. She was smart and funny and had a great personality. She and I liked a lot of the same things, and I wanted to be with her all the time. When I was at basketball practice I thought about her. When I was in school I thought about her. When I was at home I thought about her. I couldn't get her out of my mind because she had made a place in my heart.

It seemed that every waking moment this woman captivated my thoughts. There was more to it than I could really understand. There was a mystery to this consuming passion of mine. I knew her and yet I didn't, so I wanted to know her more. I wanted to know her on a level I had never really experienced with anyone else before. *Because I was in love!*

After Stephanie and I married, the love affair deepened. In fact, our togetherness created a home of our own for us. While marriage meant we could spend a lot of time together, I still had to be away at times. Stephanie didn't like me being away. She became a little jealous when I was at work or at the seminary too long. At times I had to travel to a speaking engagement. Of course, I would e-mail her and call her. But it wasn't the same. She missed me and wanted me home. And I liked it that she did. I missed her too. I missed that place of emotional security and relational intimacy that existed in my love life with the person of my dreams.

That is a small picture of what it means to set our "sights on the realities of heaven." It's not a matter of sitting around pining away and hoping for the day we're dead and in heaven. It means our priorities, our interests, and our devotion are placed in another world with another person—Jesus. And when we get too focused on earthly things, he gets jealous.

The disciple James made it clear. He wrote, "If your aim is to enjoy this world, you can't be a friend of God. What do you think the Scriptures mean when they say that the Holy Spirit, whom God has placed within us, jealously longs for us to be faithful?" (James 4:4-5). Jesus said, "No one can serve two masters. For you will hate the one and love the other, or be devoted to one and despise the other" (Matthew 6:24). And when we give our devotion, our undivided heart to earthly things, Jesus gets jealous.

Stephanie wanted me to think about her while I was away just like I wanted her to think about me. And if another woman captured my thoughts and heart, she would have been seriously offended—as she should have been. Isn't it humbling to think that Jesus is jealous if our hearts and thoughts are on earthly things rather than on him and our home with him? He wants "heaven to fill our thoughts." He wants us to keep him as our priority. He wants us to long for him as we long for our earthly lovers and our homes with them.

Living for our future homes with new bodies in the presence of Jesus isn't a matter of just daydreaming day in and day out. It's about what kind of treasures we are building and where our priorities are in this life. Paul talked about those whose "god is their appetite"—their earthly pleasures—"and all they think about is this life here on earth" (Philippians 3:19). But we who are spiritually resurrected in Christ are not about building earthly kingdoms and living our life for the pleasures this world can give. Rather, "we are citizens of heaven," Paul says, "where the Lord Jesus Christ lives. And we are eagerly waiting for him to return as our Savior. He will take these weak mortal bodies of ours and change them into glorious bodies like his own, using the same mighty power that he will use to conquer everything, everywhere" (Philippians 3:20-21). Our focus on our future doesn't take us out of this world; it simply keeps our attention where it belongs while we are here.

Jesus prayed for his disciples by saying to his Father, "I'm not asking you to take them out of the world, but to keep them safe from the evil one. They are not part of this world any more than I am. Make them pure and holy by teaching them your words of truth" (John 17:15-17). Living in this world with our hearts in the next does involve our being engaged in the business and activities going on around us. Yet the fact that our hearts are properly focused on the next enables us to be more effective in God's business right here and now—living out his truth and building up his kingdom. C.S. Lewis said it well:

> If you read history, you will find that the Christians who did most for the present world were just those who thought most about the next. The apostles themselves, who set on foot the conversion of the Roman Empire, the great men who built up the Middle Ages, the English Evangelicals who abolished the Slave Trade, all left their mark on Earth, precisely because their minds were occupied with heaven. It is since Christians have largely ceased to think of the other world that they have become so ineffective in this. Aim at heaven and you will get earth "thrown in": Aim at earth and you will get neither.[1]

King David, who was a man after God's own heart, ruled the nation of Israel well and accomplished much on earth. Though his heart was fixed on God, he still obeyed his commands concerning how to live his life on earth. In fact he paid all the more attention to living right on earth *because* his thoughts were on God. "I reflect at night on who you are, O LORD," David said, "and I obey your law because of this" (Psalm 119:55).

A Matter of Faith

Living in this world with our heart in the next doesn't happen naturally. As we said, life with all its concerns tends to consume us. To "set your sights on the realities of heaven" and keep them there requires that we live by faith. "What is faith?" the writer of Hebrews asks. "It is the confident assurance that what we hope for is going to happen. It is the evidence of things we cannot yet see" (Hebrews 11:1). To maintain a kingdom of heaven mentality requires a "confident assurance" that God is in control and that his promises are real and will be fulfilled. When we have an intelligent faith that knows why we believe, we are confident God's promises are true.

To live in this world with our heart in the next requires a faith that fixes our spiritual eyes on Jesus.

The saints of old had an intelligent faith that gave them confidence. "It was by faith that Abel brought a more acceptable offering to God than Cain...It was by faith that Enoch was taken up to heaven without dying...It was by faith that Noah built an ark to save his family...It was by faith that Abraham obeyed when God called him to leave home and go to another land...All these faithful ones died without receiving what God had promised them, but they saw it all from a distance and welcomed the promises of God" (Hebrews 11:4,5,7,8,13). These faithful followers of God lived in the world, but they were not of this world. "They were no more than foreigners and nomads here on earth...But they were looking for a better place, a heavenly homeland. That is why God is not ashamed to be called their God, for he has prepared a heavenly city for them" (Hebrews 11:13,16).

It is by an intelligent faith that we endure hardship, trials, and difficulties here on earth. It is by this kind of faith that we set our eyes and hearts on a future of joy after death. If you've lived very long, it's clear to you that death puts a cold blanket on any plans for the future. You may enjoy a pet, like a dog or cat, but it dies. Its future is snuffed out and so is your joy. A grandmother or grandfather, a brother or sister, a husband or wife breathes their last and their future is no more. Joy is snatched from us. Death does that. It is only by an intelligent faith we have confident assurance that we can see a future after death. It is only by faith we can have joy in the face of tragedy or death. Because an intelligent faith is trusting what the eyes can't see.

Max Lucado speaks of what faith sees in his book *When God Whispers Your Name*:

> Eyes see the prowling lion. Faith sees Daniel's angel.
> Eyes see storms. Faith sees Noah's rainbow.
> Eyes see giants. Faith sees Canaan.
> Your eyes see your faults. Your faith sees your Savior.
> Your eyes see your guilt. Your faith sees his blood.
> Your eyes see your grave. Your faith sees a city
>   whose builder and maker is God.[2]

We are surrounded by a world that clamors for our attention and attempts to draw our hearts in its direction. It is a world of busyness that compels us to cope with life in all its difficulties and troubles. That is the world we see. Our task is to see yet another world invisible to the eye. It can only be seen by faith. The writer of Hebrews wraps up his great chapter that lists example after example of people who longed for another country and saw it by faith by saying:

> Therefore, since we are surrounded by such a huge crowd of witnesses to the life of faith, let us strip off every weight that slows us down, especially the sin that so easily hinders our progress. And let us run with endurance the race that God has set before us. We do this by keeping our eyes on Jesus, on whom our faith depends from start to finish (Hebrews 12:1-2).

Deepening Our Longing for God

"Keeping our eyes on Jesus." That's the key. To live in this world with our heart in the next requires a faith that fixes our spiritual eyes on Jesus. He longs for us to long after him. He wants us to be homesick for him. He wants us to thirst after him. He wants us to be like King David who prayed, "As the deer pants for streams of water, so I long for you, O God. I thirst for God, the living God. When can I come and stand before him?" (Psalm 42:1-2). David goes on to pray, "O God, you are my God; I earnestly search for you. My soul thirsts for you; my whole body longs for you in this parched and weary land where there is no water" (Psalm 63:1).

Take time to cultivate your longing and thirst for God and the home he is preparing for you. The more you spend time focused on him, the more life in this temporal world takes on an eternal perspective. The things that are real and lasting come into focus. When we keep our hearts in the next world, we can experience true peace when this earthly world all around us is in turmoil.

Pastor and theologian Calvin Miller captures the secret to the true peace we can have when we see God through the power of his Holy Spirit:

God becomes visible to those who look for him in the right place. There-fore, no eye—no literal eye—can see him! No ear can hear him! No mind can conceive him! He hides his vastness only in the deepest dimensions of our inner existence.

The world around us is the world of "outer" relationships. In such outer places we make friends, achieve success—get on in the world! In this busy, worried world we have appointments, face disappointments, and force our ego-driven souls to stab at achieving power. On the surface of our lives, things frenzied and dyspeptic dominate us. But in our hearts it is quite another matter.

First Corinthians 2:10 contains one little word that lunges at us with challenge: "But God has revealed it to us by his Spirit. The Spirit searches all things, even the *deep* things of God" (NIV).

Deep is the dwelling place of God. *Deep* is the character of the ocean. Hold the metaphor for a moment and savor its lesson ahead of time. For deep is where the noisy, trashy surface of the ocean gets quiet and serene. No sound breaks the awesome silence of the ocean's heart. Most Christians, however, spend their lives being whipped tumultuously through the sur-face circumstances of their days. Their frothy lifestyles mark the surface nature of their lives. Yet those who plumb the deep things of God discover true peace for the first time.[3]

Take time out of your busy schedule to "plumb the deep things of God." Spend time with his Word. Meditate on him and cultivate your longing for him. Let him know you hunger to know him more deeply than ever. See him by faith in your new home of the future. Praise him in advance for the new body he will give you because of his resurrection. As you do you will gain a new perspective on this life and the things that really matter.

Take a moment to carefully read and meditate on the words of the psalmist David. He saw God through his eyes of faith. He lived on earth but his heart was in another world. He said:

> I have seen you in your sanctuary and gazed
>> upon your power and glory.
> Your unfailing love is better to me than life itself;
>> how I praise you!
> I will honor you as long as I live, lifting up
>> my hands to you in prayer.
> You satisfy me more than the richest of foods.
>> I will praise you with songs of joy.

I lie awake thinking of you, meditating
    on you through the night.
I think how much you have helped me; I sing
    for joy in the shadow of your protecting wings.
I follow close behind you; your strong
    right hand holds me securely (Psalm 63:2-8).

Now we see things imperfectly as in a poor mirror, but then we will see everything with perfect clarity. All that I know now is partial and incomplete, but then I will know everything completely, just as God knows me now (1 Corinthians 13:12).

Yes, dear friends, we are already God's children, and we can't even imagine what we will be like when Christ returns. But we do know that when he comes we will be like him, for we will see him as he really is. And all who believe this will keep themselves pure, just as Christ is pure (1 John 3:2-3).

TRUTH NINE

THE TRINITY

CHAPTER THIRTY-SIX

THE MEANING OF
ONE GOD IN THREE PERSONS

The Jordan River water was cold. John, now waist-deep, reached out his hand to yet another penitent waiting to be baptized. As soon as the man faced him, John recoiled. *No, this isn't going to work,* he thought. Looking his cousin straight in the eyes he said, "'I am the one who needs to be baptized by you...so why are you coming to me?' But Jesus said, 'It should be done, for we must carry out all that God requires.' So John agreed to baptize him" (Matthew 3:14-15 NLT).

John had baptized many in his short ministry, but what happened next was like nothing that had ever happened before. The moment Jesus, the Son of God, "came up out of the water, the heavens were opened and he saw the Spirit of God descending like a dove and settling on him. And a voice from heaven said, 'This is my dearly loved Son, who brings me great joy'" (Matthew 3:16-17 NLT).

There it was—an earthshaking phenomenon for all to see and hear. Three distinct persons of the Godhead made their presence known: God the Son being baptized, God the Father voicing pleasure in his Son, and God the Holy Spirit settling, like a dove, on the Son. Thus we are introduced in a highly dramatic way to the three persons of God that we call the Trinity.

The Trinity has existed eternally. Scripture records that all three of the persons of God were involved in creation. "In the beginning God created the heavens and the earth...And the Spirit of God was hovering over its surface" (Genesis 1:1-2). "In the beginning the Word already existed. He was with God, and he was God...He created everything there is. Nothing exists that he didn't make...So the Word became human and lived here on earth among us" (John 1:1-3,14). "Then God said, 'Let us make people in our image'" (Genesis 1:26).

The question naturally arises, "Does the existence of the Trinity mean there are three different Gods? Or, is there one God who shows himself in three different roles or relationships—sometimes as a father, sometimes as a son, and at other times as a representative agent?" Scripture teaches us that God is not one person with just three roles to play, but one God existing in three persons.

You and I might find the concept of three people in one difficult to comprehend. The alternative concept, of one being showing himself in multiple roles or relationships, makes more sense to us. For example, let's consider for a moment the person of Dottie McDowell. Dottie is the wife of Josh McDowell. She is also the mother of Sean McDowell. And in addition, she is the grandmother of Scottie McDowell. Here is a woman who is wife, mother, and grandmother all rolled into one person. You might say that Dottie is three in one. We don't mean, of course, that Dottie is three people. She is simply one person with three different roles or relationships.

But the Trinity is something altogether different from either of these concepts. God is neither three separate, independent beings nor one being manifested in three different roles. God exists as three persons, yet he is still one being. Christians have taught this doctrine of the Trinity from the first century on because Scripture clearly asserts that our God is a triune Godhead—one God in three persons.

There Is But One God

Moses commanded, "Hear, O Israel: The LORD our God, the LORD is one" (Deuteronomy 6:4 NIV). Isaiah the prophet declared that God said, "Believe in me and understand that I alone am God. There is no other God; there never has been and never will be. I am the LORD, and there is no other Savior" (Isaiah 43:10-11). Over and over Moses and the prophets declared that there was only one Almighty God of the universe, who was the all-knowing and ever-present Deity.

God Is Father, Son, and Holy Spirit

While Scripture clearly affirms that there is but one God, it also tells us that he co-exists as three divine persons.

Jesus is the divine Son of God. This does not mean that Jesus was created by God. In fact, Scripture tells us plainly that he has always co-existed with God (see John 1:1-3). Jesus himself declared he had eternally co-existed with his Father God. And on the basis of that declaration the Jewish leaders plotted to kill him. They said, "He had spoken of God as his Father, thereby making himself equal with God" (John 5:18). Paul the apostle declared Jesus to be deity: "Christ himself was a Jew as far as his human nature is concerned. And he is God, who rules over everything and is worthy of eternal praise!" (Romans 9:5). The writer of Hebrews says, "The Son reflects God's own glory, and everything about him represents God exactly" (Hebrews 1:3).

Therefore, God the Father co-exists with God the Son. "Christ is the visible image of the invisible God. He existed before God made anything at all and is supreme over all creation. Christ is the one through whom God created everything in heaven and earth...He existed before everything else began, and he holds all creation together" (Colossians 1:15-17). The apostle Paul refers to both the Father and Jesus as God. "It is by the command of God our Savior that I have been trusted to do this work for him... May God the Father and Christ Jesus our Savior give you grace and peace" (Titus 1:3-4). God the Father is deity. God the Son is deity.

God the Holy Spirit is also deity. The apostle Peter recognized this when he pointed out the wrongdoing of a man in the Jerusalem church (Acts 5:3-4). The Spirit has eternally co-existed with the Father and the Son and was present at creation (see Genesis 1:2). Jesus said, "I will ask the Father, and he will give you another Counselor...He is the Holy Spirit, who leads into all truth...When the Father sends the Counselor as my representative—and by the Counselor I mean the Holy Spirit—he will teach you everything" (John 14:16,26). Paul said, "When you believed in Christ, he identified you as his own by giving you the Holy Spirit whom he promised long ago" (Ephesians 1:13). Jesus called his co-existing Spirit holy because he is the Spirit of the Holy God. The Holy Spirit is the third person of the triune Godhead.

God Is Three Distinct Persons

The Scriptures quoted above tell us clearly that God is not merely one God with three different roles or relationships. He is one God in three persons interacting both with each other and with us. God the Father is a distinct person. God the Son is a distinct person. And God the Holy Spirit is a distinct person.

We have clear evidence that Jesus, God's Son, is a distinct person because he took on a human form while God the Father did not. But Jesus referred many times to his Father God as a person. He said he was with a person—his Father—before he was born a man (John 8:38). He said this person—his Father—sent him into the world (John 17:18). He said there were many rooms in his Father's house (John 14:2). He prayed to his Father (John 17:1).

Jesus also referred to the Holy Spirit as a person many times. He used the pronoun "he" when referring to him. Jesus said, "When the Spirit of truth comes, he will guide you into all truth. He will not speak on his own, but will tell you what he has heard. He will tell you about the future. He will bring me glory by telling you whatever he receives from me. All that belongs to the Father is mine; this is why I said, 'The Spirit will tell you whatever he receives from me'" (John 16:13-15 NLT). Jesus also referred to all three persons of the Trinity when he told his followers to make disciples, "baptizing them in the name of the Father and the Son and the Holy Spirit" (Matthew 28:19).

Some people believe that the Holy Spirit is simply the influence of good and not a separate entity or third person of the Trinity. This assertion seems to fly in the face of the fact that Jesus certainly referred to him as a person. Paul the apostle indicates the Holy Spirit has a mind, saying, "He who searches our hearts knows the mind of the Spirit" (Romans 8:27 NIV). Scripture also tells us he can feel. We are not to "bring sorrow to God's Holy Spirit by the way you live" (Ephesians 4:30). The Holy Spirit makes choices as to who will receive what spiritual gifts. "It is the one and only Holy Spirit who distributes these gifts" (1 Corinthians 12:11). Also, Peter told Ananias, "You lied to the Holy Spirit" (Acts 5:3). Ananias wasn't lying to an influence; he was lying to a person. Peter said to him, "You weren't lying to us but to God" (Acts 5:4).

The Oneness of the Trinity

God exists as three persons, yet he is one being. Each person—the Father, the Son, and the Holy Spirit—has a separate identity while enjoying the same essence of nature as the others, not merely similar natures in different roles. Some might think this is contradictory. It would be contradictory if the doctrine of the Trinity claimed one God and three Gods at the same time. But the Trinity is one God who eternally co-exists as three persons. God is, was, and always will be. He is almighty, perfect, holy, light, and love. The Father, Son, and Holy Spirit as three distinct persons share this one substance and essence of being God.

While the following illustrations are imperfect, they might be helpful ways to think about three in one. For example, the chemical combination H_2O can be a liquid (water), a solid (ice), or a gas (steam). Yet in each of these forms the chemical substance is one and the same. If you put an ice cube in a beaker and heat it, you will see a solid melting into liquid and then rising into a gas. As this operation is in process, you will have all three states of the H_2O chemical co-existing.

Length, width, and height are three distinct dimensions that can be specified to define a specific volume of space. The common example of a three-dimensional object is the cube. The cube exists as a single entity because the dimensions of length, width, and height combine equally to form it. Remove any one dimension and the entire structure ceases to exist. This is because each dimension is unique yet each must unite as one to maintain the essence of a cube. God exists as one in three persons. Each person shares equally in the one essence and nature of the Godhead. All three—Father, Son, and Holy Spirit—unite to form one unique substance.

We hope these illustrations, imperfect as they are, will help you get the idea of how three can be one. We must realize, however, that we finite humans cannot expect to grasp fully the essence of the infinite God.

The Eternal Relationship of Love

God, consisting as he does of three persons, shows us that intimate relationship has existed eternally. God didn't create humans because he needed a relationship; he already had relationship. He exists in relationship. The Father has always infinitely loved the Son. The Son has always infinitely loved the Father. The Holy Spirit has always infinitely loved both the Father and the Son. A continuous cycle of perfect relationships is ever being experienced within the Godhead. While we are unable to comprehend such a perfect and continuing relationship fully, all of us long to experience this kind of relationship ourselves.

God's unity in the Trinity is the secret to unlocking how relationship is meant to work.

As individuals without relationship we stand alone, incomplete in the darkness of seclusion. This is not how we were meant to exist, and that is why God said, "It is not good for the man to be alone" (Genesis 2:18). He had made humans in his image, and that image was reflective of the perfect relationship of the three persons of the Godhead—a relationship so infinitely loving that it produced an intimate oneness, a bonding, a togetherness, and a connectedness unparalleled in the universe. What he desired for his human creation was a oneness similar to his. So instead of leaving his newly created man alone, he made another human by drawing substance from the man's side. God then said, "This explains why a man leaves his father and mother and is joined to his wife, and the two are united into one" (Genesis 2:24).

Just as God is one in relationship by his very being, so he created us to be one in relationship. The oneness of the Trinity serves as more than our master model for such oneness. God's unity in the Trinity is the secret to unlocking how relationship is meant to work. While we can never comprehend God's oneness in relationship in an absolute sense, we can gain enough insight into this mystery to experience the true meaning of relationship. Uncovering the mystery of the Trinity is like peering into the very heart of God.

Listen to Jesus talk about his Father. First he says, "I assure you, the Son can do nothing by himself. He does only what he sees the Father doing" (John 5:19). "I do nothing on my own, but I speak what the Father taught me" (John 8:28). Jesus is God, yet he doesn't speak or act on his own; in fact, he says his words aren't actually his own but his Father's who works through him. "The words I say," Jesus declares, "are not my own, but my Father who lives in me does his work through me" (John 14:10).

But the strange thing is that in spite of the fact that Jesus insists he cannot do anything by himself, he goes on to say, "The Father leaves all judgment to his Son" (John 5:22). "For you [the Father] have given him [the Son] authority over everyone in all the earth" (John 17:2). "You [the Father] gave me [the Son] the glory because you loved me even before the world began" (John 17:24). God the Father gave his Son all the authority and power to do anything he wanted. Jesus even had power over his own life. He said, "I lay down my life voluntarily. For I have the right to lay it down when I want to and also the power to take it again" (John 10:18). Jesus is God, the actual creator of the universe and the one who sustains it (see Hebrews 1:2-3). Yet he says he can't do anything on his own. Why?

Does Jesus feel somehow restricted by God his Father? Is he so rigidly under the Father's authority that he dares not do anything without his Father's permission? Not at all. The relationship is one in which the Father is pleased to give everything to the Son because he loves his Son. The Son is pleased to give everything to the Father because he loves his Father. Jesus prayed, "Father, the time has come. Glorify your Son so he can give glory back to you...And I give myself entirely to you" (John 17:1,19). "The one who sent me is with me," Jesus said. "He has not deserted me. For I always do those things that are pleasing to him" (John 8:29).

Incomprehensible Unity

It is this infinite love in perfect relationship that produces a oneness beyond our comprehension. It is not a relationship with a leverage of power and authority. It is not some hierarchical chain of command. It is a circle of relationships that looks out for the best in each other because of a deep abiding love for one another. In their infinite love, the three persons of the Trinity are so intent on pleasing one another that the very essence of their beings is indistinguishable. Speaking in math terms, they are one to the infinite power.

Jesus said, "The Father and I are one" (John 10:30). He goes on to help us understand what this infinite love does to their relationship. "I am in the Father and the Father is in me" (John 14:11). He's talking about a perfect oneness, a bonded relationship that actually fuses them together to the point that Jesus can accurately say, "Anyone who has seen me has seen the Father" (John 14:9).

Let's ponder that statement for a moment. Jesus is saying his relationship with his Father is so intimate that if you see him, if you talk to him, if you trust him, if you please him, you are seeing, talking, trusting, and pleasing the Father (see John 12:44). That is oneness!

In our love relationships, we as humans try to share the joy and pain of those we love. Yet we do that imperfectly. We try to anticipate the needs of our children and meet them, yet we do that imperfectly. We try and understand the dreams and expectations of our spouses, yet we do that imperfectly. But within the Godhead, the Father perfectly anticipates the needs of the Son. The Son understands perfectly the expectations of the Father. The Holy Spirit perfectly shares the joys and pain of the Father and the Son.

It is hard to grasp, but this loving relationship between the Father, the Son, and the Holy Spirit is such an intimate oneness that they feel the same, do the same, give the same, love the same, and so on. We know, for example, that God so loved the world that "he gave his only son" to die for us. Yet Jesus said, "I lay down my life voluntarily. For I have the right to lay it down when I want to and also the power to take it again" (John 10:18). So which is it? Did the Father give his Son to die or did the Son decide on his own to give his life? To us it seems that the two options are mutually exclusive. Both cannot be true. Either the Father gave his Son to die or Jesus is the one who made the decision. The difficulty resides in the fact that we think as individuals rather than as a co-existence in perfect harmony with another. The answer is that both the Father took the initiative to give out of his love and the Son took the initiative to give out of his love, because the two are of one nature. We suggest that the incomprehensible oneness of the Godhead is not so much a result of God's awesome power as it is the divine love shared within the Trinity.

Experience the Oneness of the Trinity

Think of it: When you pray to the Father in the Son's name, you are sharing your heart with the Son and the Spirit equally. When you honor Jesus with your life of worship and devotion, you are honoring the Father and the Holy Spirit equally.

Consider this—Paul said we can know the secret things of God "because God revealed them to us by his Spirit, and his Spirit searches out everything and shows us even God's deep secrets" (1 Corinthians 2:10). He goes on to say, "But we can understand these things...for we have the mind of Christ" (1 Corinthians 2:15,16). So which of the Godhead shows us the secrets of God? The Holy Spirit or Christ?

Paul understood that when we have God's mind and his wisdom, we have the mind and wisdom of the Godhead—that of God the Father, God the Son, and God the Holy Spirit—because all three are in perfect relationship. So when you experience one, you experience all three. This isn't the same as saying all three members of the Godhead are simply interchangeable. Each person is distinct, yet they are in such perfect harmony and oneness of relationship that to know one, his nature and being, is to know the others.

Paul said to the church at Ephesus, "I fall to my knees and pray to the Father...I pray that from his glorious, unlimited resources he will give you mighty inner strength through his Holy Spirit. And I pray that Christ will be more and more at home in your hearts as you trust in him" (Ephesians 3:14,16-17). Here Paul makes reference to all three persons of the Trinity. Then he goes on to say, "May your roots go down deep into the soil of God's marvelous love…Then you will be filled with the fullness of life and power that comes from God" (Ephesians 3:17-19). So whose love are we experiencing? Is it the love of the Father, the love of Christ, or the love of the Holy Spirit? Paul makes it clear that it is the love of God—who is Father, Son, and Holy Spirit. It is God with infinite love in perfect relationship fusing all three into one nature of love and together they share that love with us.

Granted, it is impossible for us to comprehend the Trinity. We can't muster up enough imagination to grasp such a perfect union of love and relationship. We tend to think of relationships in terms of position, hierarchy, authority, and who is responsible to whom to fulfill what roles. But in God we see three persons in perfect relationship and harmony because their nature is one. The Father so loved the world that he gave his Son. The Son so loved his Father that he gave his life. The Holy Spirit so loved the Father and the Son that he gave us his Spirit (see Romans 5:5). And together they—one God—demonstrate a perfect love toward us.

Paul said, "May you experience the love of Christ, though it is so great you will never fully understand it" (Ephesians 3:19). We will "never fully understand it" perhaps because to comprehend God's love is to comprehend God—which is inconceivably beyond our human capacity. Yet the triune nature of God has been manifested to us. We see God's handiwork of creation made for us; he revealed himself in the flesh for our salvation; and we experience his empowering presence through his Spirit. Therefore:

> We believe the truth that there is one God who is eternally co-existing as the Father, Son, and Holy Spirit in a perfect relationship of oneness.

"'I am the Alpha and Omega—the beginning and the end,' says the Lord God. 'I am the one who is, who always was, and who is still to come, the Almighty One'" (Revelation 1:8). Such an almighty, awesome, and powerful God is too frightening to look upon, for God said, "no one may see me and live" (Exodus 33:20). Yet the miracle of the Trinity gives us access to this amazing God. Remember, Jesus said, "Anyone who has seen me has seen the Father!" (John 14:9). And because the Father has sent the Holy Spirit, we can know the entire Godhead on a personal basis.

■

In previous chapters we have provided evidence for the Almighty God of the universe and also for Jesus, the Son of God. Next we will provide evidences for God the Holy Spirit, who has been sent to dwell in us as the empowering source that brings us into the circle of relationship of the Godhead. For it is the Holy Spirit who enables us to experience God.

CHAPTER THIRTY-SEVEN

EVIDENCE THAT THE
HOLY SPIRIT EXISTS

Amazed. Confused. Not understanding. Uncomprehending. This is how the disciples must have been conflicted as Jesus spent his last moments with them after his resurrection. They were overjoyed when he rose from the grave, but when he said he was going back to his Father it must have saddened them. Yet in spite of the fact that he said he was leaving, he also said, "Be sure of this: I am with you always, even to the end of the age" (Matthew 28:20).

He was going away, yet he said he would be with them always. What an apparent contradiction! But because of the mystery and perfect relationship of the Trinity, Jesus would be with them through the presence of the third person of the Trinity, the Holy Spirit. "And now I will send the Holy Spirit," Jesus said, "just as my Father promised" (Luke 24:49).

Ten days later as the disciples and others (about 120 believers) were gathered in prayer, something extraordinary happened. It is a matter of historical record. The Scriptures, which are reliable, explain that "there was a sound from heaven like the roaring of a mighty windstorm in the skies above them, and it filled the house where they were meeting. Then what looked like flames or tongues of fire appeared and settled on each of them. And everyone present was filled with the Holy Spirit and began speaking in other languages, as the Holy Spirit gave them this ability" (Acts 2:2-4).

Jews from many nations had gathered in Jerusalem for the annual festival of Shavuot (*Pentecost* in Greek) and they came running out to see what all the commotion was about. To their surprise, they heard "their own language being spoken by the believers" (Acts 2:6). Then Peter stepped forward and said, "What you see this morning was predicted centuries ago by the prophet Joel:

'In the last days, God said,
I will pour out my Spirit
upon all people. Your sons and
daughters will prophesy, your
young men will see visions,
and your old men will dream
dreams'" (Acts 2:16-17).

Peter continued with a message about Jesus dying and being raised to life again for the forgiveness of sin. And that day about 3000 people became followers of Christ.

Later, Peter and John went to the temple for afternoon prayers and saw a crippled man begging for money. Peter told him, "I don't have any money for you. But I'll give you what I have. In the name of Jesus Christ of Nazareth, get up and walk" (Acts 3:6). Amazingly, the lame man leaped up and began praising God. The disciples went throughout the city preaching and doing many miracles in the name of Jesus through the power of the Holy Spirit.

God at Work Through His Spirit

What started as a band of 120 followers of Jesus grew to thousands within weeks. The message of Jesus spread beyond Jerusalem like wildfire. Each new believer became a living witness of what God could do in a person's life. It was happening exactly as Jesus had said it would. "When the Holy Spirit has come upon you, you will receive power and will tell people about me everywhere—in Jerusalem, throughout Judea, in Samaria, and to the ends of the earth" (Acts 1:8).

Transformed lives, answers to prayers, miracles performed in Jesus' name are all a result of the workings of the third person of the Trinity—the Holy Spirit.

Previously frightened and cowardly disciples had become bold preachers of Jesus and his message. They performed signs and wonders. The message they proclaimed resulted in millions of lives being transformed. This was not a result of nothing more than a vague, undefined influence of good, or some mystical force. It was God the Holy Spirit at work.

And by the third century over 20 million people had made claim to the transforming power of Christ through the Holy Spirit.[1] All this enormous growth in Christianity is evidence of God sending his promised Comforter. And for over 2000 years every true believer of Jesus has been a testimony to the living proof that the Holy Spirit is a real person who is active in the lives of people.

Transformed lives, answers to prayers, miracles performed in Jesus' name are all a result of the workings of the third person of the Trinity—the Holy Spirit. God the Father and God the Son are in heaven. In Peter's opening message on the Day of Pentecost, he declared that Jesus "sits on the throne of highest honor in heaven, at God's right hand" (Acts 2:33). So are the supernatural manifestations of God on earth a result of the Father or of the Son? Or, is it the work of God the Holy Spirit?

Because of the incomprehensible mystery of the Trinity, it is simply God at work—Father, Son, and Holy Spirit. That is why it is not inappropriate or incorrect to say that Jesus changes lives, or for a child to say, "God lives in my heart." For Jesus himself said he would never leave us, but he clearly sits at God's right hand. Yet we know he is in our hearts through the power of his Holy Spirit. In fact, Jesus said, "When I am raised to life again, you will know that I am in my Father, and you are in me, and I am in you" (John 14:20). That means the one God in his fullness dwells within us and us within him through the power of the Holy Spirit.

Although we find it impossible to grasp the absolute perfection of God's triune relationship, that does not diminish or lessen the reality of the Holy Spirit as a person in our lives. As C.S. Lewis said, it isn't necessary to understand the process of digestion in order for your food to nourish you. We might say that after Jesus ascended into heaven to sit at the Father's right hand, God the Holy Spirit became the interactive agent of God to us. Jesus said, "The Father sends the Counselor [Holy Spirit] as my representative" (John 14:26). But he is more than just a being for us to know about intellectually. Someone has suggested that when the Holy Spirit was poured out, the word *God* was not only a noun—it also became a verb. Rather than just learning who God is or following the teaching of Jesus impersonally, the Holy Spirit brings God actually into our lives. He is the active, moving nature of God that impels us to action. God the Holy Spirit is about living, loving, responding, enjoying, embracing, comforting, supporting, accepting, encouraging, respecting, disciplining, growing, empowering, and a myriad of other such verbs.

The Holy Spirit is the dynamic, active, and ever-present person of the Trinity. We experience him in our everyday living. He demonstrates himself even in our capacity to love as God loves. "If we love each other," John said, "God lives in us, and his love has been brought to full expression through us. And God has given us his Spirit as proof that we live in him and he in us" (1 John 4:12-13). The Holy Spirit is real. He evidenced himself powerfully on the Day of Pentecost two centuries ago. And his

Spirit is additional proof that we live in him, for the "Holy Spirit speaks to us deep in our hearts and tells us that we are God's children" (Romans 8:16).

Because of these things we can confidently know the truth that God the Holy Spirit exists. And because he is the active and interactive person of the Trinity that dwells within us, he is infinitely relevant to our lives. That is the subject of the next chapter.

CHAPTER THIRTY-EIGHT

THE PURPOSE OF THE HOLY SPIRIT IN OUR LIVES

M arci surveyed her bed of azaleas. She and her husband, Chris, had recently moved into a new home, and she had already begun to beautify the yard by planting her favorite flowers.

Proud of what she had done, she motioned Chris over from mowing the grass. "How does it look?" she asked eagerly.

"Yeah, it looks fine," Chris replied.

"Just 'fine'?" Marci probed. "Don't you like it?"

"It's not the flowers," Chris said. "I'm just wondering if there is enough greenery there to make the flowers stand out."

Marci dropped her head and gave a sigh of disappointment tinged with irritation. Then she slowly removed her gardening gloves. "There's just no way I can please you, is there? I just don't do anything right." She turned and headed into the house.

Chris followed her in. "Marci, you asked my opinion," he said. "I wasn't attacking you. Why do you take things so personally?"

A lot of Christians, like Marci, take criticism personally because they find it difficult to separate their performance from their personhood. Many have grown up seeking acceptance and personal approval through performance. So an innocent question like "Is there enough greenery in the flower bed?" can start up some old tapes of an authority figure in childhood saying, "Why can't you do anything right?"

Relationship Reprogramming

All of us have experienced imperfect relationships to some degree or another. It's hard to imagine relationships that aren't to some extent skewed by focusing too heavily on performance, control, rules, obedience, expectations, obligations, and so on. Too often relationships consist of little more than people trying to get their needs met by one another. Much of the way we approach relationships has been programmed from early childhood. Sadly, what many of us have experienced isn't God's idea of what an intimate relationship is all about.

> *To live out God's idea of intimate relationships, many of us will need to be reprogrammed with the true meaning of relationships.*

God's idea of an intimate relationship is about giving, yielding, trusting, and regarding another's concerns to be as significant as our own. It's about finding joy in pleasing others, and first and foremost, about pleasing the one who died for us. "Those who are dominated by the sin nature think about sinful things, but those who are controlled by the Holy Spirit think about things that please the Spirit" (Romans 8:5).

When God redeemed us he intended more than just to save us from eternal death. He plans to restore us to live as we were meant to live—in an intimate relationship with him and with one another. And that restoration begins at the moment of conversion.

But for us to live out God's idea of intimate relationships, many of us will need to be reprogrammed with the true meaning of relationships. Our ideas of relationships are not by nature God's ideas. We are by birth self-reliant, self-centered, and self-condemning. This leads us away from trusting, yielding, giving, and looking out for the best interest of another. On top of inborn tendencies, many of our childhood models have programmed us with patterns that work against forming relationships based on giving, trust, yielding, and so on.

So how does God go about reprogramming our hearts and minds to live out his kind of relationships? Jesus could have just said, "Read about how I lived my life and then go live yours the same way." He could have given us a 12-step plan to intimate relationships. Or he could have told us to "practice, practice, practice." But he said none of these things. Instead, he sent himself in the person of the Holy Spirit so we could become an intimate part of God's relational unity. And the more we participate in the Triune relationship the more we are empowered to live and love and relate like he does.

The indwelling presence of the Holy Spirit is given us to accomplish at least five relevant things in our lives.

1. To Make Us One with God

"When you believed in Christ, he identified you as his own by giving you the Holy Spirit, whom he promised long ago" (Ephesians 1:13). But as we said above, the purpose of that relationship isn't just to give you a home in heaven; the Holy Spirit is there to form a relationship of intimate oneness between you and God.

Jesus prayed to his Father for his disciples and for you "that they will be one, just as you and I are one Father—that just as you are in me and I am in you, so they will be in us...I in them and you in me, all being perfected into one" (John 17:21,23). Jesus invites you to join the circle of perfect relationship within the Godhead. The Holy Spirit takes up residence in your life with the intent to create a miraculous oneness like that which exists in the Trinity. He is fully giving himself to you as a model for you to fully give yourself to him.

The Holy Spirit hasn't come just to live in you. You are to also live in him. Jesus said, "They [each follower of Christ] will be in us." "God has given us his Spirit as proof," the apostle John said, "that we live in him and he in us" (1 John 4:13). You are invited to become an integral part of the perfect cycle of relationship enjoyed within the Trinity. It is then that this mutual giving of selves will result in an intimacy between you and God that makes living in his image as natural as breathing.

A woman named Martha struggled with the idea of giving of herself to God. Jesus and other disciples were guests in their home, and there was so much work to do. She wanted to prepare a big dinner for her special guest. Her sister, Mary, was supposed to be helping with the meal, but instead she was sitting at the feet of Jesus listening to what he had to say.

So Martha marched in and said to Jesus, "'Lord, doesn't it seem unfair to you that my sister just sits here while I do all the work? Tell her to come and help me.' But the Lord said to her, 'My dear Martha, you are so upset over all these details! There is really only one thing worth being concerned about. Mary has discovered it—and I won't take it away from her'" (Luke 10:40-42).

What had Mary discovered that Martha didn't? She discovered that there was just one priority in life worth being concerned about, and that was giving herself to Jesus. The Master was saying to Martha, "It's not your detailed endeavors I'm after; it's your personal devotion. If you give yourself to me, I'll show you how to live life as it was meant to be lived." Jesus may not be here in the flesh to teach us that, but he has given us his Spirit to lead us to a oneness—an intimate relationship that will teach us how to reorder our lives to be pleasing to him. He is in us that our joy may be complete, and as we yield and give ourselves to him, we give him joy.

It is through the power of the Holy Spirit that we "share in his divine nature" (2 Peter 1:4) and that is why we "no longer live to please [ourselves]. Instead, [we] will live to please Christ" (2 Corinthians 5:15). Living to give each other joy in a relationship is what intimacy is all about.

2. To Make Us Christlike

Scripture says, "As the Spirit of the Lord works within us, we become more and more like him and reflect his glory even more" (2 Corinthians 3:18). That is another reason the Holy Spirit takes up residence in us, so we can know him and be like him. "By his divine power, God has given us everything we need for living a godly life" (2 Peter 1:3 NLT), and the Holy Spirit helps us live out what we have already been given.

Before being empowered by the Holy Spirit, we are enslaved to sin. The apostle Paul said, "In my mind I really want to obey God's law, but because of my sinful nature I am a slave to sin" (Romans 7:25). "But you are not controlled by your sinful nature," Paul went on to say. "You are controlled by the Spirit if you have the Spirit of God living in you" (Romans 8:9).

Some have mistakenly thought that being a Christian is about *trying* to live like Jesus. The slogan of a Spirit-filled Christian isn't "we try harder." It is "we give ourselves to each other." Our goal as a Christ-follower shouldn't be focused so much on acting like Jesus as on *being* in him and with him. It's about being in relationship with him, which naturally results in acting like him. The Holy Spirit is in us to be with us and so we may be with him. It is then we begin to see through his eyes, to hear with his ears, to think like he does, and to act as he acts. As we give ourselves over to him, as Mary did to Jesus, he exercises his power to live his life through us. He is our power source.

During my junior year in college I (Sean) took a hike with some friends that is forever etched into my memory. Since I was the resident assistant for my college dorm, I decided to bring 18 of my floormates up to the mountains of San Diego. This would be a weekend retreat of bonding and fun. For a good challenge, we decided to take the three-mile hike to the top of Stonewall Mountain. While we were ready for the hike up the mountain, we were completely unprepared for the challenges of the journey down.

I had been living near the city lights of Los Angeles for only a couple of years, but already I had forgotten how dark a starry night can be in the mountains. Although we brought enough food, water, and other supplies for the trip to the top, we forgot to bring enough flashlights for a safe trek down. The sun set, dark clouds moved in, and we suddenly realized the urgency of getting home safely and quickly. By the time we gathered all our goods and set out for the trail, the night had become pitch black. When we pulled out the two flashlights that we did bring, we found out that *neither* of them worked!

Imagine 19 college men trying to climb down a dark, windy mountainside without the light needed to see what lay ahead. We began to feel a bit of panic, but we realized that if we were to make it down safely, we would have to work together. Since some of the path could be dangerous, all 19 of us held hands and inched our way down the mountain. Without the power of the flashlight, we were left to grope haltingly down the darkness of the mountain, feeling our way around boulders and crevasses. If we'd had good batteries, our trip would have been much less frustrating and dangerous. In fact, it would have been easy.[1]

When we give ourselves over to the Holy Spirit, he provides the power and light for us to walk in his ways. "When the Holy Spirit controls our lives, he will produce this kind of fruit in us: love, joy, peace, patience, kindness, goodness, faithfulness, gentleness, and self-control" (Galatians 5:22-23). The Holy Spirit living his life through us is the power source for our lives.

3. To Illuminate the Truth of Scripture

God's Word, through the power of his Spirit, "is useful to teach us what is true and to make us realize what is wrong in our lives. It straightens us out and teaches us to do what is right. It is God's way of preparing us in every way, fully equipped for every good thing God wants us to do" (2 Timothy 3:16-17). This passage tells us that God's Word contains guidelines and insights that teach us to cultivate a deeper oneness with God. It also gives us principles that outline what Christlikeness looks like in our lives. And as we focus on these guidelines and principles, it is the Holy Spirit who translates this truth into our lives.

"No one can know God's thoughts," Paul says, "except God's own Spirit. And God has actually given us his Spirit (not the world's spirit) so we can know the wonderful things God has freely given us" (1 Corinthians 2:11-12). As this passage tells us, another function of the Holy Spirit in our lives is to show us himself and his truth. He helps us understand who he wants us to be and how he wants us to love and live. And the only way to know God's heart and mind is for him to reveal it to us through his Holy Spirit. "Who can know what the Lord is thinking?" Paul asks. He answers: "We can understand these things, for we have the mind of Christ" (1 Corinthians 2:16).

The presence of the Holy Spirit in our lives does not mean pastors and teachers of the Word are not necessary. Some cite John 14:26 as support that we don't need Scripture, because the Holy Spirit will teach us everything. But the context of this passage reveals that Jesus meant these words for his disciples, not necessarily for all subsequent believers. If the Holy Spirit were our sole guide to truth, then we wouldn't need the Scriptures, let alone books like *The Unshakable Truth*. We must not simply disregard all study or the wisdom of good teachers and rely solely on the internal leading of the Spirit. This is a deeply unbiblical approach that often leads to disastrous results. Because we are fallen, our perception is often dim and foggy, and we are subject to being fooled by voices that we think may be from God but are actually from darker sources.

Paul warned the church at Corinth of false teachers who "have fooled you by disguising themselves as apostles of Christ. But I am not surprised! Even Satan can disguise himself as an angel of light" (2 Corinthians 11:13-14).

That is why it is crucial for us to heed the challenge of Paul to "be diligent [in] accurately handling the word of truth" (2 Timothy 2:15 NASB). God involves the wise and godly teachings of men and women around us to lead us into all truth. The Holy Spirit takes the truth of Scripture and ingrains it into our lives. Nonbelievers can often grasp the truth of the Bible, but it's only through the power of the Holy Spirit that the truth can take hold of our lives and transform our character.

4. To Empower Us for Service

"When the Holy Spirit has come upon you," Jesus said, "you will receive power and will tell people about me everywhere" (Acts 1:8). In fact, Jesus said that when the Holy Spirit came, his followers "will do the same works I have done, and even greater works, because I am going to be with the Father" (John 14:12). The Holy Spirit is our empowerment to do God's work.

"There are different ways God works in our lives," Paul said, "but it is the same God who does the work through all of us. A spiritual gift is given to each of us as a means of helping the entire church" (1 Corinthians 12:6-7). It is the Holy Spirit who distributes these gifts and then empowers us to use them. In Romans 12:6 Paul explains that "God has given each of us the ability to do certain things well. So if God has given you the ability to…" then Paul goes on to identify what those gifts are and how we are to use them. The point is, the Holy Spirit empowers us to serve others, spread his gospel message and, in short, do extraordinary things for his glory.

The writer of Hebrews tells us that those who lived by faith and had God's Spirit on them "shut the mouths of lions, quenched the flames of fire, and escaped death by the edge of the sword. Their weakness was turned to strength. They became strong in battle and put whole armies to flight. Women received their loved ones back again from death" (Hebrews 11:33-35). He also points out that others "were tortured, preferring to die rather than turn from God and be free" (Hebrews 11:35).

Whether God's Spirit empowers us to perform miracles or die courageously as a martyr, he is there in our lives to reflect his light to this darkened and needy world. Jesus said, "Don't hide your light under a basket! Instead, put it on a stand and let it shine for all. In the same way, let your good deeds shine out for all to see, so that everyone will praise your heavenly Father" (Matthew 5:15-16). Our focus on God's infilling of his Spirit in us does not center on the power to perform, but on praising the person of God. The Holy Spirit empowers us to give glory and honor and praise to the Father, Son, and Holy Spirit.

5. To Bring Meaning to Our Lives

We were made in God's image, and when we become intimate with God through his Holy Spirit we begin to live as God intended and be the person God designed. Paul said, "It's in Christ that we find out who we are and what we are living for" (Ephesians 1:11 MSG). "He [Christ] gives life and breath to everything, and he satisfies every need there is" (Acts 17:25). The Holy Spirit puts us on a journey to fulfill our purpose in life. Because when "his Holy Spirit speaks to us deep in our hearts and tells us we are God's children" (Romans 8:16), he is actually completing us. We were meant to live in an intimate relationship with God as his child. When we do this, through the power of the Holy Spirit, we find our true meaning and purpose.

Jesus told his disciples to obey his father's commands "so that my joy may be in you" (John 15:11 NIV). The disciples had no idea how literally he meant that phrase to be taken. His joy was to be in them, meaning he was their joy. Although he was at that moment *with* them in body, he was telling them that when the Holy Spirit came, he would be *in* them. By declaring that their joy would "be complete" (John 15:11 NIV), Jesus was saying that he was the great "completer." His life completes ours; he gives us meaning; he provides us the fulfillment and joy in living; all because the Holy Spirit is God's agent for a continuous relationship between God and ourselves. The relevance of the Holy Spirit to our lives is this: He creates in us an intimacy with God, transforms us into Christlikeness, leads us into all truth, empowers us for service, and brings true meaning and completion to life.

That's the "what," but what about the "how"? How do we actually connect with the Holy Spirit? How do we live out the life with God that he offers? How and when are we actually filled with the Holy Spirit?

While there is overwhelming agreement among evangelicals that the Holy Spirit exists, there are varied views on how and when a person receives him. Generally speaking, most Christians hold to one of two schools of thought. One view is that a believer receives the Holy Spirit at the time of conversion and then is steadily and increasingly empowered by the Spirit as he or she yields more fully to God. The other position is that there is a two-step process. The first step redeems the believer and makes him or her God's child through the power of God's Spirit. But the person is not yet filled with the Holy Spirit. The second step purifies the believer's heart by the infilling of the Holy Spirit. Some additionally believe their infilling or baptism of the Holy Spirit is accompanied by signs or evidences of that reality, for example, the speaking in tongues.

In the following chapter we deal with how to appropriate God's power through the Holy Spirit in our lives. The apostle Paul said to "let the Holy Spirit fill and control you" (Ephesians 5:18). But how do we do that so we can daily walk in the power of God's Spirit? What should be the attitude of our heart so we can reflect God's character and live a life pleasing to him? That is the subject of the next chapter.

CHAPTER THIRTY-NINE

HOW TO LIVE IN THE POWER OF THE HOLY SPIRIT

B ob! Weave! Feint!" the trainer yelled. "Now duck!"

It was too late. Jim's sparring partner landed a left cross that put him on the canvas.

"You've got to block that punch," the trainer said as Jim slowly got off the mat. "Let's go at it again. You can win the fight next week if you master the techniques."

For weeks Jim had gone through a rigorous training regimen. Push-ups. Weight lifting. Sit-ups. Running. Punching bags. Sparring. Good diet. Up early—to bed late. Jim was giving his all to win the Golden Glove—the big prize of amateur boxing.

The big night came. It was 60 seconds into the fourth round. Jim bobbed and weaved and feinted. The left cross came flying at him and he blocked it. With his opponent wide open, Jim responded with a left uppercut followed by a thunderous right hand. His opponent went down with a thud. The crowd cheered. Jim bounced back and forth waiting for the reeling boxer to get up. But he couldn't.

The referee waved his hands to signal the fight was over. And Jim leaped onto the ropes with his hands held high. He was victorious.

The power for Jim to overcome his opponent came from what he did—the push-ups, the running, the footwork, eating right, and consistent hard practice. Because in most endeavors, this kind of training and discipline is the way to achieve your goal, many people think it's also the way to achieve an effective Christian life. But achieving an empowered, effective Christlike life requires an altogether different approach—even what some might call an upside-down approach. The power for living a Christlike life doesn't depend as much on what we do as it does on what we *don't* do.

The apostle Paul wrote to the Christians in Galatia, who were confused about what it took to live the Spirit-filled, or Spirit-empowered, life: "After starting your Christian lives in the Spirit, why are you now trying to become perfect by your own human effort?…I ask you again, does God give you the Holy Spirit and work miracles among you because you obey the law of Moses?" (Galatians 3:3,5). Paul was explaining that performance and doing good didn't unleash God's power in their lives.

Yet on the other hand, Paul told Timothy to "spend your time and energy in training yourself for spiritual fitness. Physical exercise has some value, but spiritual exercise is much more important, for it promises a reward in both this life and the next" (1 Timothy 4:7-8). Here Paul seems to be saying that training and effort is required for living a Christlike life, just as it was required of the boxer Jim to win the Golden Glove. So which is it? Is the Christian life a matter of effort or merely a matter of plugging in the power of the Holy Spirit and sitting back to let him do the work? The answer, as Paul was making it clear, is that certain efforts are needed and certain efforts are not. That leaves us with the question, which efforts are required and which ones are not?

We know our efforts or good works are useless to gain our salvation (Ephesians 2:8-9), yet there *is* something we must do. Paul explains: "The Spirit gives us desires that are opposite from what the sinful nature desires. These two forces are constantly fighting each other, and your choices are never free from this conflict" (Galatians 5:17). We fallen humans must contend with an entrenched sin nature that will plague us until we die. By receiving God's Holy Spirit, we have his new nature within us, but we still must contend with that sin nature, which is resistant to and in conflict with the Holy Spirit. That is why we must train ourselves in spiritual discipline and work hard at living godly. But this is not enough. No matter how rigorous our spiritual exercise and training, we will never gain the spiritual muscle to overcome the sin nature by our own power. So while spiritual discipline is necessary to keep us focused on God's will for our lives, that is not the formula for effective godly living. It takes something more.

Giving Up Is the Key

No matter how much we try to resist our tendency toward sin, we don't have the inner strength to live the Christian life or to do great things for God. Our own power is no match for that ever-present sin nature. That is why Paul says, "Give your bodies to God. Let them be a living and holy sacrifice—the kind he will accept" (Romans 12:1). So instead of exercising our spiritual muscles in futile hopes of overpowering the sin in our lives, Paul says to sacrifice yourself. He goes on to say, "Those who belong to Christ Jesus have nailed the passions and desires of their sinful nature to his cross and crucified them there" (Galatians 5:24). This means we are to nail even our "good work efforts" and self-reliance to the cross. Then we can say with Paul, "I have been crucified with Christ. I myself no longer live, but Christ lives in me. So I live my life in this earthly body by trusting in the Son of God, who loved me and gave himself for me" (Galatians 2:19-20).

We are to bring all our ambitions, desires, hopes, and dreams, however noble they may be, and sacrifice them to God. This means we give up on our own abilities, talents, goodness, and self-help efforts

It is when we are yielding to him that he can unleash his Holy Spirit in and through our lives.

and consider them useless. We are then to place our trust in his goodness and in his strength. When we let God know we want to see him honored, not us, he sees and responds powerfully. It is when we are yielding to him that he can unleash his Holy Spirit in and through our lives.

After I (Josh) trusted Christ, I transferred from a state college to Wheaton College, a Christian school. But I really wanted to be in law school. I remember a visiting speaker telling us during a chapel service how we as students needed to bring all our gifts and talents before God and sacrifice them to him so we could be of service. He used Romans 12:1 as his text.

Many from the student body began going forward to be a "living sacrifice" for God. I didn't. In fact, I ran out of the auditorium. I told God I'd be open to giving him my gifts and talents if I had any, but I didn't. I still struggled with my stuttering; I was terrible at English; I really questioned what, if anything, I could offer God that was of value. Then the thought passed through my mind: *What if you gave God all your limitations?*

One day I left class in frustration and started walking. A block away from the seminary campus, I heard a bell ring. It was exactly 11:45 a.m.—lunchtime at the local junior high. The sound of the bell startled me, and I stopped. The doors of the school burst open, and young people came flooding out. I backed up against a telephone pole on the sidewalk as kids rushed past me in every direction. I felt momentarily paralyzed. It was as if time had stopped for me and I was watching a sea of young people move in slow motion. In that moment, my mind went to the book of Isaiah, when God asked the prophet, "Whom shall I send? And who will go for us?" (Isaiah 6:8 NIV). In my mind, those words possessed a new context. It was as if God said to me, "These young people are in crisis; they are a hurting generation, and you have what I need to help them. So, 'whom shall I send, and who will go for us?'"

At that point I prayed, "God, all I sense I have are my limitations. But if that is what you need, I'll give my all to you to reach this generation." Instantly, my struggle to have my own career in law ended. My sense of inadequacy ended. I felt the empowering presence of the Holy Spirit fill my life.

What I *didn't* do is promise God I'd get advanced youth leader training, practice my speaking, build a youth leader network, or hire a public relations firm in order to do great ministry for him. What I did do was give up trying on my own and sacrifice whatever I had to God, which wasn't much. And God in effect said back to me what he said to Paul, "My gracious favor is all you need. My power works best in your weakness" (2 Corinthians 12:9).

When you and I turn our backs on our self-reliance, our self-centeredness, or our self-condemnation and simply say, "I need you and I want to please you," God responds by living his life through us. He wants our obedience, of course, but first and foremost, he wants *us*. What he wants is a willing and yielded vessel. That is why we are told to "follow the Holy Spirit's leading in every part of our lives" (Galatians 5:25); "give yourselves completely to God" (Romans 6:13); "put aside your selfish ambitions" (Luke 9:23); and "[trust] Christ to give the victory" (1 John 5:4). It is our yielding and submitting to the Holy Spirit that allow his power and presence to be seen through our lives. Paul said, "This light and power that now shine within us—is held in perishable containers, that is, in our weak bodies. So everyone can see that our glorious power is from God and is not our own" (2 Corinthians 4:7). When we seek to honor him and not ourselves, he is pleased to exhibit his power and life through us.

Once we give up and sacrifice ourselves to him, the Holy Spirit empowers us. And that is when spiritual exercise and discipline comes into play. It is when we want the Holy Spirit's power defining our living that we need to cultivate good spiritual fitness. We do this by consistently studying his Word, going to him in constant prayer, worshipping with fellow believers, and fulfilling all the "one anothers" of Scripture, that is, love one another, accept one another, encourage one another, comfort one another, and so on. But we are never to feel we are strong in ourselves. We must ever remember the true source of our spiritual power. Confessing our weaknesses and sin should become a pattern of life.

King David struggled with his pride, his lust, and his self-centeredness. Yet in spite of all David's weakness, God said David was a man after his own heart. Why? Because David understood that God didn't want his self-serving works; he wanted his honesty and transparency. David wrote, "You would not be pleased with sacrifices, or I would bring them. If I brought you a burnt offering, you would not accept it. The sacrifice you want is a broken spirit. A broken and repentant heart, O God, you will not despise" (Psalm 51:16-17).

Because we are human and struggle with our sin nature, it means we must continually repent when we do wrong, turn from our wrongdoing (confess), and seek forgiveness of God. That is why James said, "Humble yourselves before God. Resist the Devil, and he will flee from you. Draw close to God, and God will draw close to you… Let there be tears for the wrong things you have done. Let there be sorrow and deep grief…When you bow down before the Lord and admit your dependence on him, he will lift you up and give you honor" (James 4:7-10).

So when we give ourselves to God with all our faults, failures, and weaknesses, God gives himself to us in return. And with him in our lives in the person of the Holy Spirit, we are an empowered follower of Christ. Paul summarized this when he proclaimed "let the Holy Spirit fill and control you" (Ephesians 5:18).

Discovering the Spirit-Filled Life

Dr. Bill Bright, founder of Campus Crusade for Christ International, was one of the most Spirit-filled and empowered persons we have ever known. He developed a booklet that hundreds of thousands of believers around the world have used to understand the Spirit-filled life.* In the following pages we are including a replica of that booklet.[1]

If you have yet to experience the Spirit-filled life, we invite you to trust in God, surrender to the Holy Spirit right now, and ask him to take control of your life. If you feel you have more to learn before you are ready to do this, we pray that reading the following booklet will lead you to open your life to him.

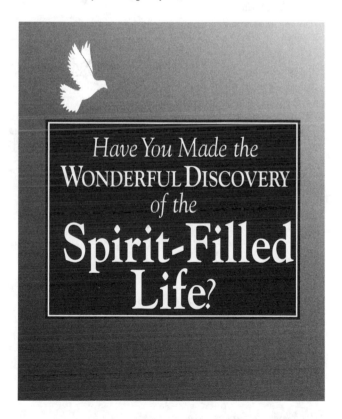

Have You Made the **WONDERFUL DISCOVERY** *of the* **Spirit-Filled Life?**

---

* The booklet is published by New Life Resources and is available in bulk at www.campuscrusade.org. Just click on ministry resources and look for "tracts & booklets."

Every day can be an exciting adventure for the Christian who knows the reality of being filled with the Holy Spirit and who lives constantly, moment by moment, under His gracious direction.

The Bible tells us that there are three kinds of people:

1. NATURAL PERSON

(One who has not received Christ)

Self-Directed Life
S – Self is on the throne
† – Christ is outside the life
● – Interests are directed by self, often resulting in discord and frustration

"A natural man does not accept the things of the Spirit of God; for they are foolishness to him, and he cannot understand them, because they are spiritually appraised" (1 Corinthians 2:14).

2. SPIRITUAL PERSON

(One who is directed and empowered by the Holy Spirit)

Christ-Directed Life
† – Christ is in the life and on the throne
S – Self is yielding to Christ
● – Interests are directed by Christ, resulting in harmony with God's plan

"He who is spiritual appraises all things… We have the mind of Christ" (1 Corinthians 2:15,16).

3. WORLDLY (CARNAL) PERSON

(One who has received Christ, but who lives in defeat because he is trying to live the Christian life in his own strength)

Self-Directed Life
S – Self is on the throne
† – Christ dethroned and not allowed to direct the life
● – Interests are directed by self, often resulting in discord and frustration

"Brothers, I could not address you as spiritual but as worldly—mere infants in Christ. I gave you milk, not solid food, for you were not yet ready for it. Indeed, you are still not ready. You are still worldly. For since there is jealousy and quarreling among you, are you not worldly? Are you not acting like mere men?" (1 Corinthians 3:1–3, NIV).

The following are four principles for living the Spirit-filled life.

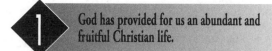

1 God has provided for us an abundant and fruitful Christian life.

Jesus said, "I have come that they may have life, and that they may have it more abundantly" (John 10:10, NKJ).

"I am the vine, you are the branches. He who abides in Me, and I in him, bears much fruit; for without Me you can do nothing" (John 15:5, NKJ).

"The fruit of the Spirit is love, joy, peace, patience, kindness, goodness, faithfulness, gentleness, self-control; against such things there is no law" (Galatians 5:22,23).

"You shall receive power when the Holy Spirit has come upon you; and you shall be My witnesses both in Jerusalem, and in all Judea and Samaria, and even to the remotest part of the earth" (Acts 1:8).

The following are some personal traits of the **spiritual person** that result from trusting God:

- Love
- Joy
- Peace
- Patience
- Kindness
- Faithfulness
- Goodness

- Life is Christ-centered
- Empowered by Holy Spirit
- Introduces others to Christ
- Has effective prayer life
- Understands God's Word
- Trusts God
- Obeys God

The degree to which these traits are manifested in the life depends on the extent to which the Christian trusts the Lord with every detail of his life, and on his maturity in Christ. One who is only beginning to understand the ministry of the Holy Spirit should not be discouraged if he is not as fruitful as more mature Christians who have known and experienced this truth for a longer period.

Why is it that most Christians are not experiencing the abundant life?

Worldly Christians cannot experience the abundant and fruitful Christian life.

The worldly (carnal) person trusts in his own efforts to live the Christian life:

◆ He is either uninformed about, or has forgotten, God's love, forgiveness, and power (Romans 5:8–10; Hebrews 10:1–25; 1 John 1; 2:1–3; 2 Peter 1:9; Acts 1:8).

◆ He has an up-and-down spiritual experience.

◆ He cannot understand himself—he wants to do what is right, but cannot.

◆ He fails to draw on the power of the Holy Spirit to live the Christian life (1 Corinthians 3:1–3; Romans 7:15–24; 8:7; Galatians 5:16–18).

Some or all of the following traits may characterize the **worldly person**—the Christian who does not fully trust God:

- Legalistic attitude
- Impure thoughts
- Jealousy
- Guilt
- Worry
- Discouragement
- Critical spirit
- Frustration
- Aimlessness

- Fear
- Ignorance of his spiritual heritage
- Unbelief
- Disobedience
- Loss of love for God and for others
- Poor prayer life
- No desire for Bible study

(The individual who professes to be a Christian but who continues to practice sin should realize that he may not be a Christian at all, according to 1 John 2:3; 3:6–9; Ephesians 5:5.)

The third truth gives us the only solution to this problem…

3 Jesus promised the abundant and fruitful life as the result of being filled (directed and empowered) by the Holy Spirit.

The Spirit-filled life is the Christ-directed life by which Christ lives His life in and through us in the power of the Holy Spirit (John 15).

◆ One becomes a Christian through the ministry of the Holy Spirit, according to John 3:1–8. From the moment of spiritual birth, the Christian is indwelt by the Holy Spirit at all times (John 1:12; Colossians 2:9,10; John 14:16,17).

◆ *Though all Christians are indwelt by the Holy Spirit, not all Christians are filled (directed and empowered) by the Holy Spirit on an ongoing basis.*

◆ The Holy Spirit is the source of the overflowing life (John 7:37–39).

◆ The Holy Spirit came to glorify Christ (John 16:1–15). When one is filled with the Holy Spirit, he is a true disciple of Christ.

◆ In His last command before His ascension, Christ promised the power of the Holy Spirit to enable us to be witnesses for Him (Acts 1:1–9).

How, then, can one be filled with the Holy Spirit?

4 We are filled with the Holy Spirit by faith; then we can experience the abundant and fruitful life that Christ promised.

You can appropriate the filling of the Holy Spirit **right now** if you:

◆ Sincerely desire to be directed and empowered by the Holy Spirit (Matthew 5:6; John 7:37–39).

◆ Confess your sins. By **faith**, thank God that He **has** forgiven all of your sins—past, present, and future—because Christ died for you (Colossians 2:13–15; 1 John 1; 2:1–3; Hebrews 10:1–17).

◆ Present every area of your life to God (Romans 12:1,2).

◆ By **faith** claim the fullness of the Holy Spirit, according to:

His command: Be filled with the Spirit.

"Do not get drunk on wine, which leads to debauchery. Instead, be filled with the Spirit" (Ephesians 5:18, NIV).

His promise: He will always answer when we pray according to His will.

"This is the confidence we have in approaching God: that if we ask anything according to his will, he hears us. And if we know that he hears us—whatever we ask—we know that we have what we asked of him" (1 John 5:14,15, NIV).

Faith can be expressed through prayer...

How to Pray in Faith to Be Filled with the Holy Spirit

We are filled with the Holy Spirit by **faith** alone. However, true prayer is one way of expressing our faith. The following is a suggested prayer:

> Dear Father, I need You. I acknowledge that I have sinned against You by directing my own life. I thank You that You have forgiven my sins through Christ's death on the cross for me. I now invite Christ to again take His place on the throne of my life. Fill me with the Holy Spirit as You **commanded** me to be filled, and as You **promised** in Your Word that You would do if I asked in faith. I pray this in the name of Jesus. As an expression of my faith, I now thank You for directing my life and for filling me with the Holy Spirit.

Does this prayer express the desire of your heart? If so, bow in prayer and trust God to fill you with the Holy Spirit **right now**.

How to Know That You Are Filled (Directed and Empowered) by the Holy Spirit

Did you ask God to fill you with the Holy Spirit? Do you know that you are now filled with the Holy Spirit? On what authority? (On the trustworthiness of God Himself and His Word: Hebrews 11:6; John 17:17.)

Do not depend on feelings. The promise of God's Word, not our feelings, is our authority. The Christian lives by faith (trust) in the trustworthiness of God Himself and His Word. This train diagram illustrates the relationship among **fact** (God and His Word), **faith** (our trust in God and His Word), and **feeling** (the result of our faith and obedience) (John 14:21).

The train will run with or without the caboose. However, it would be futile to attempt to pull the train by the caboose. In the same way, we as Christians do not depend on feelings or emotions, but we place our faith (trust) in the trustworthiness of God and the promises of His Word.

How to Walk in the Spirit

Faith (trust in God and His promises) is the only way a Christian can live the Spirit-directed life. As you continue to trust Christ moment by moment:

◆ Your life will demonstrate more and more of the fruit of the Spirit (Galatians 5:22,23) and will be more and more conformed to the image of Christ (Romans 12:2; 2 Corinthians 3:18).

◆ Your prayer life and study of God's Word will become more meaningful.

◆ You will experience His power in witnessing (Acts 1:8).

◆ You will be prepared for spiritual conflict against the world (1 John 2:15–17); against the flesh (Galatians 5:16,17); and against Satan (1 Peter 5:7–9; Ephesians 6:10–13).

◆ You will experience His power to resist temptation and sin (1 Corinthians 10:13; Philippians 4:13; Ephesians 1:19–23; 2 Timothy 1:7; Romans 6:1–16).

Spiritual Breathing

If you become aware of an area of your life (an attitude or an action) that is displeasing to the Lord, even though you are walking with Him and sincerely desiring to serve Him, simply thank God that He has forgiven your sins—past, present, and future—on the basis of Christ's death on the cross. Claim His love and forgiveness by faith and continue to have fellowship with Him.

If you retake the throne of your life through sin—a definite act of disobedience—breathe spiritually. Spiritual breathing (exhaling the impure and inhaling the pure) is an exercise in faith that enables you to experience God's love and forgiveness.

1. *Exhale:* Confess your sin—agree with God concerning your sin and thank Him for His forgiveness of it, according to 1 John 1:9 and Hebrews 10:1–25. Confession involves repentance—a change in attitude and action.

2. *Inhale:* Surrender the control of your life to Christ, and receive the fullness of the Holy Spirit by faith. Trust that He now directs and empowers you, according to the **command** of Ephesians 5:18 and the **promise** of 1 John 5:14,15.

TRUTH TEN

GOD'S KINGDOM

CHAPTER FORTY

KINGDOMS AT WAR

It was a strange time for the Judean people living under the rule of the Roman Empire. It was a time of great religious fervor, and yet a time of extreme cultural despair. Religion flourished among the leaders, who proclaimed the Scriptures with zeal. Many of the Jewish people followed their teachings to the letter. They knew of God, and most claimed to believe in him. Yet religion seemed confined within the walls of their place of worship and had little visible effect on the culture at large. Poverty within the Roman culture was rampant among the tenant families and the disenfranchised slaves and servants. The Jewish religious leaders were doing little to help the poor—widows, orphans, beggars, social outcasts, those who were heavily taxed. In fact, the moral and ethical lives of the religious elite were not significantly different from the Roman culture in which they lived.

Within this sea of societal despair, a little band of men and women saw a ray of hope. It was their Messiah, the Christ they followed in the hope that he would lead their nation out of tyranny into a new kingdom of rightness and glory. These followers of Jesus saw him and his coming kingdom as a solution to every problem they faced. They stayed with him as he taught the people, healed them, fed them, and ministered to their needs. But all the while they looked forward to the glorious day when he would assemble an army, defeat the Roman oppressors, and establish a new kingdom of prosperity and freedom.

But to their utter horror, their Master was arrested, put through a mockery of a trial, and crucified. They were stunned. Their hope for freedom from Roman bondage was cruelly dashed and, in hiding, they despaired. But then on the first day of the following week their emotions soared again when the seemingly impossible happened: Jesus arose from the dead. The little band was now back on top, wild with the hope that their long-promised kingdom was about to be established at last. What better drawing card for an enthusiastic army than to be led by a man who had defeated death! They were ready; they were excited; they could hardly wait.

They met with Jesus many times after his resurrection, and he talked often about the kingdom. Finally they asked, "Lord, are you going to free Israel now and restore our kingdom?" (Acts 1:6). He replied that his Father set such dates as those, and it was not for them to know. Furthermore, he announced that he was about to leave them again. Imagine their surprise and confusion. But he promised to send his Holy Spirit, who would empower them to spread his kingdom "in Jerusalem, throughout Judea, in Samaria, and to the ends of the earth" (Acts 1:8).

No doubt such answers confused these followers even more. Why wouldn't Jesus move to establish himself as ruler of his kingdom now? Why would he leave them in his moment of greatest triumph? And how could they establish the kingdom without its leader? Then Jesus actually ascended before their very eyes and disappeared into the clouds, and the hopes of these disciples were dashed yet again. We can only imagine their emotional turmoil as they turned and slowly descended the Mount of Olives and plodded dejectedly toward Jerusalem.

> When we live out Jesus' kingdom worldview, we are engaging in a mighty spiritual conflict to overthrow Satan's kingdom, the kingdom of this world, and establish Christ's kingdom in its place.

For a long while they must have walked silently, each nursing his own deep disappointment. Picture Philip finally breaking the heavy silence. "I just don't get it, Peter," he said. "I thought he was going to restore our kingdom."

"I don't get it either," Peter replied, shaking his head in despair. "Practically everything he taught us was about the kingdom, and I ate up every word of it. I mean, I was ready to leave my fishing business completely and follow him because I felt called to help make it all happen."

"Me too," James chimed in. "I never saw anyone put a finger on our problems like he did. He healed people, he loved them, he preached radical change, he fed the hungry. And my, how he took those religious leaders to task...He knew they didn't have anything to offer a hurting world. They are exactly what he said they were, 'white sepulchers with dead men's bones inside.' He was our hope. I thought he was going to be the leader of a movement that would change everything."[1]

Spiritual Kingdoms at War

Jesus was in fact the leader of a kingdom movement that would change everything. But Jesus' idea of the kingdom was considerably different than that of his disciples and the rest of the world. What was this "kingdom" Jesus talked about anyway?

The Roman governor, Pontius Pilate, was trying to get some clarity on that issue when Jesus was brought before him. He asked Jesus if he was the king of the Jews. The governor was trying to determine Jesus' political ambition.

"Then Jesus answered, 'I am not an earthly king. If I were, my followers would have fought when I was arrested by the Jewish leaders. But my Kingdom is not of this world'" (John 18:36). This further confused Pilate. Jesus was not an earthly king? *What other kind of king is there?* the governor probably wondered. *He's got a kingdom, but it's not of this world? How odd.*

It is odd unless you understand Jesus' concept of the kingdom. Jesus' kingdom idea was not about toppling the Roman Empire. His opposition wasn't the Romans or even the Jewish leaders. His opposition was Lucifer, his archenemy. You see, once Adam and Eve sinned it was Satan that moved in and made this present world his kingdom, the kingdom of darkness. So Jesus wasn't focused on human governments; he was focused on Satan's world order. Jesus came to earth to reclaim his lost creation and re-establish the circle of relationship between the Godhead (Father, Son, and Holy Spirit) and his human creation. The kingdom of God was to be a perfect relational order in which God's children loved and worshipped him, and together they would share in all the goodness and glory of his vast domain.

That is precisely what God desired to establish with Adam and Eve. The material world in which he placed the first couple would become his kingdom inheritance to them. This perfect kingdom on earth would be continually empowered by the unobstructed relational unity of God and humans. He, the source of all life and love and goodness, would make the kingdom of this world his kingdom, a kingdom without end.

But sin destroyed the relationship between God and humans. Before the kingdom of this world could become the eternal kingdom of God, Satan gained control. The disciple John said that "the world around us is under the power and control of the evil one" (1 John 5:19). In effect, Satan snatched the kingdom of this world away from God's children. Two kingdoms now exist—the kingdom of this world, with Satan as its king, and the kingdom of heaven with God as its King. That means that we are presently in the midst of a mighty conflict between two kingdoms warring against each other.

So the conflict isn't really political in nature as Pilate assumed. The struggle isn't even a cultural one. The primary enemy isn't wicked people or evil regimes of this world. The war is between God and his ways and Satan and his ways. And we as followers of Jesus are to be fighting this war alongside Christ. "For we are not fighting against people made of flesh and blood," the apostle Paul told us, "but against the evil rulers and authorities of the unseen world, against those mighty powers of darkness who rule this world, and against wicked spirits in the heavenly realms" (Ephesians 6:12). And when we live out Jesus' kingdom worldview, we are engaging in a mighty spiritual conflict to overthrow Satan's kingdom, the kingdom of this world, and establish Christ's kingdom in its place.

What God did when he entered human history 2000 years ago was to put Satan on notice that the kingdom of this world was going to be rescued and conquered by the kingdom of heaven. Jesus saw this world as a stolen kingdom temporarily under the rule of an enemy whose rule would one day come to an end. As C.S. Lewis put it, Christians on the earth live in "enemy occupied territory."[2] But their loyalty is to their commander, Jesus, who is the leader of a spiritual resistance movement to free them from the rule of the usurper.

Differing Worldviews

There will be a day when Jesus as conquering King will return to earth to establish his kingdom (our inheritance) as an eternal kingdom in heaven and on earth. But until that day comes, we continue to battle in the power of the Holy Spirit. It is a spiritual war between two ruling concepts or worldviews. Jesus is still King, only not an earthly ruler in the political realm. He is the King of a kingdom with a totally different set of basic assumptions—assumptions based in truth, which bring a different set of priorities, values, and behavior patterns. He made clear to Pilate just before his crucifixion that he indeed had a kingdom to rule. "I was born for that purpose," Jesus said. "And I came to bring truth to the world" (John 18:37). And that truth is in stark contrast to the basic assumptions of this present world. On the first day of Jesus' public ministry he "began to preach, 'Turn from your sins and turn to God, because the Kingdom of Heaven is near'" and from that point on "Jesus traveled throughout Galilee teaching in the synagogues, preaching everywhere the Good News about the Kingdom" (Matthew 4:17,23).

The kingdom truth Jesus proclaimed wasn't about power and politics, earthly authority and thrones, or a permanent homeland and occupied territories. His truth message was about the heart and the sin nature, attitudes and actions, love and relationships. His message called for a complete transformation of a person's life. And that life change was radical.

The people of that time hadn't heard anything like it. The Jewish law commanded them not to murder another. Yet Jesus said that to hate a person is the same as murder.

The Jewish law said not to commit adultery. Jesus said if you lust after a woman you are already an adulterer in your heart. The Jewish leaders taught to "love your neighbor and hate your enemy." Jesus said love your enemy. Jesus said that you must die to live, give in order to get, bow down in order to rise up, be last in order to be first. It didn't make sense to a lot of people then, and it doesn't make sense to a lot of people today. That's the thing about Jesus' kingdom: It is a whole new way to see God, ourselves, life, and relationships. It is a worldview defined by God and his Word. And it only makes sense to those who have been spiritually transformed and are living an empowered life in loving relationship with God.

The apostle Paul said, "God has actually given us his Spirit (not the world's spirit) so we can know the wonderful things God has freely given us…We speak words given to us by the Spirit, using the Spirit's words to explain spiritual truths. But people who aren't Christians can't understand these truths from God's Spirit. It all sounds foolish to them" (1 Corinthians 2:12-14). Jesus' worldview accurately sees what sin and separation from God have done to humans and the natural world. The dilemma of the Judean people at the time of Christ and ours today isn't primarily a material, political, or physical problem that can be solved by material, political, or physical solutions. Yes, there are real physical, economic, social, moral, ethical, and environmental problems today. Yet Jesus proclaimed that all our problems require a spiritual solution. And that spiritual solution "sounds foolish" to a lot of people.

It didn't make sense to Jesus' disciples at that time, because their priorities were upside down. They had not yet embraced the kingdom of heaven worldview. But when the Holy Spirit filled them, they viewed life and death through a new lens. They saw that Jesus had in fact established his kingdom—for his reign began when he was first planted deeply in the hearts of those who trusted in him. No longer was the kingdom simply a concept or a way of thinking. It became a way of relating to God and living within this world. And now, instead of the one person of Jesus spreading the kingdom movement, there would be multiplied thousands of Christians—"little Christs"—proclaiming the message through how they lived. Because of Christ's death, resurrection, and the indwelling presence of the Holy Spirit, the leader of the kingdom movement would now be living and preaching the kingdom through the lives of his followers.

This kingdom worldview—the Way of Jesus—may be spiritual in nature, but it affects every area of life. Jesus' worldview unlocks a very specific way of life, a way of knowing what is really true, a picture of being what God meant us to be, and the power to live that out based on our relationship with God. When we see and live by God's spiritual worldview, it combats darkness, injustice, and evil within the world. And that in turn brings resolution to the physical, economic, social, moral, ethical, and environmental problems of life. In fact, as we indicated earlier, God's new world order, which Jesus spiritually imparts to his followers today, will someday be a permanent and all-pervasive world order established in a new heaven and a new earth where there is no more sin, pain, sorrow, or death. But until the final and permanent kingdom of heaven envelops the kingdom of earth, we are to be his witnesses, the combatants against the spirit of darkness, and the messengers of Jesus' worldview, which is to be lived out for all to see.

Therefore:

> We believe the truth that Jesus' kingdom-of-God life and message forms our biblical worldview. It is this biblical worldview that not only provides us an accurate view of God, human history, life, relationships, death, and the world to come, but also a supernatural way to be and live in this present world.

Over the past 39 chapters we have begun to unlock the truths of a biblical worldview that we are to believe and live out. And while these truths are primarily spiritual in nature, they have a direct bearing on how we live and relate socially and culturally. Therefore, a kingdom-of-God worldview ought to be visibly influencing the world around us in a positive manner. And it has.

CHAPTER FORTY-ONE

EVIDENCE THAT GOD'S KINGDOM HAS POSITIVELY INFLUENCED THE WORLD

Religion poisons everything."[1] That is what contemporary atheist Christopher Hitchens has stated. Friedrich Nietzsche, a nineteenth-century atheist and author of *The Antichrist* writes:

> I *condemn* Christianity; I bring against the Christian Church the most terrible of all accusations that an accuser has ever had in his mouth. It is, to me, the greatest of all imaginable corruptions; it seeks to work the ultimate corruption, nothing untouched by its depravity; it had turned every value into worthlessness, and every truth into a lie, and every integrity into baseness of the soul.[2]

To some, Christianity is the evil emperor imposing its will on the masses and threatening to suppress the free expressions of humanity. Although there are those past and present who, under the banner of Christianity, have waged war, enslaved people, and brought disgrace on the name of Christ, this is only a small, sad corner of the whole picture. It can be demonstrated that it is Jesus' kingdom worldview that has fostered more good and provided more positive contributions to society than any other force in history. If we were to highlight just a few of the positive influences of a biblical worldview they would include:

- the high value for human life
- care for the sick in creating hospitals
- literacy and education for the masses
- abolition of slavery in the Western world
- the elevation of women
- high standards of justice and civil liberties
- benevolence and charity work
- development of art and music
- the motivation and basis for modern science

Atheists and other detractors of Christianity fail to point out that it is the human propensity to be self-centered that has brought such misery and suffering upon the masses. Christianity is actually the antidote to this propensity, for it is the message and power of Christ that addresses the core problem of self-centeredness.

Self-Centeredness vs. a Compassionate Heart for Others

Greed, corruption, abuse of power, and a basic disregard for others all spring from self-centeredness. Left unchecked, human nature will always revert to self-serving ways that seek to gain at another's expense. On the opposite side of the equation, making the interest and care of others as important as your own creates goodwill and harmony and meets human need. This is at the center of Jesus' teaching—it represents the very heart of God. Jesus said, "Do for others what you would like them to do for you. This is a summary of all that is taught in the law and the prophets" (Matthew 7:12).

Jesus had a heart of love that moved him to put others first, and it is that Christlike heart that has empowered his followers to change the world for good.

Looking out for the interests of others, especially those in need, is the primary core value of Jesus' worldview. The expression used most often to describe Jesus' heart of love was that he was "moved with compassion." When he saw the two blind men he was "moved with compassion." When he saw the leper he was "moved with compassion." When he saw the sick and the hungry he was "moved with compassion." (See Matthew 9:36; 14:14; 15:32; 20:34; Mark 1:41; 6:34; 8:2.) Jesus had a heart of love that moved him to put others first, and it is that Christlike heart that has empowered his followers to change the world for good.

At its core this biblical worldview represents a focus on caring for the interest of others. "In humility," Paul said, "consider others better than yourselves. Each of you should look not only to your own interests, but also to the interests of others" (Philippians 2:3-4 NIV). This compassion toward others is a radical message now and it was certainly so during the time of Christ. Within the Roman Empire during the first century, enslaving others was commonplace. Abortion was rampant. Parents abandoned virtually all babies that were deformed. Women had few rights and were considered the property of their husbands.

Yet during this time James, a disciple of Jesus, made a radical statement: "Pure and lasting religion in the sight of God our Father means that we must care for orphans and widows in their troubles, and refuse to let the world corrupt us" (James 2:27). These early Christians rejected the cultural practice of allowing abandoned babies and orphaned children to die on the streets. Instead, they would literally pick them up and adopt them into their own homes. What caused them to do this? It was the "moved with compassion" heart of their Lord being lived out in their lives. Early Christians believed that everyone—including the poor, the homeless, the handicapped, the sick—was made in the image of God and had infinite value, dignity, and worth. By the third and fourth century this influence of Jesus' worldview was widespread. Sherwood Wirt, author of *The Social Conscience of the Evangelical*, documents what took place under the influence of Christianity by AD 500:

> Many permanent legal reforms were set in motion by Emperors Constantine (280-337) and Justinian (483-565) that can be laid to the influence of Christianity. Licentious and cruel sports were checked; new legislation was ordered to protect the slave, the prisoner, the mutilated man, the outcast woman. Children were granted important legal rights. Infant exposure was abolished. Women were raised from a status of degradation to that of legal protection. Hospitals and orphanages were created to take care of foundlings. Personal feuds and private wars were put under restraint... Branding of slaves was halted.[3]

It was Christians with the compassionate heart of Jesus who cared for people that society had largely forgotten. It was Christians who reached out to the blind, the lame, the elderly, the mentally handicapped, and those less fortunate when no one else would. And those efforts have continued until this day.

Often great works of compassion and charity are birthed by the dedication and sacrifice of a single follower of Jesus.

Basil of Caesarea was a fourth-century bishop in Asia Minor. He wrote, "I had wasted much time on follies and spent nearly all my youth in vain labors...Suddenly, I awoke as out of a deep sleep. I beheld the wonderful light of the Gospel truth, and recognized the nothingness of the wisdom of the princes of this world."[4] With a kingdom worldview, Basil championed the cause of the outcasts of society, working with the poor, the sick, and the prostitutes. He eventually built a large complex just outside of Caesarea called the Basiliad, which included a poorhouse, hospice, and hospital. Basil's compassionate heart of Christ and work with the needy was regarded at the time as one of the great wonders of the world.

William Booth came to the slums of East London in 1865 as an itinerant evangelist. At that time there were tens of thousands living on the streets, sleeping wherever they could find shelter. Food was scarce and some 80,000 young women were prostituting themselves to survive.[5] William and Catherine Booth mobilized an army (the Salvation Army) "to transform the living hell of the homeless into communities of self-helping, self-sustaining families."[6]

Today the Salvation Army operates in 118 countries and provides services in 175 different languages. It is the largest nongovernmental provider of social services in the United Kingdom and one of the largest social aid providers in the world, helping more than 32 million people in the U.S. alone. The Christlike compassion of one couple over 140 years ago has been translated into a force of 4.5 million volunteers aiding those in need.[7]

Jean-Henri Dunant was born in Geneva, Switzerland, in 1828 and raised by devout Christian parents. As a child he would accompany his mother on her visits to care for the poor and sick in Geneva's suburbs. It was there that he witnessed the misery of those living in deep poverty. It left a lasting impression on this young Christian man.

In 1859 he traveled to Italy and witnessed the Battle of Solferino. He watched as nearly 40,000 wounded men begged for help on the battlefield. Moved with a Christlike compassion he persuaded the military leaders to release all captive medical personnel so they could tend to the wounded, friend and foe. Churches and private homes were transformed into makeshift hospitals. Dunant set about discussing formal procedures with the military for neutral medical aid during conflict for the alleviation of the suffering of the wounded.

His efforts resulted in the creation of a national Red Cross organization and the establishment of the Geneva Convention, which addressed how fighting armies would treat wounded soldiers. Today the International Federation of Red Cross is the world's largest humanitarian organization with 186 national societies as members.[8] Jesus was "moved with compassion," and for centuries he has moved his followers with compassion to alleviate the suffering of the wounded and dying.

Agnes Bojaxhiu was born in Macedonia in 1910. When she was 18 she joined the convent because she felt called by God to be a missionary. In 1948 while she was teaching high-schoolers in Calcutta she observed the suffering and poverty of those outside the convent walls. She sought permission from her superiors to leave the convent school and devote herself to working among the poorest of the poor in the slums of Calcutta.

Known as Mother Teresa, she received permission to start her own order called "The Missionaries of Charity." Today the work of Mother Teresa continues through the aid and assistance of co-workers, who became an official international association in 1969. Millions are still being reached in the former Soviet Union and eastern European countries, as well as in Asia, Africa, and Latin America.[9] The heart of a small lady moved by the great compassion of Christ brought comfort and healing to many.

Beyond any shadow of a doubt Christianity has been a powerful redemptive force for good in our world. It is Jesus' kingdom worldview that has led his followers to establish protection for infants and the unborn, child labor laws, separation of church and state, liberty and justice, care for those in need, abolition of slavery in the Western world, and modern science. They have built universities and hospitals and brought about musical innovations and the advancement of the written word.[10]

And while the accomplishments of the Basils, William Booths, Jean-Henri Dunants, and Mother Teresas of the world have been heroic and spectacular, these biblical worldview hall-of-famers represent only a fraction of the world-changing agents that have played a positive role in the world. Currently, ministries such as Samaritan's Purse, World Vision International, and Compassion International are reaching out to bring hope and healing to many. I (Sean) have had firsthand knowledge of the compassionate hearts of thousands reaching out to the former Soviet Union through Operation Carelift. This was an effort founded by my dad (Josh) to offer medical assistance and clothes to those in need. I have traveled on these mission trips and seen the positive impact in the lives of people when the love of Christ is lived out. Today that simple effort to reach the hurting in the former Soviet Union has become an international relief agency called GAIN (Global Aid International). In 2010 it was one of the very first agencies to meet the desperate needs of earthquake-ravaged Haiti.

It is these followers of Jesus, and many more, who have been unpublicized and largely unnoticed by the world who have had such a positive influence in society. It is Christ's kingdom worldview lived out in your everyday life and ours that is making a difference. As each of us embraces Jesus and lives out his ways, he is able to minister through us powerfully to make his prayer a reality:

> Our Father in heaven,
> may your name be honored.
> May your kingdom come soon.
> May your will be done here on earth,
> just as it is in heaven (Matthew 6:9-10).

CHAPTER FORTY-TWO

Determining Your Kingdom Worldview

I can't believe the gall of that guy," Mark said in a low tone as he sipped from his cup at an office coffee break.

"What guy?" Chris asked, leaning forward to learn more.

"Oh—Eric, the brilliant new VP of marketing." Mark's words dripped sarcasm. "He's out of his mind if he thinks he's going to get away with this."

"Away with what?" Chris asked impatiently. "What's going on?"

"Well, he asked me last week to get him all my ideas for the upcoming product line," Mark began. "He knew I had spent a ton of time and creative energy putting together some really great ideas. And I just found out this morning that he presented my ideas to the top brass and took all the credit for it."

"That's so wrong!" Chris responded.

"Don't think he's going to get away with it," retorted Mark. "I'm making it my personal mission to see that he goes down in flames!"

■

We've all been treated unjustly at some point in our lives. People take unfair advantage of others every day. You've heard it said that we live in a dog-eat-dog world. And it's natural to want to see justice done. But the kingdom of this world has a means of obtaining justice that's quite different from that of the kingdom of heaven. In fact, the kingdom of this world sees and acts differently on every level than Jesus' kingdom. Jesus prayed these words to his Father concerning his followers:

> They do not belong to the world, just as I do not. I'm not asking you to take them out of the world, but to keep them safe from the evil one. They are not part of this world any more than I am (John 17:14-16).

Jesus prayed that we would live in this world but not be a part of the way it thinks and lives. To do that requires that we first have a relational transformation. We are to relate no longer to the beliefs and values of this world, but instead to Christ himself. And in that redeemed relationship we believe what he says and embrace his values. From Christ's new set of values we then act in a new set of ways. Instead of, for example, setting out to get even, as Mark plans to do in our story, we are to act as Christ did when he went to the cross. "He did not retaliate when he was insulted. When he suffered, he did not threaten to get even. He left his case in the hands of God, who always judges fairly" (1 Peter 2:23).

How Mark and the rest of us act in any given situation is based on a set of basic assumptions about how life works. Mark's attitude that drove him to get even with his boss came from somewhere. It's natural for him to feel used and disrespected by his superior who claimed credit for his work. But why did Mark decide to "get even"? Something led him to that choice. The choices we make, the way we see our lives, and how we respond in every situation are based on a set of assumptions about how life works. And these assumptions define our worldview.

Why Your Worldview Matters

Each of us believes certain things about God, ourselves, and all of life, and we interpret those things through our past experiences and relationships. We all have a worldview whether we know what it is or not—because everything we think and do is filtered through our assumption of how life works.

We build those assumptions through a series of stages, and they finally emerge as actions. First, all that you have learned and everything you know, even *how* you learned it, comes out of a relationship with someone or something. You are a relational being, so much of what you are today is a direct result of who you've related to and how. Then, out of those relationships you establish what you believe. Relationships are the fertile ground in which beliefs grow. Then your beliefs shape what you value, and your values drive your actions (see diagram).

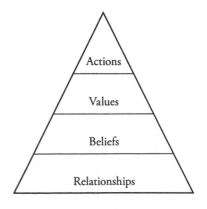

Let's look at Mark again. He grew up in an abusive home. His father wasn't around much, but when he was there, he was mean to Mark. At the age of 16, Mark fought back. He wasn't going to take it anymore. He moved in with his grandparents and finished high school. Now married and with a good job, he visits his parents now and again, but he's not relationally close to them.

Every attitude we have and every behavior we exhibit comes from this developmental process of relationships, beliefs, and values.

Out of an unhealthy relationship with his father, Mark formed some beliefs about how the world works. He developed a belief that said people care only about themselves, and they will hurt you if you get in the way. From that belief came his values, which are to place great importance on your own turf and your own accomplishments, and use them to further yourself. From that value came his mode of action, which was essentially self-protection: "kill or be killed." So Mark dealt with bullies and abusers with a "get smart, get even" course of action.

Every attitude we have and every behavior we exhibit comes from this developmental process of relationships, beliefs, and values. If you had positive and godly relationships in your formative years, you are more likely to have developed biblical values. Your view of how the world works has been formed by those relationships and is most likely still growing. Your view of the world should in fact be in a constant state of development as you grow deeper in your knowledge and relationship with God. As our beliefs and values conform to God and his Word, they are reflected in our attitudes and actions.

Most theologians and apologists would agree that our worldview comes out of our relationships, beliefs, and values. But that really doesn't define what a worldview is. Philosopher and theologian Dr. James Sire gives us a clear definition from his book *The Universe Next Door*. He states that a worldview is

> a commitment, a fundamental orientation of the heart, that can be expressed as a story or in a set of presuppositions (assumptions which may be true, partially true or utterly false) which we hold (consciously or subconsciously, consistently or inconsistently) about the basic constitution of reality, and that provides the foundation on which we live and move and have our being.[1]

Most of us arrive at our worldview without even knowing it. Yet Dr. Sire points out that there are at least eight basic issues or questions that determine the assumptions we hold about "the foundation on which we live and move and have our being."

You and I have probably already consciously or subconsciously answered those questions. They revolve around our understanding of reality, the nature of the universe, the nature of humanity, the issue of human knowing, morals and ethics, what happens to a person at death, the meaning of history, and our core commitments. If you have embraced the nine truths we have covered so far in this handbook, here is how you would answer the eight questions that define your worldview. These answers are stated in the first person as if you were answering them yourself.

1. *What is reality?* In other words, what do I consider to be ultimately real? When I stop to consider what makes anything in life real, I conclude it is God. Reality reflects the nature and character of a relational God who has created me as a relational being, and he defines my reality.

2. *How does the world exist?* I believe the personal Almighty God spoke into existence all that exists. He is the Creator God who formed the world around me and the reality in which I exist.

3. *What is a human being?* Humans are the personal creation of the relational God, made in his likeness and image with dignity and worth. Because God is three persons with infinite love in perfect relationship, I was created to live in loving relationship with God, myself, other humans, and the physical world I inhabit.

4. *Why is it possible to know anything?* An all-knowing God has given me, his creation, the capacity to know and be known. He is the source of all knowledge. All of eternity will not be enough for me to discover the infinite knowledge of God and his creation. I will only be able to scratch the surface.

5. *How do I know right from wrong?* The character and nature of God are absolutely good and right and holy. Everything that is good and right and holy flows from his character and nature, and only from them. To determine what is moral and ethical I must measure it by God and his Word as my universal standard of right and wrong.

6. *What happens to me at death?* First, I must die because sin has entered the human race and has separated me from God, the life-giver. But because God is love and because he is merciful, he has provided a way for me to be brought back into relationship with him. Therefore, because I have accepted his provision (Christ's death on the cross), when I die physically I will live eternally with him in a new heaven and earth. Otherwise, I would be separated from him in an eternal aloneness—hell.

7. *What is the meaning of human history?* History is linear, so it has a meaningful sequence of events that God interweaves and with which he

interacts to move the human saga from a beginning, through a middle, and to an end. God created time, by which human history could be chronicled, and at the beginning of time he created the world and all there is. Sin entered the world and humans died—separating them from God. God then entered the world in human form to offer redemption. During the sequence of history since the fall of man, God is in the process of restoring all things to his original design. Sin and death will be done away with, and redeemed humans will forever live to glorify God in perfect relationship with him. The meaning of human history is ultimately the working out of God's purpose on the earth, which includes a purpose for my life culminating in eternity with him.

8. *What core commitments are consistent with my worldview?* I am committed to love and worship God with all my heart, soul, and mind and love my neighbor as myself. This means I am committed to seek to know God intimately; to love my first neighbor (my family), those within Christ's body, and those in the world around me; and to engage in Christ's mission to redeem the lost until his kingdom comes.

The answers to the eight questions above form a biblical worldview based on the truths we have covered so far in this handbook. We propose that this view of life makes sense out of all the confusion, chaos, and tragedies of this world. By adopting and affirming these truths, you have just defined your own worldview. And in the next chapter we will discover how that biblical worldview defines who you are, why you are here, and where you are going.

CHAPTER FORTY-THREE

HOW YOUR WORLDVIEW DEFINES WHO YOU ARE, WHY YOU ARE HERE, AND WHERE YOU ARE GOING

Can you live in Rome and not do as the Romans do? Can you walk among sinners and not walk in sin? Can you live in the world and not be part of it?

You can, just as faithful followers of Christ have done for centuries before you, when your thinking and behavior flow out of your intimate *relationship* with God. That relationship provides you, as God's child, solid *beliefs* about him, about yourself, and about the world around us. Those beliefs create certain *values* that you then embrace. Those values reflect themselves in all your *attitudes and actions*. This is the process of forming and living out a biblical worldview that brings you that deep abiding peace and joy in life.

With that said, let's look at how this process plays out in regard to the nine truths we have covered in this book so far. What follows is but a sampling of the many ways our biblical worldview is reflected in our lives. We will address each truth we have presented thus far and walk it through the process we have highlighted above. This exercise will demonstrate how the foundational truths of Christianity give meaning to our relationships, our beliefs, our values, and our actions.

Meaning Through the Truths of Christianity

1. The Creator God Exists

The truth: A relational God exists and he created humans in his likeness and image.

Our relationship: God is a relational God who honors us enough to give us the right to choose him and his ways. He is a God who values our creativity and sense of responsibility. He has given us relationships with others and a world to nurture and care for. He is a God who loves us for who we are and gives us the capacity to love him and our fellow humans.

Our belief: We believe the truth that our Creator God is worthy of our devoted worship, and in honor of him we are to love him with all our mind, soul, and strength. Out of our love for him we are to love ourselves, one another, and the world he has given us.

Our values: We value God as the giver of life and loving relationships. We value ourselves as his temple, and we maintain ourselves physically, spiritually, and relationally. We value every person and relationship God has given us, and we value their God-given rights to life and loving relationships. We value the planet God has given us and endeavor to nurture and protect it.

Our actions: We strive to worship God and put him first in our lives continually by making his priorities our priorities.

We strive to provide for and protect our bodies, emotions, and relationships by avoiding sexual immorality and preserving our marital relationship, and by avoiding the taking of illegal drugs, putting things in our bodies that would damage the temple of God, and all other actions that would not bring honor to him.

We strive to love our neighbors by promoting social justice, taking care of the sick, meeting the needs of the needy, defending the God-given rights of others, protecting and reverencing life, and promoting peace and unity among all people.

We strive to the best of our ability to become good stewards of the talents and gifts God gave us, including the planet he gave us as our home.

2. God Gave Us His Word

The truth: God has revealed himself to us through his reliable Word, the Bible.

Our relationship: Our relational God knows us intimately, but he wants us to know him intimately in all his loving ways.

Our belief: We believe the truth that the Bible is God's revelation of himself, given to enable us to follow his ways so that we can be like him and enjoy all the blessings of an intimate relationship with him.

Our values: We value God's Word as a means to know him. We value obedience to God's Word because it informs us of the benefits we derive from a relationship with him and gives us protection from the negative consequences that result from living outside of his loving boundaries.

Our actions: We strive to study God's Word often to know him and his ways. We seek to follow his ways by obeying his commands. We do this by loving him with all our mind, soul, and strength and loving our neighbors as ourselves.

3. Sin Brought Death

The truth: The God-human love relationship came to an end through Adam and Eve's disobedience to God.

Our relationship: When the God-human relationship was broken due to Adam and Eve's disobedience, it brought death and separation from God to all the human race.

Our belief: We believe the truth that choosing our own way and deciding from within ourselves what is right or wrong, rather than believing that God is the sole arbiter of right and wrong, has resulted in death—a separation from God for all humans. This separation results in all the pain, heartache, and suffering the human race endures.

Our values: We value God and his reliable Word as the absolute standard of rightness. The essence of God's character and nature defines all that is right, perfect, holy, and good.

Our actions: We strive to humble ourselves before God, turn our backs on our self-centered ways, and submit to God's ways. As we compare our attitudes and actions to God and commit to his ways, we choose what is right and reject what is wrong. It is then we enjoy God's provision and protection.

4. God Entered Our World

The truth: God took on human form in the person of Jesus Christ to redeem us.

Our relationship: Because God is "passionate about his relationship with [us]" (Exodus 34:14), he sent his Son to die for us.

Our belief: We believe the truth that God became human in the person of Jesus Christ. He was born of the virgin Mary to redeem us and restore us to a relationship with God.

Our values: We value unconditional love and acceptance because God demonstrated his unconditional love and acceptance by entering our world to redeem us. We value compassionate understanding because Jesus demonstrated he understood us by experiencing all the joys and sufferings we as humans have experienced.

Our actions: We strive to accept others without condition by making ourselves fully available to them, entering their world of involvement, and loving them regardless of their faults. Our actions then reflect the unconditional love and acceptance of our God, who loves us with that kind of love.

5. Jesus Atones for Our Sin

The truth: Jesus laid down his life as a sacrifice for our sin.

Our relationship: God's relationship with us is a sacrificial and giving love relationship in which he forgives us when we are undeserving of forgiveness.

Our belief: We believe the truth that Jesus as the sinless Son of God atoned for our sins in his death on the cross. The offering of his blood as a loving sacrifice for sin enables a just and holy God to forgive us.

Our values: We value justice and the reality that someone is always hurt when wrong is done. We value forgiveness and realize that a sacrifice must always be made in order to forgive.

Our actions: Our love of God for sacrificing his Son for us is reflected in the sacrificing of our own comforts, our time, and our personal possessions for others. We strive to give of ourselves unselfishly until it hurts and forgive those who do wrong against us.

6. We Are Justified by Grace

The truth: None of us deserved to be forgiven of our sins. God justifies us by his grace.

Our relationship: There was nothing we could do and nothing we could offer to deserve a love relationship with God. When we were his enemy he still loved us. Our initial relationship was one-sided—he loved us when we didn't love him.

Our belief: We believe the truth that being justified before God, completely forgiven of our sins and made his child, is a result of his grace through our faith alone in Jesus as our sacrifice for sin.

Our values: We value grace—a love given when it is not deserved or when no love is given in return. We value faith—placing our trust in Jesus—the one who sacrificed his life for us. We value a love that reached out to restore a relationship when we were utterly hopeless and lost without God.

Our actions: God's amazing love and grace empower us to place our faith in Jesus to redeem us and restore us to relationship with God. We humble ourselves, turn our back on our self-centered ways of sin, and trust in Christ's sacrifice for our forgiveness of sin. We accept God's forgiveness with a heart of gratitude and devote our lives to loving him with all our mind, soul, and strength. We rejoice in our identity as his loving child.

7. Our Lives Are Changed

The truth: Our lives are continually being changed into the likeness of Christ.

Our relationship: God imparts his divine nature (godly DNA) to us, which enables us to have an intimate relationship with him and reflect his likeness and image before the world around us.

Our belief: We believe the truth that as a follower of Christ we are destined to be conformed to the likeness of Christ.

Our values: We value all the characteristics of Christlikeness—love for God, submission to him, self-sacrifice, and love for others.

Our actions: As people being conformed to Christlikeness we not only love God, but we strive to think like, be motivated like, and live like Jesus—to love others as ourselves by making the security, happiness, and welfare of others as important as our own. We strive to fulfill the "one anothers" of Scripture.

8. Jesus Rose from the Dead

The truth: Jesus had to rise from the dead for our faith to mean anything.

Our relationship: Our relationship is not with a philosophy or a way of life. Our relationship is with the living Christ, who rose from the dead and promised to give us eternal life with him.

Our belief: We believe the truth that Jesus died and rose again to redeem us and give us eternal life with him in a new heaven and a new earth.

Our values: We value our hope of eternal life. We value the assurance our faith gives us that we will live forever with God and our loved ones who have trusted in Christ.

Our actions: We live with an expectant hope and with an anticipation of what awaits us in the next life. We don't fear death, for we do not face it alone; God is with us. We do not despair when a loved one dies who has trusted in Christ. We don't live our life for this temporal world and build up treasures here. Instead we strive to store up treasures in heaven by living this life to honor and please God.

9. God Is Three in One

The truth: God is Father, Son, and Holy Spirit in perfect oneness.

Our relationship: God has manifested himself in his handiwork of creation, he has revealed himself in bodily form in Jesus, and he has now entered our very lives in the person of his Holy Spirit. The indwelling presence of the Holy Spirit makes our relationship more intimate than any other relationship can be.

Our belief: We believe the truth that God is Father, Son, and Holy Spirit, three persons with infinite love for each other in perfect relationship. We believe we are made part of this circle of relationship through the power of the indwelling presence of the Holy Spirit.

Our values: We value intimacy—an unbroken cycle of relationship between God, ourselves, and others. We value the oneness and the bond of the Father, Son, and Holy Spirit in Scripture and desire to be part of it and emulate it in all our relationships. We value the Holy Spirit of God as the one who lives in and through our lives, enabling us to think like, be motivated like, and act like Jesus.

Our actions: We strive to turn our backs on our self-centered and self-reliant ways and yield to the Holy Spirit who lives within us. We give up trying to live like Christ through our own efforts and allow the Holy Spirit to empower us so he can make us intimate with God, make us like Christ, lead us into all truth, equip us for service, and bring true meaning to our lives. We strive daily to breathe spiritually by *exhaling*: confessing sin in our lives; and *inhaling*: drawing in the life of God's Holy Spirit and yielding control of our lives completely to him.

When we embrace these truths and strive to live them out, we are adopting and following a biblical worldview. While we may not be able to live out all these truths perfectly, God is still at work in us perfecting his will in our lives. We experience his pleasure and joy because living out a biblical worldview ultimately provides the only satisfying answers to the three deepest questions of life.

Answers That Satisfy

Who Are You?

You are a human being created in the image and likeness of a relational God. But you have lost your sense of identity because of your sin, which brought death to your Father-child relationship with your Creator. God took the initiative to bring you back into relationship with him, and because you have trusted in his solution (his Son dying in your stead) *you have regained your **identity** as a transformed, born-again child of God.* You have regained your family connection to your Father God.

Why Are You Here?

Made alive to God because of Christ, you enjoy a Father-child relationship that is continually conforming you to the image of God's Son. *Your **purpose** is to bring glory and honor to your God* by living to please him. You bring him pleasure, he brings you joy.

Where Are You Going?

Sin and death, pain and suffering, still exist. Yet God is on a mission to restore all things to his original design. You have joined his mission to proclaim the good news of God's kingdom to come. One day sin and death will be brought to an end. *Your destiny is to live eternally with God and your loved ones in a new heaven and a new earth.*

■

Your biblical worldview gives you a clear sense of your identity, purpose, and destiny in life. As God empowers you to live out your worldview, he completes you, gives you a sense of meaning, and provides you an expectant hope of an eternal future. No other worldview provides so much joy. No other worldview provides such overwhelming evidence that it is true. No other worldview provides for such a glorious future.

TRUTH ELEVEN

THE CHURCH

CHAPTER FORTY-FOUR

WHAT IS
THE CHURCH?

As a kid, going to church just didn't make sense to me (Josh). About the most I got out of it was putting fifty cents in the offering basket and taking a dollar out. To me, the sermons were boring. Sitting for 45 minutes or so listening to a preacher saying things that didn't much relate to me seemed like a waste of time.

A lot of people today feel like that about church. Of course, if Jesus were literally the pastor of the church, it would make a big difference. I suppose he would be healing people left and right, feeding the hungry, and launching his eternal kingdom on earth to bring peace and joy to the whole world. Who wouldn't want to be part of that kind of a church? Well, that is what the disciples of Jesus thought too.

Launching Jesus' "Kingdom Central"?

It had been a great month. The crowds were bigger than ever. The Messiah was displaying his power, and the sick were being healed instantly. "The crowd was amazed! Those who hadn't been able to speak were talking, the crippled were made well, the lame were walking around, and those who had been blind could see again!" (Matthew 15:31)

Four thousand men, not counting women and children, had been Jesus' outdoor congregation for three days, and they were getting hungry. Jesus asked how much food the disciples had. They told him they had seven loaves and a few small fish. So again, Jesus did the seemingly impossible. He prayed over the seven loaves and the few fish and told his disciples to distribute them to the crowd. After everyone ate all they wanted the disciples gathered up the leftovers—seven large baskets full!

Jesus sent the masses home with full bellies and continued with his ministry of healing and spreading the kingdom message. When he had his small band of disciples alone he asked a central question: "Who do people say that the Son of Man is?" (Matthew 16:13). They told him some thought he was Elijah, others thought he was Jeremiah or one of the other prophets. Then came the penetrating question—the question that really mattered. "'Who do you say I am?' Simon Peter answered, 'You are the Messiah, the Son of the living God.' Jesus replied, 'You are blessed, Simon son of John, because my Father in heaven has revealed this to you...Now I say to you that you are Peter [which means "rock"], and upon this rock I will build my church, and all the powers of hell will not conquer it'" (Matthew 16:15-18).

There it was! The declaration that the disciples were looking for. Jesus said, "I will build my church." Now he would really launch his kingdom. With him healing the sick and feeding the people, the disciples would be guaranteed a megachurch in their first week of operation. This had to be great news to them. In fact, six days later Jesus took Peter, James, and John on an excursion up a mountain that further reinforced this church notion. Suddenly "Jesus' appearance was transformed so that his face shone like the sun, and his clothes became as white as light" (Matthew 17:2 NLT). And to their amazement Moses and Elijah appeared and started talking with Jesus.

This had to be it. Who could ask for anything better? Jesus would be the kingdom pastor of the great church on the mountain and Moses and Elijah would be his two associate pastors. This would be the perfect location for "Jesus' Kingdom Central"! So Peter blurted out, "Lord, it's wonderful for us to be here! If you want, I'll make three shelters as memorials—one for you, one for Moses, and one for Elijah" (Matthew 17:4).

But no sooner did Peter get his great idea out of his mouth than a bright light flashed and a voice came booming down from a cloud, "This is my dearly loved Son, who brings me great joy. Listen to him" (Matthew 17:5 NLT). The disciples were so shocked that they fell face down on the ground. Jesus came over and told them not to be afraid. When they looked up Moses and Elijah were gone. And to top it off Jesus told them they must not tell anyone what they had seen until "the Son of Man has been raised from the dead" (Matthew 17:9 NLT).

What Does the Church Look Like?

This had to be confusing and frustrating to Peter, James, and John. Even if Jesus wasn't going to defeat the Romans and rule the nation politically, he could at least stick around after his resurrection and be pastor of the Kingdom Church on the

Mount. What better way to spread the kingdom worldview than having King Jesus preach every week? And when new technologies were created he could be televised globally, launch the Jesus Facebook, and answer all questions and solve all problems online.

But there was, and is, a better way. Jesus' idea of the church wasn't about a building that would serve as "Kingdom Central." Yes, Jesus told Peter he would build the church on the declaration that he was the Messiah, the true Son of God. But when he said "church," he didn't mean a building. His word choice was *ekklesia,* which meant a gathering of people. In the culture of that time the word *ekklesia* was clearly understood to mean a public assembly of citizens. Its Hebrew counterpart meant an assembly before the Lord. Whether in Greek or Hebrew, *church* meant "the people of God," not a building.

> *With Jesus as head of his church, the kingdom would go viral—through the power of the Holy Spirit lived out in the community of his followers—and eventually every corner of the earth would be reached.*

In today's culture, *church* is most often thought of as a building or an organization. But that is far from what the disciples and apostles understood after Pentecost. Once the Holy Spirit filled them they understood the concept—the church was God's people. The church was Christ's agent to spread the kingdom message. The church was the visible representation of Christ himself.

When Jesus told his disciples to "go and make disciples of all the nations" (Matthew 28:19) he was delivering that command to his people, the church that would shortly be established. That church was given a mission, which was part of a greater mission of redemption and restoration of all things. Christ's initial step in that mission was to give his life as a ransom. He completed that through his death on the cross, but he would accomplish the rest of his mission through another means. With Jesus as head of his church, the kingdom would go viral—through the power of the Holy Spirit lived out in the community of his followers—and eventually every corner of the earth would be reached.

Jesus' new church wouldn't be a static organization, but a living organism. It wouldn't be about building an institution or a memorial, but about spreading a message and transforming the hearts of people. The New Testament uses at least six images to describe the church, none of which are about organizations, institutions, or physical buildings.

1. *The church is the new people of God.* The apostle Paul explained to the churches of Galatia that it didn't matter any longer whether the Jewish

law of circumcision was performed. "What counts," Paul said, "is whether we really have been changed into new and different people. May God's mercy and peace be upon all those who live by this principle. They are the new people of God" (Galatians 6:15-16). God had named the Jewish nation of people as his chosen people in the past, but as Paul said to the churches at Ephesus, now "Jews and Gentiles are joined together in his church. This was his plan from all eternity, and it has now been carried out through Christ Jesus our Lord" (Ephesians 3:10-11). Jesus launched his church as a community of hope for all the nations of the world.

2. *The church is God's family.* Paul explained that Gentiles are no longer strangers. He said, "You are citizens along with all of God's holy people. You are members of God's family. We are his house, built on the foundation of the apostles and the prophets. And the cornerstone is Jesus Christ himself" (Ephesians 2:19-20). As Christians we are adopted into God's family, his church. We become his children—sons and daughters of God (see Romans 8:14-17).

3. *The church is the body of Christ.* "The church is his body; it is filled by Christ, who fills everything everywhere with his presence" (Ephesians 2:23). "Just as our bodies have many parts and each part has a special function, so it is with Christ's body...And since we are all one body in Christ, we belong to each other, and each of us needs all the others" (Romans 12:4-5).

4. *The church is a holy temple where God lives.* "We who believe," Paul stated, "are carefully joined together, becoming a holy temple for the Lord. Through him you Gentiles are also joined together as part of this dwelling where God lives by his Spirit" (Ephesians 2:21-22). "Don't you realize that all of you together are the temple of God and that the Spirit of God lives in you?" (1 Corinthians 3:16).

5. *The church is Christ's pure bride.* Paul tells husbands to love their wives as Christ loves the church. "He gave up his life for her to make her holy and clean...He did this to present her to himself as a glorious church without a spot or wrinkle or any other blemish" (Ephesians 5:25-27).

6. *The church is Christ's agent to fulfill his mission to redeem the lost.* The apostle Peter said, "You are a kingdom of priests, God's holy nation, his very own possession. This is so you can show others the goodness of God" (1 Peter 2:9). Paul told the church in Corinth and the Christians throughout Greece that "God has given us the task of reconciling people to him...We are Christ's ambassadors, and God is using us to speak to you" (2 Corinthians 5:18,20).

Therefore:

> We believe the truth that the church is Christ's visible representation on earth, in which each transformed follower of Jesus is made part of his living body to individually and collectively fulfill God's redemptive purpose.

When you become a transformed follower of Jesus you do not receive a personal, private relationship between just "Jesus and you." Each of us is made part of a community of Jesus-followers—the family, Christ's body, a holy temple where the Spirit of God lives, the bride of Christ, and the agency through which Christ is reaching out to the lost world. We the church "have the same Spirit, and we have all been called to the same glorious future. There is only one Lord, one faith, one baptism, and there is only one God and Father, who is over us all and in us all and living through us all" (Ephesians 4:4-6). We are a part of his church, and that church is still alive and well in the twenty-first century.

CHAPTER FORTY-FIVE

EVIDENCE THAT GOD'S AUTHENTIC CHURCH IS ALIVE AND WELL

The church on the corner of Pershing and Maple is a white New England–style structure with a towering steeple. The church off State Road and Portage Trail is dome-shaped and seats over 5000. The church with an exit sign off the freeway glistens in the sunlight and seems to be made of crystal. There is definitely no shortage of churches in North America. In fact, there are hundreds of thousands of church buildings in the world attended by millions of people every week. So it's not difficult to believe that churches exist. Yet visible buildings with people attending services don't necessarily constitute Christ's true church.

The real church is where God lives and moves and accomplishes his purpose.

The church is a community of believers where Christ, the head, is "over us all and in us all and living through us all" (Ephesians 4:6). Jesus said, "I tell you that if two of you on earth agree about anything you ask for, it will be done for you by my Father in heaven. For where two or three come together in my name, there am I with them" (Matthew 18:19-20 NIV). The real church is where God lives and moves and accomplishes his purpose. But is the church that was birthed at Pentecost really alive today? Is there evidence that Christ is at work through his church in the twenty-first century? And if it does exist, what does it look like?

During the Passover supper Jesus told his disciples that he was going to leave them to be with his Father. Then he said, "I am giving you a new commandment: Love each other. Just as I have loved you, you should love each other. Your love for one another will prove to the world that you are my disciples [my church]" (John 13:34-35). This is what Jesus said would characterize the church—his love living in and through his followers. He said this love-filled community would be "the salt of the earth" and "the light of the world" so that the church's "good deeds [would] shine out for all to see, so that everyone will praise [their] heavenly Father" (Matthew 5:13-16).

The authentic church is this loving community that acts as "salt and light" and impacts the culture around it. That is what the early church was all about. Some, however, have pointed out that the twenty-first-century church has largely lost its mission, and that many churches are only a slight reflection of the invisible God. The late author and Christian historian Dr. Robert Webber passed along this startling quote:

- The church started as a missionary movement in Jerusalem.
- It moved to Rome and became an institution.
- It traveled to Europe and became a culture.
- It crossed the Atlantic to America and became a big business.[1]

While there may be some truth to that quote, Christ's true church is still alive and well today. It's true that "church" organizations and institutions disappoint, and many may have lost their way as God's visible expression of himself. But if you look, you can find the church active and involved in the world. Bob Roberts Jr., pastor of a megachurch and author of the book *Transformation,* said he had to travel halfway around the world to see firsthand what the church looked like. He relates this story:

> I didn't even realize how lost I was until I saw what the church was really supposed to look like. At first, I didn't even recognize it; then I wanted to rationalize it. I had to go halfway around the world to find it—in the persecuted underground house church in Asia. I had heard the stories and statistics, but I had never met anyone face to face. They were nothing like me. They were nothing like any believers I had ever met. Not just culturally, but spiritually they blew me away. Sure, their theology is fuzzy. Some don't even have whole parts of the Bible, only perhaps an entire book or a few passages. But they know God at a depth I never had nor knew anyone else who had.
>
> Worship takes on a completely new expression on the other side of the world. No sound systems, no calculated transitions, just sweaty believers crammed together into small rooms, weeping as the Holy Spirit oozes out among them, as I never before experienced. I don't know if they are charismatic or not (all I knew was it wasn't my tongue), but it doesn't matter. No

one is getting rich, and no one is fighting for control or position. If there is a favored position, it is the privilege of being the first to die. Living on the edge as they do leaves little room for insincerity or self-promotion. These people are living what I grew up hearing the church should be.

Through small, indigenous, underground house church networks, these churches are transforming lives and their cultures. They cannot be stopped. There are too many of them, and they are spreading everywhere, every day. Here's a shocker: Laypeople start these movements, not just those "called" to full-time vocational ministry. Their church planting is the result of transformed lives and not the result of a grand strategy, even though the strategy is grand.[2]

The Active Expression of the Church

Jesus' church exists today as it did in the first century. The process of its expansion is the same. Lives are transformed by Christ's saving power, those lives form a community of hope, love, and care, and they by nature become Jesus' ambassadors to proclaim his kingdom message of love and redemption to the world around them.

Much has been said and written on the purpose and role of the church.* While the following list is not exhaustive, it provides an outline of the active expression of the church as described by Scripture.

The church embodies what a community of redeemed people looks like. Jesus said we are to love one another as he loved us, for loving in this way would "prove to the world that you are my disciples" (John 13:35). The early church "met together constantly and shared everything they had" (Acts 2:44). As Christ's body today, his followers need one another, serve one another, and live in harmony together. "If one part suffers, all the parts suffer with it, and if one part is honored, all the parts are glad" (1 Corinthians 12:26). That's what love does.

When the world looks at Jesus' church they see a holy people (2 Peter 3:14), they see a people in unity (1 Corinthians 12:25), they see a people depending on one another (Romans 12:5), and they see a people caring for one another (Romans 12:15).

The church is a reflection of the triune Godhead, who is the ultimate model of infinite love in perfect relationship. The church puts flesh and actions on God. The church is the visible representation of the invisible God.

The church is a compassionate and healing presence to those in need. The church members in the book of Acts literally "sold their possessions and shared the proceeds with those in need" (Acts 2:45). James the apostle said, "Pure and lasting religion in

---

* Robert Webber, for one, has done an extensive study of the early church, how they fulfilled God's mission and how we can do the same today. Dr. Webber's book entitled *Journey to Jesus* is a valuable resource in understanding what the authentic church looks like and how Christ intends it to express itself.

the sight of God our Father means that we must care for orphans and widows in their troubles, and refuse to let the world corrupt us" (James 1:27).

The church is compassionate, like its head, Jesus, and it is there to feed the hungry, clothe the naked, care for the sick, and bring healing to those who are suffering (see Matthew 25:31-46).

Steve Baughan of Branson, Missouri, is director of a ministry specifically reaching out to addicts and the homeless. He is sometimes criticized by Christians because he doesn't necessarily preach the gospel to those in desperate need before he feeds them, clothes them, and helps get a roof over their head. Listen to Steve's response:

> Proclaiming a Christian message isn't only about quoting Scripture passages to people or walking someone through a gospel booklet. Some people have issues so intense that quoting a few selected Bible passages just doesn't cut it. I've asked, "When your house is in flames, who do you want in your driveway? A religious person quoting Scripture or a fireman using his water hose?"
>
> Deeply hurting people simply can't hear your words over the roar of their lives going up in flames. What they need is a hose that gushes forth hope, love, and compassion in action. That might look like a hot meal, a place to sleep, and a commitment to hang in there with them, preferably from someone who has walked in their shoes.
>
> I've heard people say to addicts, "Drugs or alcohol is your problem." Reality is, drugs or alcohol is their "solution." Their problem is that they are alone or hurting or disconnected without a sense of meaning or purpose. Drugs or alcohol is an attempt to drown out the hurt or whatever their deep-seated problem is. As Thomas Aquinas wrote: "There is within every soul a thirst for happiness and meaning." An addict seeks to satisfy that thirst for happiness and meaning in a bottle, a pill, or a needle.
>
> The message of Jesus that we offer says that your solution can begin in a relationship with me—I'm your friend. I am here to remove your aloneness, I'll comfort you, help carry your burden. I'll connect with you as a person of value—I'll feed you, care for you, and take you in as family. That's what Jesus did with the Samaritan woman, the tax collector, the woman caught in adultery. And that is what he does with each of us. When we are Jesus to those who are hungry for wholeness, they will taste the salt of transformation in action—they will see the attractive light of our message. The gospel message isn't just about words of truth; it's about living that truth out in specific acts of love and compassion toward others.[3]

John the apostle said, "Let us stop just saying we love each other; let us really show it by our actions. It is by our actions that we know we are living in the truth" (1 John 3:18-19).

The church is God's reconciling agent and ambassador to spread the gospel—the kingdom message. Jesus said, "You will receive power when the Holy Spirit comes on you; and you will be my witnesses in Jerusalem, and in all Judea and Samaria, and to the ends of the earth" (Acts 1:8 NIV). The church is God's means to reconcile a lost world to him (see 2 Corinthians 5:16-21). The heartbeat of the church is that of the relational heart of God, who wants to redeem and restore those who are alone and separated from him. Evangelism isn't about church growth numbers or building an organization, it's about leading people into relationship with God.

The church is an equipping agent to make disciples who make disciples. Before Jesus ascended into heaven he gave his followers what has been referred to as the Great Commission: "Go and make disciples of all the nations" (Matthew 28:19). But that command didn't say, "Go out and start churches." Bob Roberts Jr. points out the misconception of the goal of starting churches in his book *The Multiplying Church:*

> I have a vision and a dream. Let's start a thousand churches over the next ten years, each one running a minimum of two thousand members, and in just ten years we will turn America upside-down with the gospel! That would work, right? Wrong—that scenario just happened over the past ten years, and there are fewer people in church today than ever before. How can that be? How could we have spent billions to start two thousand mega-churches and yet have fewer people in church and a society that largely feels the church is antagonistic?
>
> The answer is, in part, that it's not enough just to start churches for the sake of evangelism that will end when "conversion" takes place. Books on starting churches generally operate on the premise that we need to start churches because it is the best evangelistic method that exists. That is a true statement—but an insufficient reason for starting churches. Any research regarding the state of church growth and Christianity in America says it is in decline.[4]

Starting and building up church attendance isn't the "Great Commission" goal. Jesus said "make disciples" and the process would birth churches naturally.

The apostle Paul said that the church leadership's "responsibility is to equip God's people to do his [Christ's] work and build up the church, the body of Christ, until… we will be mature and full grown in the Lord, measuring up to the full stature of Christ" (Ephesians 4:12-13). Making disciples is a process of reproduction. As Christ's disciples are formed and equipped spiritually, they begin exercising their spiritual gifts and reproduction happens: New converts are born.

Paul told Timothy how this spiritual reproduction works when he said, "The things you have heard me say…entrust to reliable men who will also be qualified to teach others" (2 Timothy 2:2 NIV). This is not unlike our physical reproduction process. The loving and intimate relationship of a married couple results in the conception and birth of a newborn child. Through the physical and emotional nurturing and formation process, that child matures to adulthood, marries, and produces offspring as well. And the process continues generation after generation.

The early church grew naturally through a spiritual-formation process of discipleship that reproduced new believers generation after generation. This was not an addition strategy of professional preachers drawing new attendees to a building; it was a multiplication process of laypeople who, as disciples, reproduced other disciples that reproduced other disciples, and so on, and so on.

As Robert Webber says,

> Discipleship is not a vocation prescribed only for ministers and other full-time staff members in the church. Discipleship is the full-time spiritual vocation of *all* God's people. Time in discipleship is time to impress upon the new convert that he or she has a calling in Jesus Christ—the calling to be a disciple all the time in every place of life…[And] if the new convert is to grow, he or she needs a womb-like experience for a period of initial gestation.[5]

This womb-like atmosphere of mentoring and discipling is a spiritual-formation process that includes training new disciples to reproduce themselves spiritually. The church is responsible for equipping believers until they are formed spiritually to maturity (see Ephesians 4:11-16). For centuries the church has accomplished this as mature believers have journeyed together with new believers to know and be and live…

- a life of faith
- a life of worship
- a life of prayer
- a life of being conformed to the image of Christ in all relationships
- a life that continually resists the sin nature (also referred to as spiritual warfare)
- a life of making godly choices
- a life of spiritual reproduction

This spiritual-formation discipleship process was how the early church functioned, and it grew naturally and rapidly. It is the church's model for making disciples today.

It is a highly relational journey that older, more mature Christians model before their families and community as they mentor a new generation of Christ-followers. It is actually a two-way street. An older generation becomes models of godliness that invest their lives into a new generation. And a new generation is trained to seek the value of receiving from an older generation. The older, more mature believers give of their experience to the younger believers, and the younger believers seek after the wisdom of the mentors. Together the church equips people to become disciples who make disciples.

When you see a group of transformed followers of Jesus who 1) embody what the redeemed community of believers look like; 2) are meeting the needs of the hurting around them; 3) are reconciling the lost to God; and 4) are equipping its saints to reproduce themselves spiritually, you are seeing Jesus' church alive and well. These believers may not be expressing all these things perfectly, but when you see these characteristics you are seeing an expression of Christ living through his people. The church is the new people of God, Christ's body, God's family—a place where God lives in his people, who are Christ's bride and his agent to fulfill his mission. That is Christ's church, and it is very much alive and visible all across the globe.

Using principles of Scripture, we have described in the last two chapters the kind of church that people in your community will respond to, the kind of church that will change people's lives. People respond to the church's missional focus and are attracted to its authentic models of love. Look around and you will find a group of people in your area that are truly Jesus' church. You may even be part of such a gathering. Jesus' church is alive and is fulfilling its purpose—that Christians demonstrate love for one another and reach out to others, bringing hope, love, healing, and salvation to a lost and needy world.

CHAPTER FORTY-SIX

THE PRIORITY
OF THE CHURCH

G rowing up, church did not mean much to me (Josh) largely because what it offered didn't relate to my life. At least I didn't think it did. I was popular, so I felt accepted. I was good at sports, so I got lots of praise. I had lots of friends, so I felt appreciated. And since I wasn't religious I didn't figure I needed church in my life.

But in reality I was a lonely person. Oh, I would make you think everyone was my best friend and I didn't have a care in the world. And while my many friends could be spread a mile wide, the friendships were really only an inch deep. On the inside I felt alone. What I didn't realize was that Jesus and his body, the church, was there to lead me to God and remove my human and spiritual aloneness.

Feeling alone isn't really an indication of sin in our lives or a mark that we are relationally inept. Aloneness is the God-given warning signal that tells us we need to experience a relationship with him and relationships with others, including his church. It is as if God placed within each of us a homing device that seeks out relationships when we begin to feel alone. And while sin does hinder us from developing the kind of relationship that removes our aloneness, sin is not the *cause* of our aloneness.

Because of original sin we are all born lost, alienated from God. And God, of course, is the solution to our sin-induced lostness. Through Christ, we can again have that originally intended relationship with God that we lost to sin. This is why some believe that "God is all they need" to remove their aloneness. But this is not the case. Remember, Adam lived in a perfect world without sin when God declared, "It is not good for the man to be alone" (Genesis 2:18). Obviously, God was there with perfect love for his human creation. Yet he knew that Adam needed relational connections with his own kind. Therefore, God created another person to join the cycle of love relationship between Father, Son, Holy Spirit, and Adam. God could have said he was all that Adam needed, but he didn't. He created a woman to help remove Adam's aloneness.

As we can see, God's intent was to prevent human aloneness by means of relationship both with himself and with a human family. He has gone on to design another means as well. He has given his devoted people, the church, the privilege and responsibility of entering into deep relationships with each other to further remove human aloneness. Therefore, with God's three provisions for relationship—family, the church, and himself, we don't have to feel alone.

Yet some people resist the idea that we have a need for anyone but God. The idea of needing others is a little humiliating to them. God is all-powerful and the source of all there is in heaven and earth, so how could anyone possibly think he or she needs anything else? To support their position, they point to the apostle Paul, who supposedly declared that all his sufficiency was in Christ alone when he said, "I can do everything through him who gives me strength" (Philippians 4:13 NIV). This passage, they say, implies that we are spiritually weak if we need anything other than God.

But that is not what Paul is saying. Notice what he says immediately after verse 13. "Yet it was good of you to share in my troubles…you sent me aid again and again when I was in need" (Philippians 4:14,16 NIV). Paul's message was "I do everything through Christ and he is pleased to involve you in that process." We clearly need God, and God makes it clear we need one another.

Together for a Grand Purpose

Scripture says that "we are all parts of his one body, and each of us has different work to do. And since we are all one body in Christ, we belong to each other, and each of us needs all the others" (Romans 12:5). God designed us to need one another when he created us in his image as relational beings. So he placed within each of us relational needs that cry out to be met in him and in one another. When these needs are met we feel joy and a sense of completeness. When they are not met we feel alone.

But there is much more to our need for God and one another than just getting our relational needs met. There is a lost world out there, and it's our task to preach and live the gospel and point it to God. The means by which God has chosen to draw people to him is this same "homing device" that reaches out to remove aloneness—relationships.

When Jesus' church is joined in unity and love for one another, Christ is lifted up and people are relationally attracted to him. Jesus said, "Your love for one another will prove to the world that you are my disciples" (John 13:35). He went on to pray for that loving oneness of his body. "My prayer for all of them," Jesus said, "is that they will be one, just as you and I are one, Father…I in them and you in me, all being perfected into one. Then the world will know that you sent me and will understand that you love them as much as you love me" (John 17:21,23).

The church becomes the true "salt of the earth" and "the light of the world" when believers are loving each other as Christ has loved each of them. The church's greatest platform for proclaiming the truth of Jesus Christ is living a life of love among one another and a life of integrity before the world. Paul said, "We try to live in such a way that no one will be hindered from finding the Lord by the way we act, and so no one can find fault with our ministry" (2 Corinthians 6:3).

In sin, alienated from God, people feel alone. The church is Christ's powerful presence on earth, calling out with open arms, "Come to me, all of you who are weary and carry heavy burdens, and I will give you rest" (Matthew 11:28). The church is the visible reflection of the invisible Christ. And when his body lives in relational unity with God and one another, God accomplishes his grand purpose of redeeming the lost.

The Priority: Meeting Spiritual Needs or Human Needs?

While Scripture makes it clear that in relationship with God and one another we meet each other's needs, just what is it that we are in need of? If relationships remove our aloneness, what needs are met to accomplish that? Our needs can be placed largely in two broad categories: human needs and spiritual needs. Human needs include such things as our emotional needs, physical needs, mental/educational and economic needs, and so on. Spiritual needs include such things as the need to be redeemed and justified by grace through faith in Jesus, the need for the Holy Spirit, the need to be consistently renewed through prayer, God's Word, and so on.

Which of these two needs—human needs or spiritual needs—do you think is the most important? Before you jump to what you may think is the obvious conclusion, consider the following story adapted from former pastor and church specialist David Ferguson's book entitled *The Never Alone Church*.

Your pastor is barely two minutes into his sermon when the side door near the front of the auditorium bursts open. Every head swivels to see two men enter, one a bedraggled "street person," and the other a thin, hollow-eyed man staggering and unsteady on his feet. Following the men enters a poorly dressed young woman with two small children. All of them walk to the front row and sit down. The street person's matted hair and beard seem to hide his face like a mask. The other man can hardly sit up straight, and the young woman has trouble getting her children to quiet down and remain seated.

The eyes of the congregation flit nervously between your pastor and these surprise visitors. The air is thick with unasked questions: Who are these people and what do they want? How did they get past the ushers in the foyer? Are they drunk or stoned on drugs? Are they going to make a disturbance in the service? Has someone thought to call the police? Yet everyone sits motionless.

Your pastor steps off the platform and walks up to the street person and says, "What's your story?" The man stands, turns toward the congregation and says, "I've been out of work for two years. I'm homeless, and I beg or steal whatever I can to keep alive."

The pastor looks at the next man and says, "And what's your story?" The sickly man makes it to his feet with some difficulty and states in a raspy voice: "I'm heavily medicated right now. I'm in the latter stages of AIDS. As a homosexual I've had multiple partners, and it's finally caught up to me."

Finally, your pastor turns to the young lady and poses the same question: "So what's your story?" The woman stands, turns toward the congregation, and says, "I'm an unmarried mother who's out of work and depending on the welfare system to make it. I don't know exactly who is the father to my children. It could be any number of men."

As the young woman sits down, your pastor looks at you and all those seated in the auditorium and asks: "What are the real needs represented in these stories and how are we to meet them?"[1]

How would you answer this question? How would your church answer it? Some people would say, "They need God first and foremost. They have a spiritual need to confess their sins. The lady needs to quit milking the welfare system, and they all need to straighten up their lives." Yet another group of people might say, "Before anything else, we need to offer these people hope. They all need unconditional acceptance, comfort, and immediate support. One needs shelter and food, two of them need an advocate to help them get back on their feet, and one needs care and comfort in his final days of life. They have human needs and we need to meet them." So the real question here is this: Should the church love these people by primarily focusing first on their spiritual needs, or should they first focus on their human needs?

Is It a Question of Priority?

This question probably wouldn't even be asked if something hadn't happened shortly after the turn of the twentieth century. For decades the church had been at the forefront of social reforms and movements to address the human needs of people without neglecting their spiritual needs. However, some leaders who began rejecting certain foundational doctrines of the church also began interpreting Christianity solely in terms of a social gospel, neglecting or ignoring the spiritual dimension. Conservatives saw this involvement in social action to the neglect of spiritual concern as a substitution for truth.

As so often happens, a reaction to one extreme tends to breed an opposite error.

After 1925, large numbers of conservative churches largely withdrew from social issues in an effort to reject liberal theology and take a stand for truth. "This shift has been called 'The Great Reversal.'"[2] The aftereffects of this shift still linger, as even today many conservative churches see a clear separation between meeting human needs and spiritual needs and have opted to focus primarily on the spiritual side. It's clear that if the church addressed only human needs and never focused on spiritual needs, there would be an imbalance. But the Great Reversal has lead to an imbalance in the opposite direction.

So what is the biblical priority? Should the church focus only on the spiritual needs of people and neglect human needs? Or does the church make spiritual needs the first priority and *then* address human needs? Or does it meet human needs first and hope the person somehow gets his spiritual needs met? Or does it meet human needs as a method of reaching a person spiritually?

Jesus Answers the Question

Christ, the head of the church, gives us the answer. The truth is, Jesus didn't make a clear distinction between human needs and spiritual needs. Jesus told his disciples: "'You must love the Lord your God with all your heart, all your soul, and all your mind.' This is the first and greatest commandment. A second is equally important: 'Love your neighbor as yourself.' All the other commandments and all the demands of the prophets are based on these two commandments" (Matthew 22:37-40). Jesus was saying we are to love God with all that we are—spiritually, emotionally, mentally, physically, economically, and so on. And we are to love others for all that they are—spiritually, emotionally, mentally, physically, economically, and so on. He didn't put human needs ahead of spiritual needs or spiritual needs ahead of human needs.

He did say, however, to love and worship him above all else, and he would in turn supply all our needs, both human and spiritual (see Matthew 6:19-34 and Philippians 4:18-20). But Jesus didn't separate out human and spiritual needs and say, "I'll meet this one first, this one second, this one third..." and so on. Jesus actually met people at the point of their need of the moment, whether it was a spiritual or human need.

> *Jesus actually met people at the point of their need of the moment, whether it was a spiritual or human need.*

Jesus didn't say to the blind man, "If you don't believe in me as your savior, then I'm not going to heal you." Nor did he say to the lame man, "I'll make you a deal: I'll repair your legs to wholeness if you have a relationship with me." Jesus was moved with compassion for the human and spiritual needs of these people and set out to meet them both.

Scripture describes an encounter between Jesus and a man named Zacchaeus. Although this man was Jewish, he was an agent of the hated Roman government. He was a tax collector. The Jewish people resented paying Roman taxes and resented even more those Jews that did the bidding of the Romans. Often these tax collectors extorted money from the people to pad their own pockets. So Zacchaeus no doubt felt rejected and criticized by his neighbors and perhaps was even fearful of reprisal. He certainly felt alone. So as a sinner he had a spiritual need to be forgiven. And being rejected by his fellow Jews, he had a human need to feel accepted.

So what did Jesus say to this rejected, cheating sinner? Zacchaeus was perched in a tree to get a better view of this Jesus of Nazareth as he walked by. When Jesus looked up at him the first thing he said was: "Quick, come down! For I must be a guest in your home today" (Luke 19:5).

Jesus couldn't have said anything more definitive to demonstrate his unconditional acceptance of this rejected tax collector than to say he was going to his home to eat with him. Eating with someone at his home in that day was the ultimate in communicating acceptance. Scripture says that "Zacchaeus quickly climbed down and took Jesus to his house in great excitement and joy. But the crowds were displeased. 'He has gone to be the guest of a notorious sinner,' they grumbled" (Luke 19:6-7).

By eating with this sinner, Jesus didn't compromise the truth. He still held that cheating and stealing are wrong. But the Master obviously didn't think Zacchaeus needed a sermon on the evils of being a cheating tax collector at his first encounter. What Jesus did was to meet Zacchaeus at the point of his need for acceptance, and the tax collector responded to him in repentance by saying: "I will give half my wealth to the poor, Lord, and if I have overcharged people on their taxes, I will give them back four times as much" (Luke 19:8). Jesus' relational approach addressed both Zacchaeus' human need and his spiritual need. That is a clear characteristic of Jesus—his love always meets people at the point of their need, both human and spiritual.

This is another way of saying that Jesus' Great Commandment to love God and to love our neighbors is inseparably linked to his Great Commission to "make disciples of all the nations" (Matthew 28:19). Disciples are to be born out of our love for God and our neighbors—by meeting people at the point of both their human and spiritual needs. In other words, our human and spiritual needs are met by a love that says, "I care about all of you, and my love will take action to meet you at the point of your physical, emotional, spiritual, economic, and all other needs." It is a love that loves the whole person. The apostle John was talking about that kind of love when he said, "Let us stop just saying we love each other; let us really show it by our actions. It is by our actions that we know we are living in the truth" (1 John 3:18-19).

CHAPTER FORTY-SEVEN

HOW THE CHURCH MEETS HUMAN AND SPIRITUAL NEEDS

Do you have need for acceptance? Do you long for approval? Are you looking for praise? If you have a pulse you have these needs. Even your dog, if you have one, has these needs. But do our desires for acceptance, approval, praise, and so on represent human needs or spiritual needs?

The fact is, they represent both. When Jesus met Zacchaeus at the point of his need for acceptance, he actually met both a human and a spiritual need. As the Master Rabbi, his unconditional acceptance produced "great excitement and joy" in Zacchaeus. He felt valued by a fellow Jew. Perhaps for the first time since taking on his job with the Roman government, he felt he was worth something as a human being. But Zacchaeus needed more than just simple acceptance by one of his own. He needed his guilt over cheating removed. And as the Son of God, Jesus had the power to remove his guilt. Jesus' unconditional acceptance did elicit repentance from Zacchaeus, and Jesus met his spiritual need for forgiveness.

Both our human and spiritual needs can actually be categorized under the single umbrella of relational needs. We have a relational need to feel accepted by God, which is a spiritual need, as well as to be accepted by others, which is a human need. We have a relational need to feel the approval of God, a spiritual need, and to feel the approval of others, a human need. We also have a relational longing for a sense of security, for praise, for attention, and so on. And each of these needs has both a spiritual and human dimension. So when we begin to meet people at the point of their relational needs, God is pleased to actually involve us in addressing both their human and spiritual needs without necessarily assigning those needs a priority.

And the exciting thing is, God has brought his church together to meet all our relational needs, both spiritual and human. Listen to Paul as he describes the church:

> God has put the body together in such a way that extra honor and care are given to those parts that have less dignity. This makes for harmony among the members, so that all the members care for each other equally. If one part suffers, all the parts suffer with it, and if one part is honored, all the parts are glad (1 Corinthians 12:24-26).

This verse makes it clear that members of the church are to care for one another lovingly, comforting each other in suffering and rejoicing with each other in good fortune. This makes us feel cared for. It also creates unity among God's people both spiritually and on the human level.

It is through the love of the whole person that God is pleased to make the church truly relevant in the lives of others.

Paul also said, "We who believe are carefully joined together, becoming a holy temple for the Lord" (Ephesians 2:21). This is a unity that goes beyond avoiding dissention and division. It is a unity that harmoniously fits your spiritual gift together with a different but complementary spiritual gift of a fellow believer. And this is done in such a way that your strengths are maximized and your weaknesses are made irrelevant. So by locking arms with those who are strong where you are weak, your weakness becomes strong. This meets your need for respect, support, and approval, and you gain a sense of completeness and competence you would never experience alone.

When members of Christ's body are fitted together in this fashion, God accomplishes great things through them. As the spiritual gift of exhortation is combined with the spiritual gift of teaching, then in turn combined with the gift of hospitality, and then with the gift of administration with the gift of evangelism, and so on, we all experience the power of God at work in a mighty way. And when each of us acts upon our need for one another, it keeps a person from stepping out front and declaring, "I'm really the important one here" or "I'm the one who's really making everything happen." Accepting that each of us is made complete within Christ's body keeps us from focusing on ourselves so we can focus on the one who is really deserving—Christ.

Loving the Whole Person

We have already identified a number of relational needs that represent both spiritual and human needs, such as acceptance, comfort, support, respect, and approval. There are many such needs identified in Scripture. David Ferguson has identified over 50 relational needs in Scripture. We will touch on ten that he covers extensively in his book *The Never Alone Church*. The better we understand these relational needs, the better we can understand how God wants to love others through us to meet the human and spiritual needs of those around us. It is through this love of the whole person that God is pleased to make the church truly relevant in the lives of others. It is "your love for one another," Jesus said, that "will prove to the world that you are my disciples [my church]" (John 13:35).

Love Meets the Need for Comfort

Love gives comfort by giving hope; easing a grief or pain; consoling; and hurting with a person.

"He [God] is the source of every mercy and the God who comforts us. He comforts us in all our troubles so that we can comfort others" (2 Corinthians 1:3-4).

Everyone at some point suffers physical, emotional, or spiritual difficulty in life. When medical treatment is given to relieve physical injury or sickness, we can be there in prayer to help the person struggling with illness or pain. We can also be there in person to provide comfort. Paul says to "mourn with those who mourn" (Romans 12:15 NIV) when a person is suffering emotionally or physically. When we do this, something supernatural takes place. "He [God] comforts us in our troubles so that we can comfort others. When others are troubled, we will be able to give them the same comfort God has given us" (2 Corinthians 1:4). When we do this, the person in pain is getting more comfort than just that which we are giving; God is ministering through us to comfort him or her as well. We, his church, are his channel of comfort and healing to those who are hurting. At that point a person is receiving the spiritual blessing of comfort from God as well as the human comfort you are giving.

As we said in a previous chapter, comforting others isn't about trying to "fix" them, discipline them, or give them a pep talk. A love that comforts is realized simply by a person being there to share in another's suffering and letting him or her know you hurt with him or her. It could be physical pain, emotional hurt, or spiritual trouble. A love that comforts allows another person to sense not only your comforting words and touch, but also that of God himself. As Paul said, "We are Christ's ambassadors, and God is using us to speak to you" (2 Corinthians 5:20).

Love Meets the Need for Attention (Care)

Love shows care or attention by taking thought of another,
conveying interest and concern, entering another's world.

"All the members [of the church] care for each
other equally" (1 Corinthians 12:25).

God showed us this kind of love when he entered our world and took on a human form to meet our human and spiritual needs. He demonstrated he cared enough to leave heaven and sacrifice himself for us. Our Christlike love of others is able to meet them at the point of their need for attention as we sacrifice our time and energy to be with them. This kind of caring for a person's human needs often readies their heart to receive Christ's spiritual message.

Love Meets the Need for Acceptance

Love offers acceptance without conditions by
loving others for who they are.

"Accept each other just as Christ has accepted you;
then God will be glorified" (Romans 15:7).

Jesus' loving acceptance of us is able to distinguish who we are from what we've done. He was able to separate Zacchaeus as the cheating tax collector from a man in need of love and acceptance. Jesus' love did two things for Zacchaeus: It accepted the man struggling with rejection, and it led Jesus to die to absolve the guilt of the cheating sinner. It is that kind of unconditional acceptance that allowed Jesus to die for all of us while we were still sinners. When we accept others without conditions, it tells them they are of great worth to us and to God. When we accept others regardless of their physical ailments, deficiencies, or handicaps, they can feel like they belong. And it can open them up to receive God's acceptance.

Love Meets the Need for Appreciation

Love expresses appreciation by praising another and
communicating gratefulness through words and deeds.

"I praise you for remembering me in
everything" (1 Corinthians 11:2 NIV).

God has made each of us with the need to be praised by others. When we express gratitude to a spouse, a child, a fellow believer, a friend, or a stranger, we are demonstrating a love that meets that person at the point of their need for appreciation. When you let people know you are deeply thankful for who they are or what they've done, you remove a little of their sense of aloneness and God is able to minister his love to them through you.

Love Meets the Need for Support

Love provides support by coming alongside another
to lift a load and help carry a problem.

"Carry each other's burdens, and in this way you will
fulfill the law of Christ" (Galatians 6:2 NIV).

People can feel most alone when they are stressed, disappointed, or feel burdened physically, emotionally, or spiritually. God can work powerfully through us as we come alongside such people and help them by lifting their load. We can do things like running an errand for them, mowing their lawn, repairing a broken item, giving financially, praying with them, helping them with homework, or anything that would ease the pressure and lighten their load. When we minister support to the human and spiritual needs of others in the Spirit of Christ, they can see both our love and God's glory. Because "as the Spirit of the Lord works within us, we become more and more like him and reflect his glory even more" (2 Corinthians 3:18).

Love Meets the Need for Encouragement

Love offers encouragement by inspiring with courage
and urging another forward to a positive goal.

"Encourage each other and build each
other up" (1 Thessalonians 5:11).

People get discouraged. They may lose hope through disappointments, rejection, or failures. We are to be there as Christ's loving ambassador to provide hope, lift the spirits of the discouraged, provide inspiration, and urge others toward positive goals. Christ's love flowing through us offers a cheerful word, an inspirational card or song, an uplifting prayer, a light moment…anything that would lift the spirits of the discouraged.

Love Meets the Need for Affection

Love shows affection that communicates care and closeness by
offering endearing words and appropriate physical touch.

"Love each other with genuine affection" (Romans 12:10).

We were created with the relational need to connect with others. And affectionate words and appropriate touching between friends go a long way toward removing our aloneness and letting others know they are cared for. Affection isn't needed just when a person is discouraged or feeling low. It is needed continually to keep a person healthy on both a human and spiritual level. Affection lets people know they are lovable. Paul told the church to "greet one another with a holy kiss" (Romans 16:16 NIV). This is still commonly done in the Middle Eastern world. In the West a handshake or hug is used. Physical affection is one of God's designs to express his love through us to others. "If we love each other, God lives in us, and his love has been brought to full expression through us" (1 John 4:12).

Love Meets the Need for Approval

Love gives approval by expressing satisfaction with a person,
demonstrating that he or she has pleased another.

"If you serve Christ with this attitude, you will please God. And
other people will approve of you, too" (Romans 14:18).

We all need to hear the words, "I'm pleased with you." When we communicate that sentiment to others through words and actions, we meet them at the point of their need for approval. Approval of another should focus more on the person's worth as a person than on his or her accomplishments. That way we place value on the qualities of the person that allow him or her to succeed. When we focus on such qualities as persistence, creativity, determination, diligence, and so on, it places attention on the person rather than on the performance. We all have a human need for approval. We also have a spiritual need for approval. Ultimately we all want to hear people and God say, "Well done, my good and faithful servant" (Matthew 25:21).

Love Meets the Need for Security

Love provides security by eliminating danger and removing
the fear of loss, want, and broken relationship.

"Perfect love expels all fear" (1 John 4:18).

When we rest in God's loving protection and provision, it gives us a sense of security. We meet people at their point of need for security when we help them feel safe and confident they will be cared for in the future.

David Ferguson, in his book *The Never Alone Church*, points out:

> Loved ones may feel *satisfied* when their needs are *currently* being met. But they feel *secure* when they have confidence that their *future* needs will be met. For example, your children are satisfied after you provide a good meal for them. But they are secure when they know your love includes a commitment to meet their future physical needs and to be there for them tomorrow, next week, and next month. Your spouse may be satisfied with

a comfortable home and nice clothes. But he or she will feel secure when your love prompts you to adequately prepare for the future, particularly through a commitment to spiritual growth and marital harmony. A friend may be satisfied when you help her pray through an important decision, but she is secure when she senses your commitment to a deep and lasting friendship.[1]

When we reach out to others with a Christlike love, they can feel safe and secure in our relationship with them. We all have the human need for security, and we have a spiritual need for security. When the apostle John said that "perfect love expels fear," he went on to say, "If we are afraid, it is for fear of judgment, and this shows that his love has not been perfected in us" (1 John 4:18). And his love is perfected in us when we are justified—declared righteous before God because of Jesus' atoning death for us. It is then we can feel absolutely secure in his love.

The apostle Paul couldn't have put it more forcefully than when he said:

> I am convinced that nothing can ever separate us from his love. Death can't, and life can't. The angels can't, and the demons can't. Our fears for today, our worries about tomorrow, and even the powers of hell can't keep God's love away. Whether we are high above the sky or in the deepest ocean, nothing in all creation will ever be able to separate us from the love of God that is revealed in Christ Jesus our Lord (Romans 8:38-39).

Love Meets the Need for Respect

Love shows respect by valuing a person highly and communicating to that person that he or she is of great worth.

"Show respect for everyone" (1 Peter 2:17).

Respecting other people is about honoring who they are and what they bring to the table. Scripture says we are to honor God, our parents, the aged, and governing rulers. Paul also says we are to "take delight in honoring one another" (Romans 12:10). When we respect another person's ideas, perspectives on things, opinions, time, wishes, and schedule we are conveying he or she is valuable to us. When you meet people's need for respect, they feel worth something, and it helps them see they are valuable to you and to God.[2]

We Never Have to Be Alone

Christ has given us his body, the church, so we can be equipped for service and minister his love to others to meet the human and spiritual needs of those around us. As a part of such a church we never have to be alone. Christ is present in our lives through the indwelling presence of God's Holy Spirit, and the members of his body are there to be with us through thick or thin.

God's church is alive and well today to offer hope as a living embodiment of Jesus' love that, among other things, says to you and a needy world:

- There is *comfort* to ease your physical hurts, to provide a shoulder to cry on, and to produce inner healing.

- There is *attention* (care) that communicates you are so important to God that he died to have a relationship with you, and his church is here to help address all your human and spiritual needs.

- There is *acceptance* that says you are loved for who you are, no matter what.

- There is *appreciation* that gives praise to you for who you are and what you've done.

- There is *support* when you need a helping hand or a shoulder to help you carry a heavy load.

- There is *encouragement* when you are struggling with disappointments, failure, or difficulty.

- There is *affection* to help you know that through it all, you are truly loved.

- There is *approval* that says, "I am pleased with you."

- There is *security* in times of danger to remove your fear of the future.

- There is *respect* that honors you for what you think and values you for the contribution you bring.

The church, Christ's body, is alive and well in order to

> equip God's people to do his work and build up the church, the body of Christ, until we come to such unity in our faith and knowledge of God's Son that we will be mature and full grown in the Lord, measuring up to the full stature of Christ. Then we will no longer be like children, forever changing our minds about what we believe because someone has told us something different or because someone has cleverly lied to us and made the lie sound like the truth. Instead, we will hold to the truth in love, becoming more and more in every way like Christ, who is the head of his body, the church (Ephesians 4:12-15).

TRUTH TWELVE

THE RETURN OF CHRIST

CHAPTER FORTY-EIGHT

OUR RESTORED HOME: HEAVEN ON EARTH

The shingles were half blown off the barn. Some of the windows were broken. The siding on one side was almost gone, and what little paint remained on the trim was faded and peeling. The barn door was sagging, indicating the entire foundation of the place was of questionable stability. Weeds of every kind overgrew the ground, which was caked with layers of dead leaves and windblown trash accumulated over the years.

I (Sean) stood there looking at the old place as my dad (Josh) swept his arm toward it and told my sisters and me that this was the 120-acre dairy farm he had called home when he was growing up just outside Union City, Michigan. I looked at the dilapidated barn, the precariously leaning corncrib, and the overgrown fields and tried to imagine what the place must have looked like in the early 1940s.

Dad could remember when his older sister would come home to visit and how he'd help make homemade ice cream on the back porch of the house. He said his mother made the best root beer in all of Michigan, and he had guzzled all the root-beer floats his parents would let him drink. Josh clearly saw more in this acreage than my sisters and I did. We saw a place in ruins; through the enhancing lens of memory he saw it as it once was.

As we walked toward the corncrib, Josh's entire demeanor changed. Pleasant thoughts of homemade ice cream and root beer quickly faded. The reality was, happy childhood memories for my father were few and far between. We were just a few feet from the old leaning shed when he abruptly stopped. As he stared at the weather-beaten structure, tears began to trickle down his face. Within seconds he was over-whelmed with emotion. He seemed paralyzed by the memories of that terrible day of shame and abandonment so many years ago. As if re-running an old movie, he seemed to see that 11-year-old boy, frightened and alone, buried inside up to his neck in corn, hiding from the humiliating scene of a drunken father out of control. It was more than he could bear, and he wept openly. My sisters and I wrapped our arms around our dad and wept with him.

I saw my dad differently that day. This old farm, now in ruins, had been his child-hood home. He had so much wanted it to be a place of peace and safety, joy and hap-piness. But home had been far from that for Josh. And on that day I understood in a deeper way just how painful his childhood had been—a ruined childhood that could never be restored to what it should have been.

Jesus Is Coming Again to Restore What Is in Ruins

Two thousand years ago God saw through human eyes an entire world in ruins. What had once been a paradise of peace and safety, joy and happiness, was now a world of pain and suffering, murder and destruction. The Son of God stood before the city filled with people who were rejecting him and grieved. "O Jerusalem, Jerusalem, the city that kills the prophets and stones God's messengers! How often I have wanted to gather your children together as a hen protects her chicks beneath her wings, but you wouldn't let me. And now look, your house is left to you, empty and desolate. For I tell you this, you will never see me again until you say, 'Bless the one who comes in the name of the Lord!'" (Matthew 23:37-39).

I (Josh) didn't have the means to restore the old McDowell dairy farm into what it once was. And even if I could have repaired the old place, I couldn't bring back my mother and father, run back the clock, and make my childhood home into a happy and loving family; that was all in the unchangeable past.

> *God has promised to renew each of his children to his original design and restore this earth to what it once was.*

But unlike us, God can restore what has been ru-ined, both the physical creation and our broken rela-tionships. As Matthew writes, "Bless the one who comes in the name of the Lord!" (23:39). For Christ will return and take this physical "house" and our earthly home that is now "empty and desolate" and completely restore it.

The apostle Paul tells us that "all creation anticipates the day when it will join God's children in glorious freedom from death and decay. For we know that all creation has been groaning as in pains of childbirth right up to the present time" (Romans 8:21-22). The old McDowell farm along with every other place on earth is going to be restored to a home that will surpass the Garden of Eden.

And what about our painful memories and disappointments in life? Paul goes on to say we all "groan to be released from pain and suffering. We, too, wait anxiously for that day when God will give us our full rights as his children, including the new bodies he has promised us" (Romans 8:23).

God will do more than just restore the earth to its pristine and perfect condition; he will restore us as well. Whether it's pain of the past or suffering in the present, God has promised to renew each of his children to his original design and restore this earth to what it once was.

Jesus Will Return to Restore the Earth

The psalmist David declares, "The earth is the Lord's, and everything in it, the world, and all who live in it" (Psalm 24:1 niv). God made the heavens and the earth and called them "very good," and he hasn't surrendered his title and right to them. They may be in ruins now, but he has definite plans to restore them to a perfect world for us to live in.

Jesus told his disciples that he was going away to prepare a place for them and for all of us. And he gave this promise: "I will come again and receive you to Myself, that where I am, there you may be also" (John 14:3 nasb). After Pentecost, Peter preached this same message to the people of Jerusalem and said that Jesus "must remain in heaven until the time for the final restoration of all things, as God promised long ago through his prophets" (Acts 3:21). And what had the prophets said about God's restoration plans?

> Look! I am creating new heavens and a new earth—so wonderful that no one will even think about the old ones anymore (Isaiah 65:17).

> The time will come when all the earth will be filled, as the waters fill the sea, with an awareness of the glory of the Lord (Habakkuk 2:14).

> "As the new heavens and the new earth that I make will endure before me," declares the Lord, "so will your name and descendants endure" (Isaiah 66:22 niv).

These promises God declared were directed to the children of Israel, but they also include us as beneficiaries. When Peter asked what was in store for the disciples that followed Jesus, he said, "At the renewal of all things, when the Son of Man sits on his glorious throne, you who have followed me will also sit on twelve thrones, judging the twelve tribes of Israel" (Matthew 19:28 NIV). Peter later wrote, "In keeping with his promise we are looking forward to a new heaven and a new earth, the home of righteousness" (2 Peter 3:13 NIV). Jesus also told us that "when the Son of Man comes in his glory," he "will say to those on his right; 'Come, you who are blessed by my Father; take your inheritance, the kingdom prepared for you since the creation of the world'" (Matthew 25:31,34 NIV).

God has not given up on his original plan. He has neither abandoned the idea of a perfect earth, nor has he laid aside his plan for his children to live in a perfect place forever. He has no intention of taking us away to some distant heaven and then destroying this earth he designed to be our home. After his resurrection, Jesus ascended into heaven with a promise to return. He will return and restore this earth to his original design. God's perfect plan is "to bring all things in heaven and on earth together under one head, even Christ" (Ephesians 1:10 NIV).

Notice that in the verse above Paul tells us that the earth, as well as heaven, will be under one head. If we who now live on the earth were to be taken into heaven, what would be left on the earth to be brought together under one head? Heaven is God's home. The earth is our home, not only now, but forever, just as God originally intended. And it is Jesus who will eternally bring us together with God and connect his home with ours. In John's revelation he saw the holy city, the New Jerusalem, coming down from God out of heaven and said, "Look, the home of God is now among his people! He will live with them, and they will be his people. God himself will be with them" (Revelation 21:3).

Theologian Randy Alcorn in his book *Heaven* puts it this way:

> There will be one cosmos, one universe united under one Lord—forever. This is the unstoppable plan of God. This is where history is headed. When God walked with Adam and Eve in the Garden, Earth was Heaven's backyard. The New Earth will even be more than that—it will be Heaven itself. And those who know Jesus will have the privilege of living there.[1]

When God's restoration project is complete we will experience a renewed earth in the perfection of the Garden of Eden. "No longer will anything be cursed" (Revelation 22:3). No more thorns or thistles to prick our bodies. No more difficulty in getting things to grow. No more "survival of the fittest" among the animals. For they will all be at peace with one another. In fact, there will be no discord or fighting or evil anywhere, because "nothing evil will be allowed to enter—no one who practices shameful idolatry and dishonesty—but only those whose names are written in the Lamb's Book of Life" (Revelation 21:27).

Jesus Will Return to Restore Our Bodies

When Christ returns he will fulfill the promise he made through Isaiah the prophet long ago.

> In that day he [God] will remove the cloud of gloom, the shadow of death that hangs over the earth. He will swallow up death forever! The Sovereign LORD will wipe away all tears. He will remove forever all insults and mockery against his land and people (Isaiah 25:7-8).

As his redeemed children, we will live forever on this perfect earth where "there will be no more death or sorrow or crying or pain. For the old world and its evils are gone forever" (Revelation 21:4). Our earthly bodies will be "transformed into heavenly bodies that will never die. When this happens...then at last the Scriptures will come true: 'Death is swallowed up in victory'" (1 Corinthians 15:53-54).

And all this, the restoration of our bodies and a new world, is dependent upon Jesus Christ returning to destroy death and, of course, his archenemy, the devil. Jesus first had to die as an atonement for our sin. And he did. He then had to conquer death through his resurrection to become our High Priest. And he did. And upon his second coming he will destroy death and the evil one to renew and restore all things.

> Only as a human being could he [Jesus] die, and only by dying could he break the power of the Devil, who had the power of death (Hebrews 2:14).

> Christ was raised first; then when Christ comes back, all his people will be raised. After that the end will come, when he will turn the Kingdom over to God the Father, having put down all enemies of every kind. For Christ must reign until he humbles all his enemies beneath his feet. And the last enemy to be destroyed is death (1 Corinthians 15:23-26).

> The Son of God appeared for this purpose, to destroy the works of the devil (1 John 3:8 NASB).

> When he has conquered all things, the Son will present himself to God, so that God, who gave his Son authority over all things, will be utterly supreme over everything everywhere (1 Corinthians 15:28).

Therefore:

> We believe the truth that Jesus will return
> to resurrect our lifeless bodies into
> everlasting bodies, abolish sin, and restore
> the earth to a perfect world where he
> will live with us forever and forever.

Jesus conquered death through his resurrection and will one day return to earth and exercise his power to cast the devil, death, and the grave into the lake of fire, known as the second death (see Revelation 20:10-15). Christ's resurrection is a prerequisite to his return and the entire restoration plan to give us new bodies and a new earth. Christ has promised to return and do this for us. And we can rest in his promise. As the writer of Hebrews said, "It is impossible for God to lie" (Hebrews 6:18).

CHAPTER FORTY-NINE

EVIDENCE FOR
LIFE AFTER DEATH

If you are looking forward to enjoying a perfectly restored earth where you will live forever with a new body, that says something very positive about your faith. Clearly you believe there is life after death. In this book, and no doubt in many other places, you have encountered strong evidence to strengthen your faith. You have seen ample evidence that Jesus conquered death and promised to raise you from the dead. So you can trust confidently in his promise.

But you may not know there is further evidence that you have an eternal soul that will live on after this life. In fact, there are many evidences that underscore the belief that there is life after death. Numerous books have been written on the subject, notably *Life After Death: The Evidence* by Dinesh D'Souza, and *Beyond Death* by J.P. Moreland and Gary Habermas. I (Sean) have an extensive chapter on this topic in my book *Is God Just a Human Invention? And Seventeen Other Questions Raised by the New Atheists*. These and other books provide many evidences for life after death. We will highlight just four in this chapter.

Eternity Planted in the Human Heart

Recently one of my (Sean's) former students relayed to me a conversation she had had on the first day of her college English class. The teacher began the class by reading an article by a science-fiction writer who believes computers and technology will produce superhumans who will take over the world by 2030. This teacher was hoping these superhumans would be environmentalists so that they would want to preserve our lesser-evolved selves. My former student raised her hand and asked, "How can a purely material thing spawn consciousness?" The teacher simply laughed and said, "Oh, I suppose you believe in the soul too?" And the whole class laughed at her.

There are a good number of educators and scientists today who believe that the physical world is the only reality and the human soul and an afterlife simply do not exist. Yet this view has not been the universal conclusion throughout history. In fact, it's the opposite. Virtually every culture from the very dawning of civilization has believed in a life beyond the grave in which some type of soul survives death of the body.

It is amazing, when you stop to think about it, that a universal belief in the afterlife has dominated historical thinking in spite of having little empirical evidence to justify it. Of course, people do have reason to believe some things they have not experienced. They believe there is a Mount Everest even if they haven't climbed its rugged heights. They believe in the Great Barrier Reef off the coast of Australia even though they have never swum the depth of the Coral Sea. It is universally accepted that hundreds of swallows travel like clockwork in a 12,000-mile round-trip from Argentina to San Juan Capistrano each year, even though most people haven't witnessed the event firsthand. In spite of the fact that most people have neither seen nor experienced these events directly, they can be empirically observed and have been for many years—some for centuries. People record physical encounters and experiences such as these in writings, pictures, and TV specials. So it's natural for others to accept them as fact because it's clear that they can be physically proven.

But it is another matter when all cultures in history up to the present affirm their belief in something that seems impossible to record or experience and live to tell about it. Why is the belief that there is life after death affirmed almost unanimously among every culture in history without empirical evidence? It seems clear that the "sense" there is a life after death has been implanted deeply within the heart of humans. Wise King Solomon said that God "has planted eternity in the human heart, but even so, people cannot see the whole scope of God's work from beginning to end" (Ecclesiastes 3:11). Though humans cannot see into the next life, the vast majority believe it's there, and they have believed that since the dawn of time.

Free Will of the Soul

In chapter 8 of my (Sean's) book on the "new atheism," *Is God Just a Human Invention?* I deal with the fact that if we didn't have a soul we would not have the capacity to choose freely. Following is an adaptation from that chapter.

In 1996, American culture critic Tom Wolfe wrote a short essay titled "Sorry, but Your Soul Just Died." He discussed a new imaging technique that enabled neuroscientists to study the brain of a patient during a thought or emotion. He said, "Since consciousness and thought are entirely physical products of your brain and nervous system—and since your brain arrived fully imprinted at birth—what makes you think you have free will? Where is it going to come from?"[1] We agree with this much of the conclusion of Wolfe's argument. If there is no soul, then free will does not exist.

If materialism is true, then a human being is simply a body. If *you* are solely a material system, then you have no inner *self* that has the capacity to choose freely between options. You have no center of consciousness to make reasoned decisions. What seems to you to be a self capable of making choices is then merely a phantom projected by the mechanical processes of your mind, which is controlled solely by material processes reacting to external stimuli. Your physical systems operate completely by external programming, not by inner decision-making. Thus, if materialism is true, you do not have any genuine ability to choose your actions. What would seem to be a choice is actually predetermined by mechanical neural processes operating according to the way nature programmed your brain.

But this seems to contradict how we experience the world. We operate as if our minds freely make decisions that are carried out by the circuitry of our brains. For instance, if a stranger stops to open the door for us, we would likely describe his thought process by saying, "The polite man made up his *mind* to stay a moment longer and hold the door open for us." We would not say, "The circuitry in his brain caused him to turn around and hold the door open." We assume he *freely* chose to open the door, which is why we would likely express our thanks. Expressing thanks for an act of kindness would make no sense if we were both simply mechanical machines acting according to the inescapable programming of our brain circuitry.

The experience of making free choices seems so authentic that people cannot act as though that sense of choosing is counterfeit. Philosopher John Searle reminds us that if a waiter presents us with a choice of either pork or veal, we cannot rightly say, "Look, I'm a determinist. I'll just have to wait and see what order happens!"[2]

Denying free will comes at a high price, for it raises troubling questions: How is love meaningful if not *freely* chosen? How can we hold people morally accountable for their actions if they could not have done otherwise? What's the point of punishment? For that matter, what's the point of reward? Our capacity for free will clearly points to the reality of the human soul.[3]

Near-Death Experiences

Pam Reynolds had little option left. She had an aneurysm on her brain stem that could not be removed through conventional medical procedures. So she chose an experimental procedure called "cardiac standstill." Surgeons put her under general anesthesia to get her brain into a nonresponsive state. Then they lowered her body temperature to 60 degrees, stopped her heart to prevent blood flow to her brain, and put her into a "clinically dead" state.

With blood drained from Pam's brain, surgeons quickly removed the aneurysm and brought her back from the brink of death. *USA Today* featured the story in a June 22, 2009, article titled "The God Choice."[4] The article quoted Pam as saying she consciously left her body and witnessed the entire operation from above the surgeons. She was able to describe intimate details of the operating room procedure, including how many surgeons and attendants were involved. She described the Midas Rex bone saw used to cut open her skull, the drill bits, blade containers, and so on. She was also able to relay specific detailed conversation between the surgeons she overheard. All the details were confirmed from the official hospital records. The doctors had no scientific explanation for Pam's "out of body" experience.

In his book *Life After Death: The Evidence,* Dinesh D'Souza references thousands of documented near-death experiences that reach as far back as the writings of Plato, 300 years before Christ. In recent times, the International Association for Near Death Studies was founded to study the phenomenon and has gathered a wide body of data from around the world. "Near death research," D'Souza points out, "now involves separate tracks of inquiry into the various categories of the near death experience—the out of body phenomenon, the tunnel of darkness, the bright light, the sensation of love and warmth, the life review, and the subsequent life transformation. What emerges from this work is how vivid and real these experiences are to the people who have them."[5]

The power of near-death experiences is not so much in the lurid details related to heaven or hell that someone may report. Rather, it's that people somehow obtain information they simply could not obtain while being medically dead. These experiences demonstrate that consciousness continues after the body ceases to function. This doesn't prove that life continues *forever* after death, but they do show that consciousness is not tied simply to the physical body.

Atheists, who make up most of the critics of near-death experiences, point out that these phenomena are not valid proofs for life after death because the people involved weren't really dead. Technically that may be so, in that the people were not dead for numerous days and then rose from the grave to give their stories. But because someone isn't permanently dead doesn't mean that they can't be temporarily dead. Some of these patients were in fact medically dead, but were able to be revived. The real point of these reports is to gather information about what comes after death. And since we are lacking access to experiences from those who are permanently dead, the next best thing is to get information from those who have been very close to death or temporarily dead.

Yet we agree that while near-death experiences may refute the position held by some who say "nothing exists after death," they still do not provide empirical evidence that the soul is immortal or indicate what the afterlife is really like. Some would contend, like the apostle Thomas after the resurrection, that they will not believe until they see better proof. To such people, scientific evidence is needed to prove the possibility that there is life after death. Well, such proof is now available.

Reality of the Unseen World

The apostle Paul wrote, "We are not fighting against people made of flesh and blood, but against the evil rulers and authorities of the unseen world...and against wicked spirits in the heavenly realms" (Ephesians 6:12). Paul speaks here of a world or a dimension that is real yet unseen to us as humans.

After Jesus died and rose from the grave, he demonstrated his ability to pass from the "seen world" into this "unseen world" at will. Remember when two of Jesus' disciples were walking to the village of Emmaus? Jesus came along and spoke with them, but they didn't recognize him. As they arrived home they invited this "stranger" to spend the evening with them. And as they were preparing to eat, they recognized that the "stranger" was actually Jesus. "And at that moment he disappeared!" (Luke 24:31). Where did he go? He had a real body, yet he vanished into an "unseen world."

When these two disciples related their experiences to the rest of the disciples, Jesus again appeared before them. They were frightened and thought they were seeing a ghost. "'Why are you frightened?' he asked. 'Why do you doubt who I am? Look at my hands. Look at my feet. You can see that it's really me. Touch me and make sure that I am not a ghost, because ghosts don't have bodies, as you see that I do" (Luke 24:38-39).

Jesus had a real body that could move from the physical dimension in which we exist into an unseen physical dimension—the "unseen world" and "the heavenly realms" that Paul referred to. The Scriptures reliably document what the disciples saw and what Jesus did and said after he rose from the dead. That alone enables us to believe with confidence there is life after death as Jesus promised. But for those who are interested, scientific evidence has now been discovered that a physical reality exists outside our human physical dimension.

At the turn of the twentieth century there was a revolution in science represented in the transition from classical to modern physics. There was a radical reformulation of the laws of space, time, and matter. This was accomplished through Einstein's theories of special and general relativity, and the laws of quantum mechanics.

Prior to the new findings in physics, scientists like British philosopher and mathematician Bertrand Russell ridiculed the idea of life after death. He contended that for life to be sustainable after death, matter must be capable of qualities radically different from any matter in our physical world. And that was thought to be impossible—that is, until Einstein and quantum mechanics proved otherwise.

Previously it was assumed that we experienced space in three dimensions and time in one dimension. Einstein brought these dimensions together and postulated that we live in the four-dimensional entity of space-time. And with quantum mechanics, the idea of our four-dimensional world of space and time opened up the idea that the behavior of matter is not completely governed by fixed laws and predictable outcomes we can observe. Instead, scientists began suggesting that we are part of a larger multidimensional world including several dimensions that are hidden from what we experience in this physical world.

Dinesh D'Souza explains this scientific phenomenon in chapter 5 of his book *Life After Death: The Evidence:*

> The idea of multiple dimensions is part of a powerful new approach to physics called string theory...In its most famous form, so-called M theory, scientists tell us that reality is divided not into four but rather eleven dimensions, ten of space and one of time. So where are the other dimensions? Well, string theorists say they are hidden dimensions somehow positioned so that they are invisible and inaccessible to us. While we can't see them, they help to account for the things that we do see. As physicist Lisa Randall puts it, "We are in this three-dimensional flatland...Our world is stuck in this three-dimensional universe, although extra dimensions exist. So we live on a three-dimensional slice of a higher-dimensional world."[6]

How do scientists account for hidden dimensions that are invisible to us? To start with, most physicists accept the notion that the vast majority of matter and energy in the universe is what they call "dark matter" and "dark energy." It is matter and energy we can't see or detect. They arrive at that conclusion because galaxies are held together in clusters, but the gravitational force of ordinary matter simply isn't strong enough to keep them together. So what keeps them from flying apart? They say it's the gravitational force of "dark matter"—matter that we cannot see. Scientists come to the same conclusion about "dark energy." They say this undetected energy force explains the increasing pace of the universe's expansion.

Two thousand years ago the writer of Hebrews said that Christ "sustains the universe by the

The evidences add up to an intelligent, reasonable faith by which we can see with spiritual eyes what Jesus promised we will experience with our new bodies on a new earth for all eternity.

mighty power of his command" (Hebrews 1:3). Today scientists confirm that, beyond our dimension, a greater source of energy exists that actually holds our physical universe together. They are also saying there is far more physical matter existing beyond our dimension than within it. They, of course, are confirming what Jesus and Scripture have been saying all along. Jesus has prepared a real place for us where he now exists, and we will one day experience with him.

What's interesting is that physicists have even calculated the percentage of matter and energy in the unseen world as compared to the seen world:

> The figure is an astounding 95 percent! Ordinary matter and energy make up a mere 5 percent of all the matter and energy in the universe. The vast majority of matter and energy in existence cannot be observed or detected with any instruments.[7]

Jesus told us there was an eternal place beyond time. He promised to bring God's home to us, which is now invisible to us and outside our dimension. He demonstrated following his resurrection that he could pass from our visible dimension to a dimension invisible to us. Now the modern science of relativity, quantum mechanics, dark matter, dark energy, and multiple universes confirms the physical reality of the "unseen world"—a world Scripture has revealed to us all along.

Dinesh D'Souza draws this conclusion:

> Modern physics has expanded our horizons and shown how life after death is possible within an existing framework of physical reality. The materialist objection has proven to be a dud; in fact, modern physics calls materialism itself into question. In a crucial area, and sometimes against the intentions of the scientists themselves, modern science has proven itself not the foe of religious believers, but an unexpected ally.[8]

There is compelling evidence for life after death. The Jesus of history lived and died and rose again, making a way for us to live after death. We all sense a living soul existing within us, just as has every society in the earth's history. Our capacity of free will confirms the existence of an immaterial soul. Near-death experiences reveal that people experience consciousness and sensation outside their physical bodies. And modern physics shows how life beyond this dimension is in fact a physical reality.

These evidences add up to an intelligent, reasonable faith by which we can see with spiritual eyes what Jesus promised we will experience with our new bodies on a new earth for all eternity. Jesus said:

Don't be troubled. You trust God, now trust in me. There are many rooms in my Father's home, and I am going to prepare a place for you. If this were not so, I would tell you plainly. When everything is ready, I will come and get you, so that you will always be with me where I am (John 14:1-3).

CHAPTER FIFTY

Experiencing Eternal Joy

Our new home was great. The smell of fresh paint was still in the air. There wasn't a single stain on the carpet. The apartment was brand-new, and Stephanie and I (Sean) were eager to move in. We did move, and while I enjoyed our new home for its freshness, its beauty, and its newness, I still reached out for the familiar. Certain things just fit who I am and how I function, and even with all the excitement and glamour of a new home, I didn't want those things to change. I wanted my desk placed in a similar position as in our last home. I liked the fact that our old, comfortable living room furniture was in our new place. I liked the newness, but I also loved and appreciated the familiar.

The home God has planned for you for all eternity will be a pristine, glorious new home, yet it will retain the comfortable familiarity you love. God is not creating a strange place for you that will require you to completely readjust your tastes and change who you are. Rather, he is restoring the old—getting rid of the scars, damage, and malfunctions inflicted by the fall. You will enjoy the restored beauty of the earth with its lush forests, majestic mountains, sparkling water, and an animal kingdom with the multitude of species no longer at odds with each other.

There will be no curse upon the New Earth, and the perfection God originally intended will emerge unsullied in all its wonder and glory. While everything will be fresh and new, you will see it as a place of complete familiarity. You will realize that this is where you were meant to be all along—in a place where you fit so perfectly that it's clear it was designed expressly to your innermost tastes. In fact, this will be exactly what God has done (see Isaiah 65; Revelation 21–22).

But more than that, your future home will be a place where you will be with your loved ones, a place where the word *family* takes on a whole new meaning. Our earthly families and friends can be great. We talk together, play together, eat together; we are there for one another. But Uncle Joe can become irritating and Aunt Sarah can talk and talk and talk. We can tire at times of being with family and friends. Yet in our new home these relational imperfections will be removed along with the imperfections of the environment. People will relate to each other exactly as they should have related all along. Indeed, there will be nothing but bliss in every aspect of our lives because we will be entering into the pure joy of God himself.

Jesus gave an illustration of what it will be like to enter into the kingdom of heaven. He said that the Master would pay us the greatest of compliments by saying, "Well done, my good and faithful servants." But there would be even more. He will go on to add, "You were faithful with a few things, I will put you in charge of many things; enter into the joy of your master" (Matthew 25:23 NASB). Our entry into the kingdom of heaven is so much more than just a reward; it is our initiation into a whole new realm of meaning and significance for our lives.

Living in the Joy of God

Jesus told his followers to remain in his love, and then he said, "I have told you this so that my joy may be in you and that your joy may be complete" (John 15:11 NIV). In our new eternal home we will enter into God's joy in a literal sense. What does this entering into God's joy look like? We get a hint of it in our experiences with our own children.

Some time ago Stephanie and I (Sean) took our family to a gigantic water park. It had twisty slides, wave machines, multicolored water caverns—the works. And I have to tell you, the little kid inside me came out. Stephanie and I played with Scottie in the wave pool, and it was a huge thrill to see our little boy having such fun. But Scottie was reluctant to play on all the elaborate enhancements to this "swimming pool." So I tried the twisty slide and the "shoot the rapids" slide first, and explored the multicolored caverns on my own. Stephanie and Scottie watched me from the shallow side of this water world of joy.

Then I came up to Scottie and said, "Son, you've got to try this stuff—it's so much fun. Let me show you what a blast this is." He was still reluctant, but he saw something in my face and heard something in my voice that said, "Come on, do this with me, please." He sensed I was saying, "Enter into the joy of your father." And when he joined me on those slides, he had a blast—or should I say, a splash. As Scottie's loving father, it really did thrill me that he had so much fun.

This is a small sample of what it must mean when God says to us, "Enter into the joy of your Master." He is thrilled that we get to experience so much joy. Our first joy will be to see him face-to-face, which will be a thrill beyond imagining. The apostle John describes his own face-to-face encounter with the God-man in all his glory, saying, "His face was as bright as the sun in all its brilliance. When I saw him, I fell at his feet as dead" (Revelation 1:16-17). Of course, without a new and transformed body we couldn't even look fully into the face of God and live (see Exodus 33:20; 1 Timothy 6:16). But with new glorified bodies we will be able to see God's glorious face. And the first thing we will

> *As when a father receives a prodigal son back home from a life on a pig farm, you will experience the thrilling ecstasy of hearing God say, "Enter into the joy of your Master."*

undoubtedly see is his expression of pure joy. To be in the presence of our God and Savior and to see him face-to-face will, in itself, be the greatest experience we will ever have.

But some readers may wonder why simply gazing into the face of God would be such a magnificent experience. We know we cannot fully explain why this will be such a joy, but it's such an important aspect of our life in God's restored kingdom that we must give it a shot.

No doubt every male reader of this book has seen the face of a beautiful woman that stopped him in his tracks. And every female has seen the face of a man who almost made her swoon. We recognize this awe in the presence of extreme beauty by using the term "stunning" to describe such faces. Now, add to this experience the factor of relationship—of love. Have you ever been in the presence of that special person—say, gazing across the table at him or her during a candlelight dinner—and thought you had never seen anything so glorious? Your breath came deeper and your heart beat faster, just to think you actually had a relationship with such a glorious creature.

Now take these experiences one step further. Think for a moment about the look of a young bride in all her radiant glory, waiting in the foyer of the church for the first chords of the "Wedding March" as she anticipates meeting her lover at the altar. She can hardly wait. Consider the gaze of a bridegroom, standing nervously with his best man as he expectantly looks down the aisle toward that door where she will soon appear. Then imagine his knees weakening with unbearable ecstasy as the music begins and that radiant face appears and approaches, filled with love and joy meant only for him. He is enraptured, transported, lifted into a realm of joy he has never imagined. This beautiful creature loves him so much that she has chosen to spend her entire life devoted to him. It is the experience one never forgets, an experience that shapes one's entire life.

The beauty of the most beautiful woman or the most handsome man in the world is merely a shadow of the beauty of the face of God, who is the source of all beauty. The love in the face of the most devoted bride or groom is merely a shadow of the love of God, who is the source and perfection of all love. To go far beyond the images of beauty and love that so overwhelm us even in this fallen world and behold the face that is the fountain of all beauty and love will simply be the greatest single moment we will ever experience. It's an experience we can presently imagine only by comparison to the weaker manifestations of love and beauty we experience on this sin-damaged earth.

The inexpressible joy you will see on God's face at your arrival home has partly to do with his sense of completion. When God created a perfect world, he "saw that it was good." But of course it was ruined by sin. So after thousands of years of watching his beloved creation endure pain and suffering, he will soon experience the joy of seeing you as one of his redeemed children entering into what he originally designed—a paradise without sin where you will enjoy him and he will enjoy you forever. As when a father receives a prodigal son back home from life on a pig farm, you will experience the thrilling ecstasy of hearing God say, "Enter into the joy of your Master."

Experiencing God's Relational Joy

When God invites you to enter into his joy, he is allowing you to share a relational experience that has previously been beyond your emotional ability to comprehend. Just as I knew Scottie would thrill at the giant waterslide, God knows full well what his infinite love in perfect relationship will mean to you, even though you cannot presently comprehend it. Adam and Eve got a taste of it for but a fleeting moment. After Christ's return God will lead you into a relational glory and goodness with him that mere mortal minds and emotions cannot comprehend. But with a new body and a full eternity at your disposal, you will have all of forever to absorb it.

Just what is this relational joy of God? It is being invited to participate in the Source of love who fills the universe. The Father has eternally loved the Son. The Son has eternally loved the Father. The Holy Spirit has eternally loved the Father and the Son. The Triune Godhead has been in perfect relationship with each other for all eternity. Yet God is inviting us into their perfect circle of relationship. The simplicity and purity of enjoying a growing love relationship with God is at this point incomprehensible to our mortal minds. But let's try to imagine it.

First, a blissful eternal life is all about knowing God. Jesus prayed to his Father and said, "This is the way to have eternal life—to know you, the only true God, and Jesus Christ, the one you sent to earth" (John 17:3). Our firsthand experience of knowing God will grow throughout eternity, and our love of him will expand to contain it. As we come to know God's nature of unconditional acceptance, we will experience a secure love beyond measure. As we learn of his infinite grace, we will capture the strength and unity of his love. As we explore the humility and servanthood of God's heart, we will come to understand his true greatness. As we come to know the true essence of the Triune God with all his infinite devotion, faithfulness, goodness, and holiness, our capacity to love and grow to be like God will produce an ever-increasing enjoyment of his infinite joy and satisfaction in our finite beings throughout the ages of eternity. It will be as if God says to each of us, "My infinite joy as the Father, Son, and Holy Spirit is now in you because you are in us, and your joy is being made complete throughout time without end." That will become your reality when Christ returns and restores all things.

Experiencing God's Creative Joy

My little Scottie saw the joy in my face when he agreed to go down the waterslide with me. But he also experienced the thrill of actually going down the waterslide. While we will experience God's relational joy, we will also thrill at literally experiencing the New Earth God is preparing for us.

Imagine Jesus showing you around some of the sights of the new earth and saying, "Oh, you've got to try this fruit. This tastes so good I want you to enjoy it with me." Or think of him saying, "I love this mountain view; come stand here with me and enjoy the magnificent splendor of this vista I've restored for you." You have a God who is excited for you. He wants you to enjoy him and all that he has created for you.

It may be hard to grasp that God desires us to really enjoy our new home with him. But he does. Paul told Timothy to tell others not to put their hope in earthly wealth "but to put their hope in God, who richly provides us with everything for our enjoyment" (1 Timothy 6:17 NIV). He created this earth for our enjoyment, but sin ruined it all. In our new home sin will be eliminated, and we will enter into the joy of God's restored creation forever.

But God's invitation to enjoy his restored creation does not mean he intends us to be mere spectators. We will not be placed in an eternal rocking chair to passively enjoy the beauty of God's handiwork. Remember that in Jesus' illustration the Master said, "You were faithful with a few things, I will put you in charge of many things" (Matthew 25:23 NASB). There will be things to do, projects we will be "in charge of."

Randy Alcorn quotes theologian Dallas Willard, who comments on Matthew 25:23:

> A place in God's creation order has been reserved for each one of us from before the beginning of cosmic existence. His plan is for us to develop, as apprentices to Jesus, to the point where we can take our place in the ongoing creativity of the universe.

Alcorn then goes on to say:

> God is grooming us for leadership. He's watching to see how we demonstrate our faithfulness. He does that through his apprenticeship program, one that prepares us for Heaven. Christ is not simply preparing a place for us; he is preparing us for that place.[1]

After God created the original earth he told Adam and Eve, "Be fruitful and increase in number; fill the earth and subdue it. Rule over the fish of the sea and the birds of the air and over every living creature that moves on the ground" (Genesis 1:28 NIV). God had a responsibility in mind for his original created family of humans, and he has a responsibility for his future redeemed children. In his vision John saw those who were washed in the blood of the Lamb given a place at "the throne of God," where they will "serve him day and night" (Revelation 7:15 NIV). So our present faithfulness to God is rewarded with future responsibilities in our new home. At first glance, this promise may not immediately appeal to you. You might think, *I'm stressed out with all the responsibilities piled on me here. I was hoping that heaven would free me from all that.*

Randy Alcorn answers this fear with an insightful perspective:

> Service is a reward, not a punishment. This idea is foreign to people who dislike their work and only put up with it until retirement. We think that faithful work should be rewarded by a vacation for the rest of our lives. But God offers us something very different: more work, more responsibilities, increased opportunities, along with greater abilities, resources, wisdom, and empowerment. We will have sharp minds, strong bodies, clear purpose, and unabated joy. The more we serve Christ now, the greater our capacity will be to serve him in Heaven.[2]

There are many things we may not know about the new heaven and new earth. What exactly we can expect to be doing for all eternity is still veiled in mystery. It is a great secret yet to be revealed. But we do know this: whatever task he has planned for you will fit you exactly. When you receive your assignment, you will suddenly understand just what your particular talents were meant to accomplish. It will be your dream job—the path to fulfillment of all your deepest ambitions.

The place we live in now is only our temporary world, and God is preparing for us a new place that will be our "dream home" because we will enter into God's relational and creative joy forever. John "heard a loud shout from the throne saying, 'Look, the home of God is now among his people! He will live with them, and they will be his people. God himself will be with them. He will remove all of their sorrows, and there will be no more death or sorrow or crying or pain. For the old world and its evils are gone forever'" (Revelation 21:3-4). Our future home will be everything we ever dreamed of and much more.

CHAPTER FIFTY-ONE

FULFILLING YOUR DESTINY

Have you ever seen the bumper sticker that reads: "Don't Follow Me, I'm Lost"? Some people live their lives wandering about with little sense of direction or sense of mission in life.

But if there was ever a person with a focused mission in life, it was Jesus. And he has passed that mission on to each of us. Jesus came to earth to lay down his life as a sacrifice to redeem us and bring us back to God and establish his kingdom. Jesus' message was all about this new kingdom to come. He "began to preach, 'Turn from your sins and turn to God, because the Kingdom of Heaven is near'" and from that point on "Jesus traveled throughout Galilee teaching in the synagogues, preaching everywhere the Good News about the Kingdom" (Matthew 4:17,23).

Practically everything Jesus said and did was an effort to contrast the two kingdoms—the kingdom of heaven and the kingdom of this world. He said to his Father that his followers "do not belong to the world" and "are not part of this world any more than I am" (John 17:14,16). Our real home isn't here. Jesus doesn't want us to get comfortable living here; that is why he said, "Don't store up treasures here on earth, where they can be eaten by moths and get rusty" (Matthew 6:19). He wants us to see this life and our temporal world from his perspective—an eternal perspective.

The apostle Paul warned us about those whose "god is their appetite"—their craving for earthly pleasures—"and all they think about is this life here on earth. But we are citizens of heaven," Paul said, "where the Lord Jesus Christ lives. And we are eagerly waiting for him to return as our Savior" (Philippians 3:19-20). Living as "citizens of heaven" while residing on this earth isn't easy, especially when we face life's trials, discouragements, and difficulties.

Living in this world but not being of this world, of course, does not insulate us from its pain and heartache. We may experience the joy of Christ in our hearts while suffering the physical pain of a disease, the financial loss of unemployment or a stock market failure, or the emotional loss of a disrupted or destroyed relationship or the death of a loved one.

We may believe that Christ's mission will be complete one day when he returns to destroy sin and death and restore us to a new heaven and earth, but that belief can sometimes grow weak in the face of tragedy. Jesus tried to prepare his own disciples for the impending tragedy of his death when he said, "Truly, you will weep and mourn over what is going to happen to me, but the world will rejoice. You will grieve, but your grief will suddenly turn to wonderful joy when you see me again...I have told you all this so that you may have peace in me. Here on earth you will have many trials and sorrows. But take heart, because I have overcome the world" (John 16:20,33).

Jesus was not caught off guard on that frightful day on Calvary. He knew that day was coming; he knew exactly what he was doing; and he was masterfully in control. That's why he told his disciples, "Don't be troubled. You trust God, now trust in me" (John 14:1). Yes, he knew he was about to die, but he also knew death would have no power over him. He was appealing to his followers to rest in him and commit their troubles to him. "Have peace in me," he said. It was as if he were saying, "I want you to know I'm in control of things. I know it won't seem like it, but trust me no matter what, for I'm going to work things out for your good and my glory. And what will seem like a disaster with my death is really for your good, because through it all I will redeem you and restore everything back to what I originally planned. I am the God of Redemption, *and* I am also the God of Restoration."

Where Am I Going?

It's not hard to see now, after the fact, that Christ was in control of the situation of his death. His resurrection from the grave proves it. And we can see how he took his torturous death and transformed it into the means of salvation for the human race. We could chide the disciples for not trusting in Christ enough and for not believing he knew what he was doing. But as we said, it's not so easy to exhibit that kind of trust in the midst of trials or tragedy. It's hard to have a spirit of gratitude, courage, and optimism unless, of course, we view this temporal world with all its trials from God's eternal perspective.

In Romans 8, the apostle Paul gives us several eternal insights. He first says, "Even we Christians, although we have the Holy Spirit within us as a foretaste of future glory, also groan to be released from pain and suffering" (Romans 8:23). This passage makes it clear that optimism doesn't come from denying our present pain. Paul goes on to say that "the Holy Spirit helps us in our distress…And we know that God causes everything to work together for the good of those who love God and are called according to his purpose for them" (Romans 8:26,28). Paul had the answer: We can place our trust in God because he is sovereign and obviously knows what he's doing. When we do this, the Holy Spirit, who lives inside each individual Christian, will cause everything to work together for good.

This does not mean that everything will work together for our comfort, or that everything will work together to spare us difficulties, pain, or trials. It is not a belief that says everything that happens to God's people in this death-cursed world is somehow good. Sickness is not good. Death is not good. Pain is not good. Sorrow, sadness, and suffering are not good. However, by trusting in God, not only as our Savior but also as our sovereign Lord who does all things well, we can be confident that he will cause all things—even the bad things that happen to us—to work together for our good and his glory. Our confidence in and conviction about a God who loves us beyond words and causes all things, even tragedies, to work together for good can produce within us a spirit of gratitude, courage, and optimism in the face of life—and death.

It is faith in a sovereign God that moves us beyond a human perspective on life to an eternal perspective. The apostle Paul was a living example of this eternal mind-set. Listen to his heart of gratitude as he shares his God-inspired letter to the church of Corinth. Read the words carefully. Note how his faith in the resurrected Christ provided him with a sense of courage and optimism, even in the most difficult of times:

> We are pressed on every side by troubles, but we are not crushed and broken. We are perplexed, but we don't give up and quit. We are hunted down, but God never abandons us. We get knocked down, but we get up again and keep going…We know that the same God who raised our Lord Jesus will also raise us with Jesus and present us to himself along with you. All of these things are for your benefit…
>
> That is why we never give up. Though our bodies are dying, our spirits are being renewed every day. For our present troubles are quite small and won't last very long. Yet they produce for us an immeasurably great glory that will last forever! So we don't look at the troubles we can see right now; rather, we look forward to what we have not yet seen. For the troubles we see will soon be over, but the joys to come will last forever (2 Corinthians 4:8-9,14-18).

What an amazing approach to life's problems! Paul didn't run from difficulties in order to avoid pain, nor did he try to deny that difficulties existed in his life. He acknowledged his suffering and viewed the trials of life from an eternal perspective, knowing that the God of all comfort was there to ease his pain (see 1 Corinthians 2:3-4).

||||||||||||||||||||||||||||||||||||||||||||||||||

God's kingdom defines where we are going. For we are destined to have our struggles, suffering, and death transformed into blessings, joy, and a life at home with God for all eternity.

||||||||||||||||||||||||||||||||||||||||||||||||||

He trusted in a sovereign God who would cause everything to work together for good. Paul's faith in a God who had everything under control enabled him to see the difficulties of this life as producing "an immeasurably great glory that will last forever!"

Because of the resurrection, we are destined to live forever in new bodies on a new earth, an existence that will be so enjoyable that anything "we suffer now is nothing compared to the glory [God] will give us later." For we "wait anxiously for that day when God will give us our full rights as his children, including the new bodies he has promised us" (Romans 8:18,23).

Our "priceless inheritance" is a state of being in which we will be given "full rights" to reign with Christ in the new kingdom of heaven on a new earth. It is a kingdom "pure and undefiled, beyond the reach of change and decay" (1 Peter 1:4). This kingdom that will completely encompass the new earth is our destiny. God's kingdom defines where we are going. *For we are destined to have our struggles, suffering, and death transformed into blessings, joy, and a life at home with God for all eternity.* We will inherit a new heaven and a new earth as our eternal home. This is our destiny.

Christ is saying to us, "Trust me. I am alive and in control of every situation. I will take your struggles and change them into blessings. I will take your suffering and turn it into joy. And as your inheritance I will give you a new heaven and a new earth as your eternal home. How can I do that? I'm the sovereign, almighty King of the universe, who can do all things and who causes everything to work together for the good of those who love me and are called according to my purpose. So trust in me, no matter what."[1]

Our Mission

Our destiny may be eternal life at home with God, but we aren't there yet. "So be truly glad!" the apostle Peter said. "There is wonderful joy ahead, even though it is necessary for you to endure many trials for a while" (1 Peter 1:6). And Peter made it clear why God is keeping us here. He has a mission for us to accomplish.

"We are looking forward to the new heavens and new earth he has promised," Peter said, "a world where everyone is right with God. And so, dear friends, while you are waiting for these things to happen, make every effort to live a pure and blameless life. And be at peace with God. And remember, the Lord is waiting so that people have time to be saved" (2 Peter 3:13-15). We may be waiting to live on the new earth, but it's not time yet. The Lord appears to be waiting to usher in that final day so that those around us still have time to trust in him. Our task here is to participate in God's mission to reach these people by living pure and blameless lives that reflect his nature and draw others to him.

"God has given us the task [or mission] of reconciling people to him" (2 Corinthians 5:18). During the years of Jesus' life on earth, "God was in Christ, reconciling the world to himself" (2 Corinthians 5:19). Now, Christ is in us, and Paul says that God "has committed to us the message of reconciliation. We are therefore Christ's ambassadors, as though God were making his appeal through us" (2 Corinthians 5:19-20 NIV). He wants to involve us in his mission of drawing people to him by the attitudes we have, the things we say, and the way we act—especially in times of adversity and trouble.

God did not cause any of the suffering or difficulties you may be going through right now. There is nothing good about pain and suffering. But God is not caught off-guard or blindsided by your suffering. He knows that in this fallen world, suffering is inevitable. Yet your sovereign God causes all of your circumstances—both the good and the bad—to work together for good. As you make Christ more and more at home in your life, the gracious, long-suffering Spirit of God can be seen in your suffering. And in those circumstances, people clearly see Christ.

We often seem to fulfill Christ's mission to reach others most effectively when we are enduring times of crisis, suffering, or persecution. Nearly all of us can exhibit love, joy, peace, patience, and so on when the wind is at our back and we're sailing high. But how many people display gratitude, courage, and optimism in the midst of a storm? Displaying these attributes in such times is what causes people to sit up and take notice: when tragedy strikes, when you're hurting, when you're mistreated.

Think of the trials, struggles, or suffering you may be going through right now. It's not a sin to feel discouraged or frustrated with the tests of life. But can you sense how God wants to be there for you with his love, support, and comfort? What gives him pleasure is to fill you so completely with an abundance of his joy and blessing during your difficulties that you actually become grateful for the trials you're experiencing. And when people see how courageous and optimistic you are during your troubled times, they will be drawn to Christ.

When we fully submit ourselves to God, we can be especially encouraged when trouble strikes or problems come our way. It is during these times that we can become aware we have been assigned a mission, if we are willing to accept it—a mission to exhibit a Christlike spirit and share the love of Christ with those around us. Far from being a cause for complaint or self-pity, we should see such instances as great compliments. God trusts us enough to bestow on us the great honor of reflecting his glory in circumstances that might discourage those who do not trust him.

As you can see, sharing Christ with others doesn't have to be thought of as a chore or obligation. Rather, it is an opportunity to reveal Christ through our lives to others. It does require, however, a basic understanding of what to say and how to share a simple presentation of the gospel as we explained in chapter 27. But once that is learned, it's a matter of developing a lifestyle that makes you a walking example of Christ. As people recognize you as a person who lives in a temporal world with an eternal perspective, they too will catch a glimpse of your King and his kingdom, the King who has prepared you "an eternal house in heaven, not built by human hands" (2 Corinthians 5:1 NIV).[2]

To help you instill within your family or church group an eternal perspective while living in a temporal world, we have provided instructions to help you prepare and carry out a Judeo-Christian celebration, the Restoration Celebration. It is based on the Feast of Tabernacles, an ancient Jewish festival that puts this present world into a godly perspective. You will find these instructions in appendix C at the end of this book.

■

SUMMARY OF PART IV

God's Truth Declaration:
I Am the God of Re-Creation—The God of Restoration

- *We believe the truth* that Jesus died on the cross for our sins and rose again to transfer us from death to life and secure our eternal salvation.

  Because there is sufficient evidence that Jesus rose from the dead, we can believe with confidence that he has the power to forgive our sins and reconcile us to God.

  Christ's resurrection also assures us that he will raise our dead bodies to live with him for all eternity.

- *We believe the truth* that there is one God who is eternally co-existing as the Father, Son, and Holy Spirit in a perfect relationship of oneness.

  The Holy Spirit is the dynamic, active, and ever-present person of the Trinity who dwells within us, making us intimate with God.

  When we yield to the Holy Spirit he makes us one with God, confirms our Christlikeness, leads us into all truth, empowers us for service, and brings meaning to our lives.

- *We believe the truth* that the kingdom-of-God message forms our biblical worldview.

  God's kingdom worldview has been a powerful influence for good in this present world for centuries, motivating people to bring aid and comfort to those in need.

  A biblical worldview provides a supernatural way for Christ-followers to live in this present world.

- *We believe the truth* that the church is Christ's visible representation on earth, in which his transformed followers individually and collectively fulfill God's redemptive plan.

  The authentic church is Christ's loving community that acts as "salt and light" to draw people to Christ and impacts the culture around it.

  Jesus' Great Commandment "to love" and Great Commission "to make disciples" are inseparably linked so that his church meets both the human and spiritual needs of people.

- *We believe the truth* that Jesus will return to give his followers resurrected bodies that will last forever; abolish sin; and restore the earth to a perfect world, where his children will live with him through all eternity.

  We can believe with confidence that Jesus will return because he has conquered death through his own resurrection.

  Until Christ returns, we as his followers are engaged in his mission to reconcile as many people as possible to God.

THE REDEMPTION CELEBRATION

*Permission is granted to the purchaser of this book to photocopy
this appendix for use in a family or group celebration activity.
This material © 2010 Josh McDowell Ministry and Sean McDowell.*

The following provides you with instructions on a mealtime celebration in praise to God for going to such miraculous and gracious lengths to redeem us. The Christmas season is an excellent time to do this. This Judeo-Christian celebration is modeled after the Jewish Passover *Haggadah* ("telling") that Jewish families have conducted for centuries.

The traditional Jewish Passover celebrates God redeeming his people from the hands of Pharaoh and out of the land of Egypt to lead them into the Promised Land. The Passover is celebrated by Jewish families year after year as a way of passing down to their children the story of the Exodus, the story of the God of Redemption. But it is more than a story or historical event to them. The stories tell who they are, where they have come from, a depiction of a specific way of life, and a way of being in the world. Jewish parents for centuries have shared with their children that God fulfilled his promise to give them a land and make them a nation. That is why they so proudly bear the name of their forefather, Israel.

You probably don't conduct a Judeo-style celebration that roots you in various meaningful historical events. Yet all of us can claim the historical and biblical roots of being the sons of Adam and daughters of Eve. So in this Redemption Celebration we trace your heritage and that of your family back to the very first couple. We show how because of their sin we are all separated from our Creator, and how Jesus came to earth in human form, an event called the incarnation, to redeem you specifically to a relationship with him. We attempt to convey this in a dramatic yet simple story form. And at the end of the celebration we enable you to offer an invitation for family members to commit or recommit their lives to God, for he is "our Redeemer from ages past" (Isaiah 63:16).

If you would like to learn more about the Passover as well as the other biblical feasts of the Lord and understand how they directly relate to your Christian faith, we encourage you to visit www.ariseinglory.org. On this Web site, Harvey Diamond, a Jewish believer in Christ as the Messiah, has done a great job of unpacking the biblical festivals and relating them in the form of an interactive devotional, called "Pathways to Glory Relational Devotional." It provides various ways of relating with God in a manner that makes them especially relevant to the Christian life.

This Redemption Celebration is best done together with two or more families. Children from three years of age and up will enjoy and get something out of this celebration. Meet ahead of time with the adults you are planning this with to go over the details, select an emcee, and to assign certain readings and responsibilities.

The celebration consists of seven elements. Walk through each of these elements with one another to practice and plan for your meal and the different readings.

1. **"The Son of God Entered Our World" (a Scripture reading).** In your planning meeting, identify someone within the group who is willing to read this passage to begin the Redemption Celebration. The reading is found on page 440, and you have permission to photocopy that page and all the pages related to this celebration. You might ask the person to practice reading the passage aloud to the group, using the photocopied page. We encourage you to *read* these readings at the celebration rather than trying to casually relate the content. This gives your evening a sense of clarity and preciseness.

2. **The "Prophet Tree."** Identify someone in your group willing to present the "Prophet Tree." This person will need to follow the instructions for creating it. For practice, ask him or her to read the presentation aloud to your planning group now, using a photocopy of pages 441–443 that you provide.

3. **The meal.** Identify someone willing to take the lead to coordinate the location of the Redemption Celebration (preferably someone's home), determine the time, decide what to eat, and so on. This person is not to do

all the work. He or she is to work with the members of your family group to coordinate the logistical details of the celebration listed on page 444. Photocopy that page and provide it to the meal coordinator.

4. **"The Saddest Story That Could Ever Be Told: The Great Separation."** Identify someone within the group who is willing to read this personalized fairy-tale-type story at the celebration. Photocopy pages 445–446 of this reading and give them to the person willing to read this story and ask him or her to do the reading now for practice. (*Note:* The reader will need to fill in the blanks depending on gender.)

5. **"The Greatest Story Ever Told: The Great Redemption."** Identify someone in your group willing to read this story at the celebration. Photocopy this reading, found on pages 447–448. This story, of course, is real and lays the foundation for your children and youth to commit or recommit their lives to Christ. The designated reader can practice by reading a photocopy.

6. **"How to Experience a Relationship with God."** Identify someone in your group who is willing to make a short and clear presentation of the gospel. This is to offer your children and youth the opportunity to commit or recommit their lives to Christ, the Redeemer. The designated reader can practice reading the photocopied presentation found on pages 449–450.

7. **"Something to Celebrate."** Identify someone in your group who is willing to conclude the Redemption Celebration by directing five people (preferably young people) to read what Jesus' coming to earth means and then close in prayer. These five readings explain the meaning of Jesus' coming to earth—and our lifelong response to our Redeemer. The designated person can practice by reading a photocopy of pages 451–453.

Conducting the Redemption Celebration

After meeting with the families you plan to have the Redemption Celebration with, you are now ready to emcee your evening event and meal. Feel free to photocopy these pages as a reference guide to your celebration.

- *Introduction.* Invite everyone to be seated at the table and say, "**Tonight we are going to have a Redemption Celebration, which is a celebration of the time when God took on human form and Jesus was born into this world. And _____ (name) is going to start us off with a Scripture reading**" ("The Son of God Entered Our World").

- Immediately following the reading, have the person responsible for the Prophet Tree make his or her presentation ("The Prophet Tree").

- Announce that it is time to eat; offer a prayer for the meal.

- At the conclusion of the meal, thank all those who helped prepare it. And then say, "**Now we want to celebrate God taking on human form—which is called the incarnation. And we want to understand why he did that—why he came to earth. So to begin, _____ (name) is going to read something. But to gain the impact of this story, I want each young person here to pretend that _____ (name) is your actual _____ (mother/father). The story is entitled 'The Saddest Story That Could Ever Be Told: The Great Separation.'**"

- After the "Great Separation" reading, sensitively gauge each person's response. Ask, "**If that story were true, how would you feel?**"

  Then say to the group, "**I can tell you how I would feel; I would feel _____.**" (Describe as honestly and vulnerably as possible how it would affect you.)

  Then say, "**The story that _____ (name) just read shows how sad our lives would be if we couldn't feel each other's love. But, while that's just a fable, it parallels a real situation, a story that's absolutely true…for every one of us. Now _____ (name) will read 'The Greatest Story Ever Told: The Great Redemption.'**"

- Following the "Great Redemption" reading the emcee says, "**Thank you, _____ (name). That is the reason God came to earth in the form of a human. It was the reason Jesus died: He wants a relationship—a close friendship connection—with you. _____ (name) will now explain to us how to experience that connection, a close relationship with God.**"

- Following the prayer of commitment/recommitment say, **"If you prayed that prayer from the heart, a miracle has taken place, and you are now a child of God—all because of Jesus."** Sensitively probe to see if anyone has prayed that prayer or wants to pray further—and respond accordingly. Then at the appropriate time say: **"Let's end our time together celebrating our redemption and what we've just experienced as we respond to the very God of Redemption."** Introduce the person that is to conduct the "Something to Celebrate" presentation.

- Close your Redemption Celebration in prayer.

The Son of God Entered Our World
(A Scripture Reading)

God sent the angel Gabriel to Nazareth, a village in Galilee, to a virgin named Mary. She was engaged to be married to a man named Joseph, a descendant of King David. Gabriel appeared to her and said, "Greetings, favored woman! The Lord is with you!"

Confused and disturbed, Mary tried to think what the angel could mean. "'Don't be frightened, Mary," the angel told her, "for God has decided to bless you! You will become pregnant and have a son, and you are to name him Jesus. He will be very great and will be called the Son of the Most High. And the Lord God will give him the throne of his ancestor David. And he will reign over Israel forever; his Kingdom will never end!"

Mary asked the angel, "But how can I have a baby? I am a virgin."

The angel replied, "The Holy Spirit will come upon you, and the power of the Most High will overshadow you. So the baby born to you will be holy, and he will be called the Son of God."

Mary responded, "I am the Lord's servant, and I am willing to accept whatever he wants. May everything you have said come true." And then the angel left (Luke 1:26-38)...

The time came for [Mary's] baby to be born. She gave birth to her first child, a son. She wrapped him snugly in strips of cloth and laid him in a manger (Luke 2:6-7).

The Prophet Tree

Instructions for Creating Your "Prophet Tree"

Before the celebration: If no one has provided you with a Prophet Tree, then take any potted houseplant or a small potted pine tree to the celebration. Prior to the celebration write or type the eight prophecies about Jesus that are listed below, including their Scripture references, on eight slips of paper approximately three by four inches. Roll the slips of paper into small four-inch rolls and tie each to a branch of the potted plant with ribbons.

Begin the Presentation

Say, "Yes, Jesus was born in a manger. But how do we know that Jesus was truly the Son of God?" (Pause for possible answers.)

"Well, God gave us a way to know for certain that Jesus was his very own Son. You see, more than 400 years before Christ was born, God had his prophets foretell a lot of very specific things about Jesus. It was like identifying him by giving us his specific address. By looking back to those prophecies we know that if the information is descriptive enough, and Jesus fits the descriptions, then we will have no doubt that Jesus was in fact God's Son.

"For example, you (name someone in the group) are one person among more than 6 billion people on this planet. If I had the task of identifying you out of the earth's total population, I could do so by learning the answers to just eight questions. Let me ask you:

1. What continent do you live on? _____

   (African continent? European continent? North American continent? and so on)

2. What country do you live in? _____

   (Canada? Germany? England? United States? and so on)

3. What province or state do you live in? _____

4. What city, borough, or town do you live in? _____

5. What street or avenue do you live on? _____

6. What is your house or apartment number? _____

7. What is your last name? _____

8. What are your first and middle names? _____

"The answers to these eight questions will enable me to separate you from the more than 6 billion other people alive today. In the same fashion, God gave us Jesus Christ's address. He provided us very specific information about who the Christ would be, where he would be born, and what would happen to him. And why? So that we would be convinced beyond a reasonable doubt that a Jewish man named Jesus who lived over 2000 years ago was who he claimed to be—the Son of the one true God."

Bring Out the Prophet Tree

Now bring out the Prophet Tree and continue by saying:

"This is called a 'Prophet Tree.' On it we have eight prophecies about Jesus that were written down and preserved hundreds of years before he was ever born." Select up to eight in the group—preferably young people—to untie the slips of paper from the tree and read what is inside. One person, of course, can read more than one prophecy. They will read:

1. He would be born in Bethlehem (Micah 5:2).

2. He would be born to a virgin (Isaiah 7:14).

3. A forerunner would announce his arrival, a "voice in the wilderness" (Isaiah 40:3).

4. He would ride victoriously into Jerusalem on a young donkey (Zechariah 9:9).

5. He would be betrayed by a friend (Psalm 41:9; Zechariah 11:12).

6. He would be crucified (his hands and feet would be pierced), but his bones would be left unbroken (Psalm 22:16; 34:20).

7. He would die (be "cut off") 483 years after the declaration to rebuild the temple in 444 BC (Daniel 9:24).

8. He would rise from the dead (Psalm 16:10).[1]

Could It All Be a Coincidence?

Continue by reading:

"Every one of these prophecies was fulfilled during Jesus' life, death, and resurrection. But couldn't that all be a coincidence? Perhaps those prophecies have been fulfilled by any number of people. Right?

"This is where the science of statistics and probabilities comes in. Professor Peter W. Stoner, in an analysis that was carefully reviewed and pronounced to be sound by the American Scientific Affiliation, states that the probability of just *eight* of those prophecies being fulfilled in one person is 1 in 10 to the seventeenth power—that's 1 in 100 quintillion.[2]

"Look at it this way: If you spread 100 quintillion silver dollars across the state of Texas, they would not only cover the entire state, they would form a pile of coins two feet deep! Now, take one more silver dollar, mark it with a big red X, toss it into that pile, and stir the whole pile thoroughly.

"Then blindfold yourself, and starting at El Paso on the western border, walk the length and breadth of that enormous state, stopping just once along the way to pick up a single silver dollar out of that two-foot-deep pile…Then take off your blindfold and look at the silver dollar in your hand. What are the chances that you would have picked the marked coin out of a pile of silver dollars the size of the Lone Star State? *The same chance that one person could have fulfilled those eight prophecies in one lifetime.*

"And that's just the beginning! More than 300 prophecies in the Old Testament were fulfilled in *one person,* Jesus Christ—and all of them were made more than 400 years prior to his birth. In other words, it is completely unreasonable to imagine that the Old Testament prophecies about Jesus could have come true in one man—unless, of course, he *is,* as he himself claimed, 'the Messiah, the Son of the blessed God' (Mark 14:61-62), the One who was and is and is to come."[3]

(The emcee thanks the presenter of the Prophet Tree, announces that it is now time to eat the meal together, and says the blessing.)

Preparing for the Redemption Celebration Meal

- **Select where to conduct your Redemption Celebration.** A person's home is preferable, depending on the size of your group and their families. Conducting the celebration at multiple sites is an option if you have a large group.

- **Select date and time of your celebration.**

- **Decide on the meal.** Consider a potluck meal in which each family brings a dish. Decide who in your group will bring what. If you plan to conduct the celebration as an annual event you might want to identify a dish or two as a special item to always have as a traditional Redemption Celebration item.

The Saddest Story That Could Ever Be Told:
The Great Separation

The emcee makes an introduction: "**Now we want to celebrate the time when God took on human form—which is called the *incarnation*. And we want to understand the reason he did that—in other words, why he came to earth. To begin, _____ (name) will read us something. But to gain the impact of this story, each young person here must pretend that _____ (name of person reading the story) is your actual mother or father. This story is entitled 'The Saddest Story That Could Ever Be Told: The Great Separation.'**

The person chosen to read stands up and begins:

"I want you to imagine with me that once upon a time, in a land far away, I was the happiest _____ (king/queen) in all the world...the happiest _____ (king/queen), in fact, in all the history of all the _____ (kings/queens) in all the world.

"This happiness was not just because I was great. It was not because I had a grand castle. It was not because I ruled a glorious kingdom. It was because on one special day, I became something even better than a great _____ (king/queen), because on that day each of you were born and I became your _____ (father/mother).

"For months, I waited for your arrival. When you finally came into the world, you were truly a unique, one-of-a-kind person who had never been seen before. Never in the history of mortal time would there be another you—so distinct, so individual, yet so connected to me.

"From the first time I scooped you up in my arms and held you close, I wanted nothing more in all the world than to love you, be close to you, and watch you grow to experience all the joys of being you. You were my child, after all, and I wanted nothing to ever come between us.

"But then...a horrible thing happened. The wicked prince of an unhappy kingdom tried to overpower me and take control of my kingdom. But he failed because I was too strong. So in anger and hatred, he chose to strike where he knew it would hurt me most. He cast an evil spell over you—a great, terrible spell.

"The evil prince's spell caused a dreadful glass wall to surround you wherever you went and whatever you did. I could still see you and hear you—for I was still the great _____ (king/queen)—but it trapped you without your knowledge. It kept you from seeing me, hearing me, touching me, or even sensing that I was there.

"Thus, unless the spell could be broken, I would never again experience the pleasure, the joy, the closeness of being with you, my very own child.

"Oh, what anguish it was for me, for I could see you, but you could not see me. I saw your first steps…but you could not hear me cheering you on. I heard your first words…but they weren't spoken to me. I watched everything you did and followed you everywhere you went…but the dreadful glass wall kept you from feeling my ever-present love for you. I wanted to share everything with you—your thrill of learning to ride a bike, your relief at passing a test in school, your excitement of winning a game—but the evil spell took all that away from me.

"I was there, too, when you were hurt. When you cried, I reached out to wipe your tears away, but you never felt the touch of my hand. When you skinned your knee, I wanted to kiss it and make it better, but you didn't even know I was there. And on those nights when you would cry yourself to sleep, I heard you. I heard you cry, 'Where is my _____ (daddy/mommy)? I want my _____ (daddy/mommy).' But you couldn't hear my sobs for you.

"Oh, what a wicked spell! I would have given my kingdom—my life!—if it would break the spell and restore you to me. But it could not be, for no one on earth could break this spell. I could only watch with a broken heart, weep for you, and wait for the Spellbreaker who could reunite you with me…and bring to an end the Saddest Story That Could Ever Be Told."[4]

Emcee transition to next reading:

After the reading, sensitively gauge each person's response. Ask, "How would it make you feel if that story were true?"

Then offer, "I can tell you how I would feel; I would feel _____."
(Describe as honestly and vulnerably as possible how it would affect you.)

Then say, "The story that _____ (name) just read shows how sad our lives would be if we couldn't feel each other's love. Yet while that's just a fable, it parallels a real situation, a story that's absolutely true…for each one of us. And _____ (name) now will read 'The Greatest Story Ever Told: The Great Redemption.'"

The Greatest Story Ever Told: The Great Redemption

"In a Middle Eastern land many years ago, where a beautiful river branched out to form four other rivers, was a pristine garden. Lush tropical trees and plants produced delicious fruits of every taste and texture. A paradise of grasses and flowers under a canopy of clouds and sky painted a breathtaking canvas. Singing birds and sparkling waterfalls created a soundtrack of sheer delight. It was perfection itself, the Garden of Eden, where the first man and the first woman lived in perfect harmony with each other and with their Creator, the Trinity of God the Father, God the Son, and God the Holy Spirit.

"From the first moments of their existence, this first couple—Adam and Eve—enjoyed a close relationship with their Creator. They talked to him just as they talked to each other. They walked with him in the garden. They laughed together, sharing the delights of paradise—reveling in the gazelle's grace, the eagle's soaring strength, the sparrow's playfulness.

"They communed with God as a dear friend and loving Father, for they were a family. And through this relationship they had everything they needed. They had love, because their love came from God. They had joy, because their joy came from God. They had peace, because their peace came from God. They had no hunger, greed, fear, or pain because God's holy presence permeated the wonderful garden. They were a perfect family.

"But then something terrible happened. A rebellious angel named Lucifer plotted in hatred to ruin the perfect family and world God had created. Lucifer, who had been cast out of heaven because he wanted to rule his own kingdom without God, persuaded the first human couple that they, too, should rule their own world without God. So he deceived them into believing that they knew better than God did. He convinced them to selfishly and sinfully choose their own ways rather than trusting in God's ways.

"Adam and Eve's sinful choice to reject God and his ways formed a dreadful wall—a wall of death—that separated them from their loving Creator and Father God. *Gone* were their shared moments of intimacy and happiness. *Gone* were the moments of laughter they enjoyed together. *Gone* was their close relationship.

"From that point on, God watched in grief and sadness as children—his children—came into the world he created without knowing him and feeling his love. He watched them every moment of the day, but they could not feel his interest. He saw them follow the sinful path of Adam and Eve, which kept every child, teenager, and adult from knowing and feeling his love.

"The perfect and holy Creator, who knew no sin, watched his sinful children—who were separated from his presence. They were now disconnected from the only source that could sustain life, love, joy, and peace. He watched as his children had to suffer the agony of war and hunger, disease and heartache, pain and suffering. Sin separated God from the cherished family he had created, and it broke his heart. But as his heart ached for his children, he already knew how he would respond.

"And this—though it is miraculous—is no fairy tale. It is absolutely true.

"God wanted to reconnect to his children and restore a relationship with them—with *you*—but God, being holy, could not relate to sin. So he devised a plan. He sent his Son into our world to become one of us—a child himself, a human baby—for you. God's own Son came to earth—in a virgin's womb, as the prophets foretold, as the shepherds learned—to cancel the curse so you could know, so you could *feel* his love for you.

"The sin of the first couple and your sin caused death, and the prince of darkness, Satan himself, held the power of death over you. Only one thing could cancel the curse of sin: A sinless human had to be willing to sacrifice himself for you. So God's Son, perfect and sinless in every way, became human. As the Bible records, 'Only as a human being could he die, and only by dying could he break the power of the Devil, who had the power of death' (Hebrews 2:14).

"He did it all for you. Though you sinned against him, he loved and accepted you. This is the meaning of redemption—to purchase you back with his blood. It shows you how much he wants a relationship with you.

"And that kind of relationship is available to anyone who responds to his offer of a never-ending, always-with-you love relationship by believing and trusting in Christ as the Son of God, your Savior, Redeemer, and friend.

"*Not* the end—but the *beginning* if you trust in Jesus the Redeemer."[5]

Emcee:

"Thank you, _____ (name). That is the reason God came to earth in the form of a human. It was the reason Jesus died—he wants to redeem you so he can have a relationship with you. _____ (name) will explain to us how to experience that relationship with God."

How to Experience a Relationship with God

(*Presenter:* Feel free to read these five points or simply use the following as a guide):

Trusting in the Redeemer—Jesus Christ—involves four things:

1. We must recognize we have a problem with God. "No one has real understanding;" the Bible says, "no one is seeking God. All have turned away from God; all have gone wrong" (Romans 3:11-12).

Recognizing our problem with God means we acknowledge that we have turned away from God and don't have enough understanding in life to decide for ourselves what is right. The Bible says it like it is: You "were once so far away from God. You were his enemies, separated from him by your evil thoughts and actions" (Colossians 1:21).

2. We must realize that Jesus Christ is our only solution. "When people sin," the Bible says, "they earn what sin pays—death" (Romans 6:23 NCV). Our problem with God has earned us death—separation from God. And we are totally incapable of solving that problem.

We can't just try harder to be good. You see, Jesus didn't come to earth to make bad people good; he came to earth to make dead people live. Romans 8:11 says, "The Spirit of God, who raised Jesus from the dead, lives in you. And just as he raised Christ from the dead, he will give life to your mortal body by this same Spirit living within you." So Christ is our only solution.

3. We need to respond to Christ's offer to redeem us. We need to be given new life. And Christ will give us new life when we agree with Jesus, who said:

> I am the way, the truth, and the life. No one can come to the Father except through me (John 14:6).

> You will die in your sins; for unless you believe that I am who I say I am, you will die in your sins (John 8:24).

> I am the resurrection and the life. Those who believe in me, even though they die like everyone else, will live again. They are given eternal life for believing in me and will never perish. Do you believe this? (John 11:25-26).

Do you really believe this? Are you convinced that Jesus Christ is who he said he is: the resurrection and the life, the only way to salvation, the only solution to your situation? Will you commit your life to him? He is ready to raise you from death to life, from separation from him to a new relationship with him. It says in John 1:12-13, "To all who believed him and accepted him, he gave the right to become children of God. They are reborn! This is not a physical birth resulting from human passion or plan—this rebirth comes from God."

4. You can rely on God to live in and through you. You may be dead to God because of your sins, but he is ready, as it says in Colossians 2:14, to "[cancel] the record that contained the charges against us. He took it and destroyed it by nailing it to Christ's cross."

If this prayer truly expresses the desire of your heart to begin a new life in Christ, you can pray these words silently to God:

- God, I recognize I have a problem with you. I have sinned against you and have gone my own way in life.

- I realize now that you are my only solution. I ask you to forgive me of all my sins. Right now I am turning away from my old life and turning to Jesus Christ as my only hope of finding a relationship with you.

- I respond right now to Jesus Christ's offer to rescue me from death. Right now I place my trust in you as my Savior and Redeemer. Right now I believe you will transform me into your child and give me an eternal relationship with you.

- I rely upon you to transfer me from death to life. You said in John 11:25 that I will be given eternal life by believing in you and that I will never perish. I believe and rely on you to transform me into your child right now.

- Thank you for doing what you said you would do. Thank you for making me your forgiven child and bringing me into a relationship with you, the one true God. Please live your life in and through me every day. I pray these things in Jesus' name. Amen.

The emcee makes a transition to the last reading by saying:

"If you prayed that prayer from the heart, a miracle has taken place, and you are now a child of God—all because of Jesus." (Sensitively probe to see if anyone has prayed that prayer or wants to pray further and respond accordingly. Then at the appropriate time say:) **"Let's end our time together by celebrating our new life and what we've just experienced as we respond to the very God of Redemption."** (Introduce the person who is to conduct the closing presentation, "Something to Celebrate.")

Something to Celebrate

Instructions: The person chosen to direct this portion should photocopy and cut out the five readings on these pages, distribute them to individuals at your celebration before it starts, and ask them to take turns reading when you call on them. Preferably, have young people at your meal read them. Follow the order from 1 to 5, and at the end of each reading the person will say, "That is worth celebrating." Prompt the entire group to then say, "He is worthy."[6]

---

1. Because of Jesus,
God Accepts Me Unconditionally

Like every other human being, I suffered the curse of death. I was born in sin, disconnected from God, and that broke his heart. And even though I sinned against him, he accepted me without condition. He wanted so much to have a love relationship with me that he was willing to set aside his glory, humble himself, and even go through a torturous death on a cross to redeem me, even though I didn't deserve it. Jesus coming to earth shows how passionate God is about enjoying a relationship...with me.

That is worth celebrating!
[The group responds: "He is worthy."]

---

2. Because of Jesus,
God Loves Me Sacrificially

Even though I was born with a sinful nature—and added to my guilt many times by sinning myself—God solved the problem of my sin in a way that satisfied his mercy *and* his justice. "He sent his own Son in a human body... [and] destroyed sin's control over [me] by giving his Son as a sacrifice for [my] sins" (Romans 8:3). In spite of my sin, God loved me enough to sacrifice himself, and he proved it by laying down his life for me!

That is worth celebrating!
[The group responds: "He is worthy."]

---

3. I Must Respond by
Living a Life of Devoted Worship of God

Christ sacrificed his life for me; I can do no different for him. Romans 12:1 says, "Give your bodies to God. Let them be a living and holy sacrifice—the kind he will accept. When you think of what he has done for you, is this too much to ask?" In Exodus 34:14 it says, "You must worship no other gods, but only the LORD, for he is a God who is passionate about his relationship with you."

That is worth celebrating!
[The group responds: "He is worthy."]

4. I Must Respond by
Living a Life of Continual Prayer to God

In Hebrews 4:15-16 Jesus is called our High Priest when it says, "This High Priest of ours understands our weaknesses, for he faced all of the same temptations we do, yet he did not sin. So let us come boldly to the throne of our gracious God. There…we will find grace to help us when we need it." Prayer allows us to share our hearts and needs with God, and he is always there for us.

That is worth celebrating!
[The group responds: "He is worthy."]

---

5. I Must Respond by
Living a Life of Confident Faith in God

In Hebrews 12:1-2 it tells us to "run with endurance the race that God has set before us. We do this by keeping our eyes on Jesus, on whom our faith depends from start to finish." We trusted in Christ to redeem us, and he did. We trust in him now to see us through the trials and difficulties of life—and he will.

That is worth celebrating!
[The group responds: "He is worthy."]

Emcee then thanks the person in charge and the five readers and closes the Redemption Celebration in a song of worship and a prayer of thanksgiving to God for sending his Son and redeeming us.

THE REVELATION CELEBRATION

The Revelation Celebration is designed as a Judeo-Christian family event that includes a meal. You will engage your children and teenagers in a fun and rewarding time illustrating that Scripture and the Holy Spirit are God's provisions to keep our relationships with him alive and fresh. The focus is on the ongoing process of coming to know God through his Word and the indwelling presence of the Holy Spirit.

This celebration is based on the Jewish holiday called the Festival of Harvest. In the Hebrew language of the Old Testament, it is called *Shavuot*. In the Greek language of the New Testament it is called *Pentecost*.

For centuries the Jewish people have gathered together in their homes to observe Shavuot by celebrating the revelation of God's written Word given to Moses on Mount Sinai. Scripture is God's revelation to us so we might know him and his ways. This is something to celebrate.

But there is something more to celebrate. After Jesus died, rose again, and ascended into heaven, 120 of his disciples and followers were gathered in an upper room. They were observing Shavuot—Pentecost—when Jesus' promised Holy Spirit filled each one of them. Jesus said it is his "Holy Spirit who leads into all truth" (John 14:17). Paul the apostle said that "God has actually given us his Spirit (not the world's spirit) so we can know the wonderful things God has freely given us" (1 Corinthians 2:12). The Holy Spirit is God's revelation of himself. He infills us so that we might know God intimately and be like him.

The Revelation Celebration is a time to celebrate God's revealed Word and the Holy Spirit, whom God sent as a means to know him on a deep relational level, because he is the "God who is passionate about his relationship with you" (Exodus 34:14).

If you would like to learn more about the Festival of Harvest as well as the other biblical feasts of the Lord and understand how they directly relate to your Christian faith, we encourage you to visit www.ariseinglory.org, the Web site of Harvey Diamond, a Jewish believer in Christ as the Messiah. He has done a great job of unpacking the biblical festivals and relating them in the form of an interactive devotional, called "Pathways to Glory Relational Devotional." It provides various ways of relating with God in a manner that makes them especially relevant to the Christian life.

The Revelation Celebration is best done together with two or more families. Children from three years of age and up will enjoy and get something out of this mealtime event. Meet ahead of time with the adults you are planning this with to go over the details and assign responsibilities.

This celebration consists of six elements. Walk through each of these elements to practice and plan for your meal and the different readings. If your group is too large to fit into one home, plan to split up and conduct more than one celebration.

The six elements of the meal celebration do not include music, so your group may want to insert the singing of hymns or worship music at various times throughout the event.

1. **"Celebrating Two Revelations of God."** Identify someone in your group who is willing to read this presentation, which explains what the Revelation Celebration is all about. The reading is found on page 460, and you have permission to photocopy those pages and all the pages related to this celebration. You might ask the person to read the material aloud to the group for practice, using the photocopied pages. We encourage you to *read* these readings at the celebration meal rather than casually relating the content. The exception is "The Verbal Relay Process" illustration.

2. **"Why We Celebrate."** Identify someone within your group who is willing to be in charge of this presentation, found on pages 461–463. Ask him or her to read it aloud now to familiarize everyone with the material.

3. **The meal.** Identify someone in your group who is willing to take the

lead to coordinate the location of the Revelation Celebration (preferably someone's home), identify the time, obtain the prescribed menu items, determine what else is served, and so on.

This person is not to do all the work. He or she is to work with group members to coordinate the logistical details of the celebration, listed on page 464. Photocopy that page and provide it to the meal coordinator.

4. "**The Verbal Relay Process.**" Identify someone in your group who is willing to conduct this illustration, found on pages 465–466. Make a photocopy of those pages and ask him or her to read them aloud to familiarize everyone with the illustration.

5. "**God's Accurate Letters of Love.**" Identify someone who is willing to read this information, found on pages 467–469. Ask him or her to read these pages aloud now to familiarize the group with this material.

6. "**From God's Heart to Yours.**" Identify someone within your group who is willing to read this presentation, found on pages 470–471. Ask him or her to read it aloud now to familiarize everyone with its content.

Conducting the Revelation Celebration

After meeting with the families you plan to have the Revelation Celebration with, you are now ready to emcee your evening event and meal. Photocopy these pages as a reference guide to your celebration.

- *Introduction:* Invite everyone to be seated at the table and say, "**Tonight we are going to have a celebration and** _____ (name) **is going to start us off**" ("Celebrating Two Revelations of God").

- Immediately following that presentation have the person responsible for the "Why We Celebrate" make his or her presentation.

- Announcement of the meal and the prayer for the meal will be given by the person presenting "Why We Celebrate."

- At the conclusion of the meal, thank all those who helped prepare it. Then say, "**Now** _____ (name) **has something to share with us**" ("The Verbal Relay Process").

- After the verbal relay presentation say, "**Now, to see how accurate the life-saving message of the Bible is, let's have** _____ (name) **read something very fascinating, entitled 'God's Accurate Letters of Love.'**"

- Following that presentation, after a moment of silence, share from your own heart how you desire to know God more through his Spirit and his Word. Encourage others to share their desires to know God more. After a time of sharing close in prayer.

Consider Reading This Prayer at the End of the Celebration

"Tonight, O Lord, we have celebrated the revelation of your Holy Word and the revelation of your Holy Spirit. You have given us your Spirit and your Word that we might know you and love you intimately. And in doing so you have enabled us to love our wives and husbands, mothers and fathers, sons and daughters, grandparents, grandchildren, and friends as you meant for us to love them—with Christlike, unselfish love.

"Help us to go away from this celebration more lovingly committed to you and to one another. And let this prayer from your apostle Paul in Ephesians 3 be our concluding prayer:

> I pray that from his glorious, unlimited resources he will give you mighty inner strength through his Holy Spirit. And I pray that Christ will be more and more at home in your hearts as you trust in him. May your roots go down deep into the soil of God's marvelous love. And may you

have the power to understand, as all God's people should, how wide, how long, how high, and how deep his love really is. May you experience the love of Christ, though it is so great you will never fully understand it. Then you will be filled with the fullness of life and power that comes from God. Now glory be to God! By his mighty power at work within us, he is able to accomplish infinitely more than we would ever dare to ask or hope. May he be given glory in the church and in Christ Jesus forever and ever through endless ages. Amen (verses 16-21).

"And everyone said…Amen!"

Celebrating Two Revelations of God

Tonight we are going to participate in what we are calling the "Revelation Celebration." It is based on a Jewish holiday. The Jewish holiday is called the Festival of Harvest. In the Greek language of the New Testament it is called *Pentecost.*

For centuries the Jewish people gathered together in their homes and observed the Festival of Harvest by celebrating the revelation of God's written Word given to Moses on Mount Sinai. God appeared to Moses and said, "I am the LORD, the merciful and gracious God. I am slow to anger and rich in unfailing love...You must worship no other gods, but only the LORD, for he is a God who is passionate about his relationship with you" (Exodus 34:6-7,14).

God gave the children of Israel and each of us his Word as his love letters on how to come to know him personally. Because humans have sinned against God, they are separated from him. The Scriptures—his written Word—are instructions on how to regain a personal love relationship with God.

Tonight we will celebrate God's revealing himself to us through his Holy Word so we can know him for who he is.

Hundreds of years after Moses, it was written in Scripture that "the Word became human and lived here on earth among us" (John 1:14). His name was Jesus. He told his followers that to redeem them he must die for their sins, but that he would arise from the dead. He also said, "I will ask the Father, and he will give you another Counselor, who will never leave you. He is the Holy Spirit, who leads into all truth" (John 14:16). And the Bible says that "God has actually given us his Spirit...so we can know the wonderful things God has freely given us" (1 Corinthians 2:12).

During the Jewish Passover celebration, Jesus was, in fact, crucified. But just as he had said, he rose again and went back to his Father God in heaven. And 50 days from the Passover, when the Festival of Harvest, or Pentecost, was observed by the Jewish people, something extraordinary happened—just as Jesus had promised. It is recorded in the second chapter of Acts.

> On the day of Pentecost, seven weeks after Jesus' resurrection, the believers were meeting together in one place. Suddenly, there was a sound from heaven like the roaring of a mighty windstorm in the skies above them, and it filled the house where they were meeting. Then, what looked like flames or tongues of fire appeared and settled on them. And every one present was filled with the Holy Spirit (Acts 2:1-4).

Tonight, we too will celebrate God's revealing himself to us by giving us his Holy Spirit.

So tonight we celebrate God's revelation of his Word. Tonight we celebrate God's revelation of his Holy Spirit.

Why We Celebrate

Instructions: At the end of this reading there are three group readings to photocopy, cut out, and distribute to three young people who will be attending your Revelation Celebration. Pull them aside and ask them to help you out with your reading. They are simply to read aloud what is written, on your cue.

Also ask the youngest child who can speak and will be attending the celebration to assist you. Ask the child to simply say, "Because," when you nod at him or her. This child will need to be able to be attentive to your reading and cues.

You will need a cluster of grapes as an object lesson and enough small clusters to give to each person at the Revelation Celebration meal. Be sure the cluster you use has a main vine clearly visible from which numerous grapes extend.

Read Aloud:

"Why do we celebrate tonight? We celebrate because God has revealed himself through the written Word and through his Holy Spirit. But what does that really mean to us?

"God's revelation through his written Word and through his Holy Spirit means everything to you and me, because the Spirit and the Word teach and empower us to accomplish the one thing we were meant to accomplish—and that is to enjoy relationships. We were created to revel in a love relationship with God and with one another because, as Exodus 34:14 says, 'He is a God who is passionate about his relationship with you.'

"I have asked _____ (name of youngest child) to assist me. Each time (he or she) says, 'Because,' I would like all of you to quote that scripture aloud in unison: 'He is a God who is passionate about his relationship with you.' Okay?"

"Why did God give you his written Word?"
(Nod to youngest child to say, "Because.")
(**Group says in unison,** "He is a God who is passionate about his relationship with you." [Repeat this again if the group is unclear what they were to do.])

"Why did God give you his Holy Spirit?"
(Nod to youngest child to say, "Because.")
(**Group says in unison,** "He is a God who is passionate about his relationship with you.")

"Why did God create you to love him and one another?"
(Nod to youngest child to say, "Because.")
(**Group says in unison,** "He is a God who is passionate about his relationship with you.")

Now nod to the teenager/young person to whom you gave Reading #1 to indicate that he or she is to read it aloud. *Note:* Before your meal event make a photocopy of all three of these readings and cut them out so you can give one to each person doing the reading.

Reading #1

We celebrate the revelation of your Holy Word, O God, for it allows us to know you for who you are. You said to Moses as recorded in Exodus 33, "I know you by name, and I'm pleased with you." And Moses replied, "If you're really pleased with me, show me your ways so I can know you." Your Holy Word reveals yourself and your ways to us. We celebrate the giving of your Holy Word tonight.

Nod to the teenager/young person with Reading #2 to indicate that he or she is to read it aloud.

Reading #2

We celebrate the revealing of your Holy Spirit, O God, on the day of Pentecost, for you have come to fill us not only with your Word, but with your presence also. You desire for us to join you in the circle of your perfect relationship. You said, "My prayer for all of them is that they will be one, just as you and I are one, Father—that just as you are in me and I am in you, so they will be in us" (John 17:21). Your Holy Spirit has come to indwell us and make us one with you. We celebrate the giving of your Holy Spirit tonight.

Nod to the teenager/young person with Reading #3 to indicate that he or she is to read it aloud.

Reading #3

Tonight we celebrate the revelation of your Spirit and your Word. And in doing so we celebrate how your love toward us and in us has enabled us to love one another as you have loved us. You said to your followers as recorded in John 14, "Love each other in the same way that I have loved you. Everyone will know that you are my disciples because of your love for each other." Your Spirit and your Word enable us to truly love as you love. We celebrate our love for one another tonight.

Pick up the cluster of grapes. Ask each person to take a small bunch from those that you have provided on a tray, and say the following.

"Jesus said, 'I am the vine; you are the branches. Those who remain in me, and I in them will produce much fruit. For apart from me you can do nothing' (John 15:5).

"Christ is the vine. We are the branches. This grape represents the fruit of his love. When we yield to God's Holy Word and the Holy Spirit living in us, we produce the fruit of Christlike loving. Each of you now take the fruit of the vine and eat it." (You pick a grape from the cluster and eat it as well.)

"Tonight we celebrate his love and our love for one another. Right now let someone know that you love him or her." (To set an example, you go over and embrace someone and say, "I love you." Once everyone has expressed a gesture of love to another, say the following.)

"Now, because of God's revelation of his Spirit and his Word, we celebrate him and our love for one another. And how do we do that? For one, by feasting!" If you decide to sing, say: "By singing and feasting." (Then lead in a song. Now offer the following prayer.)

"O God, we celebrate your Spirit and the Word tonight. We celebrate our love for one another. And as we partake of this food, bless it so that it strengthens us to honor you by loving one another as you have loved us. Amen."

Serve the meal.

The Meal Surrounding Our Celebration

- **Select where to conduct your Revelation Celebration.** A person's home is preferable, depending on the size of your group and their families. Conducting the celebration simultaneously at multiple sites is an option if you have a large group.

- **Select the date and time of your celebration.**

- **Decide on the meal.** Consider a potluck meal in which each family brings a dish. This time together is a time of feasting. Decide who in your group will bring what. As an object lesson you will need to have a large cluster of grapes at your celebration meal. Be sure that at least part of the cluster you use has a main vine clearly visible, from which numerous small bunches extend.

The Verbal Relay Process

Instructions: Prior to your celebration event write or type five labels to be placed on five small paper cups. The five labels should read, "Hyprochloric Acid," "Hygrochloric Acid," "Hylochloric Acid," "Hyfrochloric Acid," and "Hydrochloric Acid." Then put one candy mint in each cup. Also write or type the words "A Hyfrochloric Acid Pill" on a small slip of paper and fold it once to hide the wording. Then place the five cups on a tray and put the slip of paper in your pocket.

Presentation (familiarize yourself with this illustration so you don't need to read from the presentation):

Say: "**I need** _____ (name—choose a young person ten or older in your group) **and** _____ (name—an adult) **to help me.** _____ (name of young person), **you are a medical doctor with, among other things, this medication** (provide the tray with the five cups of mints).

"_____ (name of adult), **you have a fatal and rare disease called** '*melodrama fatalis*' **that can be cured by only one of these pills. I know the name of that pill and will pass it on to our fine doctor here through a verbal relay process.**" (Ask your young doctor to come to where you are standing). "**But I will relay the name of that all-important pill to** _____ (name of the person seated closest to you) **only once and ask him or her to whisper it to the person beside him or her only once. Then he or she must whisper it to the next and the next, each person saying it only once, until it is finally whispered to our fine doctor here. Now time is of the essence, so let's get this verbal relay going as quickly as possible. Remember, you can whisper what you hear only once. And of course, you cannot ask the previous person to repeat what was whispered—and we must move fast because our patient is dying.**"

(Whisper "Hyfrochloric Acid Pill" to the person next to you and get the relay going. Once the information has traveled around the table to the last person near you and your doctor, ask the person to whisper the pill's name to the doctor. Then facing your young doctor say:)

"**Now what is the word that was whispered in your ear?**" (After he or she has replied by repeating the word whispered to him or her, show your doctor friend the five labeled paper cups and have him or her again repeat the name he or she heard whispered. The name heard will undoubtedly be jumbled and unlike any of the specific labeled names. Say:) "**None of these pills match the name you said, so you must take a chance.**" (Let the doctor choose the cup bearing the name closest to what he or she heard. Then say:) "**Since this is your best guess as to the right pill, go ahead and take the chance; give this pill to our dying friend.**" (Ask the adult to eat the pill.

Then hand the folded slip of paper to the doctor from your pocket and ask him or her to read it. Then say:)

"**Does it match the pill** _____ (name of adult) **took?**" (It most likely won't. Even if it does, point out it was simply a shot in the dark and that it was an unlikely miracle the patient was saved. However, in all likelihood the right pill was not chosen. Say to the adult:) "**You are out of luck. You took the wrong pill, and so you must now 'pass away.'**" (The more the adult hams this up, the better. Then say:)

"**Let me ask all of you: What went wrong with this verbal relay process of getting the name of the cure to our expert doctor?**" (Let the group respond. All will agree the message got garbled in the process of transmission.)

"**Right. Doctor** _____ (name of young volunteer) **had no way to be sure he or she was giving poor** _____ (name of adult) **the correct remedy because the vital information he needed was distorted along the way. Without accurate, undistorted instructions, our dying patient couldn't experience the lifesaving power of that information.**

"**Now, what does this illustration tell us about those who copied the Bible by hand generation after generation?**" (Wait for a response. Lead the group to the conclusion that the words of Scripture had to be passed down accurately. Then say:)

"**That's right. If we are to read the exact lifesaving words God gave to those who first wrote them down, then those copying Scripture had to be careful to copy accurately, letter for letter, word for word.**"[1]

The emcee thanks the person for conducting the illustration and says: "**Now, to see how accurate the lifesaving message of the Bible is, let's have** _____ (name of adult) **read something very fascinating entitled 'God's Accurate Letters of Love.'**"

God's Accurate Letters of Love
(Make copies for everyone to read along.)

God spoke to men thousands of years ago and had them write down very important messages he wanted us to know. Because he loved us and wanted a relationship with us, he wanted us to know how we could get to know him. All of us as humans had sinned and were separated from him, so his Word was to become our instructions, or set of love letters from God, on how to come to know him personally.

Do we have an accurate set of love letters? Were the copies made of the original writings done accurately? Let's find out.

The Case of the Meticulous Scribes

Hand-copying of the Old Testament was the responsibility of a group of men who were trained as skilled scribes and gave their lives to writing. For many years before and after the time of Jesus it was their responsibility to copy Scripture. These particular scribes devoted themselves to making sure that the Holy Scriptures were copied letter for letter, word for word. Their rules for copying Scripture were so strict that when a copy was made it was considered to be an exact duplicate, just as if you had made it from a copy machine. When a copy was finished it was called a manuscript.

A scribe would begin his day of transcribing a manuscript by ceremonially washing his entire body. He would then robe himself in full Jewish dress before sitting down at his desk. As he wrote, if he came to the Hebrew name of God, he could not begin writing the name with a pen newly dipped in ink for fear it would smear the page. Once he began writing the name of God, he could not stop or allow himself to be distracted... even if a king were to enter the room. The scribe was obligated to continue without interruption until he finished penning the holy name of the one true God.

The Masoretic guidelines for copying manuscripts also required that

- the scroll be written on the skin of a clean animal.
- each skin contain a specified number of columns, equal throughout the entire book.
- the length of each column extend no less than 48 lines and no more than 60.
- the column breadth consist of exactly 30 letters.
- the space of a thread appear between every consonant.
- the breadth of nine consonants be inserted between each section.
- a space of three lines appear between each book.
- the fifth book of Moses (Deuteronomy) conclude exactly with a full line.

- nothing—not even the shortest word—be copied from memory, but rather be copied letter by letter.
- the scribe count the number of times each letter of the alphabet occurred in each book and compare it to the original.
- if a manuscript was found to contain even one mistake, it be discarded.[2]

God instilled in the Masoretes such a painstaking reverence for the Hebrew Scriptures in order to ensure the amazingly accurate transmission of the Bible, so you and I would have an accurate revelation of him.

The Case of the Accurate New Testament

The Hebrew scribes did not copy the manuscripts of the New Testament. So God did a new thing to ensure that the words of Jesus and his followers would be preserved accurately for us.

To tell if ancient manuscripts are reliable we 1) measure the time between the original writing and the first manuscript copy; and 2) determine how many manuscript copies are still in existence. The shorter the time between the original writing and the first copy and the more manuscripts there are, the more accurate the manuscripts are considered.

For example, virtually everything we know today about Julius Caesar's campaigns in Gaul comes from ten manuscript copies of *The Gallic Wars,* the earliest of which dates to just within 1000 years of the time it was originally written. The most reliable writing in secular history is Homer's *Iliad,* with 643 manuscripts, the earliest of which dates to within 400 years of the original writing.

Let's look at this chart of classical literature.[3]

Author	Book	Date written	Earliest copies	Time gap	Number of copies
Homer	*Iliad*	800 BC	c. 400 BC	c. 400 yrs.	643
Herodotus	*History*	480–425 BC	c. AD 900	c. 1350 yrs.	8
Thucydides	*History*	460–400 BC	c. AD 900	c. 1300 yrs.	8
Plato		400 BC	c. AD 900	c. 1300 yrs.	7
Demosthenes		300 BC	c. AD 1100	c. 1400 yrs.	200
Caesar	*Gallic Wars*	100–44 BC	c. AD 900	c. 1000 yrs.	10
Livy	*History of Rome*	59 BC–AD 17	fourth century (partial); mostly tenth century	c. 400 years c. 1000 years	1 partial 19 copies
Tacitus	*Annals*	AD 100	c. AD 1100	c. 1000 yrs.	20
Pliny Secundus	*Natural History*	AD 61–113	c. AD 850	c. 750 yrs.	7

The New Testament Has No Equal

Using this accepted standard for evaluating the reliability of ancient writings, the New Testament stands alone. It has no equal. No other book of the ancient world can even compare to the reliability of the New Testament. Take a look at this chart: [4]

Author	Book	Date written	Earliest copies	Time gap	Number of copies
John	New Testament	AD 50–100	c. AD 130	50-plus years	Fragments
The rest of the New Testament authors			c. AD 200 (books)	100 years	
			c. AD 250 (most of New Testament)	150 years	
			c. AD 325 (complete New Testament)	225 years	5600-plus Greek manuscripts
			c. AD 366–384 (Latin Vulgate translation)	284 years	
			c. AD 400–500 (other translations)	400 years	19,000-plus translated manuscripts
			TOTALS	50–400 years	24,600-plus manuscripts

There are nearly 25,000 manuscripts or fragments of manuscripts, with some dating back to within 50 years of the original writings. And none are more than 400 years newer than the originals. Incredible!

When you hold a Bible in your hand you can be sure it is the most accurate and reliable writing in all of history! God wanted you to be sure that the Bible you read is the accurate love letters he had written just for you.

From God's Heart to Yours

Instructions: Practice reading this presentation until you can read it with passion and feeling. It is designed to help those at your celebration capture God's heart for personal relationship.

Say:

"I am going to read something as though God is personally sharing his heart with us tonight."

I am the Alpha and the Omega, the beginning and the end. I am the one who is, who always was, and who is still to come, the Almighty One.

I am the infinite God who knows no boundaries or limitations. My power and knowledge and greatness are beyond your comprehension. My love and holiness and beauty are so intense that for you to see me in all my glory would overwhelm you—for as a mortal you could not see me and live. And yet…I created you to know me intimately, for I am passionate about my relationship with you.

But a relationship isn't complete unless the love cycle—each one of us knowing and being known—is completed. I want you to know that I know you, and I want you to know me.

I know everything there is to know about you. I know your favorite color, your favorite food, what music you like, the dreams you have, and the future you long for. I know your struggles and weaknesses. I am glad with you when you make right choices. I am saddened when you make wrong choices. I know you better than you know yourself, and…I love you.

But I want to ask you a question—not for my information, but for yours. Do you love me? I mean *really* love me? Be slow to answer; be sure before you speak. And before you do, let me tell you the secret to really loving me. To love me, you must come to know me. For to know me is to love me!

Learn of my mercy and my faithfulness, and you will love me. Come to know my goodness and holiness, and you will love me. Learn of my justice tempered with patience, and you will love me. Know what I love and what I hate, and you will love me. Know what saddens my heart and what gives me pleasure, and you will love me.

This is the way to have eternal life: to know me, the only true God. And the more you know me, the more you will become like me. The more you know me, the more you will praise and thank me and honor my name. And the more you know me, the more you will love others as I love them.

There are two ways to know me. The first is through my Holy Spirit. I have sent you my Spirit to live within you. Allow me to fill you with my Spirit. Make me at home in your heart. Speak to me often in your prayers. Confide your fears, your hopes, your dreams to me. Let me live my life through you. I am with you always, and I will never leave you.

The second way to know me is through the written revelation of me— my Holy Word, the collection of my love letters to you. Read my words, hide them in your heart, and know me for who I am—the one true God, your Savior, and your friend.

I long for you to communicate with me by opening your heart in prayer. As you hear the words of the following prayer, I urge you to make the prayer your own, and let the words come from your heart. Pray silently to me:

O God, you are great, but I know so little of your greatness. I know you are merciful and faithful and holy and just, but I really know so little of you.

I want to thank you for your Holy Spirit. I welcome you to be more and more at home in my heart. And I thank you for your Holy Word and for giving to me right now, this very moment, a longing to know you and a hunger to read your love letters to me.

I ask you to help me. Help me by giving me a desire to read your Word more often. As I read, help me to see you and know you in every page, so I can be like you. O God, let me honor you with my life. I sense you smiling at me right now. Thank you. Thank you for loving me. I love you too. Amen.[5]

Emcee: After a moment of silence, share from your own heart how you desire to know God more through his Spirit and his Word. Encourage others to share their desires to know God more. After a time of sharing, close in prayer.

Consider reading the prayer found at the close of your guidelines, on pages 458–459.

THE RESTORATION
CELEBRATION

*Permission is granted to the purchaser of this book to photocopy
this appendix for use in a family or group celebration activity.*
This material ©2010 Josh McDowell Ministry and Sean McDowell.

The Restoration Celebration is designed as a Judeo-Christian family event that includes a meal. You will engage your children and teenagers in a fun and rewarding time that celebrates the richness of our relationship with God through Christ here on earth, as well as illustrating that, while living here on earth is temporal, there is coming a day when a new and perfect heaven and earth will be our home for all eternity. The focus is on Jesus returning to give us our inheritance of newly restored bodies that last forever and a perfect world to live in.

This celebration is based on the Jewish holiday called the Feast of Tabernacles or Shelters (Booths). God commanded the children of Israel to live in makeshift shelters for seven days every year. "This will remind each new generation of Israelites that their ancestors had to live in shelters when I rescued them out of the land of Egypt. I, the Lord, am your God" (Leviticus 23:43).

For centuries, during the fall of the year, Jewish families have celebrated *Sukkot* (Hebrew, meaning "booth" or "hut"). For seven days they are to eat in their huts and "rejoice before the Lord your God" (Leviticus 23:40). As the seventh festival, it marks the completion of both the harvest season and the festival cycle. It therefore serves as a special time of celebrating the fullness of God's creative and redemptive work and, furthermore, the *rest* of God. It is to be a time to remember and reflect upon all God has done for us and give him glory. Yet the key significance of this festival is that it serves as a rehearsal and celebration of the future glory of God.

God gave the prophet Zechariah a vision of the coming Messiah, the restoration of Israel, and the restoration of all things. The prophet saw a time when "the Lord will be king over all the earth. On that day there will be one Lord—his name alone will be worshipped" (Zechariah 14:9). The apostle Paul spoke of a time in human history "that at the name of Jesus [the Messiah] every knee will bow, in heaven and on earth and under the earth, and every tongue will confess that Jesus Christ is Lord, to the glory of God the Father" (Philippians 2:10-11).

It is in this restoration context that Zechariah declares that "the survivors from all the nations that have attacked Jerusalem will go up year after year to worship the King, the LORD Almighty, and to celebrate the Festival of Tabernacles" (Zechariah 14:16 NIV). God had told his people "be joyful at your Feast…for the LORD your God will bless you in all your harvest and in all the work of your hands, and your joy will be complete" (Deuteronomy 16:14-15 NIV). But what Zechariah was no doubt pointing to was the ultimate joy made complete when all things would be restored to God's original design and "the tabernacle of God is among men, and He shall dwell among them" (Revelation 21:2 NASB).

At the final restoration of all things there will be no more struggling with this sin-cursed world or living in shabby huts. The prophet Isaiah declared this restoration promise of the Lord:

> I will preserve You and give You as a covenant to the people, to restore the earth, to cause them to inherit the desolate heritages (Isaiah 49 NKJV).

> "As the new heavens and the new earth that I make will endure before me," declares the LORD, "so will your name and descendants endure" (Isaiah 66:22 NIV).

> In that day he [God] will remove the gloom, the shadow of death that hangs over the earth. He will swallow up death forever! The Sovereign LORD will wipe away all tears. He will remove forever all insults and mocking against his land and people (Isaiah 25:7-8).

Your Restoration Celebration is a time to thank God not only for what he has done, but also for what he is going to do in the future: give you and your families new bodies that will never wear out and a perfect world to enjoy with him for all eternity. And, of course, Christ conquering sin and death on our behalf could not have happened without him both dying for us *and* rising from the dead. So your Restoration Celebration will include praising God for the bodily resurrection of his Son, Jesus Christ.

If you would like to learn more about the Feast of Tabernacles as well as other biblical feasts of the Lord and understand how they directly relate to your Christian faith, we encourage you to visit www.ariseinglory.org, the Web site of Harvey Diamond, a Jewish believer in Christ the Messiah. He has done a great job of unpacking the biblical festivals and relating them in the form of an interactive devotional, called "Pathways to Glory Relational Devotional." It provides various ways of relating with God in a manner that makes them especially relevant to the Christian life.

The Restoration Celebration is best done together with two or more families. Children from three years of age and up will enjoy and get something out of this mealtime event. Meet with the adults you are planning this with ahead of time to go over the details and assign responsibilities.

This celebration consists of five elements. Walk through each of these elements to practice and plan for your meal and the different readings. If your group is too large to fit into one home, plan to split up and conduct more than one celebration.

The five elements of your meal celebration do not include music. Your group may want to insert the singing of hymns or worship music at various times throughout the Celebration event.

1. **"Celebrating the God of Restoration."** Identify someone in your group who is willing to read this presentation, which explains what the Restoration Celebration is all about. The reading is found on pages 478–479, and you have permission to photocopy those pages and all the pages related to this celebration. You might ask the person to read the material aloud to the planning group for practice, using the photocopied pages. We encourage you to *read* these readings at the celebration meal, rather than casually relating the content. And in your planning you will want to discuss how elaborate you want your *sukkah* (temporary shelter) to be.

2. **"Death Had to Be Conquered."** Identify someone in your group willing to read this presentation and conduct the illustration (for which they will need to make preparations). Ask him or her to read the presentation aloud to your adults group now for practice, using a photocopy of pages 480–482 that you provide.

3. **The meal.** Identify someone willing to take the lead to coordinate the location of the Restoration Celebration (preferably someone's home), determine the time, decide what to eat, and so on. This person is not to do all the work. He or she is to work with the members of your family

group to coordinate the logistical details of the celebration, listed on page 483. Photocopy that page and provide it to the meal coordinator.

4. **"What We Treasure."** Identify someone within the group who is willing to read the presentation and facilitate discussion with your mealtime group. Photocopy pages 484–485 of this reading and provide them to the person willing to do this and ask him or her to do the reading now before your planning group for practice.

5. **"Why Say Hallelujah?"** Identify someone in your group who is willing to conclude the Restoration Celebration by facilitating discussion and directing those they will choose (preferably young people) to read what eternity will be like and then closing in prayer. The designated person can practice by reading the photocopies of pages 486–489.

Conducting the Restoration Celebration

After meeting with the families you plan to have the Restoration Celebration with, you are now ready to emcee your evening event and meal. Photocopy these pages as a reference guide to your celebration.

Note: Make sure that arrangements have been made to have the sukkah "built" and ready at the location of the celebration meal.

- *Prior to beginning the introduction:* Your group has brought "finger food" appetizers to the event. Prior to formally gathering around the table, invite people to sit under the sukkah and eat their finger food together. If your sukkah is small perhaps only two people at a time can eat under it together. While this is largely symbolic, you will make reference to it later in the evening.

- *Beginning the introduction:* Invite everyone to be seated at the table and say, **"Tonight we are going to have a celebration and _____ (name) is going to start us off"** ("Celebrating the God of Restoration").

- Immediately following that presentation ask the person responsible for "Death Had to Be Conquered" to make his or her presentation. *Note:* Announcement of the meal and prayer will be made by the person conducting this presentation.

- At the conclusion of the meal, thank all those who helped to prepare it. Then say, **"Now _____ (name) has something to share with us"** (presentation of "What We Treasure").

- After the "What We Treasure" presentation say: **"The imperfect things and everything that pleases neither God nor us are going to be destroyed. In their place will be a new and perfect world where all our dreams and hopes come true. And to end our evening just right, let's have _____ (name) lead us in an exercise"** ("Why Say Hallelujah?" presentation).

- After the "What We Treasure" presenter offers a prayer, consider closing your time in a praise song.

Celebrating the God of Restoration

Preparations/instructions: One of the key points of your celebration is to illustrate that life in this present world is temporal. This celebration is drawn from the Jewish Feast of Tabernacles, which is a reminder to the Jewish people that their ancestors lived in temporary shelters when God led them out of the desert and into the Promised Land (see Leviticus 23:43). The Restoration Celebration is a time to look forward to the new bodies and new home God is preparing for us. And in so doing, just like in the Jewish Feast of Tabernacles, a *sukkah* (temporary shelter) needs to be built.

Your sukkah doesn't have to be elaborate. It can be as simple as spreading a sheet over dining room chairs to create a makeshift tent. Or you can construct a little more substantial structure with cardboard boxes. Get your children involved and make it a fun experience. If you are conducting your celebration in warm weather consider using a tent or building a lean-to outside. Some of you could even sleep in your sukkah and make it a family time of fun.

The sukkah is important because it serves as a standing object lesson for your celebration. It reminds us that our lives and this present world and all we have are like a "mist that appears for a little while and then vanishes" (James 4:14 NIV). So when you do create your sukkah make sure it comes across as "temporary." If you are using cardboard, make holes in the top and sides that demonstrate it is in need of repair. If you build a lean-to outside leave holes in the roof so you can see the stars at night. Be sure that whatever you make, it is large enough that at least two people at a time can sit under it, because during your meal the emcee is going to ask at least two people at a time to eat in or under the sukkah.

Presentation: Read the following aloud.

> Tonight we are participating in a Restoration Celebration. We are gathering together like the children of Israel have gathered for centuries in celebration of the Feast of Tabernacles. They would live under a sukkah, or hut, for seven days to remind them that God led them from their temporary homes in the wilderness and into the Promised Land of Israel.
>
> We have our own version of a sukkah. If you haven't joined someone under the sukkah to share an appetizer, do it just prior to our meal. The sukkah is to remind us that all that we own and have on this earth is temporary—even our lives are temporary. But one day Jesus will return and make earth his home with all God's children—those who have been forgiven of their sins and have a relationship with God.
>
> But this world, our earth, and the stars and sky above us will be made new. Tonight we celebrate that while life here is temporary, Jesus will one day lead us out of this old world and give us a new one—a home

that will never grow old and decay. John, a disciple of Jesus, saw a vision of that time in our future. He saw God's home, heaven, coming down to our new earth. The Bible says:

> Look, the home of God is now among his people! He will live with them, and they will be his people. God himself will be with them. He will remove all of their sorrows, and there will be no more death or sorrow or crying or pain. For the old world and its evils are gone forever (Revelation 21:3-4).

We will have new homes that won't grow old and deteriorate. We will have new bodies too, ones that will never die. Our friends and family who have died and have trusted in Jesus will be raised to life and will live with us. Our new bodies won't suffer pain or get old or wear out. The Bible says:

> Our bodies now disappoint us, but when they are raised, they will be full of glory. They are weak now, but when they are raised, they will be full of power. They are natural bodies now, but when they are raised, they will be spiritual bodies...Every human being has an earthly body just like Adam's, but our heavenly bodies will be just like Christ's (1 Corinthians 15:43-44,48).

Our God is the God of Restoration. He will one day restore this earth back to the paradise it once was. He will restore our bodies to what he originally designed.

So tonight we will celebrate what God has said will come to pass. Tonight we will contrast the imperfect now (point to the sukkah) with the perfect to come. We will look at what is and be reminded of what will be. Tonight is our Restoration Celebration.

Death Had to Be Conquered

Preparations/instructions: To prepare for this illustration you will need duct tape and a makeshift "tomb." You will be illustrating how a body was prepared for burial in a tomb. The duct tape will be used to wrap around a volunteer's legs. You can use your sukkah as a "tomb" if it is small and you're not eating under it outside. Otherwise, use six chairs. Place one across at the top and two on each side to form a rectangular space on the floor for your volunteer to lie down in, as if in a tomb. The sixth chair is the "stone door" at the entrance.

Once you have your "tomb" assembled, choose a volunteer—preferably a young person at least seven years old. *Note:* Feel free to read the following presentation or make the words your own.

Presentation: Begin your illustration by saying something like:

"Jesus said he would return to give us new bodies and a new world. But something very important had to happen before he could fulfill his promise. In fact, our entire salvation depended upon it. He had to rise from the dead.

"Jesus was crucified and buried in a tomb. And unless he was truly the Son of God and rose from the dead, he couldn't fulfill his promise to give us eternal life in a perfect world.

"Some people say Jesus didn't rise from the dead. They don't believe he was the Son of God, and they don't believe a person can have eternal life. What they say is that Jesus really didn't die on the cross, but passed out and then revived once he was buried in the tomb. They say that, just like any other mortal, he grew to old age and died. But never rose from the grave.

"Well, tonight in our Restoration Celebration we want to increase our confidence that Jesus did in fact die and then, as God's Son, overcame death, rose again, and is returning to earth to restore all things to perfection.

"I've asked _____ (name of volunteer) to help me with something." (Ask the young person to come up and sit on the chair that will act as the "stone door" in front of the "tomb.")

"The Bible tells us that just before Jesus was taken out and crucified on a cross, he was beaten very badly. He lost a lot of blood. He then had a crown of thorns pressed down into his head. He was made to carry the heavy cross to the place of crucifixion. He was so weak he couldn't even carry the cross all the way. Then he was nailed to the cross by his hands and feet. When he cried out and died, a soldier speared him in the side to make sure he was dead. So when his disciples took Jesus down from the cross to bury him, he was really dead.

"In those days people would carefully prepare a body before placing it in a tomb. What they would do is put about 75 pounds of embalming ointment and spices on the body, then wrap it tight with linen cloth to form a mummy. This is all explained in John 19:39-40.

"Now what I'm going to do is wrap _____ (name) **with this duct tape only on the legs.**" (Have volunteer sit down and begin at his or her ankles; with his or her feet together, wrap around and around up to mid-calf. Make it tight, but not so tight as to cut off circulation.) **"Now imagine if** _____ (name) **were wrapped tight like this all the way to** (his or her) **neck. After Jesus' disciples wrapped him with the 75 pounds of ointment, it hardened like cement. So Jesus was wrapped solidly, with his legs and arms encased in the wrappings.**

"**Now,** _____ (name) **I'd like you to scoot between the chairs (or in the sukkah) and we are going to imagine this is the tomb Jesus was placed in.**" (Take hold of the chair just used by your volunteer.) **"Now this chair represents the tomb door. I'm going to place it in front of the 'tomb.' The stone in front of Jesus' tomb probably weighed one to two tons. It had to be rolled up a slotted incline by several men, and then it fell into a groove. It could only be opened from the outside.**" (Place chair in front of the sukkah or other chairs.)

"**So there Jesus was, encased in 75 pounds of hardened spices, wrapped like a mummy, and sealed in a tomb by a stone that weighed at least one ton. Now here's what some say who think Jesus was just a normal man who never really rose from the dead. They say Jesus swooned—fainted—on the cross and just passed out. And then three days in the cold, damp tomb revived him.**

"**Now remember, Jesus was beaten half to death and didn't have enough strength to even carry his own cross. He was nailed to the cross, and once he died, a soldier speared his side and as the Bible says, 'blood and water flowed out' (John 19:34). So now the cold, damp tomb revived him and he just wiggled his way out of his tight wrapping?**

"_____ (name of volunteer), **why don't you try to wiggle the wrappings off your feet. You can't use your hands, because if you were in the same situation as Jesus your hands would be strapped to your side. You can't sit up either, because you would be encased in a solid mummy suit. Just try and shake your wrappings off your feet.**" (It will be impossible for your volunteer to do it. So continue.)

"**But for argument's sake, let's assume you did revive and were able to stand up in your mummy suit.**" (Help your volunteer to his or her feet, but keep him or her within the chairs or sukkah. Then sit on the chair that is acting as your "tomb door.")

"**Now,** _____ (name), **keep your hands to your sides, hop over here, and try to move this 'one-ton tomb door' out of the way.**" (Again, your volunteer will be unable to move the chair by simply bumping it with his or her body.)

"**Well, it's clear here that it stretches the imagination to think that Jesus could** even survive his crucifixion, let alone break out of his grave clothes and somehow move a one-ton stone door from inside the tomb. The reality is, Jesus was the Son of God who died for us and rose again from the grave because he was and is God. And he is returning again to give us perfect bodies that will live forever in a perfect world.

"So tonight we are going to have a Restoration Celebration. Jesus died for us, rose again, and is coming back to give us new bodies and a new world. And how do we celebrate? For one, by feasting!" (If you decide to sing, say:) "by singing and feasting." (Then lead in a song and offer the following prayer:)

> O God, we celebrate your resurrection and your return to earth. And as we partake of this food, bless it so that it might strengthen us to praise and honor you as we look toward your return. Amen.

Note: If anyone has not yet eaten under the sukkah, invite them to have their appetizer there.

Serve the meal.

Preparing for Your Celebration Meal

- **Select where to conduct your Restoration Celebration.** A person's home is preferable, depending on the size of your group and their families. Conducting the celebration simultaneously at multiple sites is an option if you have a very large group.

- **Select the date and time of your celebration.**

- **Decide on the meal.** Consider a potluck meal in which each family brings a dish. This time together is a time of feasting. Decide who in your group will bring what food. Be sure to bring some "finger food" that can be used to eat under your sukkah—food that cannot be spilled or soil the floor.

What We Treasure

Preparation/instructions: In advance, ask an adult to be your "scribe" and write down the various dislikes that your group identifies. Also, you will need a frying pan, some lighter fluid, and matches. At the end of your presentation you will place the paper that your "scribe" writes on in the pan, dowse it with lighter fluid, and set it aflame.

Presentation: Explain to the group that you want to read a short reading aloud and then brainstorm with them what they dislike about this imperfect world and what they are going to like about the perfect world God has promised us.

Read this aloud:

"Jesus said, 'Don't store up treasures here on earth, where they can be eaten by moths and get rusty and where thieves break in and steal' (Matthew 6:19).

"Our sukkah represents everything that gets old and rusty. While we can eat under it, it won't last, and neither will anything in this present world. That is why Jesus went on to say: 'Store your treasures in heaven, where they will never become moth-eaten or rusty and where they will be safe from thieves' (Matthew 6:20).

"We store up treasures in heaven when we love God with all our hearts and our strength and our minds and love those around us like we love ourselves."

(Ask:) "What does loving God and others like ourselves look like?" (Get a response from group—for example, praying to God, reading his Word, various expressions of care and love for others, and so on.)

(Continue:) "We store up treasures in heaven when we specifically obey God's Word and make choices that please him."

(Ask:) "What does obeying God's Word look like?" (Get a response from group—for example, not lying, cheating, stealing, when we obey parents, do not swear, do not get drunk, when we stay away from bad influences, and so on.)

(Continue:) "We store up treasures in heaven when we refuse to follow our self-ish wants and desires and instead do good to others."

(Ask:) "What does denying our selfish desires and doing good to others look like?" (Get response from group—for example, doing homework instead of _____, cleaning our rooms instead of _____, doing good for a father, mother, sister, brother, friend, even an enemy, instead of _____, and so on.)

(Then say something like:) "Our Restoration Celebration is a reminder to store up treasures in heaven that will last, rather than in this world, which will not last. So let's do this. Let's make a list of the things you really don't like—things you don't want to last. And we'll write them down. But let's also name the good things we want to last—**things you want to be around you and with you in heaven."** (You can ask for one category at a time or alternate between what we don't like and what we do like.)

(But be sure to have your "scribe" write the things down that your group doesn't like. Things might be mentioned like: "I don't like homework, doing dishes, getting tired, crying, pain, breakups, accidents, crime, war, earthquakes, storms, growing old, forgetting, dying, and so on. Then ask:)

"What do we like?" (You need not write these down. But these things might include beautiful sunsets, ice cream, laughter, singing/music, various types of food, pretty clothes, to feel loved, to always have energy and strength—to never get tired, to be with loved ones who have passed away, and so on.)

Once you have completed the exercise: Take the list of what the group has said they didn't like and place it in the pan. Set the pan on the table. Sprinkle some lighter fluid on it and say:

"I'm going to ask _____ (name of adult or older young person) **to light the paper that represents all the things of this world we don't like. And as** (he or she) **lights it I want to read you these verses from the disciple Peter.**

> **Since everything around us is going to melt away, what holy, godly lives you should be living! You should look forward to that day and hurry it along—the day when God will set the heavens on fire and the elements will melt away in the flames. But we are looking forward to the new heavens and new earth he has promised, a world where everyone is right with God. And so, dear friends, while you are waiting for these things to happen, make every effort to live a pure and blameless life. And be at peace with God (2 Peter 3:11-14)."**

The emcee comments on this illustration and introduces the "Why Say Hallelujah?" presentation.

Why Say Hallelujah?

Preparations/instructions: At the end of this short reading there are five readings to be done by volunteers you select. Photocopy these pages, cut the readings out, and distribute them to some in your group prior to your meal. Involve as many young people in this exercise as possible.

These readings are cause for celebration, so you will ask the group to energetically shout "Hallelujah" at the end of each reading. Have the readings done in numeric order, 1 through 5.

Read aloud:

"We want to close out our Restoration Celebration in praise. And there is a biblical word that means praise and thanksgiving. John the apostle heard it used repeatedly in heaven. It is the word 'Hallelujah.'

"John said:

> I heard the sound of a vast crowd in heaven shouting, "Hallelujah! Salvation is from our God. Glory and power belongs to him alone…" And from the throne came a voice that said, "Praise our God, all his servants, from the least to the greatest, all who fear him." Then I heard again what sounded like the shout of a huge crowd, or the roar of the mighty ocean waves, or the crash of loud thunder: "Hallelujah! For the Lord our God, the Almighty, reigns. Let us be glad and rejoice and honor him" (Revelation 19:1-2,5-7).

"So to wrap up our celebration I have asked a number of people to read something. And after they finish I will say 'And all the people said…' and all of us will shout out the praise word *Hallelujah!* Let's practice. 'And all the people said…' (Prompt the group, if needed, to shout "Hallelujah!")

Nod to the person you gave Reading #1 to indicate that he or she is to read it aloud.

Reading #1

We have cried. We have suffered. We have been disappointed with others and in ourselves. Some of our loved ones have even died. *But there is coming a day when all will be restored*—a day when, as Revelation 21 says, "the home of God is now among his people! He will live with them and they will be his people…He will remove all of their sorrows, and there will be no more death or sorrow or crying or pain. For the old world and its evils are gone forever." [No need to read aloud the full Bible reference of Revelation 21:3-4.]

Say: "**And all the people said…**" Group shouts "Hallelujah!"
Then nod to the person who is to read Reading #2.

Reading #2

We work. We sweat. We get tired. We run and get out of breath. We grow old and wear out. *But there is coming a day when all will be restored*—a day when Isaiah 40 will be perfectly fulfilled. For it says: "Those who wait for the LORD will gain new strength; they will mount up with wings like eagles, they will run and not get tired, they will walk and not become weary." [No need to read aloud the full Bible reference of Isaiah 40:31 NASB.]

Say: "**And all the people said…**" Group shouts "Hallelujah!"
Then nod to the person who is to read Reading #3.

Reading #3

We fear we won't be accepted. We fear we won't get a good enough job. We fear things in our future. We may even fear the dark. *But there is coming a day when all will be restored*—a day when all our fears are gone. As 1 John 4 points out, "we will not be afraid on the day of judgment, but we can face [the Lord] with confidence…Such love has no fear because perfect love expels all fear." [No need to read aloud the full Bible reference of 1 John 4:17-18.]

Say: **"And all the people said…"** Group shouts "Hallelujah!"
Then nod to the person who is to read Reading #4.

Reading #4

There are wars and rumors of wars. People fight for power. People fight for wealth. People fight for houses and land. Our world of sin has known no peace. *But there is coming a day when all will be restored*—a day when King Jesus will bring everlasting peace. As Isaiah 9 says, he is called the "Wonderful Counselor, Mighty God, Everlasting Father, Prince of Peace. His ever-expanding, peaceful government will never end." [No need to read aloud the full Bible reference of Isaiah 9:6-7.]

Say: **"And all the people said…"** Group shouts "Hallelujah!"
Then nod to the person who is to read Reading #5.

Reading #5

We have had dreams. We have had desires. We have had hope. Many have not been fulfilled. We have had to live with disappointments small and large. *But there is coming a day when all will be restored*—a day when every dream and hope and desire will be fulfilled. As King David said in Psalm 37, "Take delight in the LORD, and he will give you your heart's desires." [No need to read aloud the full Bible reference of Psalm 37:4.]

Say: **"And all the people said…"** Group shouts "Hallelujah!"

(Then say:) **"Let's close with this prayer.**

"O God, you are the God of Restoration. Everything you created was good. Yet sin has brought ruin to your human creation and to the perfect world you personally crafted. And tonight we celebrate your miraculous and merciful plan to restore all things to your original design.

"What we now see and hear and taste and touch is temporal; it will not last. You have told us in your Word to 'let heaven fill [our] thoughts. Do not think only about things down here on earth.' Help us to always remember that. Life is like a mist that vanishes quickly. But when you return you will make our life eternal in a perfect world. As 1 Corinthians says, 'Now we see things imperfectly as in a poor mirror, but then we will see everything with perfect clarity. All that [we] know now is partial and incomplete, but then [we] will know everything completely, just as God knows [us] now.' Thank you, King Jesus. We welcome your return. Hallelujah and amen."

Note: Consider closing your time in a praise song.

NOTES

Chapter One—What We All Want out of Life

1. Geoffrey Cowley, "The Science of Happiness," *Newsweek*, September 12, 2002, 48.
2. J.P. Moreland and Klaus Issler, *The Lost Virtue of Happiness* (Colorado Springs, CO: NavPress, 2006), 17.
3. J.P. Moreland, *Love Your God with All Your Mind* (Colorado Springs, CO: NavPress, 1997), 81-82.
4. Josh McDowell and David H. Bellis, *Last Christian Generation* (Holiday, FL: Green Key Books, 2006), 11-3.
5. David Kinnaman and Gabe Lyons, *unChristian* (Grand Rapids, MI: Baker Books, 2007), 74.
6. Pew Research Center Study as cited in "Generation Gap Is Widest Since 1960s," Associated Press article reported by Hope Yen, *Akron (Ohio) Beacon Journal*, 29 June 2009.
7. Christian Smith, *Soul Searching: The Religious and Spiritual Lives of American Teenagers* (New York, NY: Oxford University Press, 2005), 41-45, 74.
8. See Neil Gross and Solon Simmons, "How Religious Are America's College and University Professors?" available online at http://religion.ssrc.org/reforum/Gross_Simmons.pdf.
9. Jeff Myers, *Handoff* (Dayton, TN: Legacy Worldwide, 2008), 35-36.
10. Ibid., 34.
11. Ron Sider, *The Scandal of the Evangelical Conscience* (Grand Rapids, MI: Baker, 2005), 128.
12. Smith, 89.
13. Myers, 24.

Chapter Two—Twelve Truths That Define the Christian Faith

1. Barna Research Group, Barna.org Web site article #264, "Many Churchgoers and Faith Leaders Struggle to Define Spiritual Maturity" (Ventura, CA: The Barna Research Group, Ltd., 2008), 1, 3.
2. Chuck Colson, *The Faith* (Grand Rapids, MI: Zondervan, 2008), 28.

3. Alan Hirsch, *The Forgotten Ways* (Grand Rapids, MI: Brazos Press, 2006), 18.

Chapter Three—The Real Meaning of Truth

1. Adapted from Josh McDowell, Bob Hostetler, and David H. Bellis, *Beyond Belief to Convictions* (Wheaton, IL: Tyndale House Publishers, 2002), 52-53.

2. "Hardwired to Connect: The New Scientific Case for Authoritative Communities," The Commission on Children at Risk, 2003.

3. As quoted by Sean McDowell, *Apologetics for a New Generation* (Eugene, OR: Harvest House Publishers, 2009), 142.

4. J.P. Moreland, *Love Your God with All Your Mind* (Colorado Springs, CO: NavPress, 1997), 25.

Chapter Four—Who Is God?

1. Wikipedia, article: "Age and Size of the Universe" at www.en.wikipedia.org/wiki/universe, 2009.

2. As explained in the film production "Ants! Nature's Secret Power" produced for the Science Channel by ADI Mayer Film and OMF in association with Docstar DWRBM: BWK © 2004.

3. Wikipedia, article: "The Brain" at www.en.wikipedia.org/wiki/brain, 2009.

4. Wikipedia, article: "Pantheism" at www.en.wikipedia.org/wiki/pantheism, 2009.

5. Christian Smith, *Soul Searching: The Religious and Spiritual Lives of American Teenagers* (New York, NY: Oxford University Press, 2005), 41-42.

6. Wikipedia, article: "Overview of Deism" at www.en.wikipedia.org/wiki/deism, 2009.

7. Smith, 41-42.

Chapter Five—Evidence for God's Existence

1. Frank Turek, "The Cosmological Argument," *Apologetics Study Bible for Students,* Sean McDowell, gen. ed. (Nashville, TN: Broadman and Holman Publishers, 2009). Turek is quoting from Norman L. Geisler and Frank Turek, *I Don't Have Enough Faith to Be an Atheist* (Wheaton IL: Crossway Books, 2004).

2. William Lane Craig interviewed by Lee Strobel, *The Case for a Creator* (Grand Rapids, MI: Zondervan, 2004), 109.

3. William A. Dembski and Sean McDowell, *Understanding Intelligent Design* (Eugene, OR: Harvest House Publishers, 2008), 122-123.

4. Hill Roberts and Mark Whorton, *Holman QuickSource Guide to Understanding Creation* (Nashville: B & H Publishing, 2008), 323.

5. Ibid., 109-110.

6. Ibid., 133-134.

7. Sean McDowell, *Ethix* (Nashville, TN: Broadman & Holman Publishers, 2006), 49-50; embedded citation from Fyodor Dostoyevsky, *The Brothers Karamazov* (New York, NY: Bantam Books, 1970), 95.

8. Ibid., 161-162.

9. Bertrand Russell, *Why I Am Not a Christian* (New York, NY: Simon & Schuster, 1957), 107.

10. Adapted from Josh McDowell and Thomas Williams, *In Search of Certainty* (Wheaton, IL: Tyndale House Publishers, 2003), 66.

Chapter Six—Discovering Your Identity

1. Charles W. Colson, *The Faith* (Grand Rapids, MI: Zondervan, 2008), 171.

2. Charles Caldwell Ryrie, ed., *Ryrie Study Bible* (Chicago, IL: Moody Press, 1976), 25.

Chapter Eight—Why God Gave Us His Words

1. Adapted from Josh McDowell, Bob Hostetler, David H. Bellis, *Beyond Belief to Convictions* (Wheaton, IL: Tyndale House Publishers, 2002), 157-158, 163-165; and www.seanmcdowell.org.

Chapter Nine—Evidence That God's Word Is Reliable

1. Adapted from Josh McDowell, Bob Hostetler, David H. Bellis, *Beyond Belief to Convictions* (Wheaton, IL: Tyndale House Publishers, 2002), 166-178; and www.seanmcdowell.org.

2. Josh McDowell, *The New Evidence That Demands a Verdict* (Nashville, TN: Nelson, 1999), 74.

3. Ibid., 78.

4. Ibid., 79.

5. Adapted from McDowell, *New Evidence,* chart, 38.

6. Ibid.

7. Ibid., 38-39.

8. United Bible Society, "2008 Global Summary of Scripture Distribution by Bible Societies." See www.biblesociety.org/index.php?id=21.

9. United Bible Society, "2008 Global Scripture Translation as of December 31, 2008." See www .biblesociety.org/index.php?id=22.

10. Adapted from McDowell, Hostetler, Bellis, 167-169, 176-179.

11. Sean McDowell, "Bones and Dirt," *Apologetics Study Bible for Students,* Sean McDowell, gen. ed. (Nashville, TN: Broadman & Holman Publishers, 2009).

Chapter Ten—The Protection and Provision of God's Word

1. Adapted from Josh McDowell, Bob Hostetler, and David H. Bellis, *Beyond Belief to Convictions* (Wheaton, IL: Tyndale House Publishers, 2002), 11-12.

2. Paul Copan, *True for You, but Not for Me* (Minneapolis, MN: Bethany House Publishers, 1998), 17.

3. Adapted from Sean McDowell, *Ethix: Being Bold in a Whatever World* (Nashville, TN: Broadman & Holman Publishers, 2006), 41.

4. This chapter is adapted from chapters 6 and 7 of Josh McDowell and Bob Hostetler, *Right from Wrong* (Nashville, TN: Word Publishing, 1994).

5. Bill Hybels, *Laws That Liberate* (Wheaton, IL: Victor Books, 1985), 10.

6. S.I. McMillen, *None of These Diseases* (Westwood, NJ: Spire Books, 1968), from the Preface.

Chapter Eleven—Living Under God's Protection and Enjoying His Provisions

1. This chapter is adapted from chapters 10 and 11 of Josh McDowell and Bob Hostetler, *Right from Wrong* (Nashville, TN: Word Publishing, 1994).

2. Caitlin Flanagan, "Why Marriage Matters," *Time* magazine, July 13, 2009, 47.

3. Ibid., 47.

Chapter Twelve—The First Broken Relationship

1. Adapted from Josh McDowell and Thomas Williams, *The Relational Word* (Holiday, FL: Green Key Books, 2006), 21-24.

2. Aldous Huxley, "Confessions of a Professed Atheist," *Report: Perspective on the News,* vol. 3 (June 1966), 19.

3. Christian Smith, *Soul Searching: The Religious and Spiritual Lives of American Teenagers* (New York, NY: Oxford University Press, 2005), 165.

4. Ibid., 163.

Chapter Thirteen—Evidence That Sin Has Consequences

1. *Akron (Ohio) Beacon Journal,* November 11, 2009, A1, A4, A5, B2, B3.

Chapter Fourteen—Choosing Right from Wrong

1. Adapted from Josh McDowell and Thomas Williams, *The Relational Word* (Holiday, FL: Green Key Books, 2006), 24-25.

Chapter Seventeen—Evidence that God Became Human to Redeem Us

1. C.S. Lewis, *Mere Christianity* (New York, NY: Macmillan, 1960), 40-41.

2. Diagram drawn from Josh McDowell, *The New Evidence That Demands a Verdict* (Nashville, TN: Thomas Nelson Publishers, 1999), 158.

3. William E. Lecky, *History of European Morals from Augustus to Charlemagne* (New York, NY: D. Appleton, 1903), 2:8-9.

4. Clark H. Pinnock, *Set Forth Your Case* (Nutley, NJ: Craig Press, 1967), 62.

5. Gary R. Collins, quoted in Lee Strobel, *The Case for Christ* (Grand Rapids, MI: Zondervan, 1998), 147.

6. Dan Brown, *The Da Vinci Code* (New York, NY: Doubleday, 2003), 233.

7. James A. Kleist, *The Epistles of St. Clement of Rome and St. Ignatius of Antioch,* "To the Ephesians" (Ramsey, NJ: Paulist Press, 1978).

8. Alexander Roberts, *First Apology, the Ante-Nicene Fathers,* vol. 1 (Grand Rapids, MI: Eerdmans, 1993), 184.

9. Joseph P. Smith, *St. Irenaeus: Proof of the Apostolic Preaching* (Ramsey, NJ: Paulist Press, 1978), chapter 47.

10. Pliny, *Letters and Panegyricus,* tr. Betty Radice, Loeb Classical Library (Cambridge, MA: Harvard University Press, 1969): 10.96 (2. 289).

11. J. Ed Komoszewski, M. James Sawyer, Daniel B. Wallace, *Reinventing Jesus* (Grand Rapids, MI: Kregel, 2006), 215.

12. Drawn from Josh McDowell and Sean McDowell, *More Than a Carpenter* (Wheaton, IL: Tyndale House Publishers, 2009), 30-39.

13. Origen, *Contra Celsum,* tr. Henry Chadwick (Cambridge, England: Cambridge University Press, 1980), 32.

14. Adapted from chapter 4 of Josh McDowell, Bob Hostetler, David H. Bellis, *Beyond Belief to Convictions* (Wheaton, IL: Tyndale House Publishers, 2002), 68-71.

Chapter Eighteen—What God's Unconditional Acceptance Produces

1. Gloria Gaither and William J. Gaither, "I Am Loved" (Nashville, TN: William J. Gaither, Inc., 1978), CCLI14019.

2. Drawn from chapter 5 of Josh McDowell, Bob Hostetler, David H. Bellis, *Beyond Belief to Convictions* (Wheaton, IL: Tyndale House Publishers, 2002), 92-93.

Chapter Nineteen—How to Accept Others as God Accepts Us

1. Drawn from David and Teresa Ferguson, *Never Alone* (Wheaton, IL: Tyndale House Publishers, 2001), 87-88.

2. Drawn from Josh McDowell, Bob Hostetler, David H. Bellis, *Beyond Belief to Convictions* (Wheaton, IL: Tyndale House Publishers, 2002), 147-149.

Chapter Twenty-One—Evidence That Jesus Was God's Perfect Sacrifice

1. Messianic prophecies section adapted from chapter 4 of Josh McDowell, Bob Hostetler, David H. Bellis, *Beyond Belief to Convictions* (Wheaton, IL: Tyndale House Publishers, 2002), 63-68.

2. For a detailed treatment of this prophecy, see Josh McDowell, *The New Evidence That Demands a Verdict* (Nashville: Thomas Nelson Publishers, 1999), 195-201.

3. Peter W. Stoner and Robert C. Newman, *Science Speaks* (Chicago: Moody Press, 1976), 107.

4. Ibid.

Chapter Twenty-Two—The True Meaning of Love

1. Charles Wesley (1707–1788), Robert K. Brown and Mark R. Norton, compilers, *The One Year Book of Hymns* (Wheaton, IL: Tyndale House Publishers, 1995), March 29.

Chapter Twenty-Three—How to Love Others as God Loves Us

1. Max Lucado, *3:16: The Numbers of Hope* (Nashville, TN: Thomas Nelson Publishers, 2007), 42.

2. Charles W. Colson, *The Faith* (Grand Rapids, MI: Zondervan, 2008), 164-165.

3. Jeff Myers, *Handoff* (Dayton, TN: Legacy Worldwide, 2008), 128.

Chapter Twenty-Five—Evidence That Christ Has the Power to Save Us

1. Drawn from Bascom Palmer Eye Institute, *Cataracts*, www.bpei.med.miami.edu/site/disease/disease_cataracts.asp (2009).

2. Drawn from Josh McDowell, Bob Hostetler, David H. Bellis, *Beyond Belief to Convictions* (Wheaton, IL: Tyndale House Publishers, 2002), 71-76.

Chapter Twenty-Six—The Joy of Salvation

1. Adapted from Josh McDowell, Sean McDowell, *More Than a Carpenter* (Wheaton, IL: Tyndale House Publishers, 2005), 160-165.

Chapter Twenty-Eight—Understanding Your Purpose

1. Adapted from Wikipedia, article "Caterpillar," www.wikipedia.org/wiki/caterpillar#behavior.

Chapter Twenty-Nine—Evidences of a Changed Life

1. Drawn from Jeffrey A. Bogue, *Living Naked* (Akron, OH: Living Naked Press, 2009), 123-126.
2. Drawn from Francis Collins, *The Language of God* (New York, NY: Free Press, 2006), 19-20.
3. Drawn from Jeffrey A. Bogue, *Living Naked* (Akron, OH: Living Naked Press, 2009), 42-44, 45-48.

Chapter Thirty—Seeing Yourself as God Sees You

1. Part of this list is adapted from Neil T. Anderson, *Victory Over the Darkness* (Ventura, CA: Regal Books, 1990), pp. 45-47, 57-59.
2. Adapted from Josh McDowell, *See Yourself as God Sees You* (Wheaton, IL: Tyndale House Publishers, 1999), 110-120.

Chapter Thirty-Two—The Historical Necessity of Christ's Resurrection

1. Gerd Lüdemann, *What Really Happened to Jesus: A Historical Approach to the Resurrection,* tr. John Bowden (Louisville, KY: Westminster John Knox Press, 1995), 1.

Chapter Thirty-Three—Evidence That Jesus Literally Rose from the Dead

1. Stephen T. Davis, *Risen Indeed* (Grand Rapids, MI: Eerdmans, 1993), 79-80.
2. Paul L. Maier, "The Empty Tomb as History," *Christianity Today,* March 28, 1975, p. 5.
3. Paul L. Maier, *First Easter* (New York, NY: Harper and Row, 1973), 98.
4. George Hanson, *The Resurrection and the Life* (London, England: William Clowes & Son, 1911), 24.
5. John Dominic Crossan, *Jesus: A Revolutionary Biography* (San Francisco, CA: Harper Collins, 1991), 145.
6. David Friedrich Strauss, *The Life of Jesus for People,* 2nd ed., vol. 1 (London, England: William & Norgate, 1879), 412.
7. C.H. Dodd, "The Appearances of the Risen Christ: A Study in the Form Criticism of the Gospels," in *More New Testament Studies* (Manchester, UK: University of Manchester Press, 1968), 128.
8. William Lane Craig, *The Son Rises* (Eugene, OR: Wipf and Stock Publishers, 2000), 94-95.
9. Drawn from Josh McDowell and Sean McDowell, *Evidence for the Resurrection* (Venture, CA: Regal Publishing, 2009), 195-196.
10. Adapted from Josh McDowell, Bob Hostetler, David H. Bellis, *Beyond Belief to Convictions* (Wheaton, IL: Tyndale House Publishers, 2002), 261-270.
11. As quoted in Lee Strobel, *The Case for the Real Jesus* (Grand Rapids, MI: Zondervan, 1998), 146.
12. Drawn from Josh McDowell, Sean McDowell, *More Than a Carpenter* (Wheaton, IL: Tyndale House Publishers, 2005), 134-135.
13. Drawn from McDowell, Hostetler, Bellis, 271-273.
14. Dan Cohn-Sherbok, "The Resurrection of Jesus: A Jewish View," in *Resurrection Reconsidered,* Gavin D'Costa, gen. ed. (Oxford, UK: Oneworld Publications, 1996), 200.
15. N.T. Wright, "Christian Origins and the Resurrection of Jesus: The Resurrection as a Historical Problem," *Sewanee Theological Review,* vol. 41:2 (Easter 1998), 111, emphasis added.
16. N.T. Wright, "The Transforming Reality of the Bodily Resurrection," in *The Meaning of Jesus: Two Visions* by N.T. Wright and Marcus Borg (New York: NY, HarperCollins Publishers, 1999), 115.

17. Michael Licona, "Paul on the Nature of the Resurrection Body," in *Buried Hope or Risen Savior: The Search for the Jesus Tomb,* ed. Charles L. Quarles (Nashville, TN: B&H Academic, 2008), 177-198.

18. Stephen T. Davis, *Risen Indeed* (Grand Rapids, MI: Eerdmans, 1993), 56.

19. Norman I. Geisler, *Baker Encyclopedia of Christian Apologetics* (Grand Rapids, MI: Baker Books, 1999), 662.

20. Drawn from McDowell and McDowell, *Evidence for the Resurrection,* 204-206.

21. Paul Rhodes Eddy and Gregory A. Boyd, *The Jesus Legend* (Grand Rapids, MI: Baker Books, 2007), 142.

22. T.N.D. Mettinger, *The Riddle of Resurrection: "Dying and Rising Gods" in the Ancient Near East* (Stockholm: Almqvist and Wiksell, 2001), 221.

23. McDowell and McDowell, *Evidence for the Resurrection,* 232-233.

Chapter Thirty-Four—Overcoming the Fear of Death

1. Drawn from Josh McDowell, Sean McDowell, *Evidence for the Resurrection* (Ventura, CA: Regal Publishing, 2009), 57-58.

2. Randy Alcorn, *Heaven* (Wheaton, IL: Tyndale House Publishers, 2004), 57.

3. Drawn from McDowell and McDowell, *Evidence for the Resurrection,* 64-66.

Chapter Thirty-Five—Living Bodily on Earth with Our Hearts in Heaven

1. C.S. Lewis, *Mere Christianity* (New York, NY: Collier Books, 1960), 118.

2. Max Lucado, *When God Whispers Your Name* (Dallas, TX: Word Publishing, 1994), 101.

3. Calvin Miller, *Into the Depths of God* (Minneapolis, MN: Bethany House Publishers, 2000), 15.

Chapter Thirty-Seven—Evidence That the Holy Spirit Exists

1. Alan Hirsch, *The Forgotten Ways* (Grand Rapids, MI: Brazos Press, 2006), 18.

Chapter Thirty-Eight—The Purpose of the Holy Spirit in Our Lives

1. Adapted from Sean McDowell, *Ethix* (Nashville, TN: Broadman & Holman Publishers, 2006), 15.

Chapter Thirty-Nine—How to Live in the Power of the Holy Spirit

1. Bill Bright, *Have You Made the Wonderful Discovery of the Spirit-Filled Life?* (Peachtree City, GA: New Life Resources of Campus Crusade for Christ International, 1966, 1995, 2000, 2008). *Have You Made the Wonderful Discovery of the Spirit-Filled Life?* written by Bill Bright © 1966–2010 Bright Media Foundation (BMF) and Campus Crusade for Christ International (CCCI). All rights reserved. www.campuscrusade.com. Included with permission.

Chapter Forty—Kingdoms at War

1. *God Is Up to Something* (Hamilton, OH: The WordsWorth Group, 2008), 1-2.

2. C.S. Lewis, *Mere Christianity* (New York, NY: Macmillan, 1943), 36.

Chapter Forty-One—Evidence That God's Kingdom Has Positively Influenced the World

1. Christopher Hitchens, *God Is Not Great: How Religion Poisons Everything* (New York, NY: Twelve Books, 2007), 13.

2. F.W. Nietzsche, *The Antichrist,* tr. H.L. Mencken (Torrance, CA: The Noontide Press, 1980), 180.

3. Sherwood Eliot Wirt, *The Social Conscience of the Evangelical* (New York, NY: Harper and Row, 1968), 31.

4. Basil of Caesarea, at http://en.wikipedia.org/wiki/St_Basil.

5. Charles W. Colson, *The Faith* (Grand Rapids, MI: Zondervan, 2008), 169.

6. Trevor Yaxley with Carolyn Vanderwal, *William and Catherine: The Legacy of the Booths, Founders of the Salvation Army* (Bloomington, MN: Bethany House Publishers, 2003), 221.

7. Wikipedia, article: "The Salvation Army," http://en.wikipedia.org/wiki/The_Salvation_Army, 2009.

8. Answers.com at www.answers.com/topic/henry-dunant.

9. Nobelprize.org at http://nobelprize.org/nobel_prizes/peace/laureates/1979/teresa-bio.html.

10. See the writings of Jonathan Hill, *What Has Christianity Ever Done for Us?: How It Shaped the Modern World* (Downers Grove, IL: InterVarsity Press, 2005); Rodney Stark, *For the Glory of God: How Monotheism Led to Reformations, Science, Witch-Hunts, and the End of Slavery* (Princeton, NJ: Princeton University Press, 2003); Rodney Stark, *The Victory of Reason: How Christianity Led to Freedom, Capitalism, and Western Success* (New York: Random House, 2005); and Vincent Carroll and Dave Shiflett, *Christianity on Trial: Arguments against Anti-Religious Bigotry* (San Francisco: Encounter Books, 2002).

Chapter Forty-Two—Determining Your Kingdom Worldview

1. James W. Sire, *The Universe Next Door* (Downers Grove, IL: InterVarsity Press, 2009), 20.

Chapter Forty-Five—Evidence That God's Authentic Church Is Alive and Well

1. Robert Webber, *Listening to the Beliefs of Emerging Churches* (Grand Rapids, MI: Zondervan, 2007), 9.

2. Bob Roberts Jr., *Transformation* (Grand Rapids, MI: Zondervan, 2006), 19-20.

3. *God Is Up to Something* (Hamilton, OH: The WordsWorth Group, 2008), 22-23.

4. Bob Roberts Jr., *The Multiplying Church* (Grand Rapids, MI: Zondervan, 2008), 25.

5. Robert Webber, *Journey to Jesus* (Nashville, TN: Abingdon Press, 2001), 102-103.

Chapter Forty-Six—The Priority of the Church

1. Story adapted from David Ferguson, *The Never Alone Church* (Wheaton, IL: Tyndale House Publishers, 1998), 77-78.

2. Robert Webber, *The Younger Evangelical* (Grand Rapids, MI: Baker Books, 2002), 29.

Chapter Forty-Seven—How the Church Meets Human and Spiritual Needs

1. David Ferguson, *The Never Alone Church* (Wheaton, IL: Tyndale House Publishers, 1998), 51.

2. Adapted from Ibid., 45-51.

Chapter Forty-Eight—Our Restored Home: Heaven on Earth

1. Randy Alcorn, *Heaven* (Wheaton, IL: Tyndale House Publishers, 2004), 101.

Chapter Forty-Nine—Evidence for Life After Death

1. Tom Wolfe, "Sorry, but Your Soul Just Died," originally published in *Forbes ASAP* (1996). Reprinted

with permission at http://orthodoxytoday.org/articles/Wolfe-Sorry-But-Your-Soul-Just-Died .php.

2. John Searle, *Freedom and Neurobiology* (New York: Columbia University Press, 2007).

3. Sean McDowell and Jonathan Morrow, *Is God Just a Human Invention?: And Seventeen Other Questions Raised by the New Atheists* (Grand Rapids, MI: Kregel, 2010), chapter 8.

4. Barbara Bradley Hagerty, "The God Choice," *USA Today,* June 22, 2009, 9a.

5. Dinesh D'Souza, *Life After Death: The Evidence* (Washington, DC: Regnery Publishing, 2009), 63.

6. Ibid., 78.

7. Ibid., 80.

8. Ibid., 89.

Chapter Fifty—Experiencing Eternal Joy

1. Randy Alcorn, *Heaven* (Wheaton, IL: Tyndale House Publishers, 2004), 215.

2. Ibid., 226.

Chapter Fifty-One—Fulfilling Your Destiny

1. Drawn from Josh McDowell, Bob Hostetler, David H. Bellis, *Beyond Belief to Convictions* (Wheaton, IL: Tyndale House Publishers, 2002), 246-252.

2. Ibid., 279-280.

Appendix A

1. For a detailed treatment of this prophecy see chapter 8 of Josh McDowell, *The New Evidence That Demands a Verdict* (Nashville, TN: Thomas Nelson Publishers, 1999), 164-202.

2. Peter W. Stoner and Robert C. Newman, *Science Speaks* (Chicago, IL: Moody Press, 1976), 106.

3. Adapted from Josh McDowell and David H. Bellis, *Is Christ Really God?* workbook, adult edition (Holiday, FL: Green Key Books, 2006), 110-112.

4. Ibid., 114-116.

5. Ibid., 117-118.

6. Ibid., 121-123.

Appendix B

1. Adapted from Josh McDowell, Bob Hostetler, David H. Bellis, *Beyond Belief to Convictions* (Wheaton, IL: Tyndale House Publishers, 2002), 230-232.

2. Josh McDowell, *The New Evidence That Demands a Verdict* (Nashville, TN: Nelson, 1999), 74.

3. Ibid., 38.

4. Ibid., 34-39.

5. Drawn from McDowell, Hostetler, Bellis, 235-237.

INDEX

About the Authors

As a young man, **Josh McDowell** was a skeptic of Christianity. However, while at Kellogg College in Michigan, he was challenged by a group of Christian students to intellectually examine the claims of Jesus Christ. Josh accepted the challenge and came face-to-face with the reality that Jesus was in fact the Son of God, who loved him enough to die for him. Josh committed his life to Christ, and for 50 years he has shared with the world both his testimony and the evidence that God is real and relevant to our everyday lives.

Josh received a bachelor's degree from Wheaton College and a master's degree in theology from Talbot Theological Seminary in California. He has been on staff with Campus Crusade for Christ for almost 50 years. Josh and his wife, Dottie, have been married for nearly 40 years and have four grown children and three grandchildren. They live in Southern California.

Sean McDowell is an educator, speaker, and author. He graduated summa cum laude from Talbot Theological Seminary with a double master's degree in philosophy and theology. He is the head of the Bible department at Capistrano Valley Christian School and is the national spokesman for Wheatstone Academy, an organization committed to training young people in a biblical worldview. You can read Sean's blog and contact him for speaking events at www .seanmcdowell.org.

Sean and his wife, Stephanie, have been married for ten years and have two children. They live in Southern California.

Throughout *The Unshakable Truth* you will find many mentions of *Beyond Belief to Convictions* (from Tyndale House Publishers) and *The New Evidence That Demands a Verdict* (from Thomas Nelson Publishers), as well as much material adapted from them. These two books make great companions to the one you're now holding.

Beyond Belief to Convictions will help you counter the distorted view this generation has about God and the truth. It specifically focuses on how you can instill biblical convictions in the young people you know and love—to help them stand strong in the face of today's culture. To obtain this book, visit your local Christian bookstore or go to www.TyndaleHousePublishers.com.

The New Evidence That Demands a Verdict is a comprehensive reference text on the evidence for the Christian faith. It will equip you with a relevant, ready defense for this decade and beyond. (It includes *Evidence That Demands a Verdict I* and *II* updated in one easy-reference volume.) Visit your local Christian bookstore or go to www.ThomasNelsonPublishers.com.

UNDERSTANDING INTELLIGENT DESIGN
Everything You Need to Know in Plain Language
WILLIAM A. DEMBSKI AND SEAN MCDOWELL

> *"Understanding Intelligent Design is the best book of its type."*
> **J.P. MORELAND**
> Author and distinguished professor of philosophy, Biola University

The prevailing mind-set in our schools and in the media is that everything we see came into being strictly by accident. But in this user-friendly resource, William Dembski and Sean McDowell show that many scientists are now admitting that this viewpoint is not based on facts.

Understanding Intelligent Design clearly shows what the best information is revealing—that our existence is not an accidental by-product of nature but the clear result of intelligent design.

APOLOGETICS FOR A NEW GENERATION
A Biblical and Culturally Relevant Approach to Talking About God
SEAN MCDOWELL

This generation's faith is constantly under attack from the secular media, skeptical teachers, and unbelieving peers. You may wonder, *How can I help?*

Working with young adults every day, Sean McDowell understands their situation and shares your concern. His first-rate team of contributors shows how you can walk members of the new generation through the process of...

- formulating a biblical worldview and applying scriptural principles to everyday issues
- articulating their questions and addressing their doubts in a safe environment
- becoming confident in their faith and effective in their witness

The truth never gets old, but people need to hear it in fresh, new ways. Find out how you can effectively share the answers to life's big questions with a new generation.

CONVICTION WITHOUT COMPROMISE
Standing Strong in the Core Beliefs of the Christian Faith
NORMAN GEISLER AND RON RHODES

Is it possible for Christians to know unity even when they disagree?

Is it ever all right for Christians to set aside doctrinal convictions for the sake of unity?

What is the difference between an essential teaching and a nonessential teaching?

From the earliest days of the church, Christians have struggled with questions related to unity and the handling of doctrinal differences. In this book you'll find clear guidance from Scripture about the doctrines on which it's essential for Christians to agree and the doctrines on which believers can graciously agree to disagree.

This landmark resource will equip you to take an uncompromising stand on the essentials of the Faith while promoting love and unity among true believers.

AUTHENTIC PARENTING IN A POSTMODERN CULTURE
Practical Help for Shaping Your Children's Hearts, Minds, and Souls
MARY DEMUTH

Your children are growing up in a world that's different from the one you knew as a child. Today, people are discovering and living out truth in radically new ways. Mary DeMuth points out the pitfalls of this new worldview and demonstrates how you can use its strengths to enhance your relationship with your children and prepare them to genuinely live out and effectively communicate the good news of Jesus Christ.

You can use this new way of thinking to cooperate with God's work in your family and in the world by...

- engaging your kids in conversations instead of issuing ultimatums
- seeing your children's behaviors as windows into your own spiritual life
- coaching your children instead of lecturing them
- modeling the transparent, authentic lifestyle you want for your kids
- demonstrating a life of thankfulness, creativity, and service

BECOMING WHO GOD INTENDED
A New Picture for Your Past • A Healthy Way of Managing Your Emotions • A Fresh Perspective on Relationships

DAVID ECKMAN

> *"I strongly urge you to get* Becoming Who God Intended *and put it to work in your life."*
>
> JOSH MCDOWELL

Whether you realize it or not, your imagination is filled with *pictures* of reality. The Bible indicates that these pictures reveal your true "heart beliefs"—the beliefs that actually shape your everyday feelings and reactions.

David Eckman compassionately shows you how to allow God's Spirit to build new, *biblical* pictures in your heart and imagination. As you do this, you will be able to experience healthy emotions and enjoy the life God the Father has always intended for you.

52 THINGS KIDS NEED FROM A DAD
What Fathers Can Do to Make a Lifelong Difference

JAY PAYLEITNER

> *"I'm delighted to see so many inspiring, practical, unexpected ideas for dads in one place."*
>
> JOSH MCDOWELL

Good news—you are already the perfect dad for your kids! Still, you know you can grow. In these pages, Jay Payleitner, veteran radio producer and dad of five, offers a bounty of inspiring and unexpected insights:

- *straightforward rules:* "carry photos of your kids," "dad tucks in," and "kiss your wife in the kitchen"
- *candid advice that may be tough to hear:* "get right with your own dad," "throw out your porn," and "surrender control of the TV remote"
- *weird topics that at first seem absurd:* "buy Peeps," "spin a bucket over your head," and "rent a dolphin"

Surely God—our heavenly Father—designed fatherhood to be a joy, a blessing, and a blast!

To learn more about other Harvest House books
or to read sample chapters, log on to our website:

www.harvesthousepublishers.com

HARVEST HOUSE PUBLISHERS
EUGENE, OREGON